AF896497

# HIGH RATES AND LOW TAXES

Amidst calls for a return to the high tax rates of the 1950s and 1960s, this book examines the tax dodging that accompanied it. Lacking political will to lower the rate, Congress riddled the laws with loopholes, exemptions, and preferences, while largely accepting income tax chiseling's rise in American culture. The rich and famous openly invested in tax shelters and decamped to exotic tax havens, executives revamped the compensation and retirement schemes of their corporations to suit their tax needs, and an industry of tax advisers developed to help the general public engage in their own form of tax dodging through exaggerated expense accounts, luxurious business travel on the taxpayer's dime, and self-help books, such as one that promised to reveal "how the 'insiders' get rich on tax-wise" real estate deals and other investments. Tax dodging was a part of almost every restaurant bill, feature film, and savings account. It was literally woven into the fabric of society.

STEVEN A. BANK is the Paul Hastings Professor of Business Law at UCLA School of Law. He has written extensively on the history of taxation, including *Anglo-American Corporation Taxation: Tracing the Common Roots of Divergent Approaches* (2011), *From Sword to Shield: The Transformation of the Corporate Income Tax, 1861 to Present* (2010), and *War and Taxes* (2008) (with Kirk J. Stark and Joseph J. Thorndike). His work has been awarded the John Minor Wisdom Award for Academic Excellence in Legal Scholarship, the De Brauw Blackstone Westbroek Prize, and has been selected for the Stanford/Yale Junior Faculty Forum.

## CAMBRIDGE TAX LAW

Tax law is a growing area of interest. It is included as a subdivision in many areas of study and is a key consideration in business needs throughout the world. Books in this series expose the theoretical underpinning behind the law to shed light on taxation systems, so that the questions to be asked when addressing an issue become clear. These academic books, written by leading scholars, are a central port of call for information on tax law, with content illustrated by case law and legislation. The books will be of interest to those studying law, business, economics, accounting, and finance courses.

*Series Editor*

Professor Peter Harris, Law Faculty, University of Cambridge,
Director of the Centre for Tax Law.
Professor Harris brings a wealth of experience to the series. He has taught and presented tax courses at more than a dozen different universities in as many countries and has acted as an external tax consultant for the International Monetary Fund for over twenty years.

# HIGH RATES AND LOW TAXES

## Tax Dodging in Mid-Century America

STEVEN A. BANK
*University of California, Los Angeles*

CAMBRIDGE
UNIVERSITY PRESS

CAMBRIDGE
UNIVERSITY PRESS

Shaftesbury Road, Cambridge CB2 8EA, United Kingdom

One Liberty Plaza, 20th Floor, New York, NY 10006, USA

477 Williamstown Road, Port Melbourne, VIC 3207, Australia

314–321, 3rd Floor, Plot 3, Splendor Forum, Jasola District Centre,
New Delhi – 110025, India

Cambridge University Press is part of Cambridge University Press & Assessment,
a department of the University of Cambridge.

We share the University's mission to contribute to society through the pursuit of
education, learning and research at the highest international levels of excellence.

www.cambridge.org
Information on this title: www.cambridge.org/9781009701952

DOI: 10.1017/9781009701969

© Steven A. Bank 2026

This publication is in copyright. Subject to statutory exception and to the provisions
of relevant collective licensing agreements, no reproduction of any part may take
place without the written permission of Cambridge University Press & Assessment.

When citing this work, please include a reference to the DOI 10.1017/9781009701969

First published 2026

*A catalogue record for this publication is available from the British Library*

*Library of Congress Cataloging-in-Publication Data*
Names: Bank, Steven A., 1969– author
Title: High rates and low taxes : tax dodging in mid-century America /
Steven A. Bank, University of California, Los Angeles.
Description: Cambridge, United Kingdom ; New York, NY : Cambridge
University Press, 2026. | Series: Cambridge tax law series | Includes index.
Identifiers: LCCN 2025034439 (print) | LCCN 2025034440 (ebook) | ISBN 9781009701952
hardback | ISBN 9781009701945 paperback | ISBN 9781009701969 ebook
Subjects: LCSH: Tax evasion – Law and legislation – United States – History |
Tax shelters – Law and legislation – United States – History |
Corporations – Taxation – Law and legislation – United States – Criminal
provisions | Tax havens | Taxation – Law and legislation – United States
Classification: LCC KF9350 .B36 2026 (print) | LCC KF9350 (ebook) |
DDC 345.73/02338–dc23/eng/20250725
LC record available at https://lccn.loc.gov/2025034439
LC ebook record available at https://lccn.loc.gov/2025034440

ISBN 978-1-009-70195-2 Hardback

Cambridge University Press & Assessment has no responsibility for the persistence
or accuracy of URLs for external or third-party internet websites referred to in this
publication and does not guarantee that any content on such websites is, or will remain,
accurate or appropriate.

For EU product safety concerns, contact us at Calle de José Abascal, 56, 1°, 28003 Madrid, Spain,
or email eugpsr@cambridge.org

For my wife Julie and four children, Reuben, Asher,
Simon, and Delilah

# CONTENTS

# FIGURES

# ACKNOWLEDGMENTS

This book benefitted from presentations before many audiences over the years, including the law faculties at the University of California, Los Angeles (UCLA) and Temple University, tax policy colloquiums at Duke University, the University of California, Irvine, the University of Colorado, and New York University, and conferences organized by the International Institute for Public Finance at the University of Iceland, the Institute for European Global Studies at the University of Basel, the Business History Conference, the Lowell Milken Institute for Business Law and Policy at UCLA, and the Tax Section of the American Bar Association. More individuals read early papers from which the chapters were built and offered useful comments at various points in the project's development than I can possibly thank, but I owe a particular debt of gratitude to Alice Abreu, Jim Barrall, Brian Cheffins, Kimberly Clausing, Michael Dorff, David Hasen, Gisela Hürlimann, Omri Marian, Ajay Mehrotra, Vanessa Ogle, Jason Oh, Katherine Pratt, Dorothea Rohde, Korinna Schönhärl, Sloan Speck, Kirk Stark, Joseph Thorndike, David Walker, Harwell Wells, Larry Zelenak, and Eric Zolt, as well as two anonymous referees. Several of the chapters draw or expand upon pieces published elsewhere, including "When Did Tax Avoidance Become Respectable?" 71 *Tax Law Review* 123 (2017), "Executive Pay: What Worked?" 42 *Journal of Corporation Law* 59 (2016) (with Brian R. Cheffins and Harwell Wells) and "Populist Ambivalence to Tax Evasion: The 1962 Campaign against Dividend and Interest Withholding in the US," in *Histories of Tax Evasion, Avoidance, and Resistance* (Korinna Schönhärl et al., eds., 2023). Some of the most significant contributions were from those who assisted in the research for this project, including the reference librarians at the UCLA Law Library and many student research assistants, including Brett Drucker, William Heller, Alexander Morato, John Monts, Jonathan Simmons, Jackson Sullivan, Paige Tobin, Lauren Yaple, and Brandon Zelner. Special thanks also to Rogue Machine Theatre, 5-Star Theatricals, Phantom Projects Theatre Group, the Colburn School of Performing Arts, and LA Surf SC, each of which unwittingly provided me plenty of time and space, often late into the evenings, to complete this project.

# Introduction

## "Tax Dodging" and Its Evolution

In their book, *The Triumph of Injustice: How the Rich Dodge Taxes and How to Make Them Pay*, economists Emmanuel Saez and Gabriel Zucman lamented the retreat of the United States' tax system from its heyday between the 1930s and 1970s when it was, in their words, "perhaps the most progressive in world history."[1] As seen in Figure I.1, the top rate shot up from 25 percent after World War I to more than 60 percent in the early 1930s and settled at the astronomically high rate of 91 percent for over a decade between 1951 and 1963. That turned out to be the high point for the top marginal rate. Over the next several decades the rate dropped to 70 percent, then 50 percent, and finally a low of 28 percent in the late 1980s. Although it has crept up since then, the top rate has never approached anything close to what it was at mid-century, remaining below 40 percent for the last four decades. Saez and Zucman and many others have called for a return to something approaching those high mid-century tax rates,[2] while others reject this nostalgia for a so-called "Golden Age" of taxation.[3]

[1] Emmanuel Saez and Gabriel Zucman, The Triumph of Injustice: How the Rich Dodge Taxes and How to Make Them Pay 48 (2019).

[2] Most proponents of higher marginal rates do not call for a return to the 91 percent rate. Saez and Zucman suggest a top marginal rate "in the vicinity of 75%" that would amount to an effective rate of 60 percent on average for the top 1 percent. Id. at 134. *See* Thomas Piketty, Emmanuel Saez, and Stefanie Stantcheva, *Optimal Taxation of Labor Incomes: A Tale of Three Elasticities*, 6 Am. Econ. J. Econ Pol'y 230, 232 (2014) (recommending a top rate of over 80 percent); Thomas Piketty, Capital in the Twenty-First Century 512 (2014) (same); Veronica Stracqualursi, *Ocasio-Cortez Suggests 70% Tax for Wealthy to Fund Climate Change Plan*, CNN, Jan. 4, 2019 (proposing a top rate as high as 60 to 70 percent on earnings over $10 million). This call for a return to 1950's era taxation is not new either. *See, e.g.*, Ezra Klein, *A Rich Guy's Case for Higher Taxes*, Wash. Post, April 16, 2012; Marc Linder, *I like Ike: Bringing Back Eisenhower-Era Progressive Taxation*, 67 Tax Notes 833 (1995).

[3] Arpit Gupta, *Revisiting the High Tax Rates of the 1950s*, 19 Manhattan Inst. for Pol'y Research Issue Brief 1 (April 2013). *See* Lawrence Mone, *There's No Going Back to the 1950s Tax System*, Wall St. J., April 16, 2013, James Pethokoukis, *Why We Can't Go Back to Sky-High, 1950s Tax Rates*, AEIdeas, April 18, 2012.

**Figure I.1**[4] Top marginal income tax rates, 1913–2023

Both proponents and critics of the mid-century rates acknowledge that taxpayers did not actually pay taxes at those high rates on all their income. Under our graduated rate income tax system, the marginal tax rates only apply to the dollars earned "at the margin," or above the threshold at which that stated rate begins. A more important indicator of the tax burden is what is called the "effective rate."[5] This is the percentage of an individual's annual income paid in taxes.[6] It is essentially an average of all the graduated rates

[4] All rates are from Tax Policy Center, Historical Individual Income Tax Parameters, 1913–2023 (May 11, 2023). The top rate rose to 31 percent as part of George W. Bush's infamous "Read My Lips" tax hike in 1990 and to 39.6 percent in 1993 before it was reduced to 35 percent in 2003. That rate cut expired in 2013, returning it to 39.6 percent, before it was dropped slightly to 37 percent under the Tax Cuts and Jobs Act in 2017. Id.

[5] Reuven S. Avi-Yonah, *Book Review, Why Tax the Rich? Efficiency, Equity, and Progressive Taxation*, 111 Yale L. J. 1391, 1394 (2002) (*reviewing* Does Atlas Shrug? The Economic Consequences of Taxing the Rich (Joel B. Slemrod, ed. 2000)).

[6] Joseph J. Thorndike, *Soak-the-Rich Republicans? The Persistence of High Tax Rates in the 1950s*, 66 Tax L. Rev. 761, 762 (2013).

applied to the marginal increments of income earned from first to last dollar, after taking into account the effect of deductions, credits, preferential capital gains tax rates and other methods of reducing, avoiding, or evading income taxes.[7] It is no surprise, therefore, that the effective rates at mid-century were lower than the statutory rates.

Saez and Zucman argue that while "few people paid the 80%–90% top marginal income tax rates that prevailed from the 1930s through to the 1970s," the "effective rates for the very affluent exceeded 50 percent."[8] Although it would be natural to assume that the gap between the statutory rate and the effective rate was at least in part because "tax dodging was out of control," they claim that this was not the case.[9] According to Saez and Zucman, "[President Franklin Delano] Roosevelt had pioneered, in the 1930s, the enforcement strategy that would keep tax evasion and avoidance under control for the decades that followed."[10] They conceded that "schemes to avoid taxes did regularly pop up," such as to convert ordinary income to capital gains, but they maintained that such schemes "were quickly prohibited."[11]

Where it was not as easy to shut down avoidance maneuvers or evasion was more difficult to detect, Saez and Zucman believed that strong social norms prevented abusive tax transactions. They contend, for example, that "there is no evidence, in any contemporary chronicles of how company executives lived in the 1940s, 1950s, and 1960s," that perks "such as company jets, lavish offices, gargantuan meals, 'company' seminars in Cape Cod or Aspen and so on . . . were particularly common or large."[12] From this, they surmised that "spending lavishly using corporate money was simply not the socially accepted way for company executives to behave before the 1980s."[13] Consequently, Saez and Zucman concluded that "tax dodging was kept in check" in mid-century America.[14]

This conclusion is controversial. Others have reported an effective rate that ranged between 20 and 30 percent, rather than 50 percent, by the end

[7] Avi-Yonah, *supra* note 5, at 1394.
[8] Saez and Zucman, *supra* note 1, at 48.
[9] Id. at 49.
[10] Id. at 48.
[11] Id. at 50.
[12] Id.
[13] Id.
[14] Id. at 48.

of the 1950s,[15] although some of these studies are themselves contested.[16] As Yale law professor Boris Bittker long ago pointed out, "there are . . . many different ways to compute effective tax rates, generating – despite occasional references to the 'true' or 'actual' rate – as many computations as there are commentators."[17] Nevertheless, at least one aspect of the differences in effective rate calculations in this case is readily apparent. Saez and Zucman took into account all taxes, including federal, state, and local income taxes, payroll taxes, estate taxes, corporate profits, property taxes, and sales taxes,[18] while other studies have focused exclusively on income taxes.[19] Moreover, some of these lower estimates of the effective rate include state and local income taxes, rather than just federal income taxes, and some include or omit capital gains, which means they over or understate the effective federal income tax burden.

Nevertheless, this debate over effective rates is fundamentally not about tax dodging. Proponents of the return to mid-century tax rates contend that higher tax rates on the very affluent today could help to reduce that inequality, noting that inequality was lower when tax rates were at their highest.[20] Opponents respond that the link between tax rates and inequality is not clear, arguing that the high rates were eviscerated by

15 W. Elliot Brownlee, *Historical Perspective on U.S. Tax Policy Toward the Rich*, in Does Atlas Shrug? The Economic Consequences of Taxing the Rich 60, tbl. 2.5 (Joel B. Slemrod, ed. 2000) (while the effective rate on the top 1 percent was 58.6 percent in 1944, when the top marginal rate was 94 percent, it was between 25 and 32 percent throughout the 1950s and 1960s); William V. Williams, *The Changing Progressivity of the Federal Income Tax*, 17 Nat'l Tax J. 425 (1964) (effective rate on the top earners declined from 49.3 percent in 1954 to 27.2 percent by 1961); Erika York, Income *Taxes on the Top 0.1Percent Weren't Much Higher in the 1950s*, Tax Foundation, January 23, 2019 (effective income tax rate on the top 0.1 percent was 21 percent in the 1950s); Amity Shlaes, *1950s Tax Fantasy is a Republican Nightmare*, Bloomberg, Jan. 12, 2013 (studies show the effective rate for millionaires dropped from 49 percent in 1953 to 31 percent in 1960).

16 *See* Marc Linder, *Eisenhower-Era Marxist Confiscatory Taxation: Requiem for the Rhetoric of Rate Reduction for the Rich*, 70 Tul. L. Rev. 905, 931 (1996) (critiquing Williams' methodology).

17 Boris I. Bittker, *Effective Tax Rates: Fact or Fancy?* 122 U. Pa. L. Rev. 780, 782 (1974).

18 Saez and Zucman, *supra* note 1, at 41. Commentators also note that the authors assigned all the incidence of the corporate tax on shareholders and none on consumers or workers. *See* Edward N. Wolff, *Book Review of* The Triumph of Injustice: How the Rich Dodge Taxes and How to Make Them Pay, 18 J. Econ. Inequality 441 (2020).

19 Brownlee, *Historical Perspectives on U.S. Tax Policy Toward the Rich, supra* note 15, at 60; Williams, *supra* note 15, at 426; York, *supra* note 15.

20 *See, e.g.*, Piketty, Capital in the Twenty-First Century, *supra* note 2, at 493 ("the progressive income tax . . . played a key role in the reduction of inequality in the last century.").

tax dodging,[21] while proponents insist that the wealthy were still subject to a tax burden during this period that reduced the incentives to seek or demand high compensation, which in turn allowed for a wider distribution of "the fruits of growth."[22] That has led people to take more interest in mid-century tax dodging, but mostly to either support or refute the response to calls for a return to something closer to the period's high rates on the very affluent,[23] rather than to understand how it operated on a societal level across income groups. Studies that focus on the top 1 percent overlook the way that tax dodging became entrenched as a cultural, mass market, phenomenon during this period, even before the much-discussed boom in tax shelters in the 1970s and early 1980s.[24]

This book fills in the gap in the literature by offering both a bird's eye and ground-level view of tax dodging in mid-century America. Far from being an era of vigorous tax enforcement and rigid social norms in favor of paying taxes, the 1950s and 1960s were the golden age of tax dodging in the United States. During this period, despite attempts to crackdown on abuse, celebrities pioneered or popularized a variety of tax dodging schemes, corporations structured compensation packages to allow executives to reduce their income tax burden and lobbied for new provisions that enabled them to do this more successfully, and countries such as Switzerland, Lichtenstein, the Bahamas, and the Netherlands Antilles ran advertisements in American newspapers and magazines that boasted not of their magisterial ski slopes or beautiful beaches, but of their attractive tax laws for US businesses and

21 Scott Greenberg, *Tax Rates on the Rich Were Not That Much Higher in the 1950s*, Tax Foundation Blog, Aug. 4, 2017; James Pethokoukis, *Why We Can't Go Back to Sky-High, 1950s Tax Rates*, AEI Ideas Blog, April 18, 2012; Phillip Magness, *The Progressive Tax Myth*, U.S. News & World Report, Oct. 31, 2017. Some proponents also suggest that the rich did not pay that much in income taxes during the 1950s. Nathan Newman, *Give us AOC's 70% Tax Rates – But Save the 1950s Nostalgia*, Jacobin, Oct. 7, 2019.

22 Piketty, Capital in the Twenty-First Century, *supra* note 2, at 513. Proponents also contend the rich of the 1950s were simply not as rich as they are today, which makes it an inapt comparison for the relative burden on the wealthy. Marshall Steinbaum, *Effective Progressive Tax Rates in the 1950s*, Roosevelt Institute Blog, Aug. 8, 2017.

23 *See* Joseph J. Thorndike, *Playing Fast and Loose with Lessons from the 1950s*, Tax Notes, March 25, 2013 (citing a debate between Timothy Noah in the *New Republic* and David Brooks in the *New York Times* over effective rates during the 1950s).

24 For examples of work focusing on the rise and fall of the tax shelter industry in the 1970s and 1980s, *see* Jeffrey H. Birnbaum and Alan S. Murray, Showdown at Gucci Gulch: Lawmakers, Lobbyists, and the Unlikely Triumph of Tax Reform (1987), as well as in the 1990s and beyond, *see* David Cay Johnston, Perfectly Legal: The Covert Campaign to Rig our Tax System to Benefit the Super Rich – and Cheat Everybody Else (2003).

individuals. These all served to publicize, normalize, and legitimize tax dodging, which set the stage for its democratization. Lawyers, accountants, and tax preparers entered into the tax planning business after World War II to serve individuals who previously had not even been subject to income taxes, experts published how-to tax avoidance books promising to deliver information to the ordinary man on "how the 'insiders' get rich on tax-wise" investment deals, advertisements for tax shelters started to appear in the most prominent newspapers across the country, and tax dodging tools such as deferred compensation, fringe benefits, and expense accounts spread beyond executives to the salesman and middle-level employees of the American suburb. Quite simply, during the 1950s and 1960s, tax dodging was brazenly public, sometimes outlandish, and often explicitly or implicitly condoned by politicians.

## A Prehistory

Tax dodging was not unique to mid-century America; indeed, it is as old as taxation itself. The Roman Empire famously was plagued with tax avoidance, especially at the time of its fall.[25] According to one account, "many wealthy Romans buried their jewelry or stock of gold coin" to evade the tax collector and "it was largely to avoid taxation that in the late empire all but a few merchants and bankers stopped keeping accounts."[26] In Egypt during Roman rule, it was so common to evade taxes by simply fleeing your village that there was a procedure for announcing it and keeping records of the tax fugitives.[27] Similarly, in

[25] James William Ermatinger, The Decline and Fall of the Roman Empire 69 (2004); James J. O'Donnell, The Ruin of the Roman Empire 68 (2009); Amanda Foreman, *Tax Evasion's Bite: From the Ancient World to Modern Days*, Wall St. J. Online, Sept. 23, 2015. The playwright Bernard Shaw was reported to have said that "the power of Julius Caesar was really based on his effectiveness as a tax-collector. In its later days the empire could not find men to discharge this hated duty." Robert B. House, *The Historical Background of the Tax Question*, in Studies in Taxation: North Carolina Yearbook, 1927–1928 9 (1928).

[26] Carolyn Webber & Aaron Wildavsky, A History of Taxation and Expenditure in the Western World 141 (1986). This method of tax dodging predated the Roman Empire. *See Tax-Dodging No Modern Discovery, False-Bottomed Silo at Mizpah Shows*, Christian Science Monitor, May 23, 1929, at 1 (describing the archeological finding in an area from the early Iron Age between 1200 and 800 BC of a compartment with a false bottom that was apparently "intended to evade income tax collectors.").

[27] Kerstin Droβ-Krüpe, *Not Paying Taxes in Roman Egypt*, in Histories of Tax Evasion, Avoidance, and Resistance 71, 76–77 (Korinna Schönhärl, Gisela Hürlimann and Dorothea Rohde, eds., 2023).

Japan during the Heian Period around the twelfth century, the imperial court went bankrupt because tax exemptions granted to Heian Nobles had removed most of the taxable land from the rolls.[28] In the twentieth century, Switzerland's banks rose to become a center of tax evasion for wealthy individuals seeking to hide their assets in the period immediately following World War I.[29] Assets held in Swiss financial institutions by non-Swiss residents rose tenfold between 1920 and 1938.[30] Not surprisingly, this rise is attributed mainly to taxes, with the most significant jumps following years of tax rate increases in neighboring France.[31] Britain's Inland Revenue faced a similar problem around this time, with one source calling the period from 1922 to 1936 "halcyon days for the tax avoider."[32]

American taxpayers were no less motivated to avoid taxes. In the nineteenth century, before the modern income tax even existed, property tax evasion was rampant, particularly with the rise of intangible property like stocks and bonds.[33] In one year, although the total value of taxable securities listed on the San Francisco Exchange was estimated to be more than $110 million, only $5,000 worth of these assets were reported on tax returns.[34] In Massachusetts, when assessors started to crack down on underreporting, a quarter of the value of the state's intangible wealth disappeared from Boston, only to reappear in a few neighboring towns with taxpayer-friendly assessors.[35] The situation was no better at the federal level under the Civil War-era income tax. In 1863, revenues were approximately $50 million below projections and part of the shortfall was attributed to the fact that so many people "shirk their duty in making their payments,"[36] through a combination of what tax historian

[28] Foreman, *supra* note 25.

[29] GABRIEL ZUCMAN, THE HIDDEN WEALTH OF NATIONS 8–9 (2015).

[30] Id. at 14.

[31] Id. at 15, 17.

[32] David Stopforth, *1922–36: Halcyon Days for the Tax Avoider*, BRITISH TAX REV. 88 (1992).

[33] STEVEN A. BANK, FROM SWORD TO SHIELD: THE TRANSFORMATION OF THE CORPORATE INCOME TAX, 1861 TO PRESENT 30–31 (2010); HENRY CARTER ADAMS, THE SCIENCE OF FINANCE: AN INVESTIGATION OF PUBLIC EXPENDITURES AND PUBLIC REVENUES 382 (1898).

[34] CLIFTON K. YEARLEY, THE MONEY MACHINES: THE BREAKDOWN AND REFORM OF GOVERNMENTAL AND PARTY FINANCE IN THE NORTH, 1860–1920 58 (1970).

[35] Id. at 48–49.

[36] Joseph J. Thorndike, *The Civil War Income Tax Was Failing. Could a Crackdown on Cheats Save It?* 183 TAX NOTES 1521, 1523 (2024) (quoting an opinion piece in Scientific American dated Jan. 9, 1864).

Joseph Thorndike described as "outright evasion [and] chiseling around the edges," plus the Bureau of Internal Revenue "let[ting] them get away with it."[37]

Corporations also took pains to avoid taxes on their assets. The New York Central Railroad, owned and run by Cornelius Vanderbilt, claimed to have capital of $143 million on its balance sheet, but only paid tax on $22 million of it by treating its debt as diminishing the value of its capital stock and then deducting the debt again from the diminished valuation, all in violation of New York judicial decisions that barred the practice.[38] Similarly, the Western Union Telegraph Company, by claiming that its wires and telegraph poles were not taxable as real estate, paid taxes on capital of $1.8 million despite distributing dividends on capital of $47 million.[39] These were not isolated examples. "[C]rooked accounts, dishonest bonding, underassessment, phony indebtedness, the juggling of domiciles, collusion with public officials, or bribing them were all part of the arsenal of corporate tax dodgers."[40]

Tax dodging continued under the income tax in the 1920s and 1930s. In September 1923, Representative William R. Green, a Republican from Iowa who was Chair of the House Ways and Means Committee, complained in an address before the National Tax Association that "so much ingenuity has been used in inventing methods whereby less taxes would be paid."[41] Much of it, however, often involved maneuvers that were fully, or at least technically, legal. Populist journalist Ferdinand Lundberg grudgingly conceded this point, while only thinly disguising his outrage:

> Various ways were discovered by the rich for evading these taxes. One method was to invest in tax-exempt government securities. . . . Other ways of evading taxes were to invest money abroad; to declare stock dividends and transfer cash earnings to surplus to be held against a day of low taxes for distribution; to build unnecessary plants, hotels, and office buildings; to pay inordinately high salaries to corporation officials; and to resort to technically legal subterfuges such as personal holding companies.[42]

37 Id. at 1522.

38 Id. at 62.

39 James H. Coleman, Letters &c on Corporations and Taxation 9 (n.d.; approx. 1880).

40 Yearley, *supra* note 34, at 32.

41 W.R. Green, *Problems of National Taxation*, 2 Nat'l Income Tax Mag. 5 (1924).

42 Ferdinand Lundberg, America's 60 Families 165 (1937).

Some of these examples of tax dodging probably sound uncontroversial to the modern reader,[43] but during the 1920s, they were a frequent source of criticism.[44] For example, tax-exempt securities were characterized as "the foremost and most immediate of all American governmental problems" because they served as "a refuge for large investors who seek to avoid taxation."[45] In the early 1920s, Treasury Secretary Andrew Mellon called for a constitutional amendment requiring the taxation of income from state and municipal securities and Congress even considered legislation to that effect.[46] Similarly, although the Supreme Court held that stock dividends were nontaxable in 1920,[47] critics still insisted that "there is something crooked about them, that the surpluses created and thus distributed, or redistributed, in capital, or paper evidences of capital, are a device whereby the rich man is dodging taxes."[48] Senator Smith W. Brookhart, a Progressive Republican from Iowa, announced his intention to submit a bill "to make stock dividends taxable or curtail their issuance for alleged tax-dodging purposes."[49]

These political reactions merely mirrored the public intolerance at the time for all forms of tax dodging, legitimate or otherwise. As John Sears, the author of the practitioner treatise, *Minimizing Taxes*,[50] remarked in a

[43] One notable exception is executive compensation. *See, e.g.*, Alan Rappeport, *Biden Calls for Higher Tax on Corporations and the Wealthy*, N.Y. TIMES, March 11, 2024 (proposal to deny deductions for all employee compensation by corporations in excess of $1 million); *"Outrageous" CEO Pay Targeted in New Bill from Bernie Sanders, US Democrats*, REUTERS, Jan. 22, 2024 (proposal to increase a corporation's tax rate when its CEO-to-worker pay ratio exceeded fifty to one).

[44] *Tax Dodging Easy for Rich, Impossible for Poor*, AUSTIN AMERICAN, Oct. 18, 1925, at SM11 (identifying three methods of tax dodging "all sanctioned by law": Tax-exempt securities, stock dividends, and retained earnings).

[45] William Hand, *Tax Exempt Bonds Called Nation's Foremost Problem*, WASH. POST, Feb. 12, 1923, at 4; *Tax Dodging Denied in Municipal Bonds*, N.Y. TIMES, March 17, 1928, at 27; Roy G. Blakey and Gladys C. Blakey, *Federal Tax Legislation, 1939*, 29 AM. ECON. REV. 695, 698 (1939).

[46] *Tax Dodging Check Sought by Cutting Rates on Surtaxes*, CHRISTIAN SCIENCE MONITOR, Dec. 6, 1922, at 1.

[47] Eisner v. Macomber, 252 U.S. 189, 219 (1920).

[48] Editorial, *Stock Dividends and Tax-Dodging*, BARRON'S, Dec. 25, 1922, at 9. *See Mellon Upholds Oil Stock Melon*, COURIER JOURNAL (Louisville), Oct. 21, 1922, at 3 (Mellon denied charges that Treasury had been lax in enforcing the tax laws by not going after Standard Oil Company of New Jersey for issuing a 400 percent stock dividend); *see Tax Dodging Strategy in Standard Oil Companies' Extensive Stock Dividends*, INDIANAPOLIS STAR, Oct. 18, 1922, at 1 (reporting letter Representative Frear of Wisconsin sent to Mellon calling attention to the dividend as a tax avoidance tactic).

[49] *Plans Bill to Tax Stock Dividends*, THE SUN (Baltimore), Jan. 6, 1923, at 2.

[50] JOHN H. SEARS, MINIMIZING TAXES (1922).

1921 article, "in the public mind, methods of tax reduction, saving or avoidance are often said to be confused with tax 'evasion' or tax 'dodging' and to all methods of tax saving is often imputed a moral guilt, if not a legal risk and liability."[51] In reviewing Sears' treatise in 1923, University of Minnesota law professor Henry Rottschaefer wrote that there is a "widespread popular sentiment that the skilled tax lawyer is engaged in a reprehensible business," noting that the title of Sears' book served as "the final proof of the correctness of their position."[52]

By the 1930s, with most people scarred by the Crash of 1929 and weary of the Great Depression, the public had little patience for wealthy people who found ways to reduce their taxes, even if legal. This was never more evident than in 1933 when the Senate Finance Committee on Banking and Currency, led by its chief counsel Ferdinand Pecora, held hearings on the causes of the stock market crash[53] In the course of these hearings, the public learned that financier J. P. Morgan and his partners had paid no income tax during the height of the Great Depression in 1931 and 1932.[54] As historian Joseph Thorndike recounted, "it was a stunning revelation, at least to the popular press. How could this giant of American wealth escape the income tax?"[55] Morgan was not alone either. It was disclosed that Otto Kahn of the investment firm Kuhn Loeb and Company, which was second only to the House of Morgan among American private banks, paid no income tax between 1930 and 1932.[56]

It made little difference that Morgan, Kahn, and other financiers had paid no income tax because their losses in the stock market in the 1920s had wiped out any income from the early 1930s.[57] "That point seemed lost on many reporters and lawmakers – not to mention the general public."[58] As one observer noted in the aftermath of the Pecora hearings, "it is difficult to consider the question of tax avoidance without immediately encountering the moral issue. This is particularly so because of the

[51] John H. Sears, *Effective and Lawful Avoidance of Taxes*, 8 VA. L. REV. 77 (1921).

[52] Henry Rottschaefer, *Review: Minimizing Taxes by John H. Sears*, 21 MICH. L. REV. 719 (1923).

[53] Stock Exchange Practices, Hearings Before the Sen. Comm. On Banking and Currency on S. Res. 84, 73rd Cong., 1st Sess. 3219–2235 (1933).

[54] FERDINAND PECORA, WALL STREET UNDER OATH 190 (1939).

[55] JOSEPH J. THORNDIKE, THEIR FAIR SHARE: TAXING THE RICH IN THE AGE OF FDR 85 (2013).

[56] PECORA, *supra* note 54, at 190; Theresa M. Collins, *Introducing Otto H. Kahn (1867–1934)*, 28 BUS. AND ECON. HIST. 13 (1999).

[57] THORNDIKE, THEIR FAIR SHARE, *supra* note 55, at 86.

[58] Id.

recent Congressional investigations into the incomes and tax payments of large financial houses."[59]

Thus, in 1934, Judge Learned Hand was trying to counter the bias against legal tax planning when he wrote his famous declaration in the *Gregory* case that "any one may so arrange his affairs that his taxes shall be as low as possible; he is not bound to choose that pattern which will best pay the Treasury, there is not even a patriotic duty to increase one's taxes."[60] There was also, as Professor Daniel Shaviro later observed, a "curious dual quality" to Hand's opinion in the case, with fellow Professor Assaf Likhovski agreeing that "it contained contradictory messages."[61] It was a seemingly pro-taxpayer statement in the context of a decision that sided with the government and found that literal compliance with the words of the statute providing for tax-free treatment of a reorganization of a company was insufficient "even though the facts answer the dictionary definitions of each term under in the statutory definition."[62] Thus, Hand recognized that the transaction literally complied with the statute, but still rejected it as violating the spirit of the law, concluding "[t]o dodge the shareholders' taxes is not one of the transactions contemplated as corporate 'reorganizations.'"[63] In part, this was to address a split among the judges on the three-judge panel deciding the case, which ended up swaying a literalist judge to eventually join the views of the majority.[64] In part, however, Judge Hand's line-drawing was

59 George T. Altman, *Recent Developments in Income Tax Avoidance*, 29 ILL. L. REV. 154 (1934).

60 Helvering v. Gregory, 69 F.2d 809, 810 (2d. Cir. 1934). Both the decision, and Judge Hand's aphorism in support of tax planning, were affirmed by the Supreme Court. Gregory v. Helvering 293 U.S. 465, 469 (1935) ("The legal right of a taxpayer to decrease the amount of what otherwise would be his taxes, or altogether avoid them, by means which the law permits, cannot be doubted."). Hand was not the originator of this aphorism, nor was the *Gregory* case. *See, e.g.*, Oscar W. Underwood, Jr., *Form and Substance in Tax Cases*, 16 VA. L. REV. 327, 329 (1930) ("It is now, and in fact has been for a long time, well settled that every taxpayer has a right, so long as he abstains from fraudulent or deceptive means, to so order his affairs that the least possible amount in taxes will fall upon him," citing United States v. Isham, 84 U.S. 496, 506 (1873) and Weeks v. Sibley, 269 F. 155 (N.D. Tex. 1920)).

61 Daniel Shaviro, *The Story of Knetsch: Judicial Doctrines Combating Tax Avoidance* in TAX STORIES 313, 321 (Paul Caron, ed., 2003); Assaf Likhovski, *The Story of Gregory: How are Tax Avoidance Cases Decided?* in BUSINESS TAX STORIES 89, 96 (Steven A. Bank & Kirk J. Stark, eds., 2005).

62 Gregory, 69 F.2d at 810.

63 Id. at 811.

64 Likhovski, *supra* note 61, at 95–96.

to address a larger split between the professional legal literature and the political and cultural attitudes towards tax planning.[65]

Lawyers and tax administrators had been trying to draw this avoidance/evasion line since the income tax was first enacted,[66] but it became a preoccupation of legal scholars in the 1920s and 1930s.[67] In 1921, Sears published a piece in the *Virginia Law Review* "to point out fundamental differences between methods of avoiding or reducing taxes which may safely be regarded as effective and lawful as distinguished from forbidden evasion."[68] In his treatise on the subject, Sears contended that "the term 'avoidance' of taxes is used to described some lawful action aimed to affect *taxability in the future*, as distinguished from 'evasion,' which refers to some fraud upon the revenue, past, present, or future."[69] This definition, of course, still left one to wonder what was "lawful" and what was "fraud." At least in the 1920s, both courts and scholars resolved that question by resorting to formalism and literalism.[70]

Evasion was typically described as an activity that was fully illegal, such as failing to file tax returns or hiding income and assets from the tax authorities. One 1920s tax practitioner offered the example of someone who purchased bonds for investment, but who did not disclose them to the property tax collector when asked to do so.[71] As Randolph Paul, the namesake of the New York law firm of Paul, Weiss, Rifkind, Wharton & Garrison and a Treasury official in the late 1930s and 1940s, emphasized in his *Restatement of Tax Avoidance*, evasion typically has "elements of deceit, if not fraud, more specifically, if there is evasion, there will be subterfuge, camouflage, concealment, some attempt to color or obscure event, or to make things seem other than they are."[72]

[65] Id. at 110–13, 115–20.

[66] Marvin A. Chirelstein, *Learned Hand's Contribution to the Law of Tax Avoidance*, 77 YALE L.J. 440 (1968). As far back as 1873, the Supreme Court had said, in the context of the Stamp Act of 1864, that as long as "it is not perceived that the practice is open to the charge of fraud . . . a person has the legal right . . . to avoid the tax." United States v. Isham, 84 U.S. 496, 506 (1873).

[67] Likhovski, *supra* note 61, at 111.

[68] Sears, *Effective and Lawful Avoidance of Taxes*, *supra* note 51, at 77.

[69] SEARS, MINIMIZING TAXES, *supra* note 50, at 2.

[70] Likhovski, *supra* note 61, at 106.

[71] James L. Dohr, *Avoidance vs. Evasion of Tax Liability*, 6 NAT'L INCOME TAX MAG. 370 (1928).

[72] Randolph E. Paul. *Restatement of Tax Avoidance*, in STUDIES IN FEDERAL TAXATION 9, 16–17 (1937).

Avoidance, by contrast, did not involve concealment or misrepresentation under these interpretations.[73] Sears called tax avoidance a "legally innocent method of saving," even if not everyone agreed that it was morally innocent. In its more controversial form, it may not have involved deceit, but it often involved employing aggressive techniques in which rules were bent and twisted beyond the intentions of the drafters of the original provisions. Since these techniques generally complied with the literal language of the statute, observers tended to characterize them as "loopholes." One oft-cited instance of this was the so-called "incorporated pocketbook," in which an individual formed a corporation and contributed his stocks, bonds, and income-producing assets to the corporation in exchange for all of its stock.[74] The objective was to shield his personal investment income from the high marginal rates applicable to individuals by taking advantage of the lower corporate tax rate that was meant to be an aid to businesses.[75] Sometimes, however, the term "loophole" may have been thrown around a bit too liberally. For example, one observer argued that the existence of the preferential tax rate on capital gains was a loophole because it appeared to have created the over-expansion of the 1920s, which Congress surely could not have intended.[76]

In its less controversial form, sometimes considered a different category altogether called tax planning, tax avoidance involved choosing to take advantage of available tax benefits as a means of minimizing one's taxes. For example, Sears characterized a change of domicile to a new place to avoid the taxes of the old residence, as long as the move actually occurred, as tax avoidance whether undertaken by an individual or a business such as a corporation.[77] Similarly, purchasing tax-exempt municipal bonds, rather than taxable bonds, was sometimes described as a method of avoiding taxes. Many considered it fully appropriate because it

[73] Id. at 17.

[74] Samuel Joyce Sherman, *Taxation of Corporations Used to Avoid Taxes upon Stockholders*, Part I, 13 TAX MAG. 19 (1935); Randolph E. Paul, *Motive and Intent in Tax Law*, 1 PSYCHIATRY *169*, 172 (1938). In 1913, even before the term "incorporated pocketbook" came into existence, some argued that the separate corporate tax rate was itself a loophole because Congress did not anticipate that wealthy stockholders like John D. Rockefeller and Andrew Carnegie would "escape" the graduated rates that were supposed to reach their "swollen incomes" simply because the surtax rates only applied if corporate profits were distributed to these stockholders as dividends. *Find Rich Need Not Pay Any Income Tax*, N.Y. TRIB., April 29, 1913, at 4.

[75] Id. at 19–20.

[76] F.I. Raymond, *The Capital Gains Loophole*, 10 TAX MAG. 373, 373–74 (1932).

[77] SEARS, MINIMIZING TAXES, *supra* note 50, at 5–14.

was by design in the statute.[78] Indeed, the *Wall Street Journal*, using tax-exempt securities as an example, defined tax avoidance as "the acceptance of an invitation extended by the Federal Government, the states, and the municipalities, in the form of enacted statutes, to the taxpayer to reduce his tax liability under the law."[79] As we have already seen, though, many disagreed that this was any less morally reprehensible than other forms of tax avoidance, expressing loud disagreement with the policy underlying it,[80] especially when it was used by wealthy individuals.[81]

Some used these legalistic distinctions to counter the moral outrage about tax dodging. Sears, for example, argued that "tax avoidance is right morally; that it is right for the tax payer to 'get away with whatever he can', barring misrepresentation and concealment" since by doing so this "tends to make fair what legislators have made unfair" and helps to "make manifest errors in tax legislation which should be corrected."[82] Harvard law professor John MacArthur Maguire and his student Philip Zimet explained that this "school of practice" believed that in light of the "professionally entrancing thicket of accounting methods, varying rates, challenged interpretations, constitutional controversies, administrative technicalities, etc." that were operating in "the tax jungle," taxpayers were essentially free to act in accordance with the literal language of the statute until the legislature changed the law.[83] As George Altman, a lawyer and accountant who was a lecturer in law at Northwestern, concluded, "if the government is not to be restrained by any moral aspects of taxation, why look to the taxpayer for salvation?"[84]

These legalistic line-drawing efforts did not seem to have much effect on actual practice or attitudes. *New York Times* reporter Godfrey Nelson observed that "in general tax parlance . . . the terms 'tax avoidance' and 'tax evasion' have almost come to be regarded as synonymous."[85] A 1934

78 Dohr, *supra* note 71, at 370.

79 Editorial, *Evasion vs. Avoidance*, WALL ST. J., Aug. 2, 1935, at 4.

80 *See supra* text accompany notes 42–46.

81 *See, e.g.*, Charles L.B. Lowndes, *Taxing the Income from Tax-Exempt Securities*, 32 ILL. L. REV. 643, 644 (1938) ("The exemption of interest from governmental obligations from the income tax clearly frustrates the ability-to-pay principle by allocating tax-exempt income to the maximum brackets of the tax.").

82 Sears, *Effective and Lawful Avoidance of Taxes*, *supra* note 51, at 79.

83 John MacArthur Maguire and Philip Zimet, *Hobson's Choice and Similar Practices in Federal Taxation*, 48 HARV. L. REV. 1281, 1283 (1935).

84 Altman, *supra* note 59, at 156.

85 Godfrey N. Nelson, *Rigid Law in View for Income Taxes*, N.Y. TIMES, Jan. 14, 1934, at N7.

Treasury petition before the Board of Tax Appeals illustrated this, alleging that former Treasury Secretary Andrew Mellon engaged in "fictitious" stock sales in a "comprehensive scheme of tax evasion and avoidance."[86] Trying to draw a sharp line between legal tax planning or avoidance and tax evasion may have even backfired, emboldening tax dodgers to push the line, without convincing critics to back off. By 1937, Randolph Paul lamented that "[s]ome taxpayers have reached the point of believing that tax avoidance is one of their inherent rights."[87]

Perhaps inspired by past populist attempts to go after tax dodging,[88] or for political reasons,[89] President Franklin Delano Roosevelt appealed to the popular distaste for tax avoidance and evasion by going after both in his 1937 tax message to Congress. Roosevelt explained that a study of 1936 income tax returns prepared by the Treasury Department "reveals efforts at avoidance and evasion of tax liability, so widespread and so amazing both in their boldness and their ingenuity, that further action without delay seems imperative."[90] Roosevelt noted that some of these efforts "have the color of legality; others are on the borderline of legality, others are plainly contrary even to the letter of the law," but "all are alike in that they are definitely contrary to the spirit of the law."[91]

Roosevelt couched his proposal in moralistic terms, calling these schemes "unethical" and "evil."[92] He urged Congress to ignore "efforts to befog the issue" such as by those claiming what they are doing is technically legal or are justified because they do not approve of the high income tax rates.[93] As

86 *Treasury Files New Petition in Mellon Tax Case*, ST. LOUIS POST-DISPATCH, Sept. 16, 1934, at 1. A previous tax evasion case filed against Mellon in the spring of 1934 on a different set of facts had been rejected by a grand jury and the Board of Tax Appeals in the new case eventually found him innocent of any fraud, although it did impose liability for other errors in his taxes. W. ELLIOT BROWNLEE, FEDERAL TAXATION IN AMERICA: A HISTORY 131 (3rd ed. 2016).

87 PAUL, *supra* note 72, at 76–77.

88 During his run for President as an independent candidate in 1924, Senator Robert La Follette had promised to begin "cleaning up the wide-spread tax dodging which has been permitted by democratic and republican administrations." *"Independent Bloc" to Demand Senate Probe of Income taxes Paid by Multimillionaires*, ATL. CONST., Oct. 26, 1924, at 9.

89 Some suggest that Roosevelt's decision to target tax avoidance was because he did not want to break a promise he had made to not increase income tax rates, Roy G. Blakey and Gladys C. Blakey, *The Revenue Act of 1937*, 27 AM. ECON. REV. 698 (1937), while others accused him of using it to go after political enemies. Westbrook Pegler, *Fair Enough: Tax Avoidance*, WASH. POST, Sept. 22, 1937, at 9.

90 Franklin D. Roosevelt, *Message to Congress on Tax Evasion Prevention*, June 1, 1937.

91 Id.

92 Id.

93 Id.

public finance economists Roy and Gladys Blakey commented, "the President . . . appears unwilling to distinguish between the moralities of tax evasion and those of tax avoidance, although the legitimacy of avoidance has been recognized by the courts."[94] Perhaps to emphasize his disdain for the legalistic line-drawing exercises, Roosevelt joked in a subsequent press conference that "tax evasion becomes tax avoidance when a wealthy man hires a $250,000 lawyer to change the word evasion to the word avoidance."[95] He sought to capitalize on the populist sentiments against all forms of tax dodging, rather than toe the line drawn by Judge Hand and others.

Not surprisingly, none of the fine legal distinctions made in academic, judicial, and professional circles had seeped into the popular and political discourse that Roosevelt's proposals ignited.[96] Raymond Moley, one of the architects of the New Deal who became an opponent by the end of the Great Depression, wrote that "the public cares little about the legal distinction between 'evasion' and 'avoidance': to the country as a whole a tax dodger is a tax dodger."[97] In 1938, tax lawyer Montgomery B. Angell of New York City observed that "public outcry has been raised against 'evaders and avoiders,'" with no distinction between the two.[98] As Lucius Buck, a Special Assistant to the Attorney-General, remarked, "the terms evasion and avoidance are in general lay use and are generally listed as synonymous ones, even in law dictionaries," so it hardly should have been a surprise that they were used interchangeably in the media and in popular discussions.[99] Public sentiment against all forms of tax dodging was so charged that it led one tax practitioner to ask, in light of President Roosevelt's message and the ensuing legislative activity leading up to the adoption of the Revenue Act of 1937, "is it ethical for an attorney to advise a client to take all legal means necessary to avoid the payment of a tax?"[100]

[94] Blakey and Blakey, *The Revenue Act of 1937*, *supra* note 89, at 703. *See* J. Blake Lowe and John D. Wright, *Tax Avoidance versus Tax Evasion*, BARRON'S, Aug. 20, 1937, at 20 ("In the recent congressional tax inquiry, the words 'tax avoidance' and 'tax evasion' were used both loosely and interchangeably.").

[95] Charles A. Beard, *The New Deal's Rough Road*, 42 CURRENT HISTORY *625*, 626 (1935).

[96] There were a few exceptions, but they did not seem to do much to counter Roosevelt's proposals. *See, e.g.*, David Lawrence, *Tax Avoidance Strictly Legal*, ARIZONA REPUBLIC, June 4, 1937, at 1 ("Mr. Roosevelt has introduced the novel theory that the courts of the United States must, in effect, draw no distinction between tax avoidance and tax evasion. He calls both unethical and contrary to the spirit of the law.").

[97] Raymond Moley, *The Fine Art of Avoidance*, NEWSWEEK, June 12, 1937, at 44.

[98] Montgomery B. Angell, *Tax Evasion and Tax Avoidance*, 38 COLUM. L. REV. 80 (1938).

[99] Lucius A. Buck, *Income Tax Evasion and Avoidance: Some General Considerations*, 25 GEO. L.J. 863, 865 (1937).

[100] William Cogger, *Tax Avoidance v. Tax Evasion*, 15 TAX MAG. 518 (1937).

Despite the best efforts of Judge Hand and others,[101] the distinction between avoidance and evasion had become "increasingly blurred."[102] In 1940, tax lawyer and New York University professor Harry Rudick noted, "for those who prefer to continue the logomachy, the distinction may be cynically but practically expressed in the remark that avoidance is merely successful evasion and evasion is unsuccessful avoidance."[103] Randolph Paul had offered a similarly "pragmatic" definition a few years earlier – "avoidance being what *works*, and evasion being what *fails*" – although he still sought in vain to define the two terms so as to offer a "clear cut" distinction.[104]

By the 1950s, even if many lawyers and judges still insisted that a bright line could be drawn between evasion and avoidance or planning,[105] popular opinion was no longer as clear about the immorality of either. Not only were "the terms . . . generally indistinguishable in the minds and conversations of laymen and only vaguely differentiable by lawyers,"[106] but the public's Depression-era resistance to all forms of tax minimization had started to melt away. Most people likely did not openly embrace it, but there was a growing ambivalence about tax dodging. For many people, curiosity replaced shock and envy replaced outrage.

## Why Did Popular Opinion Shift?

What accounts for the change in attitudes toward tax dodging? Not surprisingly, two developments – the rise in tax rates and the broadening of the taxpayer base – combined to make those most affected become

101 *See, e.g.*, Commissioner v. Newman, 159 F.2d 848, 850–51 (2d Cir. 1947) (Judge Hand, in dissent, wrote "[o]ver and over again courts have said that there is nothing sinister in so arranging one's affairs as to keep taxes as low as possible. Everybody does so, rich or poor; and all do right, for nobody owes any public duty to pay more than the law demands: taxes are enforced exactions, not voluntary contributions. To demand more in the name of morals is mere cant.").

102 Harry J. Rudick, *The Problem of Personal Income Tax Avoidance*, 7 L. & CONTEMP. PROBS. 243, 245, n.10 (1940).

103 Id.

104 Randolph Paul, *Restatement of Tax Avoidance*, in STUDIES IN FEDERAL TAXATION 9, 14 (1937) (italics in original).

105 *See, e.g.*, SYDNEY A. GUTKIN AND DAVID BECK , TAX AVOIDANCE VS. TAX EVASION (1958); *but see* Harrop A. Freeman, *A Problem for Professional Men: The Expanding Concept of Tax Fraud*, 45 A.B.A. J. 577, 578 (1959) ("it has long been recognized that tax evasion and avoidance are closely related and fall either side of a fine and indistinct line.").

106 GUTKIN AND BECK, *supra* note 105, at 3.

interested in tax dodging opportunities. More broadly, however, as this book will explain, it was the backsliding from these high rates through loopholes, special exemptions, and selective enforcement that led to the popular ambivalence toward tax dodging and its structural and cultural entrenchment for decades to come.

### *The Rise in the Top Tax Rates*

As previously mentioned, tax rates soared to pay for World War II and remained high in the decades following the war.[107] More importantly for the purposes of the market for tax dodging, the thresholds at which individuals crossed into the higher marginal tax brackets dropped as well, subjecting more people to those high rates. For example, in 1936, individuals with taxable incomes in excess of $1 million were subject to a 77 percent marginal income tax rate,[108] but that amounted to only sixty-one returns that year.[109] By 1954, there were 77,511 individuals subject to a 72 percentage marginal rate bracket or higher.[110] The massive increase in the number of individuals subject to a comparable rate in 1954 is attributable to the fact that the threshold beyond which income was subject to the 72 percent rate had dropped precipitously from $1 million to $44,000 as the income tax transitioned from a "class tax" to a "mass tax."[111] Even the top marginal rate of 91 percent in 1954 applied to income above $200,000 for single filers, whereas the top combined marginal rate of 79 percent in 1936 only kicked in at $5 million.[112]

One effect was that "[t]he tax-avoidance business," which had been a little less visible after the Revenue Act of 1937's crack down, "returned and boomed."[113] The high rates made tax dodging enticing, as well as

107 Steven A. Bank , Kirk J. Stark & Joseph J. Thorndike, War and Taxes 108 (2008).

108 Tax Foundation, *Historical U.S. Federal Individual Income Tax Rates & Brackets, 1862–2021* (1936 data) ("Federal Individual Income Tax Rates History").

109 U.S. Treas. Dep't, Statistics of Income for 1936, Pt. 1, at 5 (1938).

110 U.S. Treas. Dep't, Statistics of Income, Individual Income Tax Returns 1954, at 56, 57 (1957) (joint, single, and head of households).

111 Federal Individual Income Tax Rates History, *supra* note 108 (1954 data); Carolyn C. Jones, *Class Tax to Mass Tax: The Role of Propaganda in the Expansion of the Income Tax During World War II*, 37 Buffalo L. Rev. 685, 686 (1988).

112 Federal Individual Income Tax Rates History, *supra* note 108 (1954 and 1936 data).

113 Richard M. Cooperman, *The Tax Thieves of 1951, Part VI. The True Villains*, New Republic, Dec. 24, 1951, at 10, 11. *See* Roswell Magill, *The Impact of Income Tax Leakages – A Postscript to Randolph Paul*, 12 Tax L. Rev. 1, 1 (1956) ("High rates foster methods and plans for tax reduction and avoidance."); Mortimer M. Caplin, *Threats to*

cost-effective. William J. Casey and J. K. Lasser explained in their 1952 report on *Tax Sheltered Investments* that the "appalling fact is that a dollar of corporate income can shrivel down to less than a penny by the time it has passed through the wringer of the corporate income tax, the individual tax on dividends and the estate tax payable on passing savings on to one's family."[114] Not surprisingly then, Mortimer Caplin, a law professor at Virginia and future Commissioner of Internal Revenue, observed that these rates "led to increased interest in tax planning, in means for arranging one's affairs to minimize taxation, in tax avoidance."[115]

### *The Growth in the Number of Taxpayers*

The second development that helped change the public's attitude toward tax dodging was that the number of people subject to taxation rose considerably. As seen in Figure I.2, in 1940, at a time when there were 132 million people in America, there were only 7.5 million tax returns filed.[116] By 1960, the population had grown over 36 percent to 180 million, but the number of income tax returns filed had grown over 757 percent to 60 million in total.[117] This change was attributable to a drop in the exemption threshold. Whereas the income tax did not apply to a single person with earnings below $1,500 in 1928, it applied to everyone who earned over $600 from 1948 through 1969.[118] As a percentage of the labor force, a mere 5 percent of workers paid income taxes in the mid-1930s, compared to between 65 and 70 percent by the mid-1950s.[119]

*the Integrity of our Tax System*, 44 VA. L. REV. 839, 840 (1958) (High rates have "led to increased interest in tax planning, in means for arranging one's affairs to minimize taxation, in tax avoidance."); PAUL, TAXATION FOR PROSPERITY, *supra* note 35, at 279 ("A 90-percent rate proved to be a powerful stimulant to ingenuity . . . the market had never buzzed with so many schemes"). It also may have revived efforts to get states to pass resolutions calling for Congress to amend the Constitution to limit the top federal tax rate to 25 percent, with an ability to override the limit during wartime. *See* Frank E. Packard, *Put a Ceiling on Taxes!* CHANGING TIMES: THE KIPLINGER MAGAZINE, August 1951, at 43 (noting that the campaign, which started with a resolution passed in Wyoming had spread to twenty-four other states).

114 WILLIAM J. CASEY & J. K. LASSER, TAX SHELTERED INVESTMENTS 1 (1952).

115 Caplin, *supra* note 113, at 840. *See* Magill, *The Impact of Income Tax Leakages*, *supra* note 113, at 1 ("[h]igh rates foster methods and plans for tax reduction and avoidance.").

116 JEROME R. HELLERSTEIN, TAXES, LOOPHOLES & MORALS 13 (1963).

117 Id.

118 Id. Tax Policy Center, Historical Individual Income Tax Parameters, 1913–2023 (May 11, 2023).

119 JOHN F. WITTE, THE POLITICS AND DEVELOPMENT OF THE FEDERAL INCOME TAX 126, fig. 6.2 (1985).

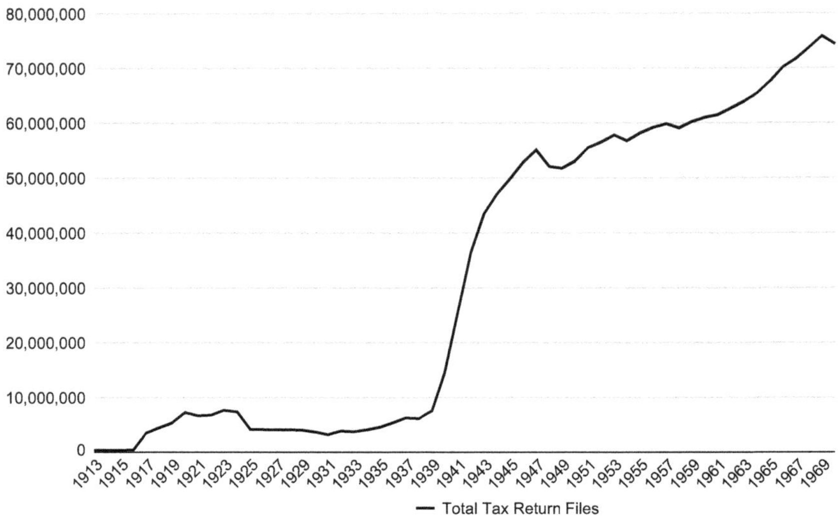


**Figure I.2** Total returns, 1913–1970[120]

Not only did the number of taxpayers increase dramatically, but rates for taxpayers in the lowest brackets also jumped significantly. Between 1932 and 1939, the lowest tax rate was 4 percent on income over $4,000. By 1941, the rate had more than doubled to 10 percent and the income threshold had dropped in half to $2,000. It jumped again to 23 percent by the end of the war in 1944. It moderated after the war, but the bottom rate remained no lower than 20 percent on income over $4,000 from 1951 to 1963.[121]

The high rates and broadened base of taxpayers contributed to the democratization of tax dodging. Tax advising rapidly transformed in response to the rise in rates and in taxpayers. During the 1920s and 1930s, this field was occupied primarily by a small number of white shoe law firms that represented the wealthiest segment of society. Tax dodging, like much of the income tax itself, was reserved for the upper crust of

[120] Historical Statistics of the United States: Earliest Times to the Present v. 5, Pt. E, 5–112 (tbl. Ea740-747), 5–113 (tbl. Ea748-757) (2006).

[121] It was 20.4 percent in 1951 and 22.2 percent in 1952 and 1953. All rates and income thresholds are from Tax Policy Center, Historical Individual Income Tax Parameters, 1913–2023 (May 11, 2023).

society, promoted by a small number of prominent New York and Washington, DC law firms and discussed in hushed tones in the dark and smokey confines of private dining rooms and clubs.[122] Taxpayers in the middle or lower brackets were unlikely to consult a tax adviser, let alone to engage in tax dodging. As the *Austin American* wrote in 1925, "ducking the income tax is easy – IF – you have the money! For the poor man, the salaried man, or the man in moderate circumstances, it is virtually impossible – at least legally."[123]

Not only did the increase in taxpayers draw lawyers and accountants into tax work, but it spawned an entirely new industry of retail tax preparation and advising services. With extensive advertising, these tax advisers introduced a whole new class of people to the tax system and, in some cases, to the methods for dodging it. These new advisers opened offices in many nontraditional spaces, such as in department stores and in shopping centers, as well as in small storefronts on quaint main streets and gritty back alleys. They wrote newspaper advice columns and do-it-yourself guides, often promising to bring the rich guy's tax dodging secrets to the little guys. Access to tax advice had never been greater.

The result was that tax dodging spread throughout society. As tax practitioner Harry Graham Balter wrote in his 1953 treatise, *Fraud under Federal Tax Law*,

> To a greater or lesser extent, nearly everyone is guilty of practicing some form of tax evasion, whether we call it "fraud" or not. Failure to report interest in bank deposits, padding of business entertainment expenses, exaggerating contributions to charity, or adding a fictitious dependent, are examples of tax evasion, unfortunately practiced on a wide scale by rich and poor alike.[124]

A decade later, New York University law professor Jerome Hellerstein observed that this sentiment had not changed, noting that "as so often happens in tax matters, the legitimate has been abused and has fostered the illegitimate."[125]

[122] THORNDIKE, THEIR FAIR SHARE, *supra* note 55, at 202.
[123] *Tax Dodging Easy for Rich, Impossible for Poor*, AUSTIN AMERICAN, Oct. 18, 1925, at SM11.
[124] HARRY GRAHAM BALTER, FRAUD UNDER FEDERAL TAX LAW 16 (2d. ed. 1953).
[125] HELLERSTEIN *supra* note 116, at 127.

## A Word about Terminology

The transformation in public attitudes is in some respects symbolized by the transformation in the use of the term "tax dodging" itself. In the nineteenth and early twentieth centuries, tax dodging was typically associated with what we would call tax evasion as a legal matter. Someone described as a "tax dodger" was considered contemptible and unpatriotic. In 1883, the *Chicago Daily Tribune* opined that "tax-dodging . . . is one of the most discouraging of many signs of the laxity of our social ties."[126] The newspaper used the term interchangeably with tax evasion, noting that "to evade the payment of the taxes due the State is, just like the disregard of the duties of serving on the jury and going to the polls, an attempt to obtain the benefits of government without giving an equivalent."[127] One writer in 1906 went a step further, describing "tax dodging" to be "as reprehensible and as conclusive evidence of disloyalty as many other treasonable acts."[128]

The negative connotation of tax dodging continued after the enactment of the income tax. In 1921, the *Atlanta Constitution* described "the tax-dodger" as "selfish and unpatriotic and dishonest,"[129] while the *Baltimore Sun* compared the tax dodger to a wartime "profiteer."[130] Although it was associated with more than simply tax evasion by this point, tax dodgers were still viewed as unpatriotic, with the *Constitution* calling a tax dodger "a thief who steals from his honest fellow-citizens the benefits that accrue from American citizenship and the protection of the American flag."[131] In 1931, the *Pittsburgh Courier* expressed similar sentiments, writing "the tax dodger is the man who delights in owning nothing to be taxed; he delights in escaping the payment of taxes . . . This type of man is not a citizen – he is a parasite."[132]

By the 1950s and 1960s, a subtle shift emerged. The term "tax dodging" was not free from stigma, but it began to be used with a kind of moral ambivalence that it did not typically have before the war. In fact, "tax dodging" had become sufficiently ambiguous that using the term was a way for observers to comment without making a legal or moral judgment about it. Even those who sought to condemn most of what people were

126 Editorial, *Tax-Dodging*, CHI. DAILY TRIB., Aug. 28, 1883, at 4.
127 Id.
128 *Review*, American Citizenship, by John S. Wise, 4 OKLA L. J. 360 (1906).
129 Editorial, *The Tax Dodgers*, ATL. CONST., June 21, 1921, at 8.
130 *Income Tax Dodgers*, THE SUN (BALTIMORE), Jan. 20, 1920, at 8.
131 *The Tax Dodgers*, *supra* note 129, at 8.
132 *Tax Dodgers*, PITT. COURIER, Jan. 10, 1931, at 10.

doing in their tax maneuvers used the tax dodging phrase, either to cover more ground or to avoid having to defend their judgment based on where it fell on the side of the now blurry line between evasion and avoidance.[133] It had become a catch-all phrase that reflected the myriad ways that some people managed to escape the taxes that hit others squarely in their pocketbooks.

This book primarily uses the term "tax dodging" both because it came into prominent use during this mid-century period, and because it avoids some of the line drawing distinctions that remain in the legal literature. It does not mean that the tax saving maneuvers discussed in this book are, or were at the time, considered illegal, immoral, risky, or somehow inappropriate. Nor does it mean that all deductions, credits, exemptions, or special allowances enacted by Congress should be considered a "loophole," which was described by one contemporary observer as "an unfair means of escape from a burden that others are obliged to bear."[134] Nevertheless, the tax maneuvers described in the chapters that follow, whether arising from "accidental" loopholes or those "put into the laws deliberately" or from the proper or improper use of certain Code provisions,[135] were primarily intended to dodge taxes or, if they were motivated at least in part by unrelated reasons, they were structured to dodge as much of the tax consequences as possible.

## A Roadmap

This book explores how the themes discussed in this introduction played out in various settings in mid-century America. Part I explores tax dodging that was high profile and influential. It starts by examining two groups that were affected by the high rates and were uniquely positioned to influence public perception of and engagement with tax dodging. The first group was comprised of Hollywood celebrities, who were some of the early users and innovators of tax dodging techniques and shelter transactions. They were income rich, unlike old money wealth who were asset rich, and they had nontax reasons to be interested both in owning, rather than renting, their talents and in

[133] *See, e.g.*, H. F. Millikin, The Prudent Man: Tax Dodging as an Art 153 (1963).

[134] Louis Eisenstein, The Ideologies of Taxation 182 (1961). Eisenstein noted that as the term "loophole" took on a negative air, the word "erosions" is "now in fashion" because it suggests "an objective appraisal." Id. at 193.

[135] Magill, *The Impact of Income Tax Leakages*, *supra* note 113, at 9–10.

diversifying their investments. Moreover, they had high profiles and were admired, which meant that their tax dodging helped to popularize some techniques that might have otherwise gone unnoticed by the public. This part of the book also discusses tax havens, a particular type of tax dodging that was prominently used by celebrities, but also became popular among wealthy taxpayers generally and the businesses that they owned. Tax havens were in part high profile both because of the people and companies that used them, but they had an allure of their own that went beyond that. Because of the extensive advertising undertaken to attract investment in havens and the exotic nature of the locations, they were attractive stories for the press and readers. The second group was comprised of corporate executives. Although not nearly as famous as celebrities, they may have been even more influential over the long run. As some of the highest income-earners, they were especially interested in the taxation of compensation and ways to structure their own company's compensation to dodge the high marginal rates. That was part of the impetus to move toward more deferred compensation, more stock-based compensation, and more noncash benefits, which were changes that spread across companies and workers at all levels.

These high-profile groups of taxpayers and transactions helped to publicize and entrench tax dodging, which, as Part II explains, led to its spread beyond the higher brackets. As previously mentioned, the creation of a tax advising industry focused on this segment of the taxpaying population and the advertising of both tax advice and self-help schemes introduced an entire generation of taxpayers to the basics of tax dodging. Some of the devices used by high profile taxpayers also became available to groups beyond the highest tax brackets. Middle-level bureaucrats and traveling salesmen, for example, took part in the generous expense account practices that were originally adopted for corporate executives. Not only did more people find ways to dodge taxes, but more people knew people who were dodging taxes, which increased their desire to seek a "loophole," "shelter," or "haven" of their own. Moreover, as the public learned of the special tax benefits Congress provided to the wealthy, they resisted bitterly when Congress sought to curtail their own small measure of tax dodging by proposing, for example, to extend withholding from wages to the interest on their savings accounts.

None of this is to say these developments were the inevitable result of high progressive rates. There were a variety of justifications for the high rates that received support across the political spectrum, from infrastructure investments to expanding federal benefit programs to enhance the social welfare safety net. When the support for the high rates wavered, however, without the corresponding political will to cut taxes directly, Congress settled for implicit tax cuts. By adopting new exceptions, creating loopholes, and watering down the measures they did adopt to address tax dodging, it both emboldened those who benefitted from it and disheartened those who were left out, leaving them to identify their own forms of tax dodging. It was the backtracking from the high rates, particularly in a nontransparent way for the benefit primarily of the rich and famous, rather than the high rates on their own, that helped to make tax dodging a social and cultural phenomenon in mid-century America.

# PART I

# High-Profile Tax Dodging

# 1

# The Golden Age of Tax Dodging: Celebrities, Hollywood, and the Publicity Effect

> In Romanoff's, on Rodeo Drive off Wilshire, where much of tomorrow's high strategy is planned over a couple of Bloody Marys and Hamburgers Fogelson, the talk is the kind of talk that might be heard if the American Stock Exchange, Sutter Creek, and the New York Cocoa Exchange had merged, taking in a Greek shipping tycoon and a French Arbitrage expert as junior partners. The straight talk about picture-making – who might star, who might script, who might direct – is laced with conversations from a different planet: conversations about charge-offs, depreciation situations, 27½% depletion allowances, exploration expensing, spin-offs, Australian sheep ranches, and Swiss corporations.[1]

In the 1950s, as one columnist recently pointed out, "the wealthiest people in the U.S. were not corporate executives . . . Rather, they were entertainers."[2] In 1958, for example, when Arthur B. Homer, the president of Bethlehem Steel, was making $623,336, Frank Sinatra made nearly $4 million.[3] Given this reality, when entertainers got together to talk amongst themselves in mid-century America, "the U.S. tax laws [were] deeply involved."[4] It should not be surprising, therefore, that when it came to tax dodging during this period, entertainers were on the cutting edge.

Entertainers often attracted a team of individuals ready to help them reduce their tax hit. As Eric Hoyt noted, "high marginal rates . . . increased the power of advisors – those agents, lawyers, accountants, and managers

[1] Eric Hodgins, *Amid Ruins of an Empire, A New Hollywood Arises*, LIFE MAG., June 10, 1957, at 147, 159.

[2] *Highest Paid U.S. Executive*, ATL. J. & CONST., May 25, 1958, at 17A; Joe Nocera, *How a 91% Rate Sparked the Golden Age of Tax Avoidance in 1950s Hollywood*, L.A. TIMES, JAN. 30, 2019.

[3] Id.

[4] Hodgins, *supra* note 1, at 159.

of other sort who could help highly paid talent navigate the rocky waters of the tax code."[5] Celebrity investment advisors such as A. Morgan Maree Jr. also became more powerful as the tax hit increased. He ran what was described as an "investment and tax firm . . . dedicated to solving" celebrities' tax problems through investments in deals that would reduce their tax hit.[6] According to one estimate, "some 50 or 60 of Hollywood's stars and other mile-high earners place their financial affairs, for a 5% fee, in [Maree's] sturdy hands."[7] Perhaps more significantly from the perspective of tax dodging, "these 'advisors' were said to have operated on a percentage basis, receiving their pay after the tax returns had been filed and apparently accepted by the government."[8] As Hoyt surmised, these contingency fee arrangements presumably "encouraged the advisors to cheat on their clients' tax returns."[9]

To contemporary observers, entertainers and other celebrities appeared to be successful in their tax dodging efforts. In a 1941 study of the income and taxes paid by a small sample of actors, writers, directors, and producers for the 1938 taxable year, Leo Rosten, who was deputy director of the US Office of War Information during World War II heading up the Office of Facts and Figures Motion Picture Division,[10] found that effective rates fell substantially below their respective marginal rates.[11] Of the individuals studied, the highest percentage of income any paid in taxes was 34.1 percent on $220,000 in income, including federal, state, and property taxes, and most of the effective rates were quite a bit lower.[12] This was in a year when the top statutory federal rate alone on income above $200,000 was 66 percent.[13] Although much of the difference reflected the general divergence between marginal and effective rates for the top 1 percent of US households at the time,[14] it

[5] Eric Hoyt, *Hollywood and the Income Tax, 1929–1955*, 22 Film History 5, 9 (2010).
[6] Hodgins, *supra* note 1, at 159.
[7] Id.
[8] *Tax Frauds in Hollywood*, N.Y. Times, Feb. 23, 1929, at 5.
[9] Hoyt, *supra* note 5, at 9.
[10] Clayton R. Koppes & Gregory D. Black, *What to Show the World: The Office of War Information and Hollywood, 1942–1945*, 64 J. Am. Hist. 87 (1977).
[11] Leo Rosten , Hollywood: The Movie Colony, the Movie Makers 92 (1941).
[12] Id.
[13] Tax Foundation, *Historical Federal U.S. Income Tax Rates and Brackets, 1862–2021* (Aug. 24, 2021), available at https://taxfoundation.org/data/all/federal/historical-income-tax-rates-brackets/ (accessed August 12, 2025).
[14] The gap between the top marginal rates and the effective rates of the richest 1 percent of all households, not just those in Hollywood, was between 40 and 60 percentage points during this period. W. Elliot Brownlee, Historical Perspective on U.S. Tax Policy Toward

is not a stretch to say that members of the entertainment industry either developed or were early adopters of many of the most common tax minimization techniques of the twentieth century.

By examining a sampling of celebrity tax dodging schemes, this chapter effectively offers a survey of the most prominent tax dodging moves of this era. Perhaps more significantly, it shows how celebrities helped to drive the demand for tax dodging techniques by publicizing and normalizing them through the force of their celebrity status. Even the government's attempts to prosecute celebrities for tax dodging and legislate against their tax maneuvers mostly just served to fuel the popularity of tax dodging among the general public.

## Celebrity Tax Dodging Techniques

Celebrity tax dodging techniques roughly fell into one of three categories, although many fell into more than one. First, claiming (and sometimes exaggerating) business deductions available to everyone. Second, using tax dodging strategies that were available to anyone, but were often easier to accomplish for an entertainer. Third, using a tax dodging strategy that was uniquely available to those in the entertainment industry. What follows is a description of some of the more popular tax dodges celebrities employed.

### *"Wardrobe Skirmishes" and Other Business Deductions*

One of the earliest and most common techniques entertainers used to dodge taxes was to aggressively classify expenses as business deductions.[15] In 1950, for instance, James Cagney tried to deduct as

the Rich, in DOES ATLAS SHRUG? THE ECONOMIC CONSEQUENCES OF TAXING THE RICH 60, tbl. 2.5 (Joel B. Slemrod ed., 2000). Moreover, this gap could not be accounted for simply because an individual's real tax rate is the average of all the marginal rates in the graduated marginal rate system, up to and including the individual's top marginal rate. *See* Thomas Hungerford, *Taxes and the Economy: An Economic Analysis of the Top Tax Rates since 1945 (Updated)* 3 (fig. 1), 4 (fig. 2) (CONGRESSIONAL RESEARCH SERVICE, Dec. 12, 2012) (comparing top marginal rates and average rates for the highest income taxpayers). *See also* Laura Saunders, *Tax Report: Tax Tricks of the Rich and Famous*, WALL ST. J., Jan. 19, 2019, B5 (citing an estimate by accountant Jay Starkman that an income of $1 million in 1952 should have resulted in an income tax of approximately $870,000, or an effective rate of 87 percent, which is a far cry from the average effective rate at the time of 32 percent).

15 Hoyt, *supra* note 5, at 7–8.

a business expense $5,000 worth of dancing lessons and $414 worth of massages.[16] Other seemingly outrageous examples included an actor who tried to claim his dentures as a business expense and an attempt by comedian W. C. Fields to deduct payments to his siblings on the grounds that it was "story preparation."[17] More routinely, virtually any "gathering of entertainment industry players," of which there were many almost every day of the week in Hollywood, was claimed as business-related.[18]

Celebrities seemed most inclined to stretch the boundaries of business expenses when it came to clothing. Actress and Hollywood gossip columnist Hedda Hopper reportedly took a $5,000 business deduction for the purchase of hats on the theory that her "obsession with fashion," reflected in the 150 hats she bought in a typical year, "became an identifiable feature of her work and her image."[19] Similarly, in 1934 film star Adrienne Ames defended her large deductions for clothing on the grounds that "an extensive wardrobe" was necessary to her career as a motion-picture actress, even for clothes used only off-screen.[20] According to Ames, she "was required to appear well-dressed because it affected her earning capacity."[21] Ames claimed that she "could wear a dress but two or three times if it was distinctive, and never more than six or twelve times if not a distinctive dress."[22] Fellow Hollywood star Madge Evans argued similarly when the government questioned her deduction of $2,485 for a mink coat, $110 for an evening gown, and other items of clothing she identified as "purchased for business use."[23] "Dress consciousness," Evans contended, "is part of the way of keeping (a star's) name before the public as much as possible."[24] She explained that the mink coat "was for other purposes than merely keeping warm in New York," such as "to look smart for actors and agents, editors and radio people she would meet . . . to please the Madge Evans fan clubs that

16 *Cagney Scraps Over Tax*, N.Y. Times, Jan. 18, 1953, at 48.

17 Rosten, *supra* note 11, at 91; Joseph J. Thorndike, *High Rates and Hollywood: A Short History of Tinseltown Tax Avoidance*, Tax Notes, Jan. 27, 2019.

18 Hoyt, *supra* note 5, at 8.

19 Mary Desjardins, *"Marion Never Looked Lovelier": Hedda Hopper's Hollywood and the Negotiation of Glamour in Post-War Hollywood*, 16 Q. Rev. of Film & Video 421, 426 (1997).

20 Says *U.S. Tax Is Too Much*, Phil. Inquirer Public Ledger, Oct. 21, 1938, at 4; *Her Complaint: Income Tax*, Baltimore Sun, Oct. 21, 1938, at 7.

21 William M. Pinkerton, *Movie Glamour Girls Regard Mink Coats as Business Necessity*, St. Petersburg Times, Feb. 25, 1939, at 11.

22 Id.

23 *Madge Evans Tells Outlays*, L.A. Times, June 18, 1938, at 8.

24 Pinkerton, *supra* note 21, at 11.

would gather around her train at mid-western stations . . . [and to] flash her mink at the dazzled autograph hounds who haunt premieres."[25] It was not only actresses who tussled with the government over clothing expenses. As Eric Hoyt noted, "these wardrobe skirmishes ... contribut[ed] to a particular star's persona and reinforc[ed] the links in popular culture between Hollywood and the income tax."[26]

## *Runaway Stars*

If a liberal interpretation of the business deduction rules was one of the more modest celebrity tax dodging techniques, moving to a tax haven was one of the more extreme techniques. Entertainers had long sought to leave California to avoid qualifying as a tax resident for state taxes.[27] "Gravel-voiced Ed 'Archie' Gardner" even took his radio show, "Duffy's Tavern," to Puerto Rico to escape taxes both in the US and in Puerto Rico under special provisions designed to encourage development in the US territory.[28] In mid-century America, however, some celebrities left the country altogether. They took advantage of a change in the law in 1951 that was designed to provide an incentive for certain skilled workers to go overseas on temporary assignment in the post–World War II years, allowing them to receive the same favorable tax treatment on personal-service income as those working abroad indefinitely.[29] They merely had to live seventeen out of eighteen months abroad,[30] which largely matched the time necessary to shoot a few movies with

[25] Id.

[26] Hoyt, *supra* note 5, at 8.

[27] *See, e.g., Actors' Device to Avoid Taxes Entails Travel,* N.Y. HERALD TRIB., Dec. 15, 1935, at E2.

[28] Charles Renshaw, Jr., *Artful "Archie,"* ATLANTA CONSTITUTION, Dec. 18, 1949, at SM18; Marvin J. Levin & Morton J. Mitosky, *Tax Saving Practices of Artists and Entertainers,* 31 TAXES 21, 27 (1953).

[29] Senate Finance Committee, *Revenue Act of 1951,* Sen. Rept 781, 82nd Cong., 1st Sess. 52–53 (1951); Eric Hoyt, *Asset or Liability? Hollywood and Tax Law,* in HOLLYWOOD AND THE LAW 183, 193 (Paul McDonald et al., eds., 2015); *30 Actors in Foreign Lands Now,* L.A. TIMES, March 15, 1953, at D1. Previously, only US citizens who were "bona fide residents of a foreign country" were entitled to exclude non-US "earned income" from their gross income. Int. Rev. Code of 1939, as amended, §116(a). George D. Webster, *Taxpayer Relief – The Revenue Act of 1951,* 37 VA. L. REV. 1039, 1055 (1951).

[30] Int. Rev. Code of 1939, as amended, §119. Some in the entertainment industry took advantage of that before 1951 too, such as Paramount executive David Rose, who was dispatched to Great Britain in 1938 to oversee the company's movie productions there indefinitely and proceeded to avoid income tax in not only the USA, but also in Great Britain under a provision exempting from income salary that was deposited in a bank in

some vacation time in-between. Celebrities used this provision to go on short-term stays in Europe and dodge the difference between US and local tax rates.[31]

This new exemption for short-term moves abroad was particularly well-suited to film stars.[32] As *Business Week* observed, "the provision wasn't designed for Hollywood's use, but movie stars were the major beneficiaries."[33] Jerome Hellerstein wrote that "[m]otion-picture and radio and TV stars found the eighteen-month deal the Santa Claus they had long been clamoring for; everybody who was anybody in Hollywood at once became enamored of pictures with foreign settings."[34] "[U]nder the new loophole," American radio shows were broadcast from the Caribbean and there were reports that "one prominent actor made a picture in Mexico during a six-week period within his eighteen month sojourn that brought him $275,000 in US tax-free income," while another star "earned $600,000 in motion pictures in France and other European countries."[35] Movie stars such as "Gary Cooper, Humphrey Bogart, Gene Kelly and various others found that they could go to Europe or Africa, do a picture of two, then bask in the sunny tax immunity on the beach at Cannes."[36] Given that film actors often moved from country to country in Europe for different shots in the same movie or for different films altogether, "some entertainment figures succeeded in avoiding both American and foreign taxes."[37] The *Los Angeles Times* reported on the then-Tax Day of March 15, 1953 that "more than 30 Hollywood film stars, many of them top performers, have left the United States to work in pictures."[38] In addition to those already mentioned, other members of the "18-month club" included celebrities such as Gregory Peck, Clark Gable, Kirk Douglas, Errol Flynn,

the USA rather than paid directly to the taxpayer in a British bank. Rose v. Commissioner, 16 T.C. 232, 238 (1951); Levin & Mitosky, *supra* note 28, at 27.

31 Michael S. Kirsch, *Taxing Citizens in a Global Economy*, 82 N.Y.U. L. Rev. 443, 457–58 (2007); Jerome R. Hellerstein, Taxes, Loopholes, & Morals 184 (1963).

32 *See* Burton W. Kanter, *The United States Income Tax Treaty Program*, 7 Nat'l Tax J. 69, 85 and n. 89 (1954) (although "this area may be considered as relatively unimportant since tax factors probably play a small role in any decision" to move abroad, "Hollywood stars who have been able to schedule overseas movie making to accord with the 18 month period required to qualify for the United States tax exemption" may be the exception to that rule).

33 No More Loophole, Business Week, Aug. 1, 1953, at 78.

34 Hellerstein, *supra* note 31, at 184.

35 Id. at 184–85.

36 *No More Loophole*, *supra* note 33, at 78.

37 Hellerstein, *supra* note 31, at 185.

38 *30 Actors in Foreign Lands Now*, *supra* note 29, at D1.

Evelyn Keyes, and Gary Cooper.[39] Although studios had independent motivations for filming in foreign locations,[40] tax was called "[a] factor of clearly major importance."[41] Perhaps just as importantly, "the average filmgoer believes" that the "real reason" for this "exodus" of celebrities is "to escape paying income tax."[42]

In the 1950s, unions complained that they were losing jobs in "the tax-inspired migration of motion-picture production."[43] A report produced by UCLA labor expert Irving Bernstein for the American Federation of Labor's Hollywood Film Council found that American-interest films made abroad increased by 40 percent in the first two years after the 1951 tax change and more than doubled in the years thereafter,[44] which the International Association of Theatrical Stage Workers blamed in part on "unpatriotic tax-exile stars for forcing shoots to take place overseas."[45] According to Bernstein, there was some truth to this: "An American-interest film made abroad normally has an American director and must have one or preferably two American stars . . . Hence the director's or the star's tax advantage will often dictate where the picture will be shot."[46] One

[39] Bob Thomas, *Stars Mull Over Plan of Escaping Paying Tax*, AUSTIN STATESMAN, Feb. 20, 1952, at 5; Hellerstein, *supra* note 31, at 185; Louis Berg, *Movies on the Move!: Did Hollywood Create a Frankenstein by Making Films Abroad?* L.A. TIMES, Aug. 16, 1953, at I14; Sheilah Graham, *Paris, Tax Exemptions Lure Stars to Europe*, ATLANTA J. & ATL. CONST., Sept. 14, 1952, at 10D.

[40] These included artistic demands, lower costs, and the needs of studios to find a way to reclaim "frozen funds," or profits stranded in Europe because of post-war currency restrictions. Hoyt, *supra* note 29, at 193; J. Howard Rutledge, *Hollywood Abroad*, WALL ST. J., Sept. 18, 1952, at 1.

[41] IRVING BERNSTEIN, Hollywood at the Crossroads: An Economic Study of the Motion Picture Industry 68 (HOLLYWOOD AF OF L FILM COUNCIL 1957).

[42] Hellerstein, *supra* note 31, at 185.

[43] Id.

[44] Bernstein, *supra* note 41, at 49, tbl. 25. *See* DANIEL STEINHART, RUNAWAY HOLLYWOOD: INTERNATIONALIZING POSTWAR PRODUCTION AND LOCATION SHOOTING 9 (2019) (finding an upward trend through 1958 upon recreating Bernstein's study based on completed productions).

[45] Andrew Dawson, *"Bring Hollywood Home!" Studio Labour, Nationalism and Internationalism, and Opposition to "Runaway Production", 1948–2003*, 84 REVUE BELGE DE PHILOLOGIE ET D'HISTOIRE 1101, 1109 (2006). One film historian called labor's effort to reduce the eighteen-month tax exemption "one of their most successful anti-runaway production efforts." Camille K. Yale, Runaway Film Production: A Critical History of Hollywood's Outsourcing Discourse 66 (PhD Dissertation 2010).

[46] Bernstein, *supra* note 41, at 69. *See* Ernest R. Larkins, An Investigation of the Relationship between the Presence of U.S. Employees Abroad and the Changes in Taxation of their Foreign Earned Income 29 (PhD Dissertation 1982 ("well-known movie personalities were taking advantage of their popular demand to insist on filming abroad where their gross income would go untaxed by the US").

producer noted that "'the [tax] inducement is so strong that many a star or director will labor abroad for a lot less than he or she will work here.' This exerts additional pull on a film company to make a picture in some other country – especially considering that the principals may represent 25% or more of the cost of a picture."[47] For example, director William Wyler pushed for the Academy Award-winning film *Roman Holiday* to be shot on location in Rome in part to take advantage of the temporary assignment tax exemption.[48] That is not surprising considering the amount of tax saved. On Gene Kelly's eighteen-month stay in Europe in 1952 he reportedly earned more than $680,000 tax free.[49] Bernstein concluded that "[i]t is the view of sophisticated observers of the motion picture industry that the net effect of these tax advantages has been to increase the number of films made abroad on a substantial scale."[50]

Although labor succeeded in getting Congress to limit the exemption amount for those temporarily living abroad in 1953,[51] some stars responded by permanently shifting their residences abroad. By 1961, the *Hollywood Reporter* noted that "[q]uite a number of US players and other talent have been living abroad, taking advantage of laws which exempt them from tax on income earned overseas if they maintain bona fide residences outside the US."[52] They may have only made up a "small proportion" of those who permanently lived and worked abroad,[53] but celebrities were high-profile and their tax-motivated moves "made for great copy in newspaper and magazine articles."[54] For example, newspapers called *Bridge on the River Kwai* actor William Holden a "runaway star" because he left for Switzerland and refused to do a film in the USA because of the tax consequences.[55] Newspapers called out other actors who joined Holden in Switzerland, including Richard Burton, Noel Coward, Peter Ustinov, David Niven, George Sanders, and Yul

[47] Rutledge, *supra* note 40, at 1.
[48] Yale, *supra* note 45, at 68.
[49] Hedda Hopper, *Looking at Hollywood: Mason to Go Abroad for Film Having an Iron Curtain Theme*, Chi. Daily Trib., Nov. 21, 1952 at A8.
[50] Bernstein, *supra* note 41, at 69.
[51] Technical Changes Act of 1953, P.L. 287 (Aug. 15, 1953) (capping the tax-exempt amount at $20,000); Hellerstein, *supra* note 31, at 185; Yale, *supra* note 45, at 74.
[52] *Overseas "Tax Havens" May End*, Hollywood Reporter, Feb. 7, 1961, at 1.
[53] Philip M. Stern, The Great Treasury Raid 138 (1964).
[54] Hellerstein, *supra* note 31, at 185.
[55] Will Taxes Spoil Rock Hudson? No, He Says, Newsday, Aug. 9, 1960, at 3C; Rick Du Brow, *William Holden Going to Live in Switzerland*, Austin American-Statesman, Aug. 15, 1969, at 7.

Brynner, as well as directors such as Norman Krasna and Robert Siodmak, producer Anatole Litvak, and writers like A. J. Cronin and Georges Simenon.[56] Charlie Chaplin, who lived near Holden's home in the town of Vevey in Switzerland, also reportedly left the country at least in part to dodge unpaid taxes.[57]

Most of these celebrity expats denied that their moves abroad were tax-motivated,[58] but their protestations fell on deaf ears. Reporters wrote that they did not "want to admit . . . that it's due to high taxes that [they] sought asylum in Switzerland or other countries which don't 'sock the rich' and charge up to 95 percent of a man's income for annual tax bills."[59] Nevertheless, the newspapers connected the dots for readers as the *Daily Boston Globe* did when an article about stars such as Errol Flynn, Van Heflin, Audrey Hepburn and her husband Mel Ferrer moving abroad was accompanied by the headline "Hollywood Stars Seek Tax Relief on Foreign Shores: Actors Plan Films Abroad to Escape High Income Taxes."[60]

Some celebrities were more open about their tax motivations for moving abroad, perhaps none more than *Maltese Falcon* director John Huston.[61] In a letter to his agent Paul Kohner in 1955, Huston, who gave up his US citizenship in 1952 to move to Ireland, conceded that the decision affected the types of films he could make:

> I would have to confess that [shooting the picture away from the USA] was only to avoid paying taxes, as there isn't a single other reason that would hold water. I wouldn't like saying this, Paul, nor, I think, would

[56] Geoffrey Bocca, *Hollywood in the Alps*, AUSTIN-AMERICAN STATESMAN, May 7, 1961, at SM4.

[57] *Chaplin Balks at U.S. Income Levy for 1953*, CHI. DAILY TRIB., Aug. 31, 1955, at 13. He later sold his Hollywood studio and again failed to pay the taxes due on the sale. *$1.1 Million Tax Bill Set Up for Charlie Chaplin*, WASH. POST, June 17, 1956, at A10. A combination of xenophobia, anti-Communism paranoia, and a scandal involving an affair and an unwanted child also led to his exile. Stern, *supra* note 53, at 138; Scott Eyman , Charlie Chaplin v. AMERICA: WHEN ART, SEX, AND POLITICS COLLIDED (2023).

[58] Marjory Adams, *Hollywood Stars Seek Tax Relief on Foreign Shoes*, DAILY BOSTON GLOBE, Sept. 20, 1959, at 79.

[59] Id. at 79. *Compare Is it a Crime to Work Abroad?* WASH. POST TIMES HERALD, July 30, 1961, at G1 (Holden protesting that "I'd live there even if my taxes were higher than in the states") *with* Du Brow, *supra* note 47, at 7 (Holden, in noting that he had considered moving to Switzerland before actually making the move, conceded that "anyone who doesn't think about the idea in this day of high taxes is crazy. But I decided against it because I wanted my boys to be raised in this country.").

[60] Adams, *supra* note 58, at 79.

[61] WILLIAM LUHR, THE MALTESE FALCON: JOHN HUSTON, DIRECTOR 3 (1995).

> people like to hear me say it ... So long as I make pictures outside the United States, I shall have to limit myself to material that doesn't call for a modern day American setting. We should consider this a rule.[62]

Considering that Huston went on to direct films such as *Moulin Rouge* and *Moby Dick*, this was apparently not much of a hardship, but it illustrates the extremes some mid-century celebrities went to dodge high taxes.

Even Hollywood studios participated in a form of tax flight, although typically without moving the entire studio out of the country. In the 1930s, many sought to leave California to dodge its high state taxes. Florida was particularly aggressive in wooing the film industry. As *Time Magazine* wrote, "Happy squeals to the effect that the cinema industry might leave California have been heard from Florida since before the real estate boom of 1923–26."[63] Some of the biggest studios in California were receptive to such entreaties, using it to keep policy-makers in line. "Every time California proposes a new tax on cinema production," the magazine continued, the cinema industry issued "disgruntled threats to go to Florida."[64] Such threats became concrete in 1935 when bills were introduced in California proposing between a 0.5 and a 1 cent per foot tax on the master film and all copies of films produced by Hollywood studios.[65] Joseph M. Schenck, president of United Artists, estimated that the bigger levy would amount to a 35 percent income tax on film studios.[66] The *Los Angeles Times* editorial board predicted that this "would almost certainly force every major producer to leave this field, despite the heavy losses moving would entail."[67] Indeed, a group of major studio heads, led by Schenck, Fox studio's Sidney R. Kent, and Metro-Goldwyn-Mayer (MGM)'s Louis B. Mayer traveled to Florida to consider Schenck's proposal.[68]

62 Hoyt, *Asset or Liability? supra* note 29, at 183 (quoting Letter from John Huston to Paul Kohner, John Huston Papers, 1162 (October 25, 1955) in Academy of Motion Picture Arts and Sciences).

63 *Cinema: Schenck Plan*, TIME MAG. ONLINE, March 18, 1935.

64 Id.

65 *Tax Threats to Films*, L.A. TIMES, Feb. 6, 1935, at A4; *California Impost Would Hit Movies*, N.Y. TIMES, Feb. 10, 1935, at E7; *New Screen Tax Sought*, L.A. TIMES, April 2, 1935, at 2.

66 *The Schenck Plan*, *supra* note 63; *No Bluff*, L.A. TIMES, March 6, 1935, at A4.

67 Id. at A4.

68 *Film Studios Prepared to Leave Coast*, HARTFORD COURANT, March 9, 1935, at 18; *Flight of Studios Faces Hollywood*, N.Y. TIMES, March 5, 1935, at 23; *Fair Tax Guarantee or We Move, Says Schenck*, Hollywood Reporter, March 29, 1935, at 1.

Other areas also sought to lure Hollywood studios in the wake of the California tax proposal. Chicago Mayor Edward Kelly traveled to California to discuss the tax situation there with movie industry leaders. He pointed out to them that "[w]hile the California income taxes go as high as 15 per cent, there is no such tax in Illinois" and argued that "Chicago and the metropolitan area have all the facilities the movies would need."[69] Delaware, New Jersey, North Carolina, and Texas all made offers to exempt studios from state taxation altogether, at least temporarily,[70] and some repeated the offers in subsequent years.[71] In the 1950s, a film set was even built in the tiny town of Brackettville, Texas, a hundred miles west of San Antonio, in an attempt to lure Hollywood studios.[72] Although the large studios generally remained in Southern California, there were reports that Paramount was considering shifting regular shooting of its films to out-of-state studio locations,[73] a practice that continues to this day as studios chase tax breaks around the world.[74]

### *Their Own Private Loophole*

Rather than relying upon existing deductions or fleeing the country, top entertainment executives used connections to enact their own private loopholes. In one famous example, Louis B. Mayer, the long-time head of MGM Studios, had a contract in which MGM agreed to pay him 10 percent of its net profits from all films even if he quit or retired.[75] When he finally did retire in 1951, MGM negotiated to pay him a lump sum payment of $2.275 million for relinquishing his rights to future profits

69 *Film Companies Invited Here to Avoid High Taxes*, Chi. Daily Trib., Oct. 24, 1935, at 13.

70 Louella O. Parsons, *Will Studios Move? Industry Awaits State Tax Action*, San Francisco Examiner, March 24, 1935, at 4E.

71 *Delaware Tax-Free Bid to Film Studios Moved*, Hollywood Reporter, March 2, 1937, at 1.

72 Don Graham, *Regional Filmmaking, Texas, and the Hollywood Tradition*, 69 Southwest Review 350, 354 (1984).

73 *Paramount to Use Long Island Studio in First Anti-tax Move*, Billboard, April 6, 1935, at 20. A few weeks later, however, Paramount denied such a move was impending in an interview with the New York correspondent of the *Los Angeles Times*. Grance Kingsley, *Studios Face Tax Wherever They Move To*, L.A. Times, April 28, 1935, at A1.

74 Winston Cho, *Canada, Georgia Benefit Most From California Runaway Productions*, Hollywood Reporter, March 21, 2022; Yale, *supra* note 45, at 3.

75 Jack Steele, *Movie, TV Stars, Save Money by Selling "Package Deals,"* Daily Boston Globe, Feb. 23, 1958, at 38.

under his contract.[76] The problem was that this type of lump sum payment would be taxed as ordinary income and, according to tax lawyer Louis Eisenstein, "relatively little would remain after taxes."[77] Instead, Mayer's lawyer lobbied the Senate Finance Committee to adopt what became known as the Louis B. Mayer provision, which appeared facially neutral, but was drafted in a way that all but said that it only applied to Mayer:

> **Sec. 1240. Taxability to Employee of Termination Payments**
> Amounts received from the assignment or release by an employee, after more than 20 years' employment, of all of his rights to receive, after termination of his employment and for a period of not less than 5 years (or for a period ending with his death), a percentage of future profits or receipts of his employer shall be considered an amount received from the sale or exchange of a capital asset held for more than 6 months if such rights were included in the terms of the employment of such employee for not less than twelve years, and if the total of the amounts received for such assignment or release are received in one taxable year and after the termination of such employment.[78]

As Phillip Stern later wrote, "[e[]ven your tax lawyer (if you have one) would probably pass over the section as meaningless, on the assumption that no client of his could ever comply with all of those 'ifs' and 'provideds.'"[79] According to Stern, that was because "Section 1240 was written with [Louis B. Mayer] specifically in mind, tailored to fit his own individual situation. It didn't mention him by name, but it might just as well have."[80]

In the 1954 version, Congress closed the loophole by limiting it to those who had included it in their terms of employment prior to the date the provision was enacted.[81] That was not before Mayer, however, had reportedly saved approximately $2 million by having his settlement taxed as capital gains rather than ordinary income.[82] Moreover, several "[o]ther highly paid executives [had] worked out contracts to fit their

[76] Id.
[77] Louis Eisenstein , The Ideologies Of Taxation 156 (1961).
[78] Internal Revenue Code of 1939, as amended, § 1240.
[79] Stern, *supra* note 53, at 45.
[80] Id.
[81] Id., at 48; Internal Revenue Code of 1954, § 1240(2) (adding a clause requiring that "such rights were included in the terms of employment of such employee before the date of enactment of this title").
[82] Stern, *supra* note 53, at 45; Eisenstein, *supra* note 77, at 156.

'termination payments' to the Mayer provision."[83] The 1954 amendment ensured that those executives who had altered their contracts to conform to the Mayer provision could keep them, but it slammed the door on others. As Eisenstein noted, tongue-in-cheek, "it would be unfair to treat them less kindly than Mr. Mayer."[84]

### *"Gentlemen Cowboys," Wildcatters, and Other Tax Shelters*

Celebrities were some of the earliest investors in so-called "tax shelters." These were designed to generate deductions to shelter a person's highly taxed ordinary income and then be eligible for the preferential capital gains rates when sold.[85] For many Hollywood stars, the easiest shelters were to either convert their expensive hobby into a deductible side business or to "deliberately become entrepreneurs in an effort to reduce their tax load."[86] One technique that was popular was "operat[ing] their horses and stable as a business enterprise."[87] Early film fan magazine *Photoplay* wrote that actors like Gary Cooper, Joel McCrea, Randolph Scott, and Joe E. Brown all raised horses, even though "heaven knows that everyone who raises horses loses money," while film stars like Mae West sold chow mein, James Cagney bottled lemon juice, and Al Jolson managed prize fighters.[88]

Another popular side business tax shelter for the Hollywood crowd was to become a "Gentleman cowboy."[89] According to one pamphlet, entitled "How to Round up a Tax-Sheltered Second Fortune by Investing in Cattle," the promoters purchased the heifers, arranged leases on land for the herd to graze, and provided the bulls.[90] Another prospectus for a cattle tax shelter pointed out that "a 69-percent-bracket taxpayer can actually end up ahead, after taxes, by $64,367 in five years," despite losing money in the enterprise.[91] As Philip Stern remarked, "it is little wonder . . . that top-bracket notables in the entertainment world, such

83 Steele, *supra* note 75, at 38.
84 EISENSTEIN, *supra* note 77, at 157.
85 Thomas W. Hanchett, *U.S. Tax Policy and the Shopping-Center Boom of the 1950s and 1960s*, 101 AM. HIST. REV. 1082, 1095 (1996); KEVIN PHILLIPS, Wealth and Democracy: A Political History of the American Rich 77 (2002).
86 ROSTEN, *supra* note 11, at 108.
87 Id.
88 Gilbert Sides, *Diamond Pin Money*, PHOTOPLAY, Feb. 1938, at 22, 84.
89 STERN, *supra* note 53, at 141.
90 Id.
91 Id. at 140.

as Alfred Hitchcock ... have developed a special fondness for brood cows."[92] The reason for this and other similar celebrity-run outside "businesses," according to *Photoplay*, was that "losing money is one of the few things you can do and make the government pay for it ... You have the fun of experimenting on a ranch or in a hat shop and most of the fifty thousand dollars you lose is the government's loss, not yours."[93]

Oil was one of the first celebrity tax shelters because of the promise of large deductions. A depletion deduction for recovering the costs of "ores and all other natural deposits" was part of the first post-Sixteenth Amendment income tax in 1913, and it was specifically extended to oil and gas wells in 1916.[94] Early on, it was used to incentivize the so-called "wildcatter" to drill for oil to fuel the growing industrial economy.[95] In his 1950 Message to Congress on Tax Policy, President Harry Truman stated that the depletion allowance was "originally introduced as a moderate measure to stimulate essential production in the first World War."[96] It was problematic, though, because it was based on the recovery of the original cost, which was often nominal since the oil was on what was called "unproven territory."[97] Congress subsequently applied a discovery value basis for cost recovery, treating the taxpayer as if he had bought the property on the effective date of the 1913 tax at its then fair market value.[98] This principle was later applied to any new acquisition of an ownership interest in oil and gas or other minerals, regardless of when purchased.[99] Valuation, however, became cumbersome.[100]

Under the Revenue Act of 1926, Congress abandoned the discovery value method and enacted the percentage oil depletion deduction, which permitted companies drilling for oil to take a flat 27.5 percent deduction each year.[101] Although the flat rate deduction was adopted for

92 Id. at 140–41.
93 Sides, *supra* note 88, at 84.
94 W. Leo Austin, *Percentage Depletion: Its Background and Legislative History*, 21 U. KAN. CITY L. REV. 22, 25 (1952).
95 Paul E. Martin, *Percentage Depletion for Oil – Saint or Sinner*, 9 BAYLOR L. REV. 247, 249 (1957). *But see* George K. Yin, *A Maritime Lawyer, Percentage Depletion, and the JCT*, 152 TAX NOTES 1695 (2016) (suggesting that the oil and gas industry was not itself the original source for adopting the provision).
96 Harry S. Truman, *Special Message to the Congress on Tax Policy* (Jan. 23, 1950).
97 Harry A. Campbell, *Depletion of Oil and Gas Properties under the Act of 1926*, 5 NAT'L INCOME TAX MAG. 51 (1927); Austin, *supra* note 94, at 25.
98 Austin, *supra* note 94, at 26.
99 Id.
100 Id. at 26–27.
101 Revenue Act of 1926, § 204(11)(c)(2).

administrative simplicity,[102] it made investing in oil quite attractive. As Joe Hyams explained, "if oil is hit, the cost of drilling is deducted," which could amount to 50–75 percent of the drilling expenses "and 27½ per cent depletion is taken off the top with no taxes. If the well is dry, the cost of drilling is deducted before taxes."[103] When they sold the well, any appreciation would then be taxed at the capital gains rate of 25 percent rather than the top individual rate of 91 percent.[104] According to Treasury Secretary John Snyder "the combination of percentage depletion and the expensing of development costs provides a mechanism for pyramiding extensive holdings in oil assets with payment of little or no income tax."[105] This became known as "drilling with tax money."[106]

Celebrities found the percentage depletion deduction so "enticing" that sought the adoption of a version of it for themselves.[107] Their investments, they argued, had some of the same income volatility and investment risks associated with oil drilling.[108] Roger Marchetti, the leading industry lobbyist for this concept,[109] argued that "film stars are just like oil wells. . . . Popularity is the source of their income, and that runs dry as quickly as an oil well does."[110] *Photoplay* subsequently called this a plea for "an allowance for exhaustion of popularity."[111] In 1958, Screen Actors Guild president Ronald Reagan pushed for this "exhaustion of popularity" deduction in testimony before the House Ways and Means Committee. Representing the Motion Picture Industry Council and the Hollywood AFL Film Council, Reagan explained that given the

[102] Peter A. Shulman, *The Making of a Tax Break: The Oil Depletion Allowance, Scientific Taxation, and Natural Resources Policy in the Early Twentieth Century*, 23 J. POL'Y 281, 288 (2011); Austin, *supra* note 94, at 27; J. P. Jackson, *Comment: Federal Income Tax Percentage Depletion of Oil and Gas Wells – Another View*, 21 TEX. L. REV. 798 (1942). Prior to 1926, the industry "had struggled to value total assets in the ground and determine how much depletion expense should be matched to each barrel of oil produced." Yuxun Willy Tan, *There's No Business Like Oil Business: The Allure of Tax Sheltered Oil Income to Hollywood's Wealthy*, 7 Iowa Hist. Rev. 37, 38 (2017).

[103] Joe Hyams, *How Big Stars Keep Their $$$*, N.Y. HERALD TRIBUNE, Feb. 15, 1959, at D3; *The Hollywood Wildcats*, TIME, Oct. 10, 1949, at 93.

[104] *The Hollywood Wildcats*, *supra* note 103, at 93.

[105] *Revenue Revision of 1950*, Hearings before the Committee on Ways and Means, House of Representatives, 81st Cong. 2d Sess. 7, 17 (Feb. 3, 1950).

[106] Id.

[107] Shulman, *supra* note 102, at 282.

[108] Id.

[109] *Tax Relief Plea to Liken Film Stars to Oil Wells*, L.A. TIMES, Jan. 3, 1938, at 1; Tan, *supra* note 102, at 39.

[110] *Tax Relief Plea to Liken Film Stars to Oil Wells*, *supra* note 109, at 1.

[111] Sides, *supra* note 88, at 85.

"diminishing market value" of actors, it was comparable to "drilling for oil or prospecting for gold" in how it was uniquely affected by the current tax laws.[112] In his written statement, Reagan proposed a tax averaging system rather than special treatment as a solution,[113] but in person, when Representative Noah Mason, a conservative Republican from Illinois, asked whether a "depreciation allowance ... on the human being" could "be used to solve your problems," Reagan quipped, "we will take almost anything we can get. We feel we are about as short lived as an oil well and twice as pretty."[114]

Although an exhaustion of popularity deduction never was adopted, many celebrities did the next best thing by investing in oil tax shelters to generate deductions that would offset their film income.[115] Celebrities like James Stewart, Gene Autry, Don Ameche, Frank Sinatra, Bing Crosby, and Bob Hope all were known to invest in oil as part of their tax dodging.[116] When newspapers reported on the "Movie-Star Millionaires," they often noted that many of the top earners like Crosby, Hope, Autry, and Irene Dunne "salted it away" in oil wells.[117] Hope reportedly netted more after tax from his half-a-million dollar oil income than from his million-and-a-half radio, film, and personal appearance income.[118] Moreover, one benefit of oil investing was that the deductions and losses could shelter radio, film, and personal appearance income even when the wells came in dry, as reportedly happened in one of the early oil investments made by Hope and Crosby.[119] There were so many films makers and stars involved in oil investing that one oilman joked that "[w]hen you see a group of movie people talking on the set, you don't know whether they're discussing an oil well or a movie."[120] The

[112] Ronald Reagan, Statement to the House Committee on Ways and Means, General Revenue Revision, 85th Cong., 1st Sess. 1980, 1982 (Jan. 27, 1958).

[113] Id. at 1985.

[114] Id. at 1991.

[115] Tan, *supra* note 102, at 39.

[116] Id. at 41; Shulman, *supra* note 102, at 281–82; Hyams, *supra* note 103, at D3; *The Hollywood Wildcats, supra* note 103, at 93; Adams, *supra* note 58, at 79; Charles Molony, *How Much Incentive Do Oilmen Need for Keeping Up Prospecting?* AUSTIN STATESMAN, Feb. 3, 1950, at 5.

[117] Liza Wilson, *Who Are the Movie-Star Millionaires?* WASH. POST, TIMES-HERALD, Sept. 27, 1959, at AW6.

[118] Sheilah Graham, *Hollywood Gossip: Chaplin May become a Citizen after 38 Years,* DAILY BOSTON GLOBE, April 8, 1950, at 15.

[119] *See* SALLY HELGESEN , WILDCATTERS: A STORY OF TEXANS, OIL, AND MONEY 89 (1981).

[120] *The Hollywood Wildcats, supra* note 103, at 93.

mingling encouraged investing in the other direction too, as oil men formed film production companies with film makers and stars in order to "acquire 'profitable' business losses for tax-deduction purposes."[121]

## *"Incorporated Talent" and "Hollywood Corporations"*

Film stars often sought to dodge the high marginal rates by holding their interest in a picture through a business organization. There were several tax advantages to using a corporation. First, the top corporate rate of 52 percent was far lower than the top individual rate of 91 percent. Second, corporations were separate assets and an ownership interest in a corporation was considered a capital asset, with sales of the stock eligible for the preferential 26 percent capital gain tax rates. In the entertainment industry, using a corporation to dodge taxes took at least two forms: (1) loan-out corporations, also known as "incorporated talent,"[122] and (2) collapsible corporations, also called "Hollywood corporations" because of their early use by entertainers.[123]

With loan-out corporations, celebrities would form personal service corporations that purported to enter into contracts with producers for the loan of actors who were under contract to the corporation to fill roles in films. Although the corporation only ever lent out the services of the celebrity who owned the corporation to a film's producers, the advantage of the scheme was that it meant the income was earned by the corporation as a fee for providing acting services, rather than by the celebrity individually as a salary, and would therefore be taxed at the much lower corporate rate than the top individual income tax rate. The corporation paid the celebrity a salary, but it was far less than the fee the corporation received from the studio, allowing the remainder to be held by the corporation for investment or loan to the celebrity, both with earnings

[121] Carey McWilliams, *The Oil Men Invade Hollywood*, THE NATION, Oct. 16, 1948, at 429. *See* Thomas F. Brady, *New Film Company Formed by Oil Man*, N.Y. TIMES, April 12, 1948, at 25 (describing an announcement by Glenn McCarthy, an oil man from Texas, about the creation of an independent film producing company with actor Robert Paige and writer Marty Collins to produce Collins' screenplay "Land of Plenty").

[122] Stanton D. Rosenbaum, *Entertainer's Corporations and Capital Gains*, 12 TAX L. REV. 33, 48, n. 63 (1956); Levin & Mitosky, *supra* note 28, at 25.

[123] STERN, *supra* note 53, at 137; Boris I. Bittker, *The Tax Treatment of Collapsible Corporations*, 13 VAND. L. REV. 129 (1959). Another early name for the device was the "Fadeout Corporation." *Hollywood Stars' Income Tax: An Ingenious Device*, THE MANCHESTER GUARDIAN (UK), Nov. 5, 1945, at 5. Sam Goldwyn is sometimes credited with the development of the collapsible corporation. Steele, *supra* note 75, at 38.

taxed at the lower corporate rate.[124] The salary was deductible and if the corporation used some of the retained earnings to purchase stock in another corporation, it could reduce the tax rate to a mere 7.8 percent because of the application of the dividends received deduction.[125] In addition, especially in later years, the loan-out structure generally provided more generous business deductions than those available to an employee individually.[126] For all these reasons, loan-out corporation were used as early as the 1930s by entertainers to dodge taxes.[127]

One particularly famous and influential use of the loan-out corporation strategy involved Charles Laughton. Laughton was an English stage and film actor best known for his role as Captain Bligh in the 1935 film *Mutiny on the Bounty* alongside Clark Gable.[128] A year prior to the film's release, Laughton formed a personal services corporation – Motion Picture and Theatrical Industries, Ltd. in England ("Industries, Ltd.").[129] Although Laughton was not a member of the board of directors of Industries, Ltd. and did not actively participate in its management, he was the sole stockholder and the only performer contracted to provide his "sole and exclusive services" to Industries, Ltd.[130] Under this arrangement, Industries Ltd. "loaned-out" Laughton to Hollywood studios that sought to use him in one of their films.[131] In one example, Paramount paid $6,000 a week to Industries, Ltd. in 1935 to secure the loan of Laughton for the film *Ruggles of Red Gap*, while Industries, Ltd. paid Laughton the more modest $750 per week under his contract.[132] This allowed the majority of the income earned for his performance to be taxed at the corporate rate, including the reinvested earnings. The

124 HELLERSTEIN, *supra* note 31, at 88.

125 The dividends received deduction exempted 85 percent of the dividend, leaving only the remaining 15 percent of the dividend subject to the 52 percent corporate rate, for an effective rate of 7.8 percent. STERN, *supra* note 53, at 136; Steven A. Bank, *When We Taxed the Pyramids*, 41 FLA. ST. U. L. REV. 39, 58–59 (2013).

126 Mary LaFrance, *The Separate Tax Status of Loan-Out Corporations*, 48 VAND. L. REV. 879, 885 (1995).

127 Emily Carman & Phillip Drake, *Doing the Deal: Talent Contracts in Hollywood* in HOLLYWOOD AND THE LAW 209, 210 (Paul McDonald, Emily Carman, Eric Hoyt & Phillip Drake, eds., 2015).

128 *Charles Laughton, Father of Talk Magazine*, SLATE, July 18, 2001.

129 Hoyt, *Asset or Liability, supra* note 29, at 191.

130 Charles Laughton v. Commissioner, 40 B.T.A. 101, 103 (1939); J. Timothy Phillips et al., *Origins of Tax Law: The History of the Personal Service Corporation*, 40 WASH. & LEE L. REV. 433, 444 (1983).

131 Hoyt, *Asset or Liability, supra* note 29, at 191.

132 Id.

Commissioner challenged the legitimacy of Industries, Ltd.,[133] arguing it was Laughton's alter ego, but the Board of Tax Appeals upheld the arrangement.[134] The Ninth Circuit affirmed on appeal, although remanding to determine whether the salary Laughton received from Industries, Ltd. was so far below what the corporation received for his services that the contract amount was in effect a single transaction paid to Laughton.[135] Notwithstanding that detail, the basic principle of the loan-out corporation was upheld, setting the precedent for others to follow.

In the mid-1930s, Congress enacted provisions that penalized what were generally referred to as "incorporated pocketbooks."[136] Under what were called the "personal holding company" rules because they applied to corporations with only a few owners, individuals were subject currently to the individual surtax rates on a high percentage of certain kinds of undistributed income such as dividends, interest, and royalties classified as "personal holding company income."[137] The problem was that Treasury was not always successful in convincing courts to apply these personal holding company rules to celebrities' loan-out corporations, in part because the statutory provision and its definition of personal holding company income was drafted too narrowly for these purposes.[138]

In 1937, Congress amended the definition of personal holding company income to include personal service contracts "if some person other tan the corporation has the right to designate (by name or by description) the individual who is to perform the services, or if the individual who is to perform the services is designated (by name or by description) in the contract."[139] This was designed to cover the "film star who draws

[133] *Seven Called Tax Dodgers by Treasury*, L.A. Times, June 19, 1937, at 1.

[134] Charles Laughton v. Commissioner, 40 B.T.A. at 107.

[135] Commissioner of Internal Revenue v. Laughton, 113 F.2d 103, 104–05 (9th Cir. 1940). There was apparently no decision on the remand. Boris I. Bittker, *Professional Associations and Federal Income Taxation: Some Questions and Comments*, 17 Tax L. Rev. 1, 5, n.8 (1961).

[136] Revenue Act of 1934, Pub. L. No. 73-216, § 351, 48 Stat. 751–52 (1934); Wallace C. Murchison, *Tax Advantages and Disadvantages of Incorporated Pocketbooks*, 28 N. C. L. Rev. 47 (1949).

[137] Randolph E. Paul, *The Taxation of Personal Holding Companies*, 31 Proc. Ann. Conf. on Tax'n of the Nat'l Tax Ass'n 403 (1938).

[138] Harry J. Rudick, *Section 102 and Personal Holding Company Provisions of the Internal Revenue Code*, 49 Yale L.J. 171, 175, 177 (1939).

[139] Revenue Act of 1937, Pub. L. No. 75-377, ch. 815, § 352(e), 50 Stat. 813, 815 (1937); Peter Miller, *Capital Gains Taxation of the Fruits of Personal Effort: Before and Under the 1954 Code*, 64 Yale L.J. 1, 3 (1954).

a modest salary from a Holding Company engaged in contracting out his services for several hundred thousands of dollars," in the definition of personal holding company income.[140]

The flaw in the reform was that the rules only applied if personal holding company income constituted 80 percent of the corporation's income for the year,[141] which allowed plenty of wiggle room to avoid the penalty. As Jerome Hellerstein observed, "if an actor handles his TV and motion picture performances through a corporation which has substantial holdings in real estate, mineral properties and other enterprises, he too can avoid the penalties of personal holding company treatment and still route his service income through his corporation."[142] Several entertainers used this strategy, including singer Tony Martin, who licensed rights to manufacture products like pajamas and perfumes for men, Groucho Marx, who developed a TV quiz game, and George Burns and Gracie Allen, who licensed their names for a furniture manufacturer to make branded "cushioned products."[143] Alternatively, a star's personal services corporation could contract for the services of everyone in the cast of the star's show, with only the star's income classified as personal holding company income, and similarly avoid hitting the personal holding company income threshold.[144] As a result of these and other methods, one tax advisor maintained that "no corporation need pay the personal holding company tax if it is familiar with the provisions of the tax law."[145] During the 1950s, the numbers appeared to back up this boast. In the 1958–59 fiscal year, only $559,000 was collected in penalty taxes under the personal holding company provisions, suggesting that few enforcement actions were either pursued or were successful.[146]

A provision enacted earlier – the accumulated earnings tax – was equally unsuccessful in shutting down celebrity loan-out corporations.[147] Part of the problem is that the provision, which imposes a penalty on a corporation that is supposed to serve as a proxy for the individual rates that would have applied if the accumulated surplus had been distributed, only applies when a corporation is "formed or availed of

[140] Paul Marcuse, *Taxation of Undistributed Profits*, 15 N.Y.U. L.Q. REV. 1, 15 (1937).
[141] Revenue Act of 1937, *supra* note 139, at §352(a).
[142] HELLERSTEIN, *supra* note 31, at 92.
[143] STERN, *supra* note 53, at 134.
[144] HELLERSTEIN, *supra* note 31, at 92.
[145] STERN, *supra* note 53, at 133.
[146] Id.
[147] Steven A. Bank, Tax, *Corporate Governance, and Norms*, 61 WASH. & LEE L. REV. 1159, 1209 (2004).

for the purpose of avoiding the income tax" on the shareholders.[148] This intent requirement can be defeated if the taxpayer offers an alternative explanation for the use of the corporation. For example, when Treasury attempted to apply it to filmmaker Cecille de Mille, who allowed most of his earnings to be reinvested inside the corporation, its arguments were rejected.[149] The Board of Tax Appeals found that the corporation was accumulating earnings to be able to finance its own films, not to evade the surtax rates, and therefore declined to impose the penalty tax in a decision hailed as crucial defeat for the government's "crusade to penalize film producers accused of dodging income taxes."[150]

The alternative to the loan-out corporation was a strategy that became known as the "collapsible corporation." This involved setting up a new corporation to produce a single film with the stock held by the producer and some of the writers and stars of the film.[151] After the film was completed and distribution contracts secured, but before the film was released to movie theaters, the corporation would be liquidated, or "collapsed," and the movie distribution rights conveyed to the stockholders as a liquidating distribution.[152] If the distribution rights had remained in the corporation after the film was released to theaters, the profits would have been subject to double taxation – first at the corporate level and a second time to shareholders at the high individual tax rates when distributed as dividends.[153] Not only did the liquidation avoid double taxation,[154] but because it was treated as a sale of the stock in exchange for the value of the holder's applicable share of the liquidated assets of the corporation, any gain was taxable at the lower capital gains

[148] I.R.C. § 533(a).

[149] Cecille B. Demille v. Commissioner, 31 B.T.A. 1161 (1935), *aff'd*, Commissioner of Internal Revenue v. Cecille B. DeMille Productions, Inc., 90 F.2d 12 (9th Cir. 1937), *cert. denied*, 302 U.S. 713 (1937).

[150] Id.; *DeMille's Vindication in Tax Claim Seen as General Victory for Personally-Owned Corp.'s*, VARIETY, Feb. 5, 1935, at 5. See Allen Rostron, *How the Board of Tax Appeals Changed Hollywood History*, 55 TAX LAW. 951, 957 (2001) (describing the case and its reverberations throughout the industry).

[151] R. Lewis Brown & Byron F. White, *Income Tax: Collapsible Corporations: Ordinary Income v. Capital Gain: Internal Revenue Code Section 117(m)*, Cal. L. Rev. 938 (1950).

[152] Id.

[153] J. Reid Hambrick, *Collapsible Corporations in Oil and Gas: Does the 1958 Act Afford Any Relief?* 28 GEO. WASH. L. REV. 815, 816 (1960).

[154] *Billboard* reminded entertainers as part of its series on tax planning that you have to "distribute the assets in kind proportionately to the stockholders" in a liquidation "and let the stockholders sell the assets themselves, thereby avoiding" the tax at the corporate level. Lewis C. Lebish, *Lose Dough on your Car, Farm, or Circus? May be Deductible*, BILLBOARD, Jan. 22, 1949, at 4.

rate. Profits from the film were offset against the stockholder's new basis, which was the value of the rights they had received in the liquidation.[155] The capital gains rate was "far more alluring" than the corporate rate for loan-out corporation, which in part explains why this transaction became "a sort of status symbol in some segments of show business."[156]

Collapsible corporations were everywhere in Hollywood in the 1940s. Producers Samuel Goldwyn and Lester Cowan, directors Sam Wood, Frank Borzage, Frank Capra, Dudley Nichols, Fritz Lang, and Leo McCarey, and movie stars Constance Bennett, Gary Cooper, James Cagney, Bing Crosby, Bette Davis, Douglas Fairbanks, Jr., Joan Fontaine, John Garfield, Paulette Goddard, Hedy Lamarr, Burgess Meredith, Pat O'Brien, Ginger Rogers, James Stewart, and John Wayne all used the collapsible corporation primarily to convert their ordinary income-producing salary into the more favorably taxed capital gains.[157] One of the most famous uses of the collapsible corporation was by Jack Benny, who incorporated his popular radio show under the name "Amusement Enterprises, Inc."[158] After setting it up, Benny sold control of the corporation to Columbia Broadcasting System (CBS) for two million dollars with an agreement for Benny to continue to appear on the show for a set period of time at an agreed-upon salary.[159] CBS also paid for the stock of Benny's company in installments, allowing Benny not only to convert ordinary income to capital gain, but defer the gain until the payments were actually made.[160] Even nonstars figured out ways to use collapsible corporations. In a series of articles in *Billboard* by Lewis Lebish, a New York accountant and lawyer, "designed to guide showbiz people thru the tax law maze" and introduce them to some of the tax dodging maneuvers employed by the

155 Boris I. Bittker & James S. Eustice, *Collapsible Corporations in a Nutshell*, 22 TAX L. REV. 127, 128 (1967).

156 STERN, *supra* note 53, at 127.

157 Hoyt, *Asset or Liability?*, *supra* note 29, at 190; *Treasury Acts to Halt Movie Stars' Racket*, CHI. DAILY TRIB., July 27, 1946, at 10; *Hollywood Stars' Income Tax*, *supra* note 123, at 5. It also gave producers, writers, and stars more control of their films, which was one factor that helped to spur the transition from the studio system to independent film production. THOMAS SCHATZ, BOOM AND BUST: AMERICAN CINEMA IN THE 1940S 181 (1977).

158 Rosenbaum, *supra* note 122, at 33.

159 Id; Saunders, *Tax Tricks of the Rich and Famous*, *supra* note 14, at B5. A few months earlier, CBS had acquired the rights to the Amos 'n' Andy radio show in a similar transaction. STERN, *supra* note 53, at 127.

160 Lewis C. Lebish, *You, Too, Can be Jack Benny: Save $$ by Capital Gains Tax*, THE BILLBOARD, Jan. 1, 1949, at 4, 45.

biggest stars,[161] Lebish focused on ways others could use business entities like corporations to shift income to capital gains, running under the headline "You, Too, Can be Jack Benny: Save $$ by Capital Gains Tax."[162]

Collapsible corporations were targeted by Treasury and Congress at various times,[163] but they survived and became a staple for tax professionals. In the Revenue Act of 1950, Congress adopted Section 341, which was supposed to force the shareholder to realize any gains on sale of the stock of the collapsible corporation as ordinary income.[164] As one lawyer in the field, however, colorfully wrote about the provision,

> Like Caliban, it was "a freckled whelp, hag-born," and has not greatly improved with age. Highly penal in nature, it was misshapen and ambiguous in its draftsmanship, leaving untouched much of the tax avoidance at which it was aimed, inflicting costly and unsuspected penalties on others quite innocent of the evils it sought to be eliminated, and creating unending uncertainty and litigation.[165]

It was readily apparent that, with a good amount of planning, collapsible corporations could still "coexist" with Section 341.[166]

Not surprisingly, entertainers continued to use business organizations to dodge taxes. One method was to form a corporation and enter into a joint venture with a studio to produce a film. In this type of transaction, "the star ... invests money in a feature, obtains partial ownership, 'produces' the feature, and eventually sells the ownership for a capital gain."[167] If the star did not invest their own money in the venture, or their share of the venture appeared to reflect their value as a performer as well as their investment, then this scheme effectively converted high-tax compensation to low-tax capital gains. *Variety* noted that within weeks of each other in 1955, film stars like Frank Sinatra, Cornel Wilde, Robert

161 Id. at 4.

162 Id.

163 *See, e.g., Treasury Acts to Halt Movie Stars' Racket*, CHI. DAILY TRIB., July 27, 1946, at 10 (enforcement letters sent to "prominent movie producers, stars, directors, and writers" about their use of collapsible corporations).

164 *See* Revenue Act of 1950, §212(a), 64 Stat. 906 (1950) (enacting Section 117(m) of the Code, which became Section 341 under the Internal Revenue Code of 1954).

165 John H. Hall, *The Consenting Collapsible Corporations – Section 341(f) of the Internal Revenue Code of 1954*, 12 UCLA L. REV. 1365 (1965).

166 Id.; *See* Levin & Mitosky, *supra* note 28, at 29 ("the writers believe that the collapsible corporation type of arrangement is not yet completely dead, in spite of the efforts of Congress to close this loophole.").

167 Hyams, *supra* note 103, at D3.

Mitchum, Joan Crawford, Rita Hayworth, and Henry Fonda all formed corporations to produce pictures for release by United Artists.[168] Some actors became known as their corporations in industry circles. In 1957, one observer noted, "William Holden is Toluca Productions, Marlon Brando is Pennebaker Productions, John Wayne is Batjac Productions, Frank Sinatra is Kent Productions, etc."[169] Others who served as heads of personal corporations included Lucille Ball and Desi Arnaz, Sid Caesar, Milton Berle, George Gobel, Jackie Gleason, and Perry Como.[170] As Kirk Douglas explained, "because of the present tax structure we have a chance at financial security only with our own companies."[171] In a review of a 1957 treatise by New York attorney Joseph Taubman entitled, *The Joint Ventures and Tax Classification*, which contained chapters on "Motion Picture Co-production Deals" and "Theatrical Business Organizations," *Variety* wrote "there's plenty of show biz interest" in joint ventures as one means of diversifying risk.[172]

### *Delay and Convert Compensation*

Even without resorting to incorporation, entertainers used techniques to delay or convert compensation to great effect.[173] Deferring compensation extended a person's compensation to a period when the post-war rates were expected to drop or when their own income might decline to a lower tax bracket, rather than keeping it "bunched" together in a single year. Even if rates did not change, deferral potentially kept a star's annual income below the thresholds for the highest rate brackets in any one period. Both advantages were particularly important for top celebrities, many of whom might have had large paydays concentrated during the height of their careers that were followed by fallow periods of less work.[174] In a radio interview, Ronald Reagan bemoaned the plight of the actor who's "had a very lean period [and] gets one of these lush breaks" and then

168 Gene Arneel, *Look, Ma, I'm a Corporation*, VARIETY, March 16, 1955, at 1.

169 BERNSTEIN, *supra* note 41, at 68.

170 Rosenbaum, *supra* note 122, at 48, n. 63.

171 Arneel, *Look Ma, I'm a Corporation*, *supra* note 168, at 1, 20.

172 *Don't Make a Move – Without a CPA*, VARIETY, June 5, 1957, at 14 (reviewing JOSEPH TAUBMAN, THE JOINT VENTURES AND TAX CLASSIFICATION (1957)).

173 A. Morgan Maree, Jr. reportedly "innovated the long-term payout of a movie star's salary over many years to best reduce the tax in a single year." *Money Manager A. Morgan Maree, III Dies*, HOLLYWOOD REPORTER, April 1, 2010.

174 Levin & Mitosky, *supra* note 28, at 29. *See* Adrian A. Kragen & Babette Barton, *The Tax Dilemma of the Entertainer*, 31 S. CAL. L. REV. 390, 390–91 (1958) (entertainers are

moves up so rapidly in the surtax bracket in the one year . . . that he doesn't benefit himself at all or get out of the hole at all, because he moves into a 75, 80, or even a 91% bracket."[175]

In one deferred compensation example, William Holden's salary for the movie *Bridge on the River Kwai* was paid over a twenty-year period.[176] This occurred because his contract called for him to be paid 10 percent of the gross profits, but, at Holden's insistence, Columbia's payments were capped at $50,000 per year.[177] Kragen and Barton noted that while Holden might have received only $325,000 after tax on an income of $2.5 million if he had been paid as the profits came in, his deferred compensation arrangement effectively simulated an annuity contract with a net return of as much as $1.5 million even if tax rates remained at the same rate as when the income was earned.[178] Milton Berle signed a thirty-year deal with the National Broadcasting Company that was simpler, but no less effective in deferring his income.[179] Under the terms of the arrangement, he agreed to perform his usual duties on television shows for the first ten years and then serve "in a 'consultive' capacity" for the remaining twenty years.[180]

A second tax dodging compensation technique – one that promised potentially "far greater tax savings" than deferral – involved the conversion of compensation to something other than salary.[181] For example, a star would negotiate to receive an asset such as a percentage of gross profits. Since it might take several years between when an actor filmed a movie and when it was released and started generating profits, they would take an advance against a percentage of the gross profits in lieu of salary in those predistribution years. This spread the income over a period of years to get some of the advantages applicable to deferred compensation,[182] but, more importantly, it allowed them to hold an asset – the profits interest – that they could sell for cash. They could

"faced with a comparatively short professional life and a concentration in that brief period of exceptionally high income from personal services.").

175 *It's YOUR Business* (ABC radio broadcast, March 31, 1957).

176 Hyams, *supra* note 103, at D3.

177 Kragen & Barton, *supra* note 174, at 397.

178 Id. at 397–98. The authors' assumption was that his income from other sources remained small over the period, so that the $50,000 per year would be subject to tax at the lower marginal rates of the graduated rate structure. Id. at 398, n.31.

179 Levin & Mitosky, *supra* note 28, at 29.

180 Id.

181 Krager & Barton, *supra* note 174, at 400.

182 Hyams, *supra* note 103, at D3.

then argue that the sales proceeds should be taxable at the capital gains rate, which was far lower than their marginal income tax rate on ordinary income like salary.

One somewhat convoluted example of this profit share approach was Jose Ferrer's payment in connection with the production of the movie *Moulin Rouge*, which was a story about the life of the painter Henri de Toulouse-Lautrec. In 1950, Ferrer acquired the rights to the stage production of this story from Pierre LaMure, the author of the book upon which it was based. These rights included a percentage of the proceeds from the sale of the motion picture rights after the presentation of the stage production. Before a play was produced, however, Ferrer was approached by director John Huston about assuming the role of Toulouse-Lautrec in a motion picture based on the book. Ferrer agreed "to abandon the theatrical production in favor of the film production provided that, if the film production were successful, I would be recompensated for my abandoning the stage production."[183] Ferrer ultimately was paid a salary, part of which was contingent on the profits from the film, for playing the starring role, and received a 17 percent interest in the net profits from the film for releasing his rights in the play. Based on testimony about the intent of the arrangement, Ferrer reported the amounts he received for releasing his rights in the play as capital gains.[184]

Another version of this conversion method was to negotiate for the sale of the intellectual property rights held by the actors in a show, such as the development of the characters they originated. This would enable the holders of those rights to sell them for capital gains, rather than receive salary associated with the airing of shows that would be subject to tax at ordinary income rates. Freeman Gosden and Charles Correll, the creators of the radio show Amos 'n' Andy, were among the earliest adopters of this technique.[185] In August of 1948, Gosden and Correll sold the intellectual property rights to their characters to Columbia Broadcasting System (CBS) for $2 million.[186] The benefit was that the sales proceeds were subject to the 25 percent capital gains rate, rather than the 77 percent

183 Commissioner v. Ferrer, 304 F.2d 125, 128 (2d. Cir. 1962).

184 Id. at 135–36.

185 Seymour S. Mintz, *Entertainers and the Capital Gains Tax*, 4 TAX L. REV. 275 (1949). Reportedly, the first time this method was used was the acquisition of Fletcher Wiley's Housewives Protective League a year earlier. Id. at 275, n. 2.

186 Charles Renshaw, Jr., *Artful "Archie."* ATLANTA CONSTITUTION, Dec. 18, 1949, at SM18.

rate on income above $1 million.[187] Moreover, CBS still signed them to a deal to continue to serve in the roles of those characters on the show at their usual salaries.[188] The key to the transaction was purportedly that the Amos 'n' Andy show "conceivably could continue without" Gosden and Correll playing the title roles on the radio show.[189] This technique, however, was soon shut down as George J. Schoeneman, Commissioner of Internal Revenue, released a statement that these types of sales were for their personal services, rather than their property.[190] The creators of Amos 'n' Andy were deemed to be safe since their deal was completed before the government pronouncement.[191] Comedian Jack Benny, however, who tried to sell his show to CBS, was denied capital gains treatment in part because "without him, the Benny show would perish."[192] The shutdown of these personal services deals, however, applied even in cases where the taxpayer and the particular character could be separated. Thus, for example, the sale by ventriloquist Edgar Bergen of the intellectual property rights associated with the characters he created – Charlie McCarthy and Mortimer Snerd – as part of a move from sale the National Broadcasting Company (NBC) to CBS fell through because the Internal Revenue Bureau failed to provide clearance.[193]

In another attempt to convert some high-taxed salary to a capital asset that could be sold for gain subject to the lower capital gains rates, film stars or directors would sometimes negotiate to own the negatives of their films after a period of years when they would be held by the studios. This "newest wrinkle" in the tax dodging arsenal reportedly was used by Cary Grant and Alfred Hitchcock, who negotiated for the right to own the negatives of the film "North by Northwest" after eight

[187] Id.

[188] Id.

[189] Mintz, *supra* note 185, at 287–88; Robert Ruark, *The Income Tax Boys Miss a Few Boats*, MINNEAPOLIS MORNING TRIBUNE, Jan. 11, 1949, at 4.

[190] *Income Tax "Capital Gains" Device officially Deflated*, BALTIMORE SUN, Jan. 4, 1949, at 4 (Schoeneman said "proposals of radio artists and others to obtain compensation for personal services under the guise of sales of property cannot be regarded as coming within the capital-gains provisions of the internal revenue code.").

[191] *Capital Gains "Loss,"* BROADCASTING, Jan. 10, 1949, at 26.

[192] Ruark, *The Income Tax Boys Miss a Few Boats*, *supra* note 189, at 4.

[193] Charles Molony, *Path to Lower Taxes Pitted with Pitfalls*, ATLANTA CONSTITUTION, Dec. 13, 1948, at 17; *Capital Gains Tax Barred in Star Deals*, WASH. POST, Jan. 4, 1949, at 4.

years.[194] Under the deal, "after that time they can sell the negative or form a corporation to reissue the negatives theatrically or [on] television," with the sales proceeds being classified as capital gains.[195]

## Crackdowns on Celebrity Tax Dodging and the Publicity Effect

In the Broadway musical *Ragtime*, one song, entitled "The Crime of the Century," is about a 1907 case in which young model Evelyn Nesbit's husband Harry Thaw was on trial for the murder of Nesbit's former lover and prominent architect Stanford White, who had allegedly seduced her when she was a teenager.[196] As one modern observer noted, "[t]he love triangle between White, Nesbit and Thaw and its violent end was fodder for the yellow journalism of the time, as the media sensationalized the story and its characters and dissected every detail."[197] Thaw may have been found not guilty by reason of insanity,[198] but Nesbit's reputation was ostensibly tattered by the lurid revelations about her life story.[199] Nevertheless, Evelyn's character in *Ragtime* appears to invoke the old adage that "all publicity is good publicity" when she sings that although "Harry's in trouble and Stanny's in Heaven . . . Evelyn gets publicity!"[200]

Treasury appeared to miscalculate this publicity effect when it targeted celebrities. These cases were chosen because they would be well-publicized, but that failed to make tax dodging less attractive. In some instances, that was because the technical nature of the tax maneuver made it difficult for the average person to understand them. In one case involving Rooney, Inc., a personal service corporation that received its income from the work of

194 Hyams, *supra* note 103, at D3.
195 Id.
196 *The Crime of the Century*, in RAGTIME (lyrics by L. Ahrens, 1977).
197 Erin Allen, *A Turn-of-the-Century "True Hollywood Story,"* LIBRARY OF CONGRESS BLOGS, April 5, 2013.
198 *Thaw Found Not Guilty by Reason of Insanity – Sent to the Asylum*, THE SEATTLE STAR, Feb. 1, 1908, at 1.
199 *Second Thaw Trial Opens Tomorrow; Prisoner Relies Upon Insanity Plea and His Girl Wife's Graphic Life Story*, WASH. TIMES, Jan. 5, 1908, at 13.
200 *The Crime of the Century*, *supra* note 196. The publicity was of questionable value to her personally, see *Seven Years of Bad Luck for Evelyn Nesbit?* BIRMINGHAM AGE-HERALD, Nov. 6, 1921, at 22 (describing her divorce from Harry Thaw and his refusal to recognize her son as his own, as well as other challenges), but she did eventually star in a movie about her life. *See* Advertisement, *Redemption: With Evelyn Nesbit Thaw and Her Son Russell*, CORDELE DISPATCH (Georgia), Jan. 19, 1918.

actor Mickey Rooney, the Bureau of Internal Revenue tried to collect $32,000 from Rooney himself, leading him to issue a statement saying "I do not owe our government one cent on account of my own taxes … Recently, the Internal Revenue Department decided to ask me to pay the tax delinquency of an old corporation with which I was once connected on a theory they refer to as 'transfer liability.' I don't believe I should pay for somebody else."[201] Effectively, the government's action only allowed the entertainer to reframe the narrative.

Even if the government won in a court of law, it often did not in the court of public opinion. An audit of the comedian duo of Bud Abbot & Lou Costello, for example, led to the disallowance of several capital gains deals, plus the loss of deductions, resulting in deficiencies that measured in the hundreds of thousands.[202] Costello settled with the government before his death, reducing his estate from millions to a mere $200,000,[203] while Abbot was reduced to working for the government to pay off his debt.[204] If there was any consequence to the publicity surrounding Abbot's tax debt, it was to evoke sympathy for his plight. As Abbot lamented when he announced his tax debt, "'They (the Government) don't split the salary,' he said. 'They take it all, and you gotta pay taxes on top of it. I owe them half a million in deductions they didn't allow."[205]

When celebrities did win their cases, as sometimes happened, it not only provided positive publicity for the celebrities, but also for their tax dodging maneuvers. Indeed, every victory involving a celebrity was trumpeted in the newspapers, likely spurring others to try the strategy too. In 1954, for example, Actor Pat O'Brien went to the Tax Court to contest a $139,000 deficiency related to his use of Terneen Productions, Inc. ("Terneen") in a collapsible corporation transaction.[206] O'Brien and several associates established Terneen to produce the film "Secret Command," in which O'Brien starred, before turning over the film to Columbia Pictures Corp. for distribution and liquidating Terneen.[207] The Tax Court sided with O'Brien, finding that Terneen was a bona fide corporation and it was actually dissolved before the box office

201 *Mickey Rooney Protests Taxes on Corporation*, L.A. TIMES, Sept. 9, 1952, at 15.
202 *Bud Abbot Loses Assets in Tax Audit*, BALTIMORE SUN, May 29, 1959, at 3.
203 Id.
204 *Abbot and Foy Team*, N.Y. TIMES, June 12, 1959, at 23.
205 Id.
206 *Pat O'Brien's Defense Ended in Tax Fight*, L.A. TIMES, Sept. 22, 1954, at A1.
207 STERN, *supra* note 53, at 137.

receipts started rolling in,[208] with newspapers proclaiming O'Brien's victory.[209]

The government attempted to stem the bleeding caused by losses, but it may only have served to further publicize those losses. In 1942, F. Hugh Herbert, an actor and playwright, wrote a play originally called "The Holy Cow," which was renamed "Kiss and Tell" and proved to be a great success on stage. When approached about turning the play into a movie, Herbert formed a corporation and decided to undertake to produce it independently through what was called the "Abbott-Herbert" corporation, ostensibly to retain creative control, but also to get capital gain tax treatment at liquidation under a collapsible corporation arrangement.[210] The government challenged the capital gains characterization and lost at the district court.[211] A mere days after the taxpayer's victory, the government announced that it planned to appeal the decision, claiming that "they were confident the Supreme Court would overturn the decision," and offering comments to the press that "even if the Herberts win on appeal ... no broad precedent would be established for other Hollywood figures to collect big refunds."[212] Making matters worse for the government, when its appeal was dismissed a few months later, the newspapers had another occasion to note "Herbert's Victory" and "the government's quiet acceptance of defeat" in a case that "attracted national attention."[213]

Even when a star's victory was limited or narrow, the newspapers often only highlighted the victory and not the details. For example, Jack Benny was assessed a deficiency for the tax reporting regarding the creation and sale of his personal services corporation, Amusement Enterprises, Inc. ("Amusement"). The Commissioner argued that even if Amusement was considered a legitimate operating corporation, only a small portion of the total contract price for the sale of Amusement to CBS – $206,000 of the total $2,260,000 received – represented the value of the stock and the remaining amount of $2,054,000 represented "the portion of the selling

[208] *Tax Court Rejects $139,000 Claim against Pat O'Brien and Partners*, L.A. TIMES, Dec. 7, 1955, at 6.

[209] *Pat O'Brien Wins Tax Fight*, ST. LOUIS POST-DISPATCH, Dec. 7, 1955, at 14A; *Pat O'Brien Film Firm Wins Income Tax Case*, EVENING STAR (Washington, D.C.), Dec. 7, 1955, at A-25.

[210] Herbert v. Riddell, 103 F. Supp. 369, 377 (S.D. Cal. 1952).

[211] Id. at 385.

[212] *U.S. to Appeal Tax Case, Treasury Confident of Winning on Hollywood Ruling*, N.Y. TIMES, March 2, 1952, at 56.

[213] Thomas M. Pryor, *Hollywood Survey*, N.Y. TIMES, Aug. 24, 1952, at X5.

price attributed to Jack Benny's services."[214] The Tax Court disagreed, concluding that the it was not "merely a cloak for a deliberate scheme of tax avoidance."[215] Legal commentators found the view somewhat incredible, noting that the court's reasoning implied that "CBS was just buying stock in Amusement Enterprises, Inc. with a calculated risk that it would procure Benny,"[216] and suggested that it likely only gives entertainers "who have a sponsor and produce their own show a substantial basis for attaining capital gains."[217] Nevertheless, newspapers did not highlight such caveats in announcing the success of Benny's tax dodging strategy.[218]

Similarly, even if the news after early victories was misleading, it often went uncorrected. In the case involving the payments to Jose Ferrer related to the profits from the movie Moulin Rouge, Ferrer won the early result. The Commissioner had challenged Ferrer's characterization of all the payments based on the film's profits as capital gains, arguing that all the payments should have been taxed as wages. The Tax Court sided with Ferrer,[219] prompting one newspaper to run with the headline "Judge Rules Jose Right, IRS Wrong."[220] The following year, however, the appellate court provided a bit more of a mixed result. Although it rejected the Commissioner's position that all payments should be taxed as ordinary income, the court reversed and remanded to determine the proper allocation, noting that not all should be capital gains either.[221] There was little reporting on this later decision in the newspapers though.

Rather than the publicity sparking a negative reaction about tax dodging and the celebrities that employed these methods, these Treasury enforcement actions appeared to boost celebrities' popularity. For example, *Variety* noted that the Jack Benny show's move "into the No. 1 Hooper [audience ratings] spot in the new ratings is attributed in large measure to the manner in which the nation's press has been front-paging the comedian's NBC-CBS capital gains

214 Benny v. Commissioner, 25 T.C. 197, 207 (1955).
215 Id. at 210.
216 Rosenbaum, *supra* note 122, at 36.
217 Id. at 48.
218 *See, e.g., Benny Wins Tax Appeal; Comedian Upheld on Capital Gain Involving $1,000,000*, N.Y. Times, Nov. 7, 1955, at 34.
219 Ferrer v. Commissioner, 35 T.C. 617, 626–27 (1961).
220 Edwin A. Lahey, *Judge Rules Jose Right, IRS Wrong*, Detroit Free Press, Feb. 2, 1961, at 28.
221 Commissioner v. Ferrer, 304 F.2d at 135–36.

switch."[222] There was little attempt to hide the tax-motivated aspect of these switches. In fact, CBS' deals with Benny, Amos 'n' Andy comedians Freeman Gosden and Charles Correll, as well as other celebrities, was characterized as being part of CBS' goal of creating a "capital gains talent roster," which they hoped would include Bing Crosby as well.[223] In part, this was because celebrities and their publicists, unlike the wealthy tax dodgers of the 1930s, encouraged, or at least did not try to avoid, publicity surrounding their tax dodging schemes. Yale law professor Boris Bittker and his student and future NYU Law Dean Norman Redlich understood the dynamics at work: "Hollywood's . . . tax avoidance may titillate the public as much as its marital lapses. There is an understanding of popular psychology in the entertainment industry's adage: 'I don't care what you write about me so long as you spell my name right.'"[224]

Sometimes, the tax scandals led commentators to openly ridicule a celebrity, but as with Evelyn Nesbit, their popularity still grew. Consider the U.S. Court of Claims' ruling that Kathleen Winsor's profits on the sale of movie rights for her romance novel *Forever Amber* to Twentieth Century-Fox Film Corporation should be taxed at capital gains rates. According to the court, Winsor was not in the business of writing or selling movie rights; rather, she had grown up writing stories "for her own amusement" and she wrote this book – her first full-length novel – not because she expected it to be published, but "primarily because she enjoyed the research and writing which went into its composition."[225]

Although scholars marveled at the legal defense of her "amateur status" as evidence of "a degree of ingenuity,"[226] journalists mocked the decision and what it said about Winsor's writing ability. Robert Ruark wrote in the *Minneapolis Morning Tribune* that "she writes a real bad one first, called 'Forever Amber,' and a worse one later called 'Star Money,' and the government decides she was killing herself

[222] *Benny's Hooper Keeping CBS' Paley Hopping*, VARIETY, Dec. 28, 1948, at 23.

[223] *Bing Crosby Next Up on CBS TV Agenda?* VARIETY, Feb. 7, 1951, at 26.

[224] Boris I. Bittker & Norman Redlich, *Corporate Liquidations and the Income Tax*, 5 TAX L. REV. 437, 438 (1950).

[225] Herwig et al. v. United States, 105 F. Supp. 384, 389 (Fed. Cl. 1952). The actual holding hewed more closely to the statutory language, with the court stating that "we do not believe that it can be justly said that Miss Winsor held her motion picture rights 'primarily for sale to customers in the ordinary course of business.'" Id. at 390.

[226] Warren S. Shine, *Some Tax Problems of Authors and Artists*, 13 TAX L. REV. 439, 440 (1958).

for her own delectation."[227] Book review columnist David Dempsey observed that the court's conclusion that she was an amateur writer "coincides with the stated opinion of a great many critics at the time the novel was published."[228] Louisville's *Courier Journal* wrote, tongue-in-cheek, in reaction to the Winsor opinion that "we can hardly wait to hear comment from certain of our acquaintances to the effect that this confirms an old opinion of theirs."[229] Cincinnati's *The Enquirer* asked "When is a writer not a writer in the eyes of the law? The answer would seem to be when she is the author of 'Forever Amber.'"[230] Notwithstanding the ridicule, Winsor thrived, with the publicity from the case helping her to secure an interview with syndicated columnist and humorist Art Buchwald in a fancy hotel in Paris and a new book contract.[231] Moreover, her *Forever Amber* book sold three million copies and Winsor came to be known as the "the woman who invented the modern best seller."[232]

In another example involving a novice author, Dwight D. Eisenhower, while still a General and not yet a President, sold the rights to his book, *Crusade in Europe*, to Doubleday for $635,000.[233] He reported it as capital gain after receiving a ruling from the Internal Revenue Service that he was not in the business of writing books.[234] This ignited outrage when it became publicly known.[235] "[W]riters all over the country protested, especially to the Bureau of Internal Revenue and to members of Congress."[236] Their protests, however, were not to reverse the decision, but to extend it to all writers.[237]

227 Robert Ruark, *Essentials for Book Writing: Typewriter, Plenty of Paper*, MINNEAPOLIS MORNING TRIBUNE, Sept. 12, 1952, at 4.

228 David Dempsey, *In and Out of Books*, N.Y. TIMES, June 22, 1952, at BR8.

229 *You May Have Said It of "Forever Amber,"* COURIER-JOURNAL, June 7, 1952, at 6.

230 *Forever Revenue*, THE ENQUIRER, June 9, 1952, at 4.

231 Art Buchwald, *Paris – and People*, N.Y. HERALD TRIB., July 3, 1952, at 11.

232 Douglas Martin, *Kathleen Winsor, 83; Wrote 'Forever Amber,'* N.Y. TIMES, May 28, 2003, at A21.

233 STERN, *supra* note 53, at 130; *Capital Gains "Loss,"* BROADCASTING, Jan. 10, 1949, at 26.

234 Id.

235 *Charges "Ike" Abuses Special U.S. Privileges*, CHI. DAILY TRIB., May 24, 1948, at 12. The controversy was re-visited once Eisenhower became a candidate for President. Drew Pearson, *I'll Chop in Both Directions, Let Chips Fall Where They May*, THE NASHVILLE TENNESSEAN, Sept. 22, 1952, at 9.

236 *Officials 'Clear' Ike in Capital Gains Deal on Book*, DETROIT FREE PRESS, Sept. 30, 1952, at 1, 2.

237 Treasury Secretary John Snyder insisted that "we treated General Eisenhower just as we would any other citizen. He asked for an interpretation of the law and we gave it to him. Any other citizen under the same circumstances would have been given the same ruling."

According to *Variety*, their complaints were mostly in the nature of "If Ike can be taxed at a lower rate, why can't I?"[238] John Harriman of the *Daily Boston Globe* reported that "Gen. Eisenhower's tax arrangement on his earnings from his memoir 'Crusade in Europe,' is turning most professional authors green with envy."[239] Robert Ruark suggested that the exemption Eisenhower qualified for should apply to professional writers too.[240]

> I congratulate Ike on his luck, but . . . It is unfortunate that professional artisans – writers, actors, musicians – spend most of their early lives on short ration, working up to the big day when they write the best seller or sign the Hollywood contract, to compensate for all the lean and bitter years. They finally hit the jackpot and then the taxman comes with a truck to lug it all away.[241]

The *Courier-Journal* even suggested that Harry Truman, who received $600,000 to contribute his memoirs in serial form to *Life Magazine*, should receive similar treatment to Eisenhower and Winsor despite the fact that the loophole Eisenhower had relied upon had since been closed.[242] According to the paper, "whatever they received for their writings was much as if they had stored experience in a savings account, and finally taken it out. To classify this as income in the same sense as an executive's continuing salary, for example, is not quite fair."[243] Indeed, commentators responded to the so-called "Eisenhower Amendment" by offering tips to authors – celebrity and non-celebrity alike – on other ways to dodge taxes, including spreading out the payments, which Truman himself employed after receiving a ruling from Treasury,[244] and holding their rights inside corporations.[245]

David Camelon, *How Eisenhower Saved $260,000 in Taxes*, ATLANTA CONSTITUTION, Jan. 16, 1949, at SM12 (quoting Treas. Sec. Snyder).

238 Id. Instead, Congress removed the loophole altogether, amending the law to tax at ordinary income rates all sales of works by a creator, with a sole exemption for patents.

239 John Harriman, *Authors' Tax Problems: Ike's Book Would Not be a "Capital Gain" Today*, DAILY BOSTON GLOBE, Oct. 17, 1952, at 30.

240 Robert Ruark, *The Income Tax Boys Miss a Few Boats*, MINNEAPOLIS MORNING TRIB., Jan. 11, 1949, at 4.

241 Id.

242 *The Trials of Amateurs Harry and Ike*, THE COURIER-JOURNAL, July 29, 1953, at 6; STERN, *supra* note 53, at 130.

243 *The Trials of Amateurs Harry and Ike*, THE COURIER-JOURNAL, July 29, 1953, at 6.

244 Harriman, *supra* note 239, at 30.

245 STERN, *supra* note 53, at 130–31.

Shining the spotlight on celebrity tax dodging only served to spark, rather than dampen, public interest in tax dodging. Celebrities helped push the market to create these innovative methods and then helped to drive the demand for them by publicizing them through the force of their own celebrity status. While many of the techniques were unattainable for the average taxpayer, celebrities glamorized them in a way that made them admirable rather than detestable.

# 2

# Havens, Refuges, Oases, and Mirages

Just as domestic tax dodging investments attracted media and popular attention, so too did foreign tax dodging investments. The difference is that while domestic tax shelters initially attracted attention because of the celebrities who were investing in these shelters, foreign tax dodging was less about the identity of the investors, which was often either shrouded in secrecy or hidden behind large faceless corporations, but about where they were investing. Most of these foreign tax dodging schemes involved investments in companies located in what have been referred to at various times in history as "havens," "refuges," or "oases" because they were in countries that imposed little to no tax and the income earned was considered outside of the reach of US tax authorities until it was returned stateside.[1]

For the average person, these investments were enticing, but unattainable, much like a "mirage." Nevertheless, the notion of finding somewhere to make income free from taxes was the holy grail of tax dodging and the phrase "tax haven" entered the popular lexicon. In part, this was because such schemes were advertised widely in national newspapers and magazines by promoters hoping to attract investors, but that alone should not have made them so iconic. These schemes resonated with so many who were unlikely to use them because they seemed exotic, involving investments in places with death-defying ski slopes and beautiful sandy island beaches. In that sense, much like with celebrities, tax havens helped to romanticize tax dodging.

[1] Sébastien Guex, *Introduction. 'Low-Tax Predators' Rather than 'Tax Havens': New Perspectives on the History of the International Tax Evasion and Avoidance Market*, in TAX EVASION AND TAX HAVENS SINCE THE NINETEENTH CENTURY 1, 20 (Sébastien Guex & Hadrien Buclin, eds., 2023); *Tax Havens: Boon to Business but a Pain to the Treasury*, NEWSWEEK, 66 (March 5, 1962). Although there is no universally accepted definition, tax havens can be broadly defined as "locations with very low tax rates and other tax attributes designed to appeal to foreign investors." Dhammika Dharmapala and James R. Hines, Jr., *Which Countries Become Tax Havens?* 93 J. PUB. ECON. 1058 (2009).

## Background

Tax havens first emerged globally long before US companies started to use them, with some suggesting that the stage was set for their emergence in the late nineteenth century.[2] Nevertheless, according to historian Vanessa Ogle, modern tax havens began to appear in Europe around World War I and in the years thereafter as "savvy lawyers and bankers discovered Switzerland, Liechtenstein, Luxembourg, the British Channel Islands, and, for the United States, the Bahamas and Bermuda, for the purpose of registering companies and trusts, or just depositing funds in bank accounts in order to benefit from zero or very low tax rates."[3] Foreign subsidiaries were established during the war as a way to better navigate diplomatic issues, but they remained popular as income taxation spread and high rates lingered after the war.[4] This was attractive not only in the US, where the first modern post-Sixteenth Amendment income tax was enacted in 1913 and became steeply progressive with the advent of World War I funding needs,[5] but in many countries in Europe as well. Between 1914 and 1924, twenty-seven countries introduced a personal income tax.[6] Some of these taxes were even more steeply progressive than in the US. The top marginal income tax rate in France, for instance, reached 90 percent in 1924.[7]

The foundation for US companies' use of tax havens, or what Ronen Palan called "the practice of competitive reduction in corporate taxation," can arguably be traced to at least two historical developments in US law.[8] First, the rise of general state incorporation laws, as distinct from special legislative charters, permitted businesses to shop for a legal

[2] Guex, *supra* note 1, at 7. *See* Robert Kearns, *U.S. Battles Offshore Tax Havens*, CHI. TRIB., June 24, 1979, at E1 ("Tax havens have been around for centuries in one form or another").

[3] Vanessa Ogle, *'Funk Money': The End of Empires, the Expansion of Tax Havens, and Decolonization as an Economic and Financial Event*, 249 PAST & PRESENT *213*, 219 (2020).

[4] Boris Gehlen and Christian Marx, *"I am a Professional Tax Evader": Multinationals, Business Groups and Tax Havens, 1950s to 1980s*, in HISTORIES OF TAX EVASION, AVOIDANCE AND RESISTANCE 221, 224 (Korinna Schönhärl, Gilsela Hürlimann and Dorothea Rohde, eds., 2023).

[5] *See* Introduction *supra*.

[6] Sébastien Lafitte, *The Emergence and Expansion of Tax Havens, 1850–2000: Insights from a New Dataset*, in TAX EVASION AND TAX HAVENS SINCE THE NINETEENTH CENTURY 37, 46 (Sébastien Guex & Hadrien Buclin, eds., 2023).

[7] Id.

[8] Ronen Palan, *Tax Havens and the Commercialization of State Sovereignty*, 56 INT'L ORGS. 151, 160 (2002); Policy Paper, *History of Tax Havens*, History & Policy, Institute of Historical Research, Senate House, London UK (Oct. 1, 2009); EMMANUEL SAEZ AND

(as opposed to business) home that had the most advantageous laws. This era of "easy incorporation" in the late nineteenth century in the United States was the beginning of the so-called "race-to-the-bottom" in which New Jersey and Delaware attempted to attract businesses to incorporate in their states by relaxing their statutory requirements and enacting certain inducements.[9] Although academics have debated whether it was a race-to-the-bottom or the top,[10] it was facilitated by the ability of businesses to incorporate in whatever state they chose, irrespective of where they were physically located or did business.[11] For corporations accustomed to strategically selecting their legal homes for reasons distinct from where they selected their business homes, it was not a big step to locate those legal homes offshore in a tax haven jurisdiction. This was crucial. As Ronen Palan wrote, "the principal attraction of tax havens and the main cause for their spectacular success lies in their ability to provide protection from national regulation and taxation without the need to physically relocate to the host country."[12]

Second, states slowly began to repeal prohibitions against owning the stock of other corporations.[13] These prohibitions were from the special charter era where legislative restrictions on a corporation's purpose were common and the ability to own stock in another corporation would have permitted these corporations to easily evade such restrictions.[14] Even after such fears faded as purpose clauses fell

GABRIEL ZUCMAN, THE TRIUMPH OF INJUSTICE: HOW THE RICH DODGE TAXES AND HOW TO MAKE THEM PAY 73 (2019). At least one additional foundational principle of corporations – the notion that a corporation is a separate legal person from its shareholders – could also be cited in this regard, but that is a principle that developed well before this period when the Supreme Court announced it in 1819. See *Dartmouth College v. Woodward*, 17 U.S. 518, 636, 657 (1819); Craig M. Boise, *Breaking Open Offshore Piggybanks: Deferral and the Utility or Amnesty*, 14 GEO. MASON L. REV. 667, 672–73 (2007).

9 Brian R. Cheffins, Steven A. Bank & Harwell Wells, *Shareholder Protection Across Time*, 68 FLA. L. REV. 691, 693 (2016); William L. Cary, *Federalism and Corporate Law: Reflections upon Delaware*, 83 YALE L.J. 663–66 (1974).

10 *See* Cheffins, Bank & Wells *supra* note 9, at 694, n. 9 (collecting sources).

11 HARRY G. HENN, HANDBOOK OF THE LAW OF CORPORATIONS AND OTHER BUSINESS ENTERPRISES 17–18 (1961).

12 Palan, *Tax Havens and the Commercialization of State Sovereignty, supra* note 8, at 163.

13 CHRISTOPHER GRANDY, NEW JERSEY AND THE FISCAL ORIGINS OF MODERN AMERICAN CORPORATE LAW 42 (1993); CHARLES S. TIPPETTS & SHAW LIVERMORE, BUSINESS ORGANIZATION AND CONTROL: CORPORATIONS AND TRUSTS IN THE UNITED STATES 213 (1932); JAMES WILLARD HURST, THE LEGITIMACY OF THE BUSINESS CORPORATION IN THE LAW OF THE UNITED STATES, 1780–1970 69 (1970).

14 HURST, *supra* note 13, at 45.

into disuse, the restrictions were maintained as concern grew about the monopoly threat from corporate holding companies.[15] It was only after the restrictions were fully moved that corporate subsidiaries became common in the US.

During the 1950s and 1960s, the federal government's push to increase private investment abroad was a modern development that laid the foundation for US businesses' use of tax havens. In the wake of the devastation of World War II, the government sought to help rebuild economies, initially in Europe, and later in the so-called "underdeveloped countries," for humanitarian reasons and to provide a bulwark against the spread of unrest and threats to democracy.[16] The Economic Cooperation Act of 1948 reflected the view that private US investment was a critical part of any foreign aid program, but it was difficult to turn that aspiration into reality.[17] In 1949, President Harry Truman acknowledged that because of "the present troubled condition of the world – the distortion of world trade, the shortage of dollars, and other aftereffects of the war – the problem of substantially increasing the flow of American capital abroad presents serious difficulties."[18] Truman noted that "private sources of funds must be encouraged to provide a major part of the capital required ... if the investment from this country is to reach proportions sufficient to carry out the objectives of our program."[19] This stance was in part a practical reaction to the political reality that, as Ethan Kapstein observed, "in the late 1940s and early 1950s, the United States had little appetite for major government-to-government foreign aid programs, despite the success of the Marshall Plan in stimulating European recovery."[20] This meant policymakers had "no choice but to rely on private capital to meet the developing world's 'gap' between

[15] WM. L. CLARK, Jr., HANDBOOK OF THE LAW OF PRIVATE CORPORATIONS 183 (I. Maurice Wormser ed., 3d ed. 1916); HARLAND PRECHEL, BIG BUSINESS AND THE STATE: HISTORICAL TRANSITIONS AND CORPORATE TRANSFORMATION, 1880S–1900S 66 (2000).

[16] PEGGY BREWER RICHMAN, TAXATION OF FOREIGN INVESTMENT INCOME: AN ECONOMIC ANALYSIS 54, 59 (1963).

[17] Economic Cooperation Act, 62 Stat. 137 (1948); Bruce E. Clubb and Vernie W. Vance, Jr., *Incentives to Private U.S. Investment Abroad under the Foreign Assistance Program*, 72 YALE L.J. 475, 476 (1963).

[18] Harry S. Truman, *Special Message to the Congress Recommending Point 4 Legislation*, June 24, 1949, Harry S. Truman Library and Museum.

[19] Id.

[20] Ethan B. Kapstein, *Private Enterprise, International Development, and the Cold War*, 22 J. OF COLD WAR STUD. 113, 123 (2020)

domestic savings and investment requirements."[21] This stance continued through much of the 1950s. As economist and former Treasury Department advisor Raymond Mikesell reported in 1957, "successive Administrations and the Congress have stated and restated the principle that the U.S. Government should place *primary* reliance on private enterprise to assist in economic development abroad."[22]

This public pressure for private foreign investment only heightened as the country became concerned about the possible spread of communism.[23] President Dwight Eisenhower advised Congress in a special message in January of 1955 "an increased flow of United States private investment funds abroad, especially to the underdeveloped areas, could contribute much to the expansion of two-way international trade."[24] Eisenhower added that not only would this allow such countries to acquire the goods (presumably from the US) "so badly needed by them to achieve sound economic growth and higher living standards," but "this would do much to offset the false but alluring promises of the Communists."[25] Private industry associations got the message. As the National Planning Association's International Committee noted in 1957, "private American investment abroad helps to foster that mutual compatibility of values and institutions between the United States and the lesser developed nations of Asia, Africa, and Latin America, which is important to the future freedom and progress not only of our own country but of the entire free world as well."[26]

The US tax treatment of income earned abroad further facilitated this push to increase private investment in foreign countries. Under the system in place at the time, corporations were taxed in the US on their worldwide income, but that only applied to the income earned by the corporation as a legal entity.[27] If the corporation established a sales office in a foreign country, that income would be currently subject to tax in the

21 Id. at 124.

22 Raymond F. Mikesell, PROMOTING UNITED STATES PRIVATE INVESTMENT ABROAD, National Planning Association Planning Pamphlet No. 101 1 (Oct. 1957).

23 This started as early as the late 1940s. Kapstein, *supra* note 20, at 114.

24 President Dwight D. Eisenhower, *Special Message to the Congress on Foreign Economic Policy of the United States*, Jan. 10, 1955.

25 Id.

26 *Policy Statement by the NPA International Committee* in Raymond F. Mikesell, PROMOTING UNITED STATES PRIVATE INVESTMENT ABROAD, National Planning Association Planning Pamphlet No. 101 v (Oct. 1957).

27 Stanley S. Surrey, *The United States Taxation Foreign Income*, 1 J. L. & ECON. 72 (1958); Louis Shere, *Current Proposals for Modifying United States Tax Law on Taxation of Foreign Source Income*, 52 PROC. ANN. CONF. ON TAX'N, NAT'L TAX ASS'N 319, 325–26 (1959).

US because it was income of the corporation. If, however, the corporation established a subsidiary in that foreign country, the foreign subsidiary would be liable for any tax due in the jurisdiction where it was located, but the parent corporation would not be separately liable for tax in the US on its foreign subsidiary's income until that income was distributed to the US in the form of a dividend or the parent sold its stock in the subsidiary.[28]

Deferral did not offer much of an advantage to US corporations if the foreign rate was the same or higher than the US rate. They paid tax in the foreign country on income earned there and risked double taxation upon repatriation of the money to the US Congress enacted a foreign tax credit at the end of World War I to avoid the double taxation and had also stepped up its pursuit of tax treaties with jurisdictions abroad to obtain reciprocal foreign tax credits if the foreign jurisdiction did not have its own version of a foreign tax credit.[29] Nevertheless, mitigating a tax impediment was hardly an incentive for corporations to invest abroad.

The real advantage to deferring taxation on profits earned from foreign subsidiaries only came if the foreign jurisdiction levied few or no taxes, like in a tax haven. That way, the foreign subsidiary would avoid taxes domestically on its income and the parent corporation would avoid taxes in the US indefinitely if the income remained in the tax haven. The tax dodging effect of this was magnified, according to Treasury Secretary Douglas Dillon, because "U.S. companies frequently attribute a disproportionate share of the profits to the trading, licensing, and servicing companies established in tax haven countries."[30] They would either sell items to their foreign subsidiary at a low price and then the subsidiary would resell at a big profit that would go untaxed in the US until returned in the form of a dividend or some other payment or the subsidiary would sell the item to

[28] Surrey, *supra* note 27, at 75; Shere, *supra* note 27, at 326. The money itself could literally be deposited in a bank in the US by the subsidiary, but would still not be subject to taxation until it was legally distributed to the US corporate parent because it was the property of a legal entity incorporated in a non-US jurisdiction and it was not earned in the US. Surrey, *supra* note 27, at 75–76.

[29] Michael J. Graetz and Michael M. O'Hear, *The "Original Intent" of U.S. International Taxation*, 46 Duke L. J. 1021, 1022–23 (1997); Richman, *supra* note 16, at 54. Prior to 1918, foreign taxes were treated like state and local income taxes and only deductible against federal income taxes, rather than credited dollar-for-dollar. Surrey, *supra* note 27, at 73.

[30] *Statement by Secretary of the Treasury Dillon before the House Committee on Ways and Means on the President's Tax Program, May 3, 1961*, in Annual Report of the Secretary of the Treasury on the State of Finances for the fiscal year ended June 30, 1961, 313, 322 (1962) ("Dillon Ways and Means Statement").

its American parent at a big mark-up that would leave the profits in the low tax jurisdiction.[31] As Senator Al Gore Sr. observed in questioning a representative of the Joy Manufacturing Company about its foreign subsidiaries during a Senate Finance Committee hearing, "the affairs of your company with respect to its overseas holdings have been managed so as to make the operations in high-tax countries show a bare profit, whereas the profit in tax-haven countries is maximized."[32] Secretary Dillon explained to the Ways and Means Committee that this profit shifting was "extremely difficult if not impossible for the Internal Revenue Service to police effectively."[33]

If the parent corporation did want to repatriate the profits, it could do so by selling the stock of the foreign subsidiary, which would give rise to capital gains. Earnings that would have been taxed at a 52 percent rate would be cut in half to 25 percent.[34] These advantages led economist Peggy Brewer Richman (later Musgrave) to blame deferral for creating "an elaborate system of tax avoidance, whereby much of U.S. business abroad is organized in the form of base and holding companies set up in countries which impose a low or zero tax on the domestic income of such base companies and exempt income earned abroad."[35]

Even with the tax haven loophole, businesses wanted more. In the late 1940s and early 1950s, business groups lobbied to expand the deferral benefit to include foreign branches of US corporations, rather than just foreign subsidiaries.[36] Because of the foreign tax credit, foreign branches, which were just divisions of the US corporation operating abroad, did not have double taxation, but branch income was not eligible for deferral. If it was subject to tax at a higher rate in the country where it was earned than if it had been earned directly in the US, then the US corporation would be worse off operating the foreign branch. Business groups also sought an across-the-board reduction for foreign corporate income from the prevailing 52 percent corporate tax rate. This kind of a special exception was already in effect for businesses operating in Latin America as what were called "Western Hemisphere Trade Corporations" under the Revenue

31 Burton Crane, *Tax Havens Draw Many Companies*, N.Y. TIMES, Aug. 19, 1956, at 1.

32 JEROME R. HELLERSTEIN, TAXES, LOOPHOLES & MORALS 164 (1963).

33 *Dillon Ways And Means Statement, supra* note 30, at 322.

34 *"Tax Havens" – One Reason U.S. Firms Are Going Abroad*, U.S. NEWS & WORLD REPORT, May 30, 1960, at 112.

35 RICHMAN, *supra* note 16, at 51.

36 MARINA VON NEUMANN WHITMAN, GOVERNMENT RISK-SHARING IN FOREIGN INVESTMENT 49–50 (1965).

Act of 1942 and in Pre-Maoist China under the China Trade Act of 1922.[37] Economist Marinna von Neumann Whitman explained that these proposals "would not only have a tremendous psychological incentive effect, but would also permit returns to increase to a point where they would outweigh the extra risks of foreign investment and would eliminate the competitive disadvantage American companies suffer when competing abroad against other foreign corporations paying no taxes in their home country" because they did not tax corporations on their worldwide income.[38] Although neither of these proposals were adopted,[39] tax haven investing remained enticing, especially as high postwar tax rates continued.

In 1956, the *New York Times* reported that "American corporations – and to a smaller extent – individuals are rushing to found companies abroad" to take advantage of the promise of "great tax savings."[40] By the 1960s, setting up a subsidiary in a tax haven was considered "a standard device employed by companies engaged in foreign operations."[41] Paul Seghers of the New York Board of Trade told the Senate Committee on Commerce that tax benefits had proven effective in spurring foreign investment: "many relatively small U.S. manufacturers have, in recent years, undertaken export activities (and consequently increased their production of goods for export) because, under existing law, profits realized by a foreign subsidiary are subject to U.S. tax only when received by a U.S. parent corporation as dividends."[42] According to Seghers, "the expectation of using such profits to build up sales abroad has acted as a most effective inducement to make efforts and risk capital in making export sales, which otherwise would not have appeared attractive."[43]

This success did not come without controversy though. In effect, American companies leveraged the US government's desire to facilitate

[37] Id. at 50; Kapstein, *supra* note 20, at 124–25; Richman, *supra* note 16, at 53. Stanley Surrey, Harvard Law Professor and later Assistant Secretary of the Treasury for Tax Policy, called the Western Hemisphere Trade Corporations provision "one of the accidents of tax history," noting that it was never intended to last beyond World War II or to benefit companies beyond those actually operating in Latin America, rather than exporters. Surrey, *supra* note 27, at 79.

[38] Von Neumann Whitman, *supra* note 36, at 50.

[39] Id. at 50, n. 15.

[40] Crane, *supra* note 31, at 1.

[41] Hellerstein, *supra* note 32, at 163.

[42] Hearings before the Committee on Commerce, U.S. Senate, 87th Cong., 1st Sess., on S. 1729, A Bill to Promote the Foreign Commerce of the United States and for Related Purposes 56, 57–58 (1961) (statement of Paul Seghers, New York Board of Trade) (*Senate Foreign Commerce Hearings*).

[43] Id. at 58.

investment in foreign countries to pursue tax dodging.[44] Accountant J. S. Seidman observed that "our country is caught between two pressures. One is our wish to help foreign countries with investments. We have been making tax treaties to facilitate these. The other is our realization of what these tax treaties may be doing to our tax base."[45]

## Popular Tax Haven Destinations for US Corporations and Investors

As a result of these developments, tax haven countries like Panama, the Bahamas, Tangier, Liberia, Liechtenstein, Switzerland, Venezuela, and the Netherlands Antilles began actively marketing themselves to US corporations and investors.[46] These and other tax haven jurisdictions competed for tax dodging investors by taking out full-page advertisements, distributing pamphlets widely, and enlisting lawyers, accountants and investment professionals to help market and facilitate investment in their countries.[47] As one observer noted in 1957, "so large is the tax-haven business that already a number of lawyers and accountants in New York specialize in the operation."[48] US tax professionals often teamed up with lawyers and accountants in tax haven jurisdictions in their marketing efforts. In one example, prospective investors received a pamphlet jointly written by an attorney in New York and an accountant in the Bahamas, describing the tax benefits of setting up corporate subsidiaries in the island nation.[49]

Given the extent to which tax havens were promoted, it is little wonder that thousands of corporations set up foreign subsidiaries to reduce their tax burden during the latter half of the 1950s.[50] In a survey of 350 firms conducted by the National Industrial Conference Board, one-third had

44 Hellerstein, *supra* note 32, at 163.

45 Crane, *supra* note 31, at 1 (quoting Seidman).

46 Mitchell Gordon, *Tax Havens: More Countries Bid to Attract Tax-Wary American Businessmen*, Wall St. J., Feb. 7, 1956, at 1; George E. Sokolsky, *These Days ... Tax Havens by Treaty*, Wash. Post and Times Herald, Sept. 23, 1957, at A17; Robert Metz, *Users of 'Tax Havens' Abroad Batten Down for Political Gale*, N.Y. Times, Feb. 26, 1961, at F1, F14; Hellerstein, *supra* note 32, at 165.

47 *See, e.g.*, Mitchell Gordon, *Tax Havens: More Countries Bid to Attract Tax-Wary American Businessmen*, Wall St. J., Feb. 7, 1956, at 1 (identifying countries); George Sokolsky, *How to Get Rich*, Wash. Post & Times Herald, Oct. 15, 1957, at A13.

48 Sokolsky, *Tax Havens by Treaty*, *supra* note 46, at A17.

49 *See, e.g.*, Sokolsky, *supra* note 47, at A13.

50 *Corporations Find Snug Tax Havens Abroad*, L.A. Times, Dec. 31, 1961, at B3; Hellerstein, *supra* note 32, at 168.

foreign subsidiaries operating in tax havens such as Panama, Switzerland, and the Bahamas.[51] Jerome Hellerstein reported that 4,000 foreign subsidiaries of US corporations were incorporated between 1954 and 1959, with over 1,000 in Switzerland and 600 in Liberia.[52] According to a Joint Committee on Internal Revenue Taxation prepared a report for the Senate Finance Committee,[53] 531 foreign subsidiaries had been organized in 52 countries between January 1, 1960 and May 31, 1961.[54] Three of the most popular destinations for newly formed foreign subsidiaries of US corporations were Panama, Switzerland, and the Bahamas,[55] which were each popularly identified as tax haven jurisdictions and offer a useful look at how offshore tax dodging operated during this period.[56]

## Panama

Panama was an early example of a Caribbean tax haven.[57] In a letter to President Franklin Delano Roosevelt in 1937, Treasury Secretary Henry Morgenthau characterized Panama as "fertile territory" for US companies seeking a tax haven, noting that "their corporation laws make it more difficult to ascertain who the actual stockholders are."[58] By the 1950s, it had become a "favorite spot" for US corporations seeking a tax haven.[59] Experts considered Panama, along with Liberia and Puerto Rico, as being "almost ideal,"[60] with one speaker at a luncheon of the New York Board

51 *Corporations Find Snug Tax Havens Abroad*, *supra* note 50, at B4.

52 Hellerstein, *supra* note 32, at 165, 168.

53 Joint Committee on Internal Revenue Taxation, Tax Effects of Conducting Foreign Business Through Foreign Corporations, prepared for the use of the U.S Committee on Finance, U.S. Senate, July 21, 1961 ("Joint Committee Report on Tax Havens").

54 Id. at 2.

55 Id. Despite the Joint Committee's recognition of the significance of Switzerland as a tax haven destination for US businesses, Steven Dean noted that Stanley Surrey, while Assistant Secretary of the Treasury for Tax Policy, neglected to publicly call out Switzerland, which Dean characterized as a concession to a racially biased view "that preferred to imagine another – more colorful – target" for their tax haven reform efforts. Steven Dean, *Surrey's Silence: Subpart F and the Swiss Subsidiary Tax that Never Was*, 86 L. & Contemp. Probs. 73, 76 (2023).

56 See *Corporations Find Snug Tax Havens Abroad*, *supra* note 50, at B3.

57 Armando Jose Garcia Pires, *The Business Model of The British Virgin Islands and Panama* 7 Working Paper No. 31/13, Norwegian Center for Taxation (Sept. 2013).

58 Robert W. Wales, *Tax Policy in Relation to Foreign Business Income: The Revenue Act of 1962*, 40 Taxes 961 (1962) (quoting Morgenthau).

59 James Russell, *Dummy Firms Organized: New Overseas Trick Exposed to Escape U.S. Income Taxes*, Hartford Courant, Dec. 31, 1961, at 18B.

60 Crane, *supra* note 31, at 11.

of Trade's international trade section in 1956 claiming "Panama . . . offers some of the best advantages" for what were sometimes called "profit sanctuary corporations."[61] Under Panamanian law, profits earned by a Panama-based corporation abroad were not taxed and there was no excess profits or capital gains taxation within the country.[62] Panama also did not tax or prohibit accumulated earnings or undistributed profits.[63] For a few hundred dollars, companies could set up a foreign subsidiary without requiring any of its officers or directors to relocate and local management firms handled all of the subsidiary's paperwork within the country.[64]

Panama not only treated income earned abroad favorably, but it was ideal for shifting profits on sales in the US from the American parent company to the Panamanian subsidiary. In one example involving the sale of coffee, a US food chain was buying coffee beans from South America for 30 cents per pound and then selling the processed coffee beans for 50 cents in the US, making a 10 cent profit per pound – after accounting for costs of preparing the coffee for sale – which was subject to a 52 percent tax in the US.[65] To reduce that tax burden, the US food chain set up a subsidiary in Panama to purchase the coffee from South America and then mark-up the price to 40 cents when re-selling the coffee to the US parent company. This shifted the company's profit from the US parent on the sale to domestic customers to the Panamanian subsidiary on its sale of the coffee to the parent, meaning it was effectively tax-free because Panama companies were not subject to tax on income earned from sales abroad.[66] Companies employed a similar strategy to shift profits on items manufactured in the US for export to high tax countries in Western Europe, using a Panamanian subsidiary to buy the items and sell them to independent distributors in other countries.[67] This way, they not only dodged US and Panamanian taxation because of the latter's exemption for taxes on items sold abroad, but also the high taxes in the countries of sale.[68] By 1961, 200 Panamanian subsidiaries of US

61 *U.S. Concerns Eye Profit Havens*, N.Y. TIMES, May 10, 1956, at 42; Richard Booth, *Foreign Tax Havens Are Found by Many*, WASH. POST, Apr. 5, 1969, at C6.

62 *Corporations Find Snug Tax Havens Abroad*, *supra* note 50, at B3.

63 *U.S Concerns Eye Profit Havens*, *supra* note 61, at 42.

64 *Corporations Find Snug Tax Havens Abroad*, *supra* note 50, at B3.

65 *Tax Havens: Boon to Business*, *supra* note 1, at 66.

66 Id.

67 Joint Committee Report on Tax Havens, *supra* note 53, at 9.

68 Id. at 10 (the result was that "the export profit is not taxed when it is earned, by either the United States, the country of destination, or Panama.").

corporations had been organized,[69] with 46 organized in 1960 and 1961 alone.[70] In 1962, George Westerman, Panama's ambassador to the United Nations from 1956 to 1960, estimated that if the US ever ended the tax-deferral of income earned by US subsidiaries in Panama, it would cost Panama 3 to 4 percent of its gross national income and 5,000 jobs.[71]

There was a risk that using a Panamanian subsidiary as a middleman of sorts could be ignored on the grounds that the subsidiary, or at least its role in the transaction, was a sham. Companies sought to avoid this by employing a management company located in Panama to perform certain ministerial tasks in the country, such as accounting, clerical, and legal services or to transfer title to and from the Panamanian company.[72] As one of the tax services at the time reportedly opined in recommending US companies employ such a management company, "the service is 'worth the price of admission' since it shows that your company is truly an operating entity in Panama – not merely a 'paper company.'"[73]

The price for tax deferral was that the profits needed to stay with the Panamanian subsidiary, but that did not prevent the US corporation from using those profits. In addition to reinvesting them in its overseas operations in Panama or elsewhere,[74] the parent company could borrow against the subsidiaries' holdings through low interest rate loans, avoiding tax on the income and providing a deduction on the interest.[75] When a parent company did want to fully bring back the principal, it could "collapse" the corporation by liquidating it and distributing the assets to the parent in exchange for the complete cancellation of the stock.[76] This converted profits that would have been taxed at the ordinary corporate rate of 52 percent to capital gain that would be taxed at the more modest 25 percent rate.[77] Although Congress had enacted legislation under the 1954 Code to restrict the use of these so-called "collapsible corporations," it only applied if the corporation was "formed or availed of" with the intent of collapsing it before the parent corporation realized the income

69 *Corporations Find Snug Tax Havens Abroad*, *supra* note 50, at B3.
70 Joint Committee Report on Tax Havens, *supra* note 53, at App. E, Table I, p. 49.
71 *Tax Havens: Boon to Business*, *supra* note 1, at 67.
72 Id. at 16.
73 Id. at 16.
74 *Tax Havens: Boon to Business*, *supra* note 1, at 66 ("It can use the money to buy coffee plantations or to build overseas warehouses and processing plants").
75 *Corporations Find Snug Tax Havens Abroad*, *supra* note 50, at B3.
76 Michael K. Ryan, *Collapsible Corporations*, 20 William & Mary Annual Tax Conf. 24 (1973).
77 Id. at 25.

on the profits earned by the subsidiary under a provision that was "neither well conceived nor well drafted . . . offer[ing] too much freedom for tax avoidance."[78]

### *Switzerland*

Switzerland was one of the earliest European tax havens, emerging fully in the years up to and following World War I.[79] Part of this was attributable to the rise of the banking industry with the establishment of the Swiss Bankers Association in 1912, the underwriting of the Swiss government, which had committed to pay fairly high interest rates, and the backstop of the Swiss National Bank starting in 1907 as a guard against financial crisis.[80] This was cemented with the Banking Act of 1934, which reinforced the bank secrecy that has been considered a "pillar of the offshore world."[81]

With an established financial industry already designed to attract capital, it was well-positioned to take advantage of rising wartime tax rates to establish itself as a tax haven. Unlike in Panama, however, Switzerland had a federal structure, so the tax advantages were not uniformly distributed. Individual "cantons," which are like American states, had their own taxing authorities and, much like in America, competed to attract businesses to their jurisdiction.[82] For example, although the canton of Zurich was the banking center, it "was not keen on offering tax privileges" to these offshore holding companies, making the banking advantages less valuable.[83] "The city's financial elite," however, "used the more amenable and much poorer rural cantons of Glarus and Zug, which redrafted their laws on the advice of lawyers and bankers from Zurich" to make them more useful as tax havens.[84] As a result, Switzerland's status as one of the oldest tax havens "flourished" between World Wars I and II "when political and economic instability as well as

[78] I.R.C. § 341 (1954); Adrian W. Dewind & Robert Anthoine, *Collapsible Corporations*, 56 Colum. L. Rev. 475, 534 (1956).

[79] Ogle, *Funk Money, supra* note 3, at 219; Ronen Palen, *History of Tax Havens,* History & Pol'y (Inst. for Hist Res. Policy Paper), Oct. 1, 2009; Gabriel Zucman, The Hidden Wealth of Nations: The Scourge of Tax Havens 8–9 (2015); Sébastian Guex, *The Emergence of the Swiss Tax Haven, 1816–1914*, 96 Bus. Hist. Rev. 353, 370 (2022).

[80] Zucman, *supra* note 79, at 9.

[81] Palen, *History of Tax Havens*, *supra* note 79.

[82] This competition extended to business codes. Palan, *Tax Havens and the Commercialization of State Sovereignty*, *supra* note 8, at 161.

[83] Palan, *History of Tax Havens*, *supra* note 79.

[84] Id.

newly introduced income taxes sent German, Italian, French and other money to bank accounts and holding companies in Switzerland."[85]

By the late 1950s and early 1960s, while US corporations were subject to tax on income earned domestically at a rate of 52 percent, the rate of tax on income earned in Switzerland was only 8 percent.[86] Moreover, if the US corporation set up a Swiss subsidiary as a holding company to own the stock of the subsidiaries operating plants in other parts of Europe, the Swiss holding company would pay no taxes on those profits because they were earned outside of the country and it could bring those profits back into Switzerland as well without taxation.[87] It is thus not surprising that Switzerland was so popular among those looking for a tax haven. Between September 1, 1959, and December 1960, 217 subsidiaries were organized in Switzerland, with 90 organized in the six-month period from September 1, 1959, to March 31, 1960.[88] In one example, a US parent corporation transferred all its patents and copyrights and assigned all its royalties to a foreign subsidiary for $22. Over the following year, the subsidiary earned $1.5 million in gross royalties and fees from licensing the intellectual property, none of which were taxable in the US because they were earned by a foreign subsidiary and had not been repatriated to the US.[89]

In its report on tax havens, the Joint Committee concluded that tax dodging was a motivating factor for US investment in Switzerland.[90] For example, Zug, was a "small, remote canton in which," according the report, "there is substantially no business activity."[91] Nevertheless, as the report explained, Zug had long used "tax-exemption laws . . . to attract 'domiciliary companies,'" which it defined as a company "which has a Swiss corporate charter, but which does not have an office or place of business in Switzerland and which does not carry on business in Switzerland."[92] Although the Joint Committee noted that "it is difficult to determine or

[85] Ogle, *Funk Money*, *supra* note 3, at 222.

[86] *56 Firms went to Zug, U.S. Tax Haven Mecca*, N.Y. Herald Trib., Apr. 15, 1962, at 29.

[87] *"Tax Havens" - One Reason U.S. Firms are Going Abroad*, U.S. News & World Report, May 30, 1960, at 112.

[88] *Joint Committee Tax Haven Report*, *supra* note 53, at 31 (tbl. II).

[89] *56 Firms Went to Zug*, *supra* note 86, at 29.

[90] *Joint Committee Tax Haven Report*, *supra* note 53, at 2.

[91] Id. at 2–3; Lee Silberman, *Fading Tax Haven? Proposal in Congress Could Hobble American Ventures in Bahamas*, Wall St. J., March 29, 1962, at 1.

[92] *Joint Committee Tax Haven Report*, *supra* note 53, at 3. This type of an exemption for domicile or so-called "letterbox" companies did not originate with Zug. Glarius reportedly adopted it as early as 1903, followed soon after by other Swiss cantons St. Gallen and Schaffhausen. Guex, *Low-Tax Predators*, *supra* note 1, at 9.

even to infer, whether, or to what extent, deferral of U.S. income taxes motivated the creation of the foreign subsidiary," the implication was that Zug would be particularly attractive for a tax haven investment since "it is clear that the value of deferring U.S. taxes is greater when there is no foreign tax or where the foreign tax is small," as was the case with Zug.[93] Thus, it should not have been surprising that of the seventy-one new subsidiaries of US corporations formed in Switzerland in 1960 and the first half of 1961, fifty-six of them were located in Zug.[94] Zug became so overcrowded that in 1963 it started discouraging companies from locating foreign subsidiaries there, repealing some of its tax advantages because of scarcity in housing, office space, and secretarial support.[95]

### *Bahamas*

The Bahamas was an early destination for US tax dodgers, who were spurred on in part by the rising tax rates enacted during the New Deal.[96] According to the US Treasury Department, in 1935 and 1936, sixty-four foreign personal holding companies were established in the Bahamas, with another twenty-two set-up in the first two months of 1937 alone.[97] It was after World War II, however, that Bahamas' status as a tax haven jurisdiction was cemented.[98] Given its close proximity to the US and its "near tax vacuum" because, unlike in Panama, it levied no income taxes even on domestic profits,[99] it was logical that the Bahamas would become a "principal tax haven" for American business in the 1950s and 1960s.[100] As one reporter noted, "[w]ith so much to offer the less fortunate nations of the world, it is not surprising that tax avoidance is cheerfully and frankly promoted as the country's second biggest industry."[101]

In most cases, the Bahaman subsidiaries were mere shell or "dummy" corporations. They were easy to form under Bahamian law with minimal

93 *Joint Committee Tax Haven Report*, *supra* note 53, at 5.

94 Id. at App. E, Table I, at 50; *Swiss "Tax Haven" for U.S. Firms Reported*, L.A. TIMES, Apr. 15, 1962, at 9.

95 Peter Grose, *Swiss Tax Haven Now Overloaded*, N.Y. TIMES, Sept. 13, 1963, at 52.

96 Ogle, *Funk Money*, *supra* note 3, at 227.

97 Wales, *supra* note 58, at 961.

98 Id.

99 Silberman, *Fading Tax Haven?*, *supra* note 91, at 1; Crane, *supra* note 31, at 11.

100 James Russell, *U.S. Companies Sprout Dummy Firms Abroad*, CINCINNATI ENQUIRER, Jan. 2, 1962, at 31.

101 Stephen Aris, *The Bahamas' Liberal Tax Laws Attracting Millions of Dollars*, L.A. TIMES, Nov. 7, 1966, at B13.

expense. The subsidiaries had to file articles of association and establish a registered office, but these services were readily supplied by the one of the thirteen major trust companies or the many lawyers located in Nassau that represented foreign subsidiaries for precisely these purposes.[102] These trust companies or lawyers effectively operated domestic management corporations overseeing hundreds of such companies. The Bahamas International Trust Company, for instance, represented seventy-six companies from the United States alone between 1958 and 1963.[103] One reporter noted that "on the wall of a building in downtown Nassau, in the Bahamas, are more than 100 signs identifying an upstairs office as the legal headquarters of more than 100 companies."[104] While the vast majority of American corporations operating in the Bahamas did so through these dummy or "suitcase" corporations, around two dozen of them, mostly subsidiaries of the more prominent US businesses, were run by employees of the companies themselves.[105] United States Steel's subsidiary in the Bahamas, Navios Corp., for example, had around sixty employees, while Bethlehem Steel had forty employees.[106]

Many of the Bahamian subsidiaries were used as go-betweens for trading companies located in the US. If an overseas customer wanted to purchase a product from the US parent company, the US parent would sell the item to the Bahamian subsidiary, often at cost to eliminate any profit earned in the U.S., and then the subsidiary would sell the item to the overseas customer at the regular sales price and retain the profits in the Bahamas.[107] Alternatively, the US parent would make the sale itself, but the Bahamian subsidiary would collect a commission on the transaction for serving as the middleman, divert some of the profit to the Bahamas.[108] Either way, the Bahamian subsidiary's involvement in the transaction was on paper only. The actual delivery of the items purchased would be made directly from the US parent to the overseas customer, while the bill was sent to the customer from the subsidiary in the Bahamas.[109]

Another popular use of these Bahamian subsidiaries was as reinsurance corporations.[110] A reinsurance corporation is effectively used to

[102] Id. at B13–B14.
[103] Ogle, *Funk Money*, *supra* note 3, at 231.
[104] Russell, *U.S. Companies Sprout Dummy Firms Abroad*, *supra* note 100, at 31.
[105] Silberman, *Fading Tax Haven?*, *supra* note 91, at 1.
[106] Russell, *U.S. Companies Sprout Dummy Firms Abroad*, *supra* note 100, at 31.
[107] Silberman, *Fading Tax Haven?*, *supra* note 91, at 14.
[108] Id.
[109] Id.
[110] Id.

diversify the risk associated with holding an insurance policy. The reinsurer takes on some of the risk in exchange for receiving some of the profit. In a tax haven, however, the reinsurance corporation may be more about shifting profits than about shifting risk. A US insurance corporation would set up a reinsurance subsidiary in the Bahamas and then sell a portion of an insurance policy to its subsidiary. The profits associated with that portion of the insurance policy would remain untaxed in the Bahamas until repatriated to the US and that could be postponed indefinitely, especially if the profits were reinvested in something like Bahamian real estate.[111] This could also be accomplished through a captive insurance company, which is an insurance company that is owned by a US business as a form of self-insurance, that is organized in the Bahamas. The US parent would pay deductible premiums to the Bahamian captive insurance subsidiary and then the subsidiary would pay, at a lower premium, a reinsurer to cover that risk as well, which would generate a profit that would be free of tax because it was generated in the Bahamas.[112]

Although there were more foreign subsidiaries in Panama, the Bahamas was ambitious and its rise as a tax haven may have had a more lasting effect.[113] In 1966, Harold Revington, manager of the Bahamas International Trust in Nassau, proclaimed "we like to think of ourselves as the future Zurich of the Western World."[114] The legal and financial infrastructure that developed in the Bahamas during this period helped to seed tax havens throughout the Caribbean region, including the Cayman Islands, the British Virgin Islands, and Antigua.[115]

## Reform Attempts

The increasing use of tax havens appeared to go too far for the Administration. In President John F. Kennedy's tax message to Congress in April 1961, he noted that "profits earned abroad by American firms operating through foreign subsidiaries are, under present tax laws, subject to U.S. tax only when they are return to the parent

111 Id.

112 Charles R. Irish, *Tax Havens*, 15 VAND. J. TRANSNAT'L L. 449, 470 (1982).

113 *Bahamas Role as Tax Haven May be Ending*, BOSTON GLOBE, Jan. 13, 1963, at 59 (reporting that there were believed to be 30,000 companies in Panama, versus 500 in the Bahamas).

114 Aris, *supra* note 101, at B13 (quoting Revington).

115 Ogle, *Funk Money*, *supra* note 3, at 227.

company in the form of dividends," which, he reminded listeners, has in some cases "made possible indefinite postponement of the U.S. tax; and, in those countries where income taxes are lower than in the United States, the ability to defer payment of U.S. tax by retaining income in the subsidiary companies provides a tax advantage for companies operating oversea subsidiaries that is not available to companies solely operating in the United States."[116] Kennedy acknowledged that "many American investors properly made use of this deferral in the conduct of their foreign investment," but said "changing conditions now make continuance of the privilege undesirable."[117]

The biggest problem, according to Kennedy, was that tax deferral was not being used to subsidize legitimate foreign investment, but instead to prop up abusive tax haven transactions that hurt the US economy. As Boris Gehlen and Christian Marx observed, "US domestic tax policy initially favoured the emergence of tax havens and the financing strategy of MNEs [multinational enterprises], but when the negative effects on the domestic economy became apparent, the U.S. pushed for a change in the bilateral agreements with tax havens" and adjusted their tax policy accordingly.[118] Specifically mentioning Switzerland, Kennedy noted that many foreign subsidiaries of US firms use

> artificial arrangements between parent and subsidiary regarding intercompany pricing, the transfer of patent licensing rights, the shifting of management fees, and similar practices which maximize the accumulation of profits in the tax haven ... to exploit the multiplicity of foreign tax systems and international agreements in order to reduce sharply or eliminate completely their tax liabilities both at home and abroad.[119]

The result of this tax-motivated foreign investment, Kennedy contended, was a disruption to the "efficient allocation of international resources" and a negative effect on the US "already adverse balance of payments."[120]

Given the declining postwar justification for foreign investment in developed countries like Europe, and the negative effects of inefficient

[116] Message from the President of the United States relative to our Federal Tax System, April 20, 1961, in President's Tax Message along with Principled Statement, Detailed Explanation, and Supporting Documents submitted by the Secretary of the Treasury at Hearings conducted by the Committee on Ways and Means, House of Representatives, May 3, 1961, at 1, 6 ("President's Message").

[117] Id.

[118] Gehlen & Marx, *supra* note 4, at 226–27.

[119] President's Message, *supra* note 116, at 6.

[120] Id.

tax-motivated foreign investment, Kennedy told Congress that "we can no long afford existing tax treatment of foreign income."[121] He proposed that we "tax each year American corporations [and 'individual shareholders of closely held corporations'] on their current share of the undistributed profits realized in that year by subsidiary corporations in economically advanced countries," which would subject them to the same tax as they would on domestic operations because of the credit for taxes paid on foreign income.[122] Kennedy proposed to continue the tax deferral privilege for investment in "developing economies," noting that "the free world has a strong obligation to assist in the development of these economies and private investment has an important contribution to make."[123] He distinguished between developing economies and "tax havens," however, proposing "the elimination of tax deferral privileges for those forms of activities, such as trading, licensing, insurance, and others, that typically seek out tax haven methods of operation," by which he presumably was referring to investments in countries that did not tax the profits of foreign subsidiaries at all.[124] According to Kennedy, "*there is no valid reason to permit their remaining untaxed regardless of the country in which they are located.*"[125]

Companies with subsidiaries in tax havens found themselves on the defensive. The president of Rockwell Manufacturing Company, for example, took out a large advertisement stating the case for locating its subsidiaries in so-called "tax haven" jurisdictions.[126] John J. Powers, Jr., president of Pfizer International, pointedly remarked that the President's proposal reflected "a certain residual naïveté" on the question of international trade by discouraging foreign direct investment at a time when it encouraged exports.[127] A tax lawyer suggested that this would affect investment in new countries too:

> For fifteen years, the Commerce and State departments have been campaigning for more exports and heavier investment abroad. Now

121 Id.

122 Id. at 7. The proposal to tax shareholders, including individual shareholders of closely held corporations, currently on income earned by foreign subsidiaries, was assailed as potentially raising constitutional concerns. Richard J. Horwich, *The Constitutionality of Subpart F of the Internal Revenue Code*, 19 U. MIAMI L. REV. 400 (1964); John A. Eichler, *Taxation of Foreign Subsidiaries under the Revenue Act of 1962 – A Note on Proposed Legislation*, 30 GEO. WASH. L. REV. 950, 962–63 (1962).

123 Gehlen & Marx, *supra* note 4, at 7.

124 President's Message, *supra* note 116, at 7.

125 Id. (italics in original).

126 *Display Ad 43*, WALL ST. J., April 21, 1961, at 10.

127 *Tax Havens: Boon to Business*, *supra* note 1, at 68.

> that the money invested in the formerly unproductive economies of Europe is paying off, the government wants to change the rules. Under these circumstances, you can hardly expect business to invest in the newly developing countries as Washington is urging now.[128]

The National City Bank of New York took a different tack, arguing that it was a "delusion" to charge that these investments were about tax dodging, claiming that "the dominant practice is to remit the maximum of profits consistent with the capital needs of the foreign subsidiary."[129] Similarly, the president of an engineering firm contended that it was "nonsense" to attribute foreign investment to tax dodging, noting that his firm had opened up an office in Zug, Switzerland to provide technical personnel for its European subsidiaries and if it was located there for tax dodging reasons, it was about dodging European taxes rather than those levied in the US.[130]

Some businesses invoked Cold War rhetoric in favor of tax haven investing, arguing it helped foster good foreign relations. One businessman testified before a Congressional Committee that the tax breaks that facilitated foreign investment in these tax havens was essential for "the Nation to meet the economic challenge now posed by the Soviet Union and ... to demonstrate abroad the benefits of free enterprise."[131] H. J. Heinz II, the president of the Heinz food packing company, which earned over 50 percent of its profits through its foreign subsidiaries, declared "[t]he growth of direct investment by American enterprise has improved the efficiency and increased the profits of U.S. business and the income of its shareholders," but it has also "gained friends and partners for the United States."[132] Paul D. Seghers, president of the Institute on US Taxation of Foreign Income, argued, "any attempt to circumscribe the tax advantages enjoyed by foreign subsidiaries ... would conflict with the Administration's policy of encouraging 'business expansion abroad and closer commercial relations with our neighbors in the free world.'"[133]

128 Id.
129 Russell, *Global Trade*, *supra* note 100, at A29.
130 William Clark, *Foreign 'Tax Haven' Talk is Nonsense, says Knight*, Chi. Daily Trib., May 2, 1962, at C6 (quoting Lester B. Knight).
131 Hellerstein, *supra* note 32, at 173.
132 *Tax Havens: Boon to Business*, *supra* note 1, at 67.
133 Russell, *Global Trade*, *supra* note 100, at A29 (quoting and paraphrasing Seghers in part).

President Kennedy's proposals were ultimately rejected in favor of a milder approach.[134] Under the "watered down" version of proposals enacted in the Revenue Act of 1962,[135] Congress adopted what became known as Subpart F, which required certain US shareholders of what were called Controlled Foreign Corporations, or foreign corporations that were substantially owned or controlled by US individuals, corporations, partnerships, or trusts, to include in their gross income their allocable share of certain income, comprised of income from related party transactions that were known as foreign base company income and certain service income.[136] The theory was that this technical and targeted version of Kennedy's original proposal would be a more "precisely fitting concept against tax haven deferral consistent with economic conditions of the time."[137] In truth, however, it was just narrowly tailored enough to allow tax haven investing to survive. Many companies restructured their operations to continue to take advantage of tax haven benefits and tax havens themselves adjusted their laws to ensure they remained attractive.[138]

134 JOHN F. WITTE, THE POLITICS AND DEVELOPMENT OF THE FEDERAL INCOME TAX 156–58 (1985); Eichler, *supra* note 122, at 983; Robert Metz, *Tax Men to Fight for Their 'Havens,'* N.Y. TIMES, Nov. 19, 1961, at F1; *Senate Rejects Tax-Bill Shift Easing Plan on Profits Abroad*, N.Y. TIMES, Sept. 1, 1962, at 8; HELLERSTEIN, *supra* note 32, at 169–70, 179–80. *See* Robert Metz, *Tax Revision Due for Swiss Havens*, N.Y. TIMES, Oct. 7, 1962, at F1 ("Specialists who have analyzed the final version of the measure say it is not nearly so bad as it might have been.").

135 *If 1962 Tax Reforms Are Enacted They Will be Less Than Sought*, THE AUSTIN STATESMAN, Aug. 28, 1962, at 4.

136 I.R.C. §§ 951–964. Adam H. Rosenzweig, *Why Are There Tax Havens?* 52 WM. & MARY L. REV. 923, 973–76 (2010); C. Richard Baker, *A New Look at Subpart F*, 54 TAXES 572 (1976); Ira T. Wender, *Tax Planning for International Operations under the Revenue Act of 1962: A Case Study*, 41 TAXES: THE TAX MAGAZINE 835 (1963).

137 Gerhard Kraft and Diana Beck, *Fifty Years of Subpart F Revisited in Light of Modified Economic Conditions*, 40 INTERTAX 683 (2012). The House Ways and Means Committee was unable to vote a bill out of committee based on Kennedy's original proposal and instead asked Treasury to draft legislation that would limit its application to foreign-owned subsidiaries that could be classified as tax haven businesses. Treasury Department, Press Release, *Treasury Releases Draft of Proposed "Tax Haven" Legislation*, July 28, 1961, in PRESS RELEASES OF THE UNITED STATES DEPARTMENT OF THE TREASURY, v. 126; Lawrence M. Stone, *Taxation on Private Investments Abroad – Legal Aspects (*Part 1*)*, PROC. OF THE 1962 INSTITUTE ON PRIVATE INVESTMENTS ABROAD AND FOREIGN TRADE, Southwestern Legal Foundation 195 (1962).

138 Lee Silberman, Tax Haven Turmoil, Wall St. J., Jan. 10, 1963, at 1; Eileen P. Carron, *Tax-Haven Role Stressed in Bahamas*, N.Y. TIMES, Jan. 17, 1964, at 73; Walter A. Slowinski, *Tax Havens: Dead or Alive*, 19 PROC. ANN. TUL. TAX INST. 450 (1970).

## Domestic Tax Havens

Kennedy's reforms not only failed to end tax haven investing, but they also did not deal with domestic tax havens. States and territories, and even counties and cities,[139] that competed on tax treatment also garnered that title in America. Nevada, for example, which to this day has no state taxes on income, capital gains, gifts, or inheritances,[140] was perhaps the boldest in the use of tax policy as a tool to lure the "tax-oppressed . . . wealthy refugees from high-tax states, such as New York and California, to establish legal residence in Nevada."[141] Some of this migration was motivated by the same factors that influenced the foreign tax haven movement – the effect of increasing taxes in other jurisdictions. Thus, business owners and corporations cited things like the impact of Utah's estate taxes on owners of stock in the Union Pacific Railroad, which was at the time incorporated in Utah, and the move by Kentucky to increase the taxes levied upon the Southern Pacific Railroad, which held a special charter in that state.[142] Nevada's tax haven status was not based exclusively on how it treated the traditional subjects of federal taxation such as income or estate taxes though. In 1960, a state constitutional amendment made permanent what was called a "free port law." This allowed companies to store or process goods in the state without being subject to property or inventory taxation.[143] As a consequence, shipments by rail, truck, and air increased tenfold as dozens of major companies set up warehouses or facilities in the state to reduce their personal property taxes.[144] This led neighboring states like Utah and Arizona to enact similar laws in attempt to compete for this business.[145]

On the US territorial side, Puerto Rico was the most aggressive in using tax benefits to attract business and was commonly referred to as a tax

[139] For example, to attract industry after World War II, Middlesex County, New Jersey called itself a "veritable tax haven" with low real estate taxes and "non-existent" state individual and corporate income taxes, corporate earnings taxes, sales taxes. *Display Ad 62*, N.Y. Times, Dec. 17, 1944, at E10. *See Display Ad 194*, N.Y. Times, Dec. 4, 1945, at 45.

[140] Beverly Moran, *The Second War between the States: How the United States Became the World's Best Tax Haven*, 16 L. & Dev'pt. Rev. 295, 312 (2023).

[141] Lewis B. Reynolds, *Nevada: Tax Haven: State Grows Richer as "Refugee" Funds Enter Business, Farming There*, Wall St. J., April 10, 1946, at 1.

[142] Id.

[143] *Another Kind of Bonanza in Nevada*, Boston Globe, Feb. 20, 1967, at 18.

[144] Id.

[145] Id.

haven, although it itself eschewed that title.[146] In an attempt to counter the effects of the post–World War I recession and encourage investment in Puerto Rico and other possessions, the US enacted what was referred to as a "possessions tax" exemption or credit.[147] Under this provision, US corporations primarily operating an active trade or business in Puerto Rico or another possession of the US got the same deferral available to US corporations setting up subsidiaries in foreign countries.[148] Because of this special treatment, the *Chicago Daily Tribune* called Puerto Rico "an income tax haven 961 miles off the Florida coast," noting that not only did the federal income tax not apply to operations in Puerto Rico, but the island territory provided a complete exemption from the Puerto Rican corporate income tax.[149] Companies could also get a five- to ten-year exemption from property taxation as part of a program called "Operation Bootstrap," which reportedly led to 553 plants being built on the island between 1947 and 1959.[150]

Puerto Rico's tax advantages only increased after Congress enacted its international tax reforms in 1962.[151] Under the Revenue Act of 1962, there was a specific carveout from the controlled foreign corporation rules for "any corporation created or organized in the Commonwealth of Puerto Rico . . . or under the laws of the Commonwealth of Puerto Rico" if 80 percent or more of the income in the preceding three years was derived from sources within Puerto Rico and 50 percent or more was derived from the active conduct of a manufacturing operation or certain other businesses in Puerto Rico.[152] As one columnist for the *Los Angeles Times* subsequently observed, "United States companies invested in Puerto Rico may find themselves in the favorable position of being one of the few areas of the world unaffected by" the new changes in the tax

146 *See* George Natanson, *Puerto Rico: Calm Port for Tax-Tossed Business*, L.A. TIMES, Jan. 13, 1963, at H1 ("Puerto Rican government authorities are quick to point out that the Commonwealth's favorable investment possibilities created by the new code does not make the island a 'tax haven.'").

147 I.R.C. § 931 (1954). Diane Lourdes Dick, *U.S. Tax Imperialism in Puerto Rico*, 65 AM. U. L. REV. 1, 6–7 (2015); RICHMAN, *supra* note 16 at 52–53.

148 Richman, *supra* note 16, at 53. According to Stanley Surrey, because of a misinterpretation of the 1921 law, Treasury considered the income of a US corporation actively doing business in Puerto Rico as exempt rather than merely deferred and treated it as such. Surrey, *supra* note 27, at 78.

149 *Investors' Guide: Tax Inducements of Puerto Rico Spur Business Growth*, CHICAGO DAILY TRIB., May 8, 1960, at A8.

150 Id.

151 *See supra* notes 135–137.

152 Revenue Act of 1962, Pub. L. 87–834, 76 Stat. 960, 1017, Sec. 957(c).

laws.[153] Combined with other provisions already in the Code, one commentator suggested that all US possessions "are accorded more favorable treatment than other parts of the world," under the new law, "but even among United States possessions Puerto Rico occupies a favored position."[154] Moreover, US companies could easily satisfy the requirement that they generate 80 percent of their income in Puerto Rico by selling to foreign customers in Puerto Rico rather than in the buyers' home countries.[155]

## Marketing and the Mirage of Tax Havens

Some assume that tax dodgers simply stumbled upon tax havens. As Sebastien Guex, a professor at the University of Lausanne in Switzerland, wrote in his history of tax havens, the whole notion of tax "havens," or as one member of the Belgian Parliament, Louis Franck, described it in a speech in 1913, "oases in the midst of the invasive and often aggressive taxation of the large neighbouring countries," implies passivity.[156] "Under this view," Guex continues, "[t]he expressions that have become commonplace – tax 'havens', 'refuges' or 'oases' are evidence of the notion that tax havens are the passive, almost involuntary product of decisions made and implemented by tax evaders or avoiders alone."[157] The implication is that US taxpayers stumbled upon countries that had adopted tax and banking laws for reasons that made sense in their domestic markets, but turned out coincidentally to be favorable for US investors in search of respite from the high mid-century tax rates.

Guex proposed that we instead consider tax haven jurisdictions as "low-tax predators."[158] According to Guex, these tax havens are "the products of a deliberate and active policy of important, even central, sectors within the ruling class of certain states. . . . These sectors not only respond to demand with supply but tend to go further. As with any market, they also try to create or stimulate demand."[159] In effect, being a tax haven was an economic development strategy. As one modern

153 Natanson, *supra* note 146, at H1.
154 Zoltan M. Mihaly, *Tax Advantages of Doing Business in Puerto Rico*, 16 STAN. L. REV. 75, 75 (1963).
155 Natanson, *supra* note 146, at H11.
156 Guex, *Low-Tax Predators*, *supra* note 1, at 10 (quoting Franck).
157 Id. at 20.
158 Id. at 29.
159 Id. at 20.

observer noted, "the incorporation business is a key driver in tax haven economic development: it provides jobs for law firms as well as government registration clerks and their support staffs, and generates a steady stream of income for countries who attract the clients by not levying taxes on any income to these corporations."[160]

The fact that demand for tax havens was cultivated does not mean that most tax haven jurisdictions originally set out to become a tax haven. As Ronen Palan wrote, "modern tax havens . . . evolved slowly and haphazardly; states appear to have stumbled upon the various attributes of tax havens, such as bank secrecy laws, low taxation, and 'liberal' corporation laws."[161] According to Palan, "only by the 1930s had a select number of tax havens – including Switzerland, Liechtenstein, the Bahamas, and Bermuda – begun to integrate the diverse elements into a core component of their development strategies."[162] Within a few decades, however, that began to change.

In the 1950s and 1960s, countries began using their economic development offices to actively promote their status as tax havens. They often did so by creating a "mirage" that associated tax haven investing with exotic tourism. In one example, the Jamaica Industrial Development Corporation, which was formed by the government of Jamaica in 1952 to help attract businesses to develop their economy,[163] ran a large advertisement in the *New York Times* to promote investment in the island.[164] It not only highlighted that Jamaica was a "tax haven for 'off-shore' based companies," but boasted that the island had "the ideal climate, the sandy beaches, [and] the azure waters" and it invited readers to "see Jamaica for yourself."[165] In another example, Monaco brought in Martin Dale of the U.S. State Department to run the Monaco Economic Development Corporation. Even though Dale claimed that "Monaco does not intend to set itself up as just another tax haven," the French government accused Monaco of using its economic development arm to induce companies to establish headquarters in the principality to avoid taxes in France, America, and

[160] Charles A. Dainoff, Outlaw Paradise: Why Countries Become Tax Havens 40 (2021).
[161] Palan, *Tax Havens and the Commercialization of State Sovereignty*, *supra* note 8, at 159.
[162] Id.
[163] Carol S. Holzberg, *Notes and Queries on Industrial Development: Illustrations from Jamaica*, 28 Social and Econ. Stud. 100, 105 (1979).
[164] *Display Ad 19*, N.Y. Times, Jan. 21, 1961, at 27.
[165] Id.

many other places.[166] Prince Ranier of Monaco sent to the largest corporations in places like the US, Britain, Germany, Switzerland, and Italy "brochures which are at once sumptuous and weighed down with facts."[167] They promised to pair Monaco's tax advantages with benefits of a luxury resort complete with amenities such as "a helicopter landing ground, tennis courts and more apartments" in the "gamblers' Mecca."[168] Malta, described as "the island of happy retirement," with "little income tax and plenty of sunshine," was another country that used its economic development arm plus a legislative change that exempted foreign-owned companies from Maltese taxes to try to create "a dreamland for foreign companies that want to avoid the high taxes and regulations of their home lands."[169] This continued to spread into the 1970s. Sri Lanka, called "the last garden paradise in a price-inflated world," tried to market itself as a haven for retirees in part because of the absence of an income tax for people who were not employed.[170]

Attorneys, accountants, bankers, and other advisors also promoted the tax haven industry in their countries. In one example, a Grand Cayman company called International Directors, Ltd. advertised a book in the classified advertisements for the *Chicago Tribune* titled "How to Save Money by Incorporating in a Tax Haven."[171] It promised "special sections for exporters, commodity dealers, investors [and] professions."[172] Similarly, Caribbean Ventures, Ltd., a property investment advisory service, distributed a newsletter promising to give readers "INSIDE FACTS on ... tax havens and investment opportunities in the

[166] Robert McKeown, *Trouble in Grace's Paradise*, Weekend Magazine, THE SUN (Vancouver), Dec. 29, 1962, at 2, 4; Robert Alden, *The Chips are Down for Monaco*, N. Y. TIMES, July 15, 1962, at 140. For an example of the use of Monaco by a US corporation, see Hearings Before the Senate Finance Committee on H.R. 10650, 87th Cong. 2d Sess., 3974–90 (1962) (testimony of J. D. A. Morrow, Chairman of the Finance Committee of Joy Manufacturing); Martin Norr, *Monaco: Biography of a Tax Haven*, 19 Tax L. Rev. 469, 475 (1964).

[167] David Mason, *Gamblers Out of Luck in Monaco*, SOUTH CHINA MORNING POST, Nov. 7, 1961, at 16.

[168] Id.

[169] Anne Sharpley, *The Cloud Haning Over this Settlers' Paradise*, EVENING STANDARD, Nov. 14, 1967, at 7; George Melloan, *Malta Drafting Offshore Companies Act and Maritime Law to Lure Foreign Firms*, WALL ST. J., Nov. 4, 1969, at 31.

[170] Richard Joseph, *The Last Garden Paradise in a Price-Inflated World*, WASH. POST, April 28, 1974, at K6.

[171] *Classified Ad 14*, CHI. TRIB., Oct. 14, 1975, at C9.

[172] Id.

Caribbean and Bahamas."[173] In another, a company called Enterprise Publishing Co. advertised a book by Midas Malone entitled "How to Do Business Tax Free!"[174] The publishers also included the traditional lure of mixing the financial benefits with the ability to actually enjoy the island lifestyle. The full page advertisement by Enterprise Publishing Co. in the *New York Times* included island resort imagery – a sketching of a man standing on the beach wearing a sport coat with elbow patches and holding a drink while talking to a women in a swimsuit lying on a beach chair in front of a coconut tree with the ocean in front of them and a sailboat in the distance.[175] Readers were told to "picture yourself in these surroundings with time and money to do all the things you want to do – no cares or worries ... You can do all this simply by doing your business tax free."[176] To get all of this, buyers were promised the opportunity to "Find Your OWN Tax Haven! And a new way of life simply and easily using any of the world's most exotic places" with the book, which the publisher claimed came "complete with tear-out forms – everything that is needed."[177]

Even within the US, governments and local development offices engaged in advertising campaigns to highlight their status as tax havens. Sometimes, they were able to combine their campaigns with the tourism bureaus by connecting the tax haven status with the vacation resort image. For instance, the Greater Reno Chamber of Commerce created a mock show bill, complete with men in suits and briefcases lined up like show girls, to advertise "Reno's Big New Hit Show: Industrial Opportunities of 1968."[178] In the advertisement, Reno bragged about being called a "multi-million dollar tax haven" by the *Chicago Daily News* and highlighted a dozen big-name companies that were operating there to take advantage of these opportunities.[179]

Puerto Rico was more business-like in promoting its tax haven advantages, perhaps in part because it sought to avoid that label.[180] According to the *Chicago Daily Tribune*, "Puerto Rico went out and sold its advantages to the mainland investor by means of a carefully prepared,

[173] *Display Ad 274*, L.A. Times, June 2, 1968, at J9.
[174] *Display Ad 1075*, N.Y. Times, Nov. 21, 1976, at 264.
[175] Id.
[176] Id.
[177] Id.
[178] *Display Ad 26*, Wall St. J., July 8, 1968, at 8.
[179] Id.
[180] *See supra* note 146.

comprehensive, and vigorously prosecuted promotional campaign."[181] Nevertheless, even Teodoro Moscoso, the Administrator of Economic Development for Puerto Rico, couldn't help but mention that the territory was a "lovely Caribbean island" in an advertisement that included a table explaining the differences in after-tax profits for a company operating in Puerto Rico versus on the mainland.[182]

Newspapers and magazines contributed to tax havens' association with resorts. Readers were bombarded with pictures of luxurious beaches or snow-capped mountains in stories on tax havens. The photos implied that generally mundane paper transactions involving tax and accounting maneuvers were actually glamorous adventures. Richard Booth invoked this image in a typical pre-Tax Day column published in the *Washington Post.* Writing below a political cartoon of a corpulent, sunglass-wearing, taxpayer lying in a hammock between two palm trees with a cigar in his mouth, Booth started by pointing out that somewhere "there are those for whom April 15 holds not terror." For example, in addition to "the gang at the jail-house" and "the crooks-at-large," there are "those uncounted thousands of city slickers who have stashed away a goodly bundle in a foreign tax haven."[183] The *Los Angeles Times* claimed that the Bahamas, a chain of islands with thousands of square miles of "the clearest, most colorful waters in the world" was an example of "the perfect tax haven."[184] Similarly, the *Wall Street Journal* opened a story from Nassau, Bahamas about tax haven regulation by describing the "native women [who] sit under gaily colored parasols plaiting and selling straw handbags, hats and other accessories" on "picturesque Rawson Square," across from the construction on opposite sides of the square of two new commercial buildings the island's "growing importance as an international financial center."[185] In another column about the Bahamas, readers were reminded that although its capital city of Nassau was "better known for its ambling surreys and throngs of happy tourists with ready cash," it had "become one of the world's most important repositories for 'hot' money," or cash "stashed for purposes of concealment from tax

181 *Investors' Guide: Tax Inducements of Puerto Rico Spur Business Growth*, CHICAGO DAILY TRIB., May 8, 1960, at A8.

182 George Sokolsky, *These Days ... Puerto Rican Tax Haven*, WASH. POST AND TIME HERALD, April 24, 1957, at A11.

183 Richard Booth, *Foreign Tax Havens Are Found by Many*, WASH. POST, Apr. 5, 1969, at C6.

184 Stephen Aris, *The Bahamas' Liberal Tax Laws Attracting Millions of Dollars*, L.A. TIMES, Nov. 7, 1966, at B13.

185 Silberman, *Fading Tax Haven?*, *supra* note 91, at 1.

collectors."[186] A *Chicago Tribune* headline for a story on tax havens described them as "Sunny," as if those dodging their taxes did so while catching some rays by the pool or on the beach.[187] When tax havens such as the Bahamas were threatened by proposed legislation in the US, the headline writers continued to press the tropical imagery, with the *New York Times* noting that "Users of 'Tax Havens' Abroad Batten down for Political Gale."[188]

Even in more wintry climates, tax havens were portrayed as luxurious and glamorous escapes from the real world. For example, *Newsweek* described Liechtenstein, a "mountainous, crescent-shaped principality," as a "paradise for profits."[189] The *Wall Street Journal* asked "Do you dream of low taxes and secret ways to outwit your competitors? . . . Many corporations are finding all this and Alpine scenery, too, in tiny Liechtenstein a picture-book nation of princes and castles on the borders of Switzerland and Austria."[190] *Forbes* evoked an even more fantastical image of fairy tales and mythology when it suggested that Zurich was run by "gnomes" that helped American investors dodge taxes.[191]

The media went so far as to imply that the glamorous lifestyle was a part and parcel of tax haven investing. For example, the *Boston Globe* suggested that tax havens targeted wealthy Americans vacationing on their beaches as suitable investors. "For the locals," the *Globe* observed, "the procedure is simple. First, persuade a millionaire to take his winter vacation in the Bahamas. When he has arrived and is relaxing on the beach, apprise him both of the tax situation and of some interesting investment possibilities."[192] Another reporter, writing about the deferral of US tax, speculated without offering any evidence that "[t]he money may never be repatriated – the owners of relatively small businesses may retire to these tax havens."[193]

186 Carl Livingston, *'Hot' Money Pours into the Bahamas*, WASH. POST TIMES HERALD, Jan. 28, 1964, at A21.

187 Robert Kearns, *Sunny Tax Havens Prove Magnet for Many Taxpayers*, CHI. TRIB., April 29, 1979, at N1.

188 Robert Metz, *Users of 'Tax Havens' Abroad Batten Down for Political Gale*, N.Y. TIMES, Feb. 26, 1961, at F1.

189 *Liechtenstein: Paradise for Profits*, NEWSWEEK, Oct. 10, 1966, at 93.

190 Mitchell Gordon, *Tax Haven: Little Liechtenstein Lures Army of U.S. and Foreign Subsidiaries*, WALL ST. J., July 7, 1954, at 1.

191 *The Gnomes of Zurich*, FORBES, June 1, 1967, at 23.

192 *Bahamas Role as Tax Haven May be Ending*, BOSTON GLOBE, Jan. 13, 1963, at 59.

193 Metz, *Users of 'Tax Havens' Abroad Batten Down for Political Gale*, *supra* note 188, at F1.

While tax haven promoters used the vacation resort imagery to sell their financial transactions, island realtors used the perception of tax savings associated with tax havens to sell their properties. In one advertisement, a real estate firm was selling a "CARIBBEAN ISLAND PARADISE" on the Grand Cayman Island.[194] In addition to noting that it was a "rare land investment opportunity . . . only an hour by air from Miami," the seller reminded prospective buyers that this was a "tax-free haven."[195] In another, a realtor advertised a "popular hideaway resort hotel on the island of Providenciales in the friendly U.S. dollar tax haven Turks & Caicos."[196] Mitchell's Creek Gardens, a residential development in the Cayman Islands, took out a three-quarter page advertisement in *Variety* magazine, a journal covering Hollywood and the entertainment industry.[197] Rather than using a movie star to promote its homes in a movie industry magazine, though, it turned instead to "international banker and financier Jean Doucet," who noted that one of the prominent features of living in the area was not only that the Cayman Islands was "an island paradise," but it was "the world's leading tax haven by destiny."[198] Queens Cove Freeport in the Bahamas even posted an advertisement in the *New York Times* offering "Free! Round Trip Jet Flight" to inspect the possible investment sites in this "new tax haven."[199] It included a map with a sketching of sunbathers and a couple jogging on the beach by the palm trees to mark the spot where it was located.

This same resort-style imagery was used by developers selling land in domestic tax haven states. In one advertisement for the home sites in a golf course residential community on the north shore of Lake Tahoe, the promoters did not just remind readers that the community was located on the Nevada, rather than California, side of the lake.[200] Next to an illustration of a golfer hitting a ball out of the rough and onto the green next to a lake with a sailboat and mountains in the distance, the advertisement for Incline Village's Fairway Estates made sure to tell them that the community was "All within Nevada's Tax Haven," which was a reference to the state's lack of an income tax.[201] In another

194 *Display Ad 2*, CHICAGO DEFENDER, Sept. 24, 1966, at 2.
195 Id.
196 *Classified Ad 1184*, N.Y. TIMES, March 23, 1975, at 213.
197 *"The World Is His Oyster . . . Mitchell's Creek Gardens Is His Home,"* VARIETY, Aug. 24, 1974, at 27.
198 Id.
199 *Display Ad 169*, N.Y. TIMES, July 28, 1968, at 114.
200 SAN FRANCISCO EXAMINER, June 23, 1963, at 77.
201 Id.

advertisement, the brokers selling land in Charleston Park Ranchos made similar claims about living in the southern part of the state, emphasizing that buyers would be "strategically located near Las Vegas and Lake Mead," where they promised that you "will enjoy 365 days of exciting Western living – hunting, fishing, boating, water skiing, golf, and the colorful Helldorado days," while also enjoying the fact that "skyrocketing taxes in most states have made Nevada a true **Haven for the Tax Weary**."[202] "In Charleston Park Ranchos," the advertisement continued, "you pay no state income tax, gift taxes, inheritance taxes or corporation taxes."[203]

This blitz of advertisements, articles, and other publicity about tax havens normalized them for the average person. This may have helped to spur people who would not otherwise benefit from tax haven investing to dodge taxes in other ways. For example, professionals like doctors and lawyers, who generated large amounts of income with a minimum of deductible expenses, were particularly eager to find a way to take advantage of the tax benefits enjoyed by corporations in tax havens transactions. The problem was that such service businesses could not take advantage of offshore opportunities unless their patients and clients moved with them. Instead, they began setting up personal service corporations – or what were called a "'tax haven for the professions" – to try to get their own version of corporate tax benefits.[204] For personal service corporations, the tax advantage was not the exemption enjoyed by a foreign subsidiary in a tax haven, but rather the ability to adopt a pension plan and defer some of their service income.[205] Whereas they could only set aside a maximum of $2,500 and up to 10 percent of earnings as a self-employed individual, in a corporation these professionals could defer up to 15 percent of their earnings in a pension with no fixed dollar maximum and use a profit-sharing plan to set aside even more.[206] Given the high individual rates, deferring compensation until retirement, plus capital gains rates on payouts that was not available on self-employed plans, was particularly attractive.[207] Moreover, the

[202] *Display Ad 431*, WASH. POST TIME HERALD, Nov. 29, 1959, at 236 (bold in original).

[203] Id.

[204] *"Tax Haven for the Professions? New Headache for Revenue Men*, U.S. NEWS & WORLD REPORT, July 7, 1969, at 70.

[205] Id.; J. Timothy Phillips, James S. McNider, III, & Daniel E. Riley, *Origins of Tax Law: The History of the Personal Service Corporation*, 40 WASH. & LEE L. REV. 433, 435 (1983).

[206] *Tax Haven for the Professions?*, *supra* note 204, at 70–71.

[207] Id. at 71.

personal service corporations were still eligible to be taxed under Subchapter S of the Code as small business corporations, which would allow them to avoid the corporate tax.[208] It's little wonder that they were viewed as a domestic version of tax havens for professionals.

The phrase "tax havens" became synonymous with tax breaks generally, even if they did not meet the conventional understanding of the term. For example, Inez Robb, a nationally syndicated columnist and former war correspondent in World War II,[209] wrote a tongue-in-cheek piece seeking to be included in the "tax haven" of "the 27½% per cent depletion allowance, tax-wise, enjoyed by the oil industry."[210] "All I'm trying to do," Robb claimed "is get under the tax tent with the big boys."[211] Similarly, one private seller of an apartment building in a "thriving Southern city" described it as "a wonderful tax haven to shelter dividend income," which referred to the fact that the "FHA interest payments of only 4½% interest" that the buyer would assume, plus any depreciation associated with the operation of the building as a rental, would be deductible against the income.[212] Another classified advertisement seeking investors for an apartment building project in Sherman Oaks, California called it a "tax haven investment," probably through the utilization of their share of depreciation deductions as partners in a partnership.[213] Each of these were examples where "tax shelter" might have been a more appropriate term because they were counting on businesses losses or deductible expenses to offset other income, rather than to exempt income from tax altogether. Nevertheless, writers chose to use "tax haven" instead, perhaps to conjure up the exotic imagery associated with the term.

Not only was the phrase "tax haven" used to suggest a transaction had tax benefits, but to imply that it was financially savvy. Many classified advertisements used the term "tax haven" without any explanation of how it applied to the item on sale. Not only did they assume that the term itself would be understood by a potential buyer, but they understood that it would be viewed favorably. For example, an advertisement for a plot of 168 acres of "scenic view land in an area of future growth" was headlined by the

[208] Id. at 70.
[209] *Inez Robb, an Ex-Columnist, Dies; Was a World War II Correspondent*, N.Y. TIMES, April 6, 1979, at D13.
[210] Inez Robb, *Pity Us Poor Country Clubbers*, DETROIT FREE PRESS, May 23, 1961, at 11.
[211] Id.
[212] *Classified Ad 32*, WALL ST. J., Aug. 25, 1961, at 7.
[213] *Display Ad 79*, L.A. Times, Dec. 8, 1960, at C15.

term "TAX HAVEN."[214] Similarly, the owner of real estate in Wisconsin placed a classified advertisement in the *Chicago Tribune* for 110 acres of farmland under the headline "Leveraged Tax Haven and Inflation Wedge."[215] An advertisement in the *Los Angeles Times* claimed to offer a "Tax Haven for a Home Avocation," which involved the sale of "a collection of the finest orchid plants."[216] One advertisement even described a house offered "For Rent Only" as a "Greenwich Tax Haven," perhaps because the state of Connecticut did not adopt a state income tax until 1991, although this was not stated in the advertisement.[217] It seemed that the term "tax haven," was used in any case where the seller could arguably claim that they might save on taxes in that location. For example, the seller of a home in Yonkers, New York listed a residential home under the title "A Tax Haven."[218] Since New York had a state income tax, the seller was apparently focusing on the relatively low property taxes, writing that, "with rising taxes everywhere it's hard to find a well located home in a good residential neighborhood like this one with ... taxes under $1,000."[219]

***

Tax havens did not just survive the Revenue Act of 1962, but they adapted and continued to expand. If the 1950s and 1960s were considered pivotal in "the proliferation and growth of established and newly emerging havens," with the U.S. effectively stimulating the development of many new tax havens,[220] a new phase of expansion for tax havens commenced in the 1970s and 1980s.[221] One tax practitioner, speaking in 1970, announced that "tax havens are very much alive and thriving. In fact, the number of such jurisdictions appears to be on the increase."[222] Despite the US and other countries enacting multiple reforms, and multinational companies and individuals that invest in them suffering withering criticism,[223] economist Thomas Piketty noted that "the overall importance of tax havens has

[214] *Classified Ad 25*, L.A. TIMES, Nov. 22, 1968, at D21.
[215] *Classified Ad No. 29, "Leveraged Tax Haven and Inflation Wedge,"* CHI. TRIB., Dec. 29, 1968, at D8.
[216] *Display Ad No. 39*, L.A. TIMES, June 21, 1966, at B13.
[217] *Classified Act 656*, N.Y. TIMES, Nov. 13, 1966, at 417.
[218] *Classified Ad 51*, N.Y. TIMES, Dec. 1, 1962, at 26.
[219] Id.
[220] Ogle, *supra* note 3, at 219.
[221] Id.; Gehlen & Marx, *supra* note 4, at 228.
[222] Slowinski, *supra* note 138, at 450.
[223] Jason Walsh, *Google, Apple Draw Transatlantic Ire over "Double Irish" Tax Haven*, CHRISTIAN SCIENCE MONITOR, May 21, 2013, at 5; Matthew Collin, *The Impact of Tax Blacklisting*, World Bank, Policy Research Working Paper 10435 (May 2023).

continued to rise" well into the twenty-first century.[224] One study concluded that "despite a number of anti-tax avoidance, disclosure, and information exchange regimes in place, [Multinational Enterprises'] operations in tax havens are substantial and MNEs still attribute relatively large portions of their tax base (at least scaled by employment) to tax havens."[225] Another found that one of the primary attacks on tax havens – "the 2000 international anti-tax haven naming and shaming campaign – had the opposite effect, increasing FDI [Foreign Direct Investment] flows to tax havens in the years following the campaign."[226]

Not only have tax havens survived, but the media continues to use the enticing imagery that characterized mid-century coverage of tax havens. *Forbes* ran a piece entitled "In Pictures: Tax Havens of the World," showing off the exclusive neighborhoods, beautiful golf courses, glittering beaches, and towering ski slopes.[227] Similarly, two Italian photographers traveled to tax havens over a three-year period to "capture the low-tax lifestyle," with *The Guardian* publishing some of their photos that featured infinity pools, jetpacks, mansions with carefully manicured hedges, luxury yachts, and one of the world's largest casinos.[228] A *Los Angeles Times* editorial about corporate use of offshore tax havens may not have had the glamorous photos, but it was titled "Tax Loophole, with a Beach."[229] Beyond labels, media coverage often gives as much attention to the revelations on how billionaires have used havens to hide their "yachts [and] jets of iconic beauty" as to how they used them to dodge taxes.[230] As was true in mid-century America, the popular response is just as frequently envy as outrage.

224 Thomas Piketty, *Foreword*, in ZUCMAN, *supra* note 79, at x.

225 Marcel Olbert, Christoph Spengel, and Stefan Weck, *Multinational Firms in Tax Havens: Corporate Motives, Regulatory Countermeasures, and Recent Statistics*, in RESEARCH HANDBOOK ON THE ECONOMICS OF TAX HAVENS 4 (Arjan Lejour and Dirk Schindler, eds., 2024). A series of documents from firms that assisted companies and people in moving assets to places with high privacy for tax dodging and privacy reasons – named the Panama (2016), Paradise (2017), and Pandora Papers (2021) – also offers evidence of the continued relevance of tax havens. Dainoff, *supra* note 160, at 140; International Consortium of Investigative Journalists, *The Paradise Papers: Secrets of the Global Elite*, Nov. 5, 2017; Rick Gladstone, *Pandora Papers: A Leaked Bomb with Uncertain Fallout*, N.Y. TIMES, Oct. 5, 2021, at A8; *After Pandora*, WASH. POST, Oct. 9, 2021, at A18.

226 Dainoff, *supra* note 160, at 137.

227 *In Pictures: Tax Havens of the World*, FORBES, March 16, 2007.

228 *Inside the World's Greatest Tax Havens: in Pictures*, THE GUARDIAN, Aug. 10, 2015.

229 *Tax Loophole, with a Beach*, L.A. TIMES, Feb. 24, 2002, at M4.

230 Peter Whoriskey and Agustin Amendariz, *Influence-Buying, Tax Avoidance, and Yachts*, WASH. POST, Oct. 7, 2021, at A1.

# 3

# Executive Pay and the Legitimization of Tax Dodging

Like celebrities, corporate executives received most of their compensation prior to World War II from salaries and cash bonuses. Both groups were focused on dodging the high marginal income tax rates, but corporate executives may have been even more influential than celebrities in making tax dodging legitimate. Not only were they able to change the compensation policies of their own corporations, where they sat on the board of directors and held sway over the design of their own pay packages and those of their employees, but they helped to influence compensation, benefit and perquisite, and reimbursement policies at their peers as well.[1] Perhaps more importantly, executives pushed for legislative endorsement of their tax-preferred compensation strategies in exchange for expanding access beyond the managerial class through the application of nondiscrimination principles. In that sense, while celebrities helped to publicize and normalize tax dodging for the masses, and wealthy tax haven users romanticized it, corporations and their executives helped to not only legalize and legitimize some of the techniques, but to propagate them in a way that brought tax dodging directly to the masses.

## Introduction

### *The Early History of Executive Pay*

The highly paid corporate executive is a distinctly modern phenomenon. For most of the nineteenth century, corporations were privately held and the owners managed the business.[2] These owners "built up their fortunes

[1] *See, e.g.*, James J. Sweeny, *Incentives, Options and Other Lures in the Nation's Top 100*, 37 Bus. Mgmt 14 (1970) ("In designing executive income packages, keeping up with the Joneses may be vital, especially when the 'Joneses' are the world's toughest competitors, America's biggest corporations.").

[2] Harwell Wells, *"No Man Can Be Worth $1,000,000 a Year": The Fight Over Executive Compensation in 1930s America*, 44 U. Rich. L. Rev. 689, 695–702 (2010).

not through salaries or other direct compensation from their companies, but through stock ownership and the profits of expansion and promotion."[3] That began to change during a merger movement at the turn of the century as public corporations started to replace private ones and managerial structures evolved.[4] Early professional managers, however, were not highly paid.[5] According to a survey of 400 manufacturing companies conducted by economists Frank Taussig and Walter Barker for the period from 1904 to 1914, executives in the largest group of companies having capital in excess of $1.5 million averaged $9,958 in annual salary,[6] or approximately $317,367 in annual salary in 2024 dollars.[7] Even when the comparison is restricted to the equivalent of the modern chief executive officer at a large company, the salaries were relatively modest. According to one study, the presidents of four railroads were paid $75,000 annually in 1914,[8] or approximately $2.3 million in 2024 dollars,[9] as compared with the average compensation of $16.7 million for chief executive officers of S&P 500 companies.[10]

Not only were early managers' salaries not exorbitant, but they were typically fixed rather than variable. Executives often worked for as many as five to ten years with "few and infrequent changes" to their pay.[11] Nor, unlike their European counterparts, did they typically get bonuses or a share of profits before World War I.[12] The "American view," so-to-speak, was that "managers receive stipulated wages; the 'profits' go to the stockholders."[13] In Taussig and Barker's study, only 13 percent of all

[3] George Thomas Washington and V. Henry Rothschild , Compensating the Corporate Executive 5 (1951).

[4] Steven A. Bank, Brian R. Cheffins & Harwell Wells, *Executive Pay: What Worked?* 42 J. Corp. L. 59, 64 (2016); Naomi R. Lamoreaux, The Great Merger Movement in American Business, 1895–1904 1–2 (1988);

[5] John Calhoun Baker, Executive Salaries and Bonus Plans 2 (1938) (prior to World War I, "there was a general feeling among those who wrote on this subject that management, as distinct from ownership, was not adequately recognized or paid.").

[6] F. W. Taussig and W. S. Barker, *American Corporations and Their Executives: A Statistical Inquiry*, 40 Q. J. Econ. 1, 19 (1925).

[7] U.S. Bureau of Labor Statistics, Inflation Calculator (calculated using 1913 as the reference point).

[8] Washington and Rothschild, *supra* note 3, at 5, n.7

[9] U.S. Bureau of Labor Statistics, Inflation Calculator.

[10] Ross Kerber, *CEO Pay Averaged $16.7 Million Last Year at S&P 500 Companies, a Decline*, Reuters, Aug. 3, 2023.

[11] Taussig and Barker, *supra* note 6, at 20 (describing executive salaries as "stable . . . as those of superintendents or engineers").

[12] Id. at 28; Baker, *supra* note 5, at viii.

[13] Taussig and Baker, *supra* note 6, at 28.

companies reported paying any kind of additional compensation beyond salaries, and only 5 percent regularly provided such additional compensation based on the performance of the business.[14]

During the 1920s and into the early 1930s, the status and pay of the professional manager started to improve. According to one report, "[t]he corporation president of this new type became a public figure, taking an active part in the life of the community. His influence increased steadily, but so also did his responsibilities."[15] Although data was still limited, compensation increased commensurately with this new influence and responsibility, with reports suggesting that "average executive compensation in large industry appear[ed] to have risen steadily."[16] More significantly, the composition of compensation changed. While salaries generally remained fixed for individual executives,[17] bonus and profit-sharing plans came into "wide use."[18] According to Harvard Business School Professor John Calhoun Baker, 64 percent of firms in a random sample of 100 large manufacturing companies listed on the New York Stock Exchange paid a bonus linked to firm performance in addition to salary in 1928 and about half of all executives in these firms received at least some bonus.[19] Some companies even provided stock-based compensation, including stock rights or options, as a bonus or a supplement to salary, but this was still exceedingly rare.[20]

The downside to this higher profile and compensation was that it drew attention to executives after the stock market crash and the onset of the Great Depression. The economic crisis fueled lawsuits and hearings involving some of the biggest corporations that revealed for the first time the compensation figures paid to executives in these corporations. One lawsuit revealed that George Washington Hill, president of the American Tobacco Company, received a salary of $168,000 and a bonus of $850,000 for total compensation of $1,018,000 in 1931 because of a bylaw provision paying the president 2.5 percent of the annual profits.[21] Another lawsuit filed against Eugene Grace, president of

[14] Id. at 28–29.

[15] WASHINGTON AND ROTHSCHILD, *supra* note 3, at 5.

[16] Id.

[17] BAKER, *supra* note 5, at 20.

[18] WASHINGTON AND ROTHSCHILD, *supra* note 3, at 6; Wells, *supra* note 2, at 700.

[19] BAKER, *supra* note 5, at 16.

[20] BAKER, *supra* note 5, at 186–87, 195–97; Wells, *supra* note 2, at 700–01.

[21] *Salary Limit Action Looms*, DAILY BOSTON GLOBE, Oct. 19, 1933, at 1; *Complaint Filed to Curb Hill's Tobacco Bonus*, N.Y. HERALD TRIB., April 5, 1931, at 18. These lawsuits led to noteworthy federal and state cases whether the American Tobacco Company had

Bethlehem Steel Corporation, disclosed that he received $1,626,753 in salary and bonus in 1929 and $5,745,307 for the period from 1925 to 1930.[22] One particularly scandalous revelation from the highly publicized Pecora Hearings before the Senate Committee on Banking and Currency in 1933 was that National City Bank chairman Charles Mitchell, who had received a relatively small annual salary of $25,000 in 1929, he also received a combined bonus of $3.5 million between 1927 and 1929 from the bank and the affiliated National City Company for which he served as chair.[23]

Although these compensation packages exceeding $1 million were extreme outliers,[24] they attracted attention as Congress sought to collect more data on executive pay and calls for salary limits became louder.[25] Salary limits were never enacted,[26] but the government did pursue other reforms, most notably requiring disclosure of executive compensation. Originally, this took place as part of a Federal Trade Commission report on the compensation of corporate officers and directors that was prepared pursuant to a Senate resolution after the revelations in the so-called Pecora Hearings.[27] Soon after, disclosure was required as part of newly adopted federal securities laws.[28]

### *Taxation and the Great Compression*

Following, and perhaps at least in part as an effect of, this controversy over executive compensation in the 1930s, there was a great reversal in executive pay. During the 1940s, the average pretax compensation for top executives of large publicly traded manufacturing companies declined 11 percent.[29] Even in the 1950s and 1960s, when the post–World War II

committed waste by agreeing to provide such large profit-sharing percentages to its president and vice-presidents. Rogers v. Hill, 289 U.S. 582 (1933); Heller et al. v. Boylan et al., 29 N.Y.S. 2d 653 (1941).

22 *Suit Asks Steel Heads Pay Back $36,493,668*, N.Y. HERALD TRIB., Jan. 14, 1931, at 32; *Grace's Large Pay Stirs Bonus Debate*, N.Y. TIMES, July 27, 1930, at 33.

23 *Mitchell Received Bonus of $3,500,000*, WASH. POST, Feb. 22, 1933, at 1; Wells, *supra* note 2, at 713–15.

24 Bank, Cheffins and Wells, *supra* note 4, at 64.

25 *Salary Limit Action Looms*, DAILY BOSTON GLOBE, Oct. 19, 1933, at 1; L. H. Robbins, *Inquiry into High Salaries Pressed by the Government*, N.Y. TIMES, Oct. 29, 1933, at XX3.

26 Wells, *supra* note 2, at 749–56.

27 WASHINGTON & ROTHSCHILD, *supra* note 3, at 6–7.

28 Bank, Cheffins, and Wells, *supra* note 4, at 64.

29 Carola Frydman & Raven Molloy, *Pay Cuts for the Boss: Executive Compensation in the 1940s*, 72 J. ECON. HIST, 225, 239 (2012).

economy boomed, executive compensation grew by an anemic 0.8 percent after inflation.[30] At the same time that executive compensation was declining or remaining flat, compensation for hourly workers was increasing.[31] The result was that not only did executive pay decline in real terms, but the gap between the compensation of executives and workers closed over the course of the decade.[32] This was the beginning of what has been called the "Great Compression" in pay levels from the 1940s through the 1960s and early 1970s.[33]

Several modern scholars attribute the Great Compression to the high mid-century income tax rates. Economist Thomas Piketty wrote that executives in US businesses during the 1950s and 1960s "had little reason to fight for such raises, and other interested parties were less inclined to accept them, because 80–90 percent of the increase would in any case go directly to the government" in the form of taxes.[34] Economist Anthony Atkinson suggests that this theory, which Piketty calls the "bargaining power explanation,"[35] may also have been responsible for a similar stagnation in executive pay in Britain during this period.[36]

Although there were other factors that restrained growth in executive pay,[37] tax appeared to get the most attention among contemporary observers. Arch Patton, a management consultant at McKinsey & Company who was one of the first to specialize in executive compensation,[38] stated that "[t]here is considerable evidence that many highly paid executives – who normally constitute the decision-making group – have not wanted cash salary increases in recent years because

30 Carola Frydman & Raven E. Saks, *Executive Compensation: A New View from a Long-Term Perspective, 1936–2005*, 23 REV. FIN. STUD. 2099, 2099–100, 2106–07 (2010); Harwell Wells, *U.S. Executive Compensation in Historical Perspective* in RESEARCH HANDBOOK ON EXECUTIVE PAY 41, 46 (Randall S. Thomas and Jennifer G. Hill, eds., 2012).

31 Harold Walsh, *March of Finance: Executives Forgotten Men at Payroll Level, Says Patton*, L.A. TIMES, Dec. 13, 1951, at A19.

32 Frydman & Molloy, *supra* note 29, at 227;Claudia Goldin & Robert A. Margo, *The Great Compression: The Wage Structure in the United States at Mid-Century*, 107 Q.J. ECON. 1, 1–2 (1992).

33 Goldin & Margo, *supra* note 32, at 1–2.

34 PIKETTY, *supra* note 2, at 510.

35 Id.

36 ANTHONY B. ATKINSON , INEQUALITY: WHAT CAN BE DONE? 186 (2015).

37 *See* Bank, Cheffins & Wells, *supra* note 4, at 106 (citing the market for managerial talent and norms as the most likely factors). *Executives Facing Pay Raise Problem*, N.Y. TIMES, Sept. 4, 1952, at 39.

38 Dana Canedy, *Arch Patton, 88; Devised First Survey of Top Executives' Pay*, N.Y. TIMES, Nov. 13, 1996, at 16.

they feel that so little is left after taxes."[39] In a 1959 study of executive compensation, economist David Roberts agreed with Patton, reporting that high income tax rates were "widely credited with partial responsibility for the failure of executive earnings gains to keep pace with those in other occupations."[40] According to Roberts, "the corporation is allegedly discouraged from making increases which add to its costs and confer little after taxes benefit upon the executive."[41]

The anecdotal data may support the role of high tax rates in the Great Compression, but the empirical evidence is more limited. In a sample of large corporations between 1946 and 2005, economists Carola Frydman and Raven Molloy examined salaries, bonuses, and stock options paid to top executives and found a correlation between tax rates and the median total compensation of executives.[42] They did not, however, find a causal relationship, noting that changes in tax rates did not produce changes in pay level in the short or long term.[43] Moreover, the correlation did not hold-up strongly throughout the period. There were tax rate changes that arguably should have spurred a significant increase in salary-based compensation for executives, such as the drop in the top marginal rate from 70 percent to 60 percent on "earned income" in 1971, and then to 50 percent thereafter, but total compensation numbers only moved slightly, if at all.[44]

This does not mean that high tax rates had little or no effect on executive compensation. Rather than leaving money on the table, executives pushed their companies to enable them to dodge taxes by altering the mix of compensation away from an exclusive reliance on salaries and bonuses. They were eventually so successful that many of the innovations developed are now standard parts of the compensation packages of all employees, not just executives, and they are rarely, if ever, discussed as tax dodging.

39 Arch Patton, *Executive Compensation: Tax Gimmicks vs. Tax Incentives*, 31 Harv. Bus. Rev. 113, 114 (1953).

40 David R. Roberts, Executive Compensation 155 (1959).

41 Id.

42 Carola Frydman & Raven S. Molloy, *Does Tax Policy Affect Executive Compensation? Evidence from Postwar Tax Reforms*, 95 J. Pub. Econ. 1425, 1426 (2011).

43 Id.

44 Bank, Cheffins & Wells, *supra* note 4, at 76. Under the Tax Reform Act of 1969, tax on earned incomes such as a salary and bonuses was reduced from 70 percent to 50 percent from 1971 to 1981, while so-called "unearned" income such as interest and dividends remained taxed at 70 percent. Graef Crystal, Financial Motivation for Executives 185 (1970).

## Executive Tax Dodging Tactics

When the first post–Sixteenth Amendment income tax was enacted in 1913, executives sought to avoid the tax by getting their employers to pay directly. For example, the American Woolen Company adopted a resolution in 1916 committing to pay any taxes due to the company's officers on account of their salaries so that they would receive such compensation in full and without deduction for the taxes paid by the company.[45] The Supreme Court held that such payments should be taxable to the officers notwithstanding that they did not necessarily negotiate for them and they never received them directly.[46]

In the 1920s and early 1930s, executives attempted to dodge the effects of the income tax through outright evasion. For example, Charles Mitchell, the National City Bank chair whose compensation had stirred controversy during the Pecora Hearings, was soon after charged with tax evasion after admitting during the hearings that he sold National City stock to his wife and then bought it back in the same year to generate a deductible loss of almost $2.8 million that wiped out his taxable income for 1929.[47] This kind of clearly illegal tax dodging continued after this period,[48] but in an era of mandatory disclosure of executive compensation as well as mandatory withholding of taxes on the cash compensation, it was unlikely to account for a significant portion of the gap between nominal and real compensation.

45 Old Colony Trust Co. v. Commissioner, 279 U.S. 716, 729 (1929).

46 Id. William Wood, the president of American Woolen Company and whose pay was the subject of this case, was paid exceedingly well for the time – more than $1 million per year in the 1920s, but he was fired by the board of directors amidst accusations of stealing from the company and he committed suicide in 1926. *William M. Wood, N.E. Mill Magnate Commits Suicide*, HARTFORD COURANT, Feb. 3, 1926, at 1.

47 *Tax Dodging Deal Aired*, L.A. TIMES, Feb. 22, 1933, at 1; *Mitchell Paid No Tax in 1929*, DAILY BOSTON GLOBE, Feb. 22, 1933, at 1; *Mitchell Will Face Grand Jury Inquiry*, N.Y. TIMES, March 19, 1933, at 1; *Mitchell Arrested as Tax Evader; Washington Orders a Quick Trial*, N.Y. TIMES, March 22, 1933, at 1.

48 *See, e.g., Executive* Sentence, N.Y. TIMES, June 9, 1960, at 23 (president of the Stamford Rolling Mills Company sentenced to prison for making false statements on his income tax return); Executive *is Indicted*, N.Y. TIMES, Jan. 10, 1959, at 38 (indictment of the president of the Welsbach Corporation for failing to report over $100,000 of income on his tax return); *Tax Scandals of '50 Echoed*, BALTIMORE SUN, Sept. 10, 1953, at 4 (indictment of president and vice-president of Lafayette Steel Co. on tax evasion in a case connected to misconduct by an earlier scandal involving IRS agents taking bribes from taxpayers).

As the patriotic fervor of World War II receded and the high marginal rates remained, executives began to focus more intently on their tax plight. Patton called this "the tax obsession."[49] He noted that income taxes had "been a nagging problem for the relatively high paid executive ever since Congress adopted the progressive income tax," but ever since the top marginal rates were dramatically increased during World War II and remained high thereafter, "the compensation of industry's executives has been increasingly weighted in terms of the tax implications."[50] George Thomas Washington and Henry Rothschild concurred with this assessment, writing in the 1951 edition of their treatise that after World War II, "[h]igh taxes, always important in the negotiation of the executive's employment contract, became . . . the single most important factor in that regard."[51] In 1953, in one article outlining American business' six goals for executive compensation, four of the six related to tax issues.[52]

Cash compensation became so disfavored that some executives actively sought to avoid it. In 1947, E. B. Tilton, the president of the Vilter Manufacturing Company in Milwaukee, Wisconsin, went so far as to publicly announce that "due to excessive and confiscatory individual income taxes" he would decline compensation for the final two months of the year.[53] Although more a publicity stunt to air his grievances against what he characterized as a system designed "to support the politicians, loafers, and deadbeats of the entire world" than a legitimate strategy, turning down a salary increase did not necessarily mean an executive was, as one columnist put it, "ready for the psychiatrist's couch."[54] In 1945, the *Chicago Daily Tribune* reported that some executives "are leaving high salaried jobs with big corporations to accept positions paying smaller salaries but carrying with them other compensation."[55]

49 Patton, *Tax Gimmicks*, *supra* note 39, at 113.

50 Id.

51 WASHINGTON & ROTHSCHILD, *supra* note 3, at 8.

52 J. K. Lasser & Meyer M. Goldstein, *Meeting the Six Goals of Executive Compensation*, DUN'S REV., June 1953, at 25. The six goals were (1) Maximum security, (2) Maximum hedge against inflation, (3) No Tax at all, (4) If that can't be done, at least capital gains tax rate, (5) If that's not possible either, at least defer taxes, and (6) Assume all costs in a way that is not taxed to the executive. Id.

53 *Executive Cuts Own Pay Because of High Taxes*, N.Y. TIMES, June 28, 1947, at 9.

54 Alex Joiner, *Many Executives Prefer Raises in Pension Form*, ATLANTA CONSTITUTION, June 30, 1953, at 21.

55 Thomas Furlong, *Lower Salary May Attract Key Executive*, CHI. DAILY TRIB., April 24, 1945, at 21.

As a result, there was a strong demand for methods to increase executive compensation in a tax friendly way.[56] For instance, in a discussion of how companies were coping with "the big tax bite," *Business Week* reported that "many companies (were) changing their ideas of how an executive might be paid."[57] The nature of the change was described by a practitioner in 1954:

> It is no longer enough merely to increase the salary or bonus or to write a share of the profits into the executive's contract. High income tax rates leave him very little of any additional compensation. ... These conditions result in a great deal of pressure being exerted on employers to work out new methods of compensating executives which will prove attractive tax-wise.[58]

An in-house lawyer at E. I. DuPont de Nemours and Co. echoed this sentiment, observing that "[t]ax planners have devoted much time to devising a plan for compensating executives which will alleviate the effect of the high individual surtax."[59]

Tax professionals helped to stoke the fires for corporations and their executives seeking to restructure their executive compensation. Arch Patton, one of the first full-time executive pay consultants, reported that "increasingly onerous taxes ... led to the development of highly skilled technicians who deal in tax code interpretation, in law, in actuarial analysis, in trusteeship, in insurance, and so on."[60] These specialists were especially important in executive compensation. Rutgers law professor Warren Freedman wrote that "[a]ny practical man will admit that the tax lawyer and the accountant have more to do with attracting and holding competent, high-salaried, key executives in an enterprise than the offers, board of directors, or stockholders."[61] According to Patton, there was "an increasing drumfire of speeches, magazine articles, and new dispatches explaining in detail how after-tax income can be increased (in other words, how taxes can be reduced)."[62] Indeed, "[t]he most popular speaker at an industry association meeting

[56] Edwin Nichols, *Tax Can Complicate Executive Pay Plans*, CHI. DAILY TRIB., Jan. 27, 1963, at A3.

[57] *Ideas Shift on Executive Pay*, Bus. Wk., June 16, 1956, at 85.

[58] William C. Childs, *Deferred-Compensation Plans for Executives*, 1954 INS. L. J. 25.

[59] Roy A. Wentz, *Remedying the Effect of Taxation on Management Ownership of Corporate Stock*, 48 NW. U. L. REV. 442, 443 (1953).

[60] John E. Balkcom, *Executive Compensation: A History of Imbalance in Public Controls, Shareholder Interests and Executive Rewards*, DIRECTORS & BOARDS, Spring 1977, at 4, 19 (quoting Patton).

[61] Warren Freedman, *A Restatement of Tax Incentives in Compensating High-Salaried Executives*, 4 RUTGERS L. REV. 617 (1950).

[62] Patton, *supra* note 39, at 113.

these days is apt to be a tax expert, whetting the appetite of his executive audience by recounting the plain and fancy devices for 'saving' on taxes."[63]

There is evidence that executives were successful in shifting parts of their compensation to forms that were tax preferred. Economist Wilbur Lewellen examined total compensation, not just salaries and bonuses, of the top five executives between 1940 and 1963 in a sample of fifty of the largest publicly traded manufacturing companies in the country as part of a National Bureau of Economic Research study.[64] According to Lewellen, while average after-tax salary and bonus-based compensation increased only moderately during the 1950s, rising from $60,364 in 1950 to $65,866 by 1960,[65] average total after-tax total compensation increased from $79,011 in 1950 to $133,249 by 1960.[66] Lewellen explained the difference as a result of "a persistent trend toward the use – and liberalization – of forms of reward other than salary and bonus."[67] "The traditional salary and bonus payments," Lewellen concluded, "no longer constitute the bulk of top executives' compensation … Corporations have come to rely much more heavily on noncurrent – and less severely taxed – forms of reward for men who are to be compensated at very high levels."[68] In fact, "[o]f the total after-tax rewards received by such men during the ten years from 1940 through 1949, 72 per cent was in the form of salary and bonus. In the nine-year interval beginning in 1955, the corresponding figure was only 38 per cent."[69] A similar shift toward deferred and contingent forms of compensation was observed in a study of the largest retailers over the same period.[70] The tax dodging tactics generally fell into one of three categories: (1) defer, (2), convert, or (3) divert.

## Defer

Deferring compensation existed before the high mid-century tax rates,[71] but it was particularly attractive at mid-century. The compensation

[63] Id.

[64] Wilbur Lewellen, *The Pattern of Compensation Over Time*, in EXECUTIVE COMPENSATION IN LARGE INDUSTRIAL CORPORATIONS 6 (Wilbur Lewellen, ed. 1968).

[65] Id. at 126, tbl. 2.

[66] Id. at 129, tbl. 3.

[67] Id. at 131.

[68] Id. at 136.

[69] Id.

[70] Wilbur G. Lewellen, *Tax Minimization and Executive Compensation Plans*, in DANIEL M. HOLLAND ET AL., TAX IMPACTS ON COMPENSATION 104, 107–08 (1969).

[71] *See, e.g.*, J. K. Lasser and V. Henry Rothschild, *Deferred Compensation for Executives*, 33 HARV. BUS. REV. 89, 91 (1955) ("While the deferred benefit plan has undoubtedly been

would still be fully taxable at ordinary income rates when recognized for tax purposes, but the assumption was that either the rates would be lower by then or the executive would be in a lower tax bracket because they were retired.[72] Moreover, even if the rates remained the same, executives benefitted from the time value of money advantage of having the money secured and earning income in the meantime. Essentially, the goal was not to dodge paying taxes altogether, but rather to avoid "extremes in taxes" by spreading the income out over a longer period.[73] There were a variety of mechanisms to accomplish this kind of deferral.

### *Deferred Contingent Compensation*

The simplest form of deferral was to delay the payment of cash for a period of years. Arch Patton remarked that the high rates prompted "[a] number of companies [to] set up tax-deferred bonus plans, sometimes called deferred contingent compensation contracts. These generally involve money or stock that is set aside in a fund for payment to the executive upon death or retirement."[74] According to one study, 90 percent of all New York Stock Exchange-listed companies as of July 31, 1954, had adopted some form of deferred compensation plan or had granted deferred compensation to one or more individual executives.[75]

There were several challenges to using deferred compensation as a solution to the high tax rates. Most significantly, the payments had to be contingent to avoid the application of the economic benefit doctrine, which was an exception to the cash method of accounting that deemed an item of income to be received, even if it was not yet paid, if it created a current economic benefit.[76] The question was what contingency would create enough uncertainty to avoid imparting a current economic benefit

increasing in popularity, it is by no means a new phenomenon," citing the General Motors Bonus Plan adopted in 1918).

72 Id.; Harold Walsh, *March of Finance: Executive Pay Study Shows Need for Careful Planning*, L.A. TIMES, Oct. 2, 1952, at A10; Raymond A. Hoffman, *Executives' Compensation*, LABOR L. J. 97, 101 (Feb. 1952).

73 *Pay Rise May Mean Decreased Income*, N.Y. TIMES, Nov. 20, 1952, at 55.

74 Arch Patton, *Incentive Compensation for Executives*, 29 HARV. BUS. REV. 35, 43 (1951). *See* CHALLIS A. HALL, JR., EFFECTS OF TAXATION: EXECUTIVE AND RETIREMENT PLANS 64 (1951) (suggesting that the tax advantages "were of great importance as factors contributing to the recent growth of deferred-type compensation plans").

75 Lasser & Rothschild, *supra*, note 71, at 89.

76 *See* Commissioner v. Smith, 324 U.S. 177, 181 (1945) ("Section 22(a) of the Revenue Act is broad enough to include in taxable income any economic or financial benefit conferred on the employee as compensation, whatever the form or mode by which it is effected.")

while still being unlikely enough to occur that the executive would accept it as a condition of receiving the compensation. Continued employment was generally satisfactory for the first part,[77] but not the second because it meant that the company's board of directors had the power to take away the compensation. Therefore, most plans in the 1950s were conditioned on things like an agreement not to compete during retirement and to be available for consultation, both of which were untested, and practitioners deemed them risky since they were within the control of the executive to satisfy them.[78] Patton concluded that the tax-free treatment of the deferred compensation contract appeared to be a "tax loophole that may not remain open for long."[79]

One potentially more attractive variant on the deferred contingent compensation contract was for the employer to purchase what was called "split-dollar" life insurance upon the life of a top executive.[80] The employer retained the cash surrender value on the policy, but if the executive agreed to pay the difference between the gross premium, less any dividends, and the cash surrender value of the policy for any taxable year, then the executive could acquire separate ownership rights to the policy and be entitled to name his own beneficiary for the proceeds attributable to the difference between the policy's face amount and its cash surrender value.[81] In 1955, Treasury issued a revenue ruling concluding that the insurance benefit received by the executive under this arrangement was not compensation, but rather akin to an annual loan of the cash surrender value, and therefore tax-free.[82]

Another reportedly "widely used" method of providing deferred compensation of salary was through a device called the "individual salary continuation contract."[83] Rather than paying later for work currently performed, which potentially raised economic benefit questions if the funds were secured, employers under these contracts agreed now to pay

77 Wentz, *supra* note 59, at 452.

78 Id. at 452–53.

79 Patton, *Incentive Compensation*, *supra* note 76, at 43.

80 Clarence E. Bonnett, Jr., *Compensation Planning for the Executive*, 9 Tax Executive 26, 38 (1956). *See* Leslie Mills, *Recent Developments in the Taxation of Executive Compensation*, 34 Taxes 882, 883 (1956) ("The use of interest-free loans combined with the purchase of life insurance on the lives of specifically designated employees has received considerable attention lately.").

81 J. Grant MacDonnell, *A Struggle to Reward Good Executives*, 2 CA Mgmt Rev. 25, 31 (1960).

82 Rev. Rul. 55-713, 1955-2 C.B. 23 (Dec. 23, 1955).

83 Hoffman, *Executives Compensation*, *supra* note 72, at 101.

later for work performed after retirement, which typically consisted of providing consulting services.[84] The principal disadvantage of this approach was the risk that the executive would die too soon, which would stop the payments. A provision to continue the payments after death would negate the idea that they were for work to be performed by the retired executive.[85]

### *Pensions and the Non-Discrimination Principle*

Pensions, which shift compensation from an employee's working years to their retirement years, were one of the earliest forms of deferred compensation. With some of the earliest American pensions adopted in the 1870s and 1880s when there was no federal income tax,[86] they were primarily used as a crude form of charity for workers,[87] or as an inducement for retirement,[88] not to provide tax benefits.[89] A close examination of their evolution over the first half of the twentieth century helps to explain how they transformed into tax dodging mechanisms for executives and, eventually, for all employees.

In the absence of a statutory exemption, companies were theoretically supposed to deduct payments to pension trusts and employees were required to include them as income even if the payments were deferred.[90] Nevertheless, the conventional wisdom was that executives could still avoid taxation under well-designed plans as long it came within one of the exceptions to the judicial doctrines of constructive receipt and economic benefit. In the case of the constructive receipt doctrine, which holds that an individual is taxed on income that is

[84] Id.; Louis Eisenstein, *A Case of Deferred Compensation*, 4 TAX L. REV. 391, 416 (1949).

[85] Hoffman, *Executives Compensation, supra* note 72, at 101.

[86] The earliest pension plans adopted in the United States came in the 1870s and 1880s, including one by the American Express Company in 1885. MURRAY WEBB LATIMER, INDUSTRIAL PENSION SYSTEMS IN THE UNITED STATES AND CANADA 21–22 (1932).

[87] WASHINGTON & ROTHSCHILD, *supra* note 3, at 193; Thomas N. Tarleau, *Development of Legislation on Pension Trusts*, 77 J. ACCOUNTANCY 376 (1944).

[88] RAINARD B. ROBBINS , IMPACT OF TAXES ON INDUSTRIAL PENSION PLANS 14–15 (1949). ("For many years employers were frank in their contention that their contributions toward pensions were not intended as compensation ... [Instead,] the effects of aging are such that the time comes when an employer can afford to pension an employee to keep him away from the plant – recognizing, of course, that public sentiment prevents dismissal.")

[89] James A. Wooten, *The "Original Intent" of the Federal Tax Treatment of Private Pension Plans*, TAX NOTES, Dec. 6, 1999, at 1305, 1307.

[90] Tarleau, *supra* note 87, at 376.

made available to him, the theory was that it was not made available to the executive if the plan or contract, which was entered into before the executive earned the money, provided that it would not pay out until a later date for valid business reasons.[91] For most pensions and other deferred compensation arrangements, there were a variety of reasons this made sense for the employer, ranging from the use of the money in the interim to the provision of a benefit that would be deemed attractive in recruiting and retaining executives. In the case of the economic benefit doctrine, much like with the deferred contingent compensation contract, the theory was that the benefit was contingent upon continuing to work at the company.[92] The risk of forfeiture negated the current economic benefit under the view that it would be "inequitable" to tax the executive currently "where there was so much doubt that the eventual pension would be paid to the employee."[93]

In part to make sure private and governmental pension plans operated on a level playing field,[94] Department of Internal Revenue pronouncements were initially used to offer more guidance than the courts could provide. This guidance, however, was focused on the tax treatment of the employer rather than the employee. In 1914, "amounts paid for pensions to retired employees or to their families or other dependents" were deemed "proper deductions for ordinary and necessary business expenses,"[95] while in 1919 "donations by a corporation to a pension funds for the benefit of its officers and employees" were deemed deductible as "donations to a charitable institution."[96] Not only were employees still subject to tax under these pronouncements, but employers were governed by the matching principle so that their deduction was conditioned on the employee's inclusion.[97]

It was not until 1921 that Congress extended the tax benefits to employees as well.[98] At first, it only excluded contributions to "a trust

[91] WASHINGTON & ROTHSCHILD, *supra* note 3, at 126.

[92] Id. at 178–79.

[93] Tarleau, *supra* note 87, at 376.

[94] Albert Handy, *Private Pension Plans and the Federal Revenue Act*, 16 N.Y. U. L. Q. REV. 408, 411 (1939) ("For some eighteen years private profit sharing and pension plans have received a certain amount of encouragement from the Department of Internal Revenue in order that they may not function at a disadvantage when compared with governmental systems.").

[95] T.D. 2090, 16 Treas. Dec. Int. Rev. 259, 281 Dec. 14, 1914).

[96] O.D. 2-19-165, 1 C.B. 224 (1919).

[97] CHRISTOPHER HOWARD, THE HIDDEN WELFARE STATE: TAX EXPENDITURES AND SOCIAL POLICY IN THE UNITED STATES 55 (1997).

[98] Revenue Act of 1921, ch. 136, § 219(f), 42 Stat. 247.

created by an employer as part of a stock bonus or profit-sharing plan."[99] Although Treasury officials interpreted this to apply to contributions to pension trusts as well,[100] the provision was not formally amended to include trusts created as part of pension plans until 1926.[101] Employers were only required to make the pensions available to "some or all" of their employees, which permitted them to limit their pensions to officers and other executives.[102] As a result, the interests of corporations and their executives in structuring executive compensation in a tax-sensitive way became aligned.

In the late 1930s, the favorable tax treatment of deferred compensation became the target of President Franklin D. Roosevelt's assault on tax dodging. Rather than being used to incentivize employers to adopt pension plans as a means "for ensuring the welfare of their older workers," as some contended was its purpose,[103] there was concern it was becoming a tool for tax dodging. Charles Russell, Deputy Commissioner of Internal Revenue reported to the Joint Committee on Tax Evasion and Avoidance that "some corporations are attempting to pass what really amounts to compensation or bonuses into pension trusts, thus postponing the taxation thereof until the period of their retirement, at which time it is expected that their individual brackets will be much lower because they will not be receiving salaries."[104]

Not only were pensions being used to dodge taxes on compensation, but they were designed to only benefit officers and directors. According to Treasury, the exemption enacted in 1926 was "twisted into a means of tax avoidance by the creation of pension trusts which include as beneficiaries only small groups of officers and directors who are in the high

99 Tarleau, *supra* note 87, at 376–77 (quoting Section 219(f)).

100 Howard, *supra* note 97, at 60.

101 Revenue Act of 1926, ch. 27, § 219(f), 44 Stat. 33–34; Tarleau, *supra* note 87, at 377 (discussing the provision that had been renumbered section 165).

102 Howard, *supra* note 97, at 61.

103 There is some question as to whether that was the original intention. At the time, some observers assumed that this was the case. *See* Tax Evasion and Avoidance, Hearings before the Joint Committee on Tax Evasion and Avoidance, 75th Cong. 1st Sess. 306 (1937) (statement of Undersecretary of the Treasury, Roswell Magill) ("the pension trust provision was put in I believe back in 1921 originally, to encourage a sort of social security on the part of individual corporations for the benefit of their own employees."). James Wooten, however, argues that it was to rectify a bias against deferred compensation vis-à-vis wage and salary income under the new income tax laws. Wooten, *supra* note 89, at 1306.

104 Robbins, *supra* note 88, at 27 (quoting Russell).

income brackets."[105] Roswell Magill, Roosevelt's Undersecretary of the Treasury, added that one corporation had adopted a pension plan "whereby a favored few of the employees and the principal stockholders will have placed in these funds to their credit each year, without it being taxed, an amount equal to approximately 60 per cent of their actual salaries."[106] Roosevelt called for Congress to prohibit deductions for payments to pension plans that were exclusively or primarily for the benefit of executives and stockholders.[107] Congress failed to act on this recommendation,[108] despite Russell's warning that "we are fearful that improper use of the provision is being stimulated by propaganda at a rapid rate."[109]

With top rates rising in the late 1930s and early 1940s, many corporations began to adopt pension plans that "expressly included executives."[110] During 1940 and 1941 alone, proposals for pension plans and retirement annuity plans were submitted for stockholder approval at more than thirty top corporations.[111] Some corporations bypassed formal pension plans and opted instead for individual contracts with their executives where they agreed to pay a portion of their pay at some later point.[112] These contracts were generally unfunded and unsecured and were mere promises to pay compensation in the future.[113]

In 1941, as the House Ways and Means Committee was beginning to review the Revenue Bill of 1942, Treasury's General Counsel Randolph Paul again highlighted the pension tax dodging problem.[114] Treasury had unsuccessfully tried to interpret the statutory language so that "only trusts having a wide coverage of employees" would be eligible for the exclusion from income,[115] but courts

[105] Tax Evasion and Avoidance, Hearings before the Joint Committee on Tax Evasion and Avoidance, 75th Cong. 1st Sess. 5 (1937) (Letter from the Secretary of the Treasury to President Roosevelt, dated May 29, 1937).

[106] Tarleau, *supra* note 87, at 377.

[107] Jerome R. Hellerstein, *Federal Tax Policy during the Roosevelt Era*, 5 LAW. GUILD REV. 160, 164 (1945).

[108] PAUL, TAXATION IN THE UNITED STATES, *supra* note 36, at 208.

[109] ROBBINS, *supra* note 88, at 28.

[110] WASHINGTON & ROTHSCHILD, *supra* note 3, at 170.

[111] GEORGE THOMAS WASHINGTON, CORPORATE EXECUTIVES' COMPENSATION 131, n. 2 (1942).

[112] WASHINGTON & ROTHSCHILD, *supra* note 3, at 170.

[113] Id.

[114] Tarleau, *supra* note 87, at 379.

[115] Id.; Robert R. Frei & James G. Archer, *Taxation and Regulation of Pension Plans under the Internal Revenue Code*, 1967 U. ILL. L.F 691, 699–700 (1967).

rejected this.[116] In one example, the court approved a bank's deferred compensation plan "created for the exclusive benefit of the senior executives," which meant that only seven highly paid employees were eligible to participate.[117] Paul recommended that in order to receive tax preferential status, all pension contributions should be immediately vested, they should generally cover at least 70 percent of a company's full-time employees, and any contributions above $7,500 should be taxed currently to the beneficiary.[118]

The Committee at least partially agreed with Paul, stating that the Code provision governing the tax treatment of pension contributions and payments "has been considerably abused by the use of discriminatory plans which either cover only a small percentage of the employees or else favor the higher paid or stockholding employees as against the lower-paid or nonstockholding employees."[119] The Committee recommended legislation to remedy this situation, noting that "[u]nder present law, it is contended the officers of a corporation may set up pension plans for themselves and make no provision for the other employees. Such actions are not in keeping with the purpose of this provision."[120]

In the Revenue Act of 1942, Congress enacted the first statute to attempt to provide comprehensive regulation of the tax treatment of pension plans.[121] Because of a "deluge" of protests from employers, however, the final statute was "hardly recognizable when compared with Paul's original suggestions."[122] It did remove from the tax-exempt category the "so-called 'key-men' trusts" that were designed to exclusively benefit executives, but it also created new retirement vehicles that offered opportunities for executives to defer compensation. For example, the Act permitted deferred profit-sharing retirement trusts, which allowed corporations to make tax-deductible contributions to provide continuous income to employees after retirement.[123] Profit-sharing contracts for specific executives had

116 Moore v. Commissioner, 45 B.T.A. 1073, 1077–1078 (1941); Albert W. Harris et al., 40 B.T.A. 1381 (1939), dismissing the case for the reasons given in Albert W. Harris, 10 B.T.A. Memo 864-A (1939), 1939 P-H B.T.A. Memo. Dec. par. 39-472 at 39-807.

117 Albert W. Harris, 1939 P-H B.T.A. Memo at 39-811.

118 Leon L. Rice, Jr., *Employee Trusts under the Revenue Act of 1942*, 20 TAXES 721 (1942).

119 H. Rep. No. 2333, 77th Cong., 1st Sess. (1942), 1942–2 Cum. Bull. 372, 413.

120 Id.

121 Revenue Act of 1942, ch. 619, §162, Pub. L. No. 77–753, 56 Stat. 798, 862 (1942).

122 Rice, *supra* note 118, at 721.

123 Thomas P. Swift, *Interest Growing in Profit Sharing*, N.Y. TIMES, Nov. 8, 1950, at 57.

existed for decades,[124] but this type of profit-sharing plan became particularly attractive both because it was consistent with the push to use performance-based compensation for executives,[125] and because it limited corporate contributions to good times, rather than requiring them in both good and bad times as with pensions.[126]

More significantly, the 1942 Act provided exceptions to the nondiscrimination requirement that still allowed plans to be focused on executives. The only requirement was that at least a majority of full-time employees also participated or the plan did not discriminate in favor of "employees who are officers, shareholders, persons whose principal duties consist in supervising the work of other employees, or highly compensated employees."[127] Under the subsequently issued Treasury Regulations, this nondiscrimination standard could be met "even though coverage is limited to employees who have either reached a designated age, been employed for a designated number of years, are employed in designated departments or are in other classifications, provided the effect is not discriminatory in favor of the high-paid group."[128]

Notwithstanding these exceptions, the nondiscrimination requirement did help push many executives to provide pensions to all of their employees as a way to politically insulate their own pension.[129] When coupled with the passage of the Social Security Act in 1935, which "made millions pension conscious," there was "extraordinary interest" following the passage of the 1942 Act "in the subject of pension plans for employees."[130] Between January 1942 and 1945,

[124] Frances Beatrice Brower, Profit Sharing for Executives, Nat'l Indus. Conf. Board, Studies in Personnel Policy No. 6 11–15 (1938); Washington & Rothschild, *supra* note 3, at 38.

[125] Miguel A. de Capriles, *Fifteen-Year Survey of Corporate Developments, 1944–1959*, 13 Vand. L. Rev. 1, 9 (1959); Wesley Smith, *The March of Finance*, L.A. Times, Dec. 1, 1940, at 13.

[126] J. E. McMahon, *Profit-Sharing Retirement Plans Advanced as Result of Increased Corporation Taxes*, N.Y. Times, Feb. 24, 1952, at F1.

[127] Revenue Act of 1942, ch. 619, §162, 56 Stat. 862, *amending* Int. Rev. Code § 165(a)(4); Frei & Archer, *supra* note 115, at 700; Rice, *supra* note 118, at 722. Under the statute, either 70 percent of all the employees or 80 percent of 70 percent of all eligible employees, excluding people employed five years or less, part-time, and seasonal employees, meaning that as long as 56 percent of the employees were covered by the pension plan, it would meet the requirements. Id. You could also create a separate plan for employees not covered by Social Security, which would not be considered discriminatory in favor of executives. Id.

[128] Frei & Archer, *supra* note 115, at 701.

[129] Walter D. Freyburger, *Pension Plans: The Philosophy of Section 165(a)*, 22 Taxes 60 (1944).

[130] Id.

more than 6,000 new pension plans were adopted.[131] According to one study conducted by Rainard Robbins of the Industrial Relations Counselors, a nonprofit established to study industry policies, not only did the data "show clearly the rapid growth of pension plans in recent years, especially during the two years following September 1, 1942," but "the contributions are more than four times as large, as a percentage of payroll, as they were under plans established prior to 1930."[132]

There was some concern that these new pension plans would only be temporary as a means of dodging the high wartime tax rates. In 1943, tax lawyer Leon Rice reported that "[i]n these times of abnormal profits and high income and excess profits taxes the Federal tax officials are fully aware of the fact that many plans are likely to be adopted primarily, if not entirely, for tax saving purposes, with the idea that upon the return to normalcy they will be abandoned."[133] This would have provided executives with the tax benefits of deferred compensation during the period of high rates when it was most beneficial, but deprive other employees of the long-term retirement benefits they thought they were receiving alongside the tax advantages.

To guard against companies abandoning pension plans, the Treasury Regulation interpreting the new pension provision warned "[t]he term 'plan' implies a permanent as distinguished from a temporary program."[134] Although it acknowledged that "the employer may reserve the right to change or terminate the plan, and to discontinue contributions thereunder," it warned "if the plan is abandoned for any cause other than business necessity within a few years after it has taken effect, this will be evidence that the plan from its inception was not a bona fide program for the exclusive benefit of employees in general."[135] The Regulation emphasized that this was especially the case for "a pension plan under which pensions were fully funded for the highly paid employees or others in favor whom discrimination is prohibited under section 165(a), and which was

[131] William R. White, *Income Taxes on Beneficiaries of Pension and Profit-Sharing Plans*, 14 Fordham L. Rev. 165, 165–66 (1945).

[132] Robbins, *supra* note 88, at 8.

[133] Leon L. Rice Jr., *The Recent Pension Trust Regulations*, 21 Taxes 486 (1943).

[134] T.D. 5278, 1943-13-11482, in 1943 C.B. 478, 481, amending Treas. Reg. § 19.165(a)(1)-1(a).

[135] Id.

abandoned soon after the pensions for such favored employees had been provided."[136]

Perhaps as evidence Congress was more about facilitating tax deferral than incentivizing retirement planning, employees and self-employed individuals were repeatedly denied tax benefits for setting up pension plans of their own. In 1951, Representative Eugene Keogh, a Democrat from New York, introduced the first in a long line of bills proposing to allow individuals to create their own tax-deferred retirement funds.[137] The Senate, however, rejected all such proposals for over a decade.[138] Even when relief was finally granted in 1962, the restrictions were significant and the tax benefits limited.[139] As a result, they were not widely used.[140]

Given political concern about the revenue loss from self-employment retirement plans, executives aligned with the opponents, perhaps because they believed the revenue cost could lead to reforms that imperiled their own pensions.[141] In 1955, for example, when hearings were held over one such bill introducing a proposed self-employment pension alternative, William J. Grede, president of a large foundry company and chairman of the Taxation Committee of the National Association of Manufacturers, testified in opposition despite the fact that his company used and benefitted from a pension and profit-sharing plan.[142] He argued that the proposal to extend pensions to self-employed persons was an example of "tax gadgeteering" in the sense that it was proposed "in place of attacking the rate structure" itself.[143] When questioned further, Grede did not concede that his plan was a tax gadget, arguing that "under the present rate structure" they are devices "in the competitive market to give you an opportunity to get people to come to work for you."[144] This was

[136] Id.

[137] H.R. 4371 and H.R. 4373, 82nd Cong., 1st Sess. (1951).

[138] Frei & Archer, *supra* note 115, at 716.

[139] Deductions were capped at $1,250 on contributions and only on earned, not passive, income of at least $25,000, capital gains treatment was denied on lump sum distributions, and there was no death benefit or sick-pay exclusion (Leslie M. Rapp, *The Self-Employed Individuals Tax Retirement Act of 1962*, 18 TAX L. REV. 351, 353–59 (1963)).

[140] Frei & Archer, *supra* note 115, at 717, n.148.

[141] Leslie M. Rapp, *The Quest for Tax Equality for Private Pension Plans: A Short History of the Jenkins-Keogh Bill*, 14 TAX L. REV. 55, 61 (1958).

[142] Individual Retirement Act of 1955, Hearings before the Committee on Ways and Means on H.R. 10, 84th Cong., 1st Sess. 1, 123, 146–48 (1955).

[143] Id. at 124.

[144] Id. at 149.

the kind of exchange that illustrated the sense that unless the government forced them to do otherwise executives were willing to pull up the ladders behind themselves when it came to tax dodging.

For executives, the pension had become a compensation substitute to dodge the high tax rates. As *U.S. News & World Report* observed in 1950, "[b]igger pensions are being used more and more by corporate directors as a possible way around the tax problems of executives."[145] Patton reported one example where the President and Vice President of a company were receiving the same cash salary in 1953 that they had received in 1940.[146] The explanation was twofold: "(a) the fact that these men are in high tax brackets and (b) the recent adoption of an unusually favorable pension plan, which defers income."[147] He considered pensions in the category of "gimmicks," though, saying "you can't compete for executive talent today without a gimmick."[148] It was not that pensions were necessarily problematic or exclusively tax motivated, but they were increasingly being used "in a way that permits unfriendly critics to charge 'tax dodging.'"[149]

## Convert

With the top rate on ordinary income at 91 percent and the capital gains rate at 26 percent, executives were keen to find a way to convert some or all their compensation to capital gains. One way was to shift pay from cash to stock. Companies were already interested in stock-based compensation to incentivize employee performance and executives were often interested because the appreciation would be taxed as capital gains, even though the initial award would be taxed as ordinary income. As tax rates rose, though, stock-based compensation became less attractive for both parties. The immediate tax hit forced the executive to sell the stock to cover the high tax on the value of the bonus, which meant that he could no longer benefit from the preferential capital gains treatment on the appreciation and the company no longer could benefit from the incentive effects. To counteract the tax effect, the company would have to gross-up its stock award

145 *Pensions vs. Pay Raises as a Lire for Executives*, U.S. NEWS & WORLD REPORT, June 2, 1950, at 18.

146 Patton, *Tax Gimmicks*, *supra* note 39, at 114.

147 Id.

148 Id. at 114. *See also* LEONARD RANDOLPH BURGESS, TOP EXECUTIVE PAY PACKAGE 56 (1963).

149 Patton, *Tax Gimmicks*, *supra* note 39, at 113.

considerably.[150] General Motors, which had long offered a stock bonus program, switched from paying bonuses entirely in stock to paying four-fifths of the bonus in cash and only one-fifth in stock.[151] Others reacted similarly.[152]

One potential way to avoid the tax problem was to switch to stock options. As long as the strike price was equal to the option price at grant, the assumption was that the receipt of the option was not taxable and any subsequent rise in value after grant and exercise would be taxable at the capital gains rate.[153] In 1945, however, the Supreme Court delivered a "rather disturbing decision" in *Commissioner v. Smith.*[154] Under *Smith*, the Court held that in a grant of a compensatory stock option, the recipient would be taxable at the exercise of the option on the difference between the then-current market value and the strike price.[155] As a result of this decision, and the Treasury regulations that were issued to implement it,[156] "the practice of granting stock options to key officers was practically suspended" for the succeeding five years.[157]

After lobbying from the National Association of Manufacturers, the United States Chamber of Commerce, and other business groups,[158] Congress in the Revenue Act of 1950 created a new scheme that aimed to restore options to their pre-*Smith* treatment.[159] Under the Act, an executive receiving what were called "restricted stock options" would not be taxed at the time of receipt on the value of the option or at the time of exercise upon receipt of the stock.[160] The intention was that the executive would only be taxed at the time of sale on the difference between the sales price and the strike price (on an option in which the strike price had been

150 Wentz, *supra* note 59, at 444.

151 Thomas H. Sanders, Effects of Taxation on Executives 89 (1951); Lasser & Rothschild, *supra* note 71, at 91.

152 Wentz, *supra* note 59, at 444.

153 Hoffman, *Executives' Compensation*, *supra* note 72, at 101–02.

154 324 U.S. 177 (1945); Hoffman, *Executives' Compensation*, *supra* note 72, at 97.

155 Id. at 182.

156 Treas. Dec. 5507, 1946–1 C.B. 18. *See* Brower, *supra* note 124, at 6 (citing the 1945 decision and a 1946 ruling of the Bureau of Internal Revenue).

157 Sanders, *supra* note 151, at 122; Wentz, *supra* note 59, at 459.

158 Sanders, *supra* note 151, at 124; Charles S. Lyon, *Employee Stock Options under the Revenue Act of 1950*, 51 Colum. L. Rev. 1, 15–16 (1951).

159 Revenue Act of 1950, Pub. L. 814, 81st Cong., 2d Sess. Ch. 994, §218 (adding I.R.C. § 130A).

160 The Court in *Smith* had left open the possibility that the receipt of the option would be taxable, but the legislative history suggests that Congress intended to eliminate that possibility. *See* S. Rep. No. 2375, 81st Cong., 2d Sess., 1950–2 C.B. 483, 526.

set at the fair market value on the date of grant) and that gain would be considered capital gain.[161] Because, however, of the perceived difficulty in identifying the precise fair market value of the stock in nonpublicly traded corporations, and even of identifying the fair market value for publicly traded stock whose price is volatile on the date the option is granted, Congress provided for some "leeway."[162] Thus, for an option granted with a strike price between 85 and 95 percent of the fair market value on the date of grant, the gain attributable to that spread would still be taxed at ordinary income rates.[163] Otherwise, as long as the strike price was no less than 85 percent of fair market value, the executive was less than a 10 percent shareholder of the corporation, and the executive held his stock for at least two years after the option grant and at least six months after exercise, the tax treatment of employee stock options on the post-grant appreciation returned to its pre-1945 state.[164]

Interestingly, the 1950 Act did not contemplate any kind of non-discrimination requirement. As New York tax lawyer John Alexander pointed out soon after enactment, the only requirement was that the option grant be "to an individual, for any reason connected with his employment by a corporation."[165] Alexander concluded that this language, which focused on the individual, makes it "clear that no 'plan' is necessary and that discrimination in favor of a highly paid employee is not a reason for denying the special statutory treatment."[166] In many cases, these newly adopted stock options were explicitly limited to executives. For example, United States Steel Corporation ratified a stock option plan in 1951 in which it was reported that "about 300 key management employees are expected to participate."[167] Similarly, stock option plans were adopted for "key executives" by Douglas Aircraft and for "management employees" by Colt's Manufacturing Company.[168] Even before the

[161] Id. The concern with taxing at exercise under *Smith* was that the executive would not have the cash to pay the tax and would have to sell the stock, which would defeat the purpose of using stock-based compensation to incentivize executives to be interested in the company's success. Chester C. Hilinski, *Some Comments on the Revenue Act of 1950*, 99 U. PA. L. REV. 455, 467–68 (1950).

[162] Reece A. Gardner, *Employee Stock Options*, 50 MICH. L. REV. 409, 415 (1952).

[163] I.R.C. § 130A(b) (1950).

[164] I.R.C. § 130A(d)(1) (1950).

[165] John H. Alexander, *Employee Stock Options and the 1950 Revenue Act*, 6 TAX L. REV. 165, 177 (1951) (quoting I.R.C. § 130A(d)(1)).

[166] Id.

[167] *Stock Option Tax Plan*, CHI. DAILY TRIB., June 30, 1951, at B4.

[168] *Douglas Aircraft Plans Stock Split*, N.Y. TIMES, Feb. 14, 1951, at 42; *Colt's Capital Increase by Transfer from Surplus*, HARTFORD COURANT, April 24, 1953, at 30.

passage of the 1950 Act, United Airlines adopted a plan that allowed executives to purchase a special class of "management stock," but they had what was classified as an option to convert that to regular common stock after a set number of years.[169]

Critics charged that these plans increased the possibility that stock option grants would be motivated by tax dodging, rather than business reasons. This was primarily because the stock could be sold six months after the shares were transferred to the executive. The argument was that this "failed to encourage development of a proprietary interest" in the company on the part of the executive,[170] which was ostensibly one of the main nontax business justifications for stock-based compensation. Alexander, however, argued that the statute contained restrictions on the use of the option "which are directed at the problem of trying to limit the use of options to those cases where they will be employed as incentive devices rather than as a means of permitting an 'insider' to take a quick profit taxable at capital gains rates."[171]

The passage of the Revenue Act of 1950 had an immediate effect on the use of stock options. Arch Patton exclaimed that "the 1950 tax law has given the stock option a new lease on life as an executive incentive."[172] A National Industrial Conference Board study of ninety-one companies found that eighty-six adopted stock option plans using the restricted stock options approved under the 1950 Act in the year after its enactment.[173] By 1964, there were 714 stock option plans among New York Stock Exchange-listed companies, compared to 269 in 1954 and only 8 before 1950.[174] Companies such as Allied Stores, Columbia Broadcasting Systems, National Cash Register, U.S Steel Corp., Standard Oil, Sinclair Oil, Sears Roebuck, and May Department Stores all were reported to have adopted stock option plans in the "big stock option rush" created by the 1950 Act.[175] More

169 J. K. Lasser, *The Tax Clinic: Two Stock Purchase Plans Submitted by United Airlines and Federated Stores*, 90 J. Accountancy 146 (1950).

170 James A. Feddersen & Sidney L. Harring, *Stock Compensation Plans*, 1971 Wis. L. Rev. 854, 857 (1971).

171 Alexander, *supra* note 165, at 178, n. 58.

172 Patton, *Incentive Compensation*, *supra* note 76, at 43.

173 Brower, *supra* note 124, at 7, n. 2; *Use of Stock Options Gains as Taxes Rise*, Chi. Daily Trib., Nov. 21, 1951, at B7.

174 Edwin H. Baker, *Employee Stock Option Plans under the Revenue Act of 1964*, 20 Tax L. Rev. 77, 78 (1964).

175 Lindley H. Clark, Jr., *Better-Paid Bosses: More Companies Boost Executive Pay Through Above-Salary Benefits*, Wall St. J., July 9, 1951, at 1.

recent studies with a longer time horizon have confirmed these early reports. Carola Frydman and Raven Saks found that more than 40 percent of the companies they studied adopted a restricted stock option plan within five years of the passage of the Revenue Act of 1950.[176]

Companies and executives that did not like the restrictions imposed upon stock options insisted there continued to be a nonstatutory path to granting tax-favorable stock options even after *Smith*. This was based on the belief that the pre-1945 distinction between "compensatory" and "proprietary" options remained, with *Smith* applying only to the former. Some lower courts had suggested that "proprietary" options, or options granted not to substitute for salary but to ensure that the executive would take an ownership interest in the company and therefore think about it in long-range terms, would not be taxable because they were for the benefit of the employer rather than to compensate the employee.[177] Treasury, in a controversial set of rulings and regulations after the *Smith* decision, had argued that *Smith* had eliminated the distinction altogether, but practitioners had contended that Treasury had exceeded its scope of authority in these pronouncements.[178] The Court eventually rejected the notion of a proprietary option in 1956,[179] however, making restricted stock options the primary avenue for tax-preferred stock compensation. Throughout the 1960s, these statutory stock options, as well as nonqualified options for those who found the restrictions too onerous, continued to be "one of the most popular forms of executive compensation."[180]

At the same time stock options were highly popular, companies began to include restricted stock in executive compensation packages. This combined the defer and convert strategies. By placing restrictions on the stock, companies hoped to defer the tax hit until the restrictions

176 Carola Frydman & Raven E. Saks, *Executive Compensation: A New View From a Long-Term Perspective, 1936–2005*, 23 Rev. Fin. Stud. 2099, 2107 (2010).

177 Lyon, *supra* note 158, at 5–6, 12–14; Note, *Taxability of Stock Option Determined by Employer's Intent*, 54 Colum. L. Rev. 1303, 1303 (1954). The distinction originated in a number of pre-1945 cases decided by the Board of Tax Appeals. *See, e.g.*, *Geeseman v. Commissioner*, 38 B.T.A. 258 (1939), acq. 1939–1 C.B. 13; *Springford v. Commissioner*, 41 B.T.A. 1001) (1940), acq. 1940–1 C.B. 4. See Mills, *supra* note 80, at 885.

178 Treas. Dec. 5507, 1946–1 C.B. 18; Gilbert A. Schneider, *Comment, Taxation - Employee Stock Options Under the Revenue Act of 1950*, 34 Marq. L. Rev. 211, 212–13 (1950).

179 *Commissioner v. LoBue*, 351 U.S. 243 (1956).

180 William M. Linden, *Comment, The Tax Bargain in Executive Compensation*, 47 Tex. L. Rev. 405, 409 (1969). See Joseph E. Bachelder, *What Has Happened to Stock Options?* N.Y. L. J., Sept. 19, 2014, at 3 ("During the 1960s, stock options continued to be the most used form of long-term equity incentive award.").

lapsed. Although the tax would be ordinary income, it would be based on the lesser of the fair market value of the stock at the time of grant or exercise, meaning any post-grant appreciation would be deferred until sale and taxed as capital gains.[181] Moreover, one benefit was that the stock would retain value even in a poor stock market, unlike options, which would become worthless if the stock dropped below the strike price.[182] Treasury regulations had specifically approved certain restrictions as sufficient to defer the tax, including a requirement that the executive offer the stock back to the corporation either at the same price the executive paid for it in stock purchase programs or at the stock's book value in stock grant programs.[183] Treasury also subsequently issued a revenue ruling approving the deferred realization if the stock could not be sold without the consent of the Board.[184]

In the early 1960s, President John F. Kennedy targeted stock options as part of his assault on tax dodging. In his tax message to Congress, Kennedy said that "[t]he existing sprawling scope of this preferential treatment [for capital gains] has led to serious economic distortions and has encouraged tax avoidance maneuvers sometimes characterized as the 'capital gains route.'"[185] Kennedy highlighted restricted stock options, noting that providing capital gains treatment for executive compensation "can no longer be said to be either desirable or necessary."[186] He recommended that "the spread between the option price and the value of the stock at the date the option is exercised be taxed at ordinary income rates at the time the option is exercised."[187]

The problem, as one Treasury official indicated in testimony before the Senate Finance Committee in 1961, was that the law "has not operated to encourage employees to acquire a proprietary interest in the business" as was expected when enacted in 1950.[188] Instead, "present law merely provides a way in which compensation can be paid to selected employees without the payment of ordinary income tax and with no possible incentive effect through continued holding of the stock" because it is

181 Linden, *supra* note 180, at 408–09.

182 Bachelder, *supra* note 180, at 3.

183 Treas. Reg. § 1.61–2(d)(5) (1957); Treas. Reg. § 1.421–6(d)(2) (1959).

184 Rev. Rul. 68–86, 1968–1 C.B. 184.

185 John F. Kennedy, *Special Message to the Congress on Tax Reduction and Reform*, Jan. 24, 1963.

186 Id.

187 Id.

188 *Treasury Aide Avoids Stand on Ending Stock Option Tax Benefits*, Wall St. J., July 21, 1961, at 8.

generally sold immediately after the minimum holding period has expired.[189] As Thomas M. Ware, president of the International Minerals & Chemical Corporation, summarized the charge in a speech to the National Business Conference, "[t]he question, as some critics put it, is 'Do stock options exist to give a few executives quick, tax-eased profits?'"[190]

The House Ways and Means Committee proposed "sharp restrictions" on the use of stock options "to provide extra compensation for company officials in high tax brackets."[191] It emphasized that the restrictions were "aimed at stock options available to designated company officials" as distinguished from broadly available plans, noting that the reforms "would not affect stock-purchase plans that benefit all employees of a concern."[192] As with pensions, by imposing restrictions on only stock options that were designated specifically for executives, the intent was to introduce a nondiscrimination principle to force companies to adopt stock option plans more broadly accessible to all employees.

Restricted stock options were replaced with "qualified stock options" in the Revenue Act of 1964, which included new restrictions such as requiring that the options be "at the money."[193] Observers predicted, however, that the few additional requirements would "not impair its usefulness as a device to avoid income taxes."[194] Most significantly, there was no movement to apply any kind of nondiscrimination requirement to qualified stock options. As one practitioner noted, "[t]he committee reports . . . make it clear that qualified stock options are intended to be incentive devised for key employees to be granted on a discriminatory basis to those employees who influence the fortunes of the company by their individual efforts."[195]

Instead of imposing a nondiscrimination requirement, Congress adopted a new program alongside the qualified stock option called an "employee

[189] Id.

[190] *Stock Options: A Business Leader Makes an Eloquent Case for the Defense*, BARRON'S NAT'L BUS. & FIN. WEEKLY, June 19, 1961, at 5 (reprinting Ware's speech).

[191] John D. Morris, *House Panel Votes to Cut Tax Benefit for Stock Options*, N.Y. TIMES, May 30, 1963, at 1.

[192] Id.

[193] Revenue Act of 1964, § 221, 78 Stat. 63 (1964).

[194] Charles L. B. Lowndes, *The Revenue Act of 1964: A Critical Appraisal*, 4 DUKE L.J. 667, 684 (1964).

[195] Baker, *supra* note 174, at 79.

stock purchase plan."[196] The "key requirement and distinguishing feature" of these plans was that they be nondiscriminatory.[197] The Ways and Means Committee reported that some companies were already offering something similar to non-executive employees under the restricted stock option program, but for reasons sufficiently different than the program designed for executives that it decided to create a separate scheme for tax purposes.[198] Under this new program, employees were taxed neither at grant nor at exercise as long as they remained continuously employed and meet the stock holding requirements,[199] and were required to make them available to all employees, with some limited exceptions for new, part-time, seasonal, and "officers, supervisors and highly compensated employees."[200] The nondiscrimination requirement for employee stock purchase plans was actually stricter than the one in place for pensions since there was no alternative path that would permit a corporation to adopt a nondiscriminatory plan limited to a specific class or category of employee as was permitted for pensions.[201]

## Divert

Unlike deferring or converting compensation income, where executives would still have to pay tax eventually on the compensation and the employer's deduction might be limited or delayed, diverting compensation into nontaxable categories such as fringe benefits was considered "the ultimate tax shelter."[202] One practitioner noted that that they

196 A few companies had offered something called an "executive stock purchase plan" after the 1950 Act was passed, but this was an agreement to purchase the stock, rather than an option, and it was limited to executives. Brower, *supra* note 124, at 7.

197 James L. Truitt, *The Employee Stock Purchase Plan*, 52 A.B.A. L.J. 879 (1966).

198 Report of the Committee on Ways and Means, House of Representatives to Revenue Act of 1963 to accompany H.R. 83, 88th Cong., 1st Sess. 64 (1963) ("1963 Ways & Means Report"). The Committee's view was that companies offering stock purchase options for all employees were effectively just trying to raise capital by offering a discount roughly commensurate with the reduction in costs from not having to do a stock offering, whereas executive stock option programs were geared towards aligning the incentives of managers with stockholders. Id.

199 Truitt, *supra* note 197, at 881. Employees were required to remain employed until at least three months before exercise and could not sell the stock if acquired within two years from grant or six months from the date of exercise, while executives under qualified stock options were required to hold the stock for three years to ensure they were acquiring a "stake in the business." Id.; 1963 Ways & Means Report, *supra* note 198, at 64.

200 See I.R.C. §§ 423(b)(4); Baker, *supra* note 174, at 84–85.

201 Baker, *supra* note 174, at 85.

202 William H. Hoffman, Jr., *Tax Influences in Shaping the Executive Pay Package*, 40 TAXES 386, 390 (1962).

potentially provided the "most ideal tax treatment," in the sense that "it is hoped the reward which is accorded the employee does not become subject to tax to him, and the employer is entitled to a full deduction."[203] No individual executive was going to be able to shift that much of his compensation to fringe benefits, but as *Boston Globe* columnist Jack Steele noted in a series on tax dodging, "fringe benefits do not provide tax savings as big or as sensational as those that wealthy taxpayers get from depletion allowances or capital gains," but "the total taxes avoided by these devices are substantial."[204]

The term "fringe benefit" was largely unknown before World War II. It reportedly "sprang up" amidst wages freezes during the war as shorthand for "money costs and employee benefits that were on the periphery of, but actually outside, direct wage payments."[205] In his study of the composition of executive pay packages, Leonard Burgess referred to these benefits as "pay elements not included in the package," in part because they were difficult to measure.[206] As they grew in prominence, "fringe benefits" sometimes was used to refer to all of these non-salary or wage benefits, including the deferred compensation, profit-sharing plans and stock options discussed in the prior two sections, and sometimes it was only intended to cover the non-statutory benefits that were not accounted for in government reporting.[207]

Dartmouth management professor C. W. Sargent divided employee fringe benefits into five main categories.[208] Many of these have become so established in modern society that they are not even considered "fringe" anymore. These included (1) "Pay for time not worked," such as vacations, holidays, sick and maternity leaves, personal leave, and paid time off to serve as a juror, to vote, or to serve as a witness on a case; (2) "Monetary awards and prizes for special activities and performances,"

203 Mills, *supra* note 80, at 883.

204 Jack Steele, *Fringe Benefits to Employees Cost Uncle $1 Billion*," DAILY BOSTON GLOBE, Feb. 20, 1958, at 32.

205 Austin M. Fisher & John F. Chapman, *Big Costs of Little Fringes*, 32 HARV. BUS. REV. 35 (1954). According to one contemporary source, the first use of the term was in 1943 when the regional chairman of the National War Labor Board referred to non-wage or salary rates as "fringe issues" rather than "auxiliary pay" or something similar and the characterization caught on. James C. Hill, *Stabilization of Fringe Benefits*, 7 INDUS. & LAB. RELATIONS REV. 221 (1954).

206 BURGESS, *supra* note 148, at 95.

207 Fisher & Chapman, *supra* note 205, at 35.

208 C.W. SARGENT, FRINGE BENEFITS, DO WE KNOW ENOUGH ABOUT THEM 13–14 (1953).

such as bonuses for attendance, quality, safety, morale; (3) "Bonuses, contributions, and profit sharing, for which the employee renders no direct regular or special service," which included savings or "thrift" plan contributions, discounts on purchases of the company's stock, severance pay, military induction or service bonuses, educational subsidies unrelated to an employee's job or college scholarships for an employee's children; (4) "Payments to provide employee security and financial protection against various hazards and contingencies," such as unemployment insurance and workmen's compensation, disability insurance, and employee welfare fund contributions; and (5) "Practices and services that benefit employees primarily," including credit unions, employee discounts, financing services, and cafeterias.[209] In addition to all of the above, a typical mid-century benefit package for executives might have included life and medical insurance, the use of company cars and jets, and dining and country club memberships.[210]

In the first half of the twentieth century, employers and employees generally relied upon judicial decisions and administrative pronouncements, rather than legislation, for the nontaxation of fringe benefits. In 1919, for example, Treasury ruled that seamen who had been provided "board and lodging in addition to their cash compensation" should not be taxed on the value of it because it was "supplied for the convenience of the employer."[211] Treasury soon amended its regulations to codify this "convenience of the employer" principle, noting more generally that "[w]hen living quarters such as camps are furnished to employees for the convenience of the employer, the ratable value need not be added to the cash compensation of the employee."[212] This "convenience of the employer" principle was eventually interpreted to cover a broad range of meal and lodging-related fringe benefits,[213] including for hospital workers,[214] live-in domestic help,[215] public health trainees,[216]

209 Id.

210 Id.; Hoffman, *Tax Influences*, *supra* note 202, at 390; Henry W. Trimble, Jr., *Executive Compensation – Corporate Considerations*, ABA SEC. REAL PROP. & TR. PROC. 23, 24 (1960); Mills, *supra* note 80, at 883; *Use of Stock Options Gains as Taxes Rise*, *supra* note 173, at B7; Steele, *supra* note 204, at 32.

211 O.D. 265, 1 C.B. 71 (1919).

212 T.D. 2992, 2 C.B. 76 (2020); Treas. Reg. §213, Art. 33.

213 J. Henry Landman, *The Taxability of Fringe Benefits*, 33 TAXES 173, 177 (1955).

214 O.D. 915, 4 C.B. 85 (1921).

215 I.T. 2253, V-1 C.B. 32 (1926).

216 I.T. 3756, 1945 C.B. 64.

ex-servicemen,[217] army officers,[218] plantation managers,[219] hotel managers,[220] sanitarium employees,[221] and apartment managers.[222]

Treasury relied upon different rationales for exempting other types of fringe benefits. Awards for past achievement, such as a prize or a testimonial dinner, that were not paid to discharge a contractual obligation or to otherwise provide payment for services rendered, were classified as nontaxable gifts.[223] On the other hand, a company cafeteria that provided free lunches to employees was not taxed under the view that it promoted employee health, welfare, contentment, and loyalty to the employer.[224] The same rationale was applied to employee recreation facilities.[225]

The exemptions seemed to be based more on political or logistical grounds than any principled rationale. One group of commentators, noting that there were regulations that provided for the taxation of the value of something received in return for services, suggested that the failure to enforce normal tax conventions for fringe benefits seemed to be related to a combination of "a lack of awareness of the extent of these fringe benefits and therefore their potential revenue consequences; a general but often irrational 'feeling' that these benefits should not be taxes; and, perhaps, a lack of competent guides to valuation in this area."[226] Another commentator later noted that because of "a lack of clear guidelines in the law," the public perceived, or rather misperceived, "that all fringe benefits are exempt from taxation."[227]

One of the more commonly offered fringe benefits – life insurance – was initially considered taxable under the constructive receipt and economic benefit doctrines. If a corporation purchased a life insurance policy for the benefit of an executive, the company could deduct the premiums paid, but the executive had to include them in income at the same time. The theory was effectively one of constructive receipt or

217 58 Stat. 284, I.T. 3702, 1944 C.B. 74.
218 Jones v. U.S., 60 Ct. Cl. 552 (1925).
219 Green v. Kanne, 38-1 U.S.T.C. ¶ 9206 (D. Haw. 1938).
220 Benaglia v. Commissioner, 36 B.T.A. 838 (1937).
221 R. Shad Bennett, 12 T.C.M. 31 (1942).
222 Lloyd N. Farnham, 6 T.C.M. 1049 (1947).
223 Rev. Rul. 54-110, 1954-1 C.B. 28 (1954); G.C.M. 5881, 13-1 C.B. 68 (1929).
224 S.S.T. 302, 1938-1 C.B. 456 (1938); Rev. Rul. 57-471, 1957-2 C.B. 630 (1957).
225 Id.
226 Joseph H. Guttentag, E. Deane Leonard, and William Y. Rodewald, *Federal Income Taxation of Fringe Benefits: A Specific Proposal*, 6 NAT'L TAX J. 250, 251 (1953).
227 David M. Graf, *Taxation of Fringe Benefits*, 27 S. TEX. L. REV. 251 (1985).

substance over form in that "the executive is deemed to have received the payment and immediately paid it out for a policy of life insurance."[228] In 1920, however, Treasury Regulations held that premiums for group life insurance policies for employees were not taxable to employees. The regulations provided that "[p]remiums paid by an employer on policies of group life insurance covering the lives of his employees, the beneficiaries of which are designated by the employees, are not income to the employees."[229] By 1936, there was a question whether life insurance policies purchased by employers for individual employees could receive the same treatment as group policies, but Treasury rejected that stance, establishing a distinction between individual and group employer-provided life insurance that effectively created a nondiscrimination incentive.[230] Medical care and hospitalization provided under group policies were accorded similar treatment, with employers permitted to deduct them as business expenses and employees entitled to exclude them from income.[231]

The early 1950s was an inflection point for the taxation of fringe benefits. As fringe benefits "proliferat[ed]" in the years after World War II to evade wage freezes, their tax exemption became controversial.[232] There was concern that Treasury would try to crack down on the taxability of fringe benefits.[233] Reports ominously warned that the Service "has turned a hard eye on the whole area of fringe benefits."[234] In April 1954, the Internal Revenue Service (IRS) ordered its staff to implement a program that would apply the economic benefit doctrine to capture income tax on things like the appreciation in value of

228 Washington & Rothschild, *supra* note 3, at 225; Commissioner v. Bonwit, 87 F.2d 764, 766 (2d Cir. 1937).

229 T.D. 2992, 1920–2 C.B. 76 (amending Article 33 of Regulation 45). In 1950, Treasury did make a distinction between term and permanent life insurance policies, with the exemption for group life only applicable in the case of the former, but Washington and Rothschild suggested that because of the work required to enforce this distinction, it would be effectively a "nuisance tax" and "Treasury may well continue to ignore" it. Washington & Rothschild, *supra* note 3, at 226.

230 Gen'l Counsel Mem. 16069, 1936–1 C.B. 84

231 Bureau Letter, Oct. 26, 1943, 3 CCH Fed. Tax Serv. ¶ 6587 (1943) (Letter from the Timothy Mooney, Bureau of Internal Revenue to Russell L. Davenport, Holyoke, Mass., in response to an inquiry).

232 Graf, *supra* note 227, at 251; Guttentag, Leonard, & Rodewald, *supra* note 226, at 250; *Singed Fringe*, Wall St. J., Nov. 17, 1953, at 1.

233 *Tax Spread Predicted*, N.Y. Times, Feb. 26, 1954, at 30.

234 Douglas Larsen, *Study Fringe Benefits for New Income Taxes*, Austin Statesmen, Oct. 6, 1953, at 4.

the inventories donated to charity and observers believed that could extend to fringe benefits too.[235]

Initially, the IRS focused on the low-end fringe benefits paid to employees, rather than the high-end fringe benefits only executives received. These low-end benefits included free meals for employees, craft training, tools, and work clothes, medical services and hospitalization, discounts on company products, housing and recreational facilities,[236] which the IRS proposed to tax by adding the market value of these benefits to each employee's income.[237] The IRS even contended that the "very existence" of pension and hospitalization plans was "a form of income on which covered employees should be taxed," separate and apart from any payments received or made on their behalf under the plans.[238]

Targeting low-end, employee-focused, fringe benefits was immediately criticized. Although there was a horizontal equity rationale for treating all employees the same whether they received free lunches or not,[239] commentators called proposals to tax noncash benefits impractical.[240] As one op-ed in the *Atlanta Constitution* asked, in an all-you-can eat company cafeteria, "will there be a different scale for the hearty eater and the frugal? What about people who are on a diet? And what about those who only say they are?"[241] The op-ed also mocked the pettiness of going after the little guy, pointing out that market values aren't the same "at Joe's beanery as at the tony place on Main Street."[242] The answer was that Treasury did not seem to care that much when it came to coming after regular employees for tax dodging. As the op-ed continued, "[l]ittle of that will bother the tax boys, though, for a slide rule can fix for them any 'market value' they want."[243] The US Chamber of Commerce predicted that if they overcame the logistics and implemented this proposal, "employees will wind up poorer than they think."[244]

235 Landman, *supra* note 213, at 178–79.

236 *Taxing the Fringes*, WALL ST. J., May 6, 1953, at 12; *Tax Report*, Wall St. J., April 29, 1953, at 1.

237 *Taxing the Fringes*, *supra* note 236, at 12.

238 *Revenue Bureau Studies Taxing "Fringe Benefits,"* N.Y. TIMES, April 25, 1952, at 32.

239 *Tax Report*, *supra* note 236, at 1.

240 *Tax Spread Predicted*, *supra* note 233, at 30.

241 *Tax People Eyeing the Appetite Now*, ATL. CONST., May 26, 1953, at 4.

242 Id.

243 Id; *Taxing the Fringes*, *supra* note 236, at 12.

244 *Study Shows Wage Hidden in Benefits*, L.A. TIMES, Nov. 9, 1952, at A12.

The pushback against targeting fringe benefits seemed to have worked, as Congress officially codified the exemption for some fringe benefits, including insurance, sick or injury pay, and meals and lodging provided for the convenience of the employer, under the 1954 Internal Revenue Code.[245] It was not until thirty years later, however, that Congress enacted a comprehensive scheme to address many incidental fringe benefits.[246] In the meantime, non-statutory exemptions for many fringe benefits remained.

Although fringe benefits were not subject to a nondiscrimination requirement,[247] many became widely available to a company's employees. There were several reasons. First, although benefits such as company cars or trips could easily be restricted to executives, others that executives might want such as recreational facilities, parking, employee discounts, or coffee in the break room were sufficiently inexpensive and open that it was easier to provide it to everyone than to enforce exclusions.[248] Moreover, fringe benefits offered some of the same incentive or productivity benefits for rank-and-file employees as executives, including increased morale, and reduced absenteeism.[249]

Second, unions had pressured to make fringe benefits more widely available ever since World War II. Wage freezes had limited their access to raises and they sought the same kinds of tax preferred alternate forms of compensation executives were receiving.[250] This continued long after the war.[251] Unions often insisted that some of the more prominent fringe benefits, such as paid vacations and insurance, be covered by their union contract.[252] Indeed, one labor expert wrote that fringe

245 I.R.C. §§ 101 (death benefits), 104 (compensation for injuries or sickness), 105 (amounts received under accident and health plans), 106 (employer contributions to accident and health plans), 119 (meals or lodging furnished for the convenience of the employer), 120 (statutory subsistence allowance received by police); Bonnett, Jr., *supra* note 80, at 28–29; Landman, *supra* note 213, at 187.

246 Tax Reform Act of 1984, Pub. L. No. 98-369, 98 Stat. 494 § 531 (enacting Section 132 of the Internal Revenue Code); Graf, *supra* note 227, at 262–271.

247 Bonnett, Jr., *supra* note 80, at 29 (citing the Senate Committee Report, which provided that the benefits are eligible for the exclusion "regardless of whether the employer's plan covers one employee or a group of employees.").

248 Mills, *supra* note 80, at 883.

249 Guttentag, Leonard & Rodewald, *supra* note 226, at 251.

250 Id.; Jack Steele, *Fringe Benefits to Employees Cost Uncle $1 Billion a Year*, DAILY BOSTON GLOBE, Feb. 20, 1958, at 32.

251 Fisher & Chapman, *Big Costs of Little Fringes*, *supra* note 205, at 39.

252 HAROLD STIEGLITZ, FRINGE BENEFIT PACKAGES 6 (1954). This was buttressed by two cases in the late 1940s holding that pensions and group health insurance, respectively, were mandatory subjects of collective bargaining. *See* Inland Steel Co. v. National Labor

benefits were frequently "the crucial factor in a particular collective bargaining situation."[253] They also negotiated for increases in their benefits, often in preference to increased cash compensation.[254] In 1956, more than one-quarter of all pensions and less than half of health and welfare plans were adjusted after union negotiations.[255] By the first half of the 1960s, those numbers increased to one-third and half of all of the corresponding pension and health and welfare plans.[256] Given the competitive marketplace, these union-negotiated benefits led many nonunion companies to offer them as well, although perhaps not always at the same rate.[257]

Finally, benefits provided exclusively to executives were problematic. Unions called it a form of "executive featherbedding," with Albert J. Hayes, president of the International Association of Machinists, specifically mentioning "inflated expense accounts," "country-club memberships," "company-paid yacht cruises and hunting trips."[258] It may have been easier to expand access to more of their benefits than to create conflict by restricting them to executives, or, as one contemporary observer suggested, it may have been the product of "increased social consciousness of both labor and management."[259] Perhaps more importantly, revenue agents were suspicious of fringe benefits that offered a tax-motivated way to finance personal consumption with tax-subsidized dollars. Restricting fringe benefits to executives risked unwanted scrutiny.[260] Making fringe benefits available to all employees was viewed as the price for offering executives the benefits they sought.

Relations Board, 170 F.2d 247 (7th Cir. 1948) (pensions); W.W. Cross & Co. v. National Labor Relations Board, 174 F.2d 875 (1st Cir. 1949) (group health insurance).

253 Arthur M. Ross, *Fringe Benefits Today and Tomorrow*, 7 LAB. L.J. 476 (1956).

254 Id.; Richard A. Lester, *Benefits as a Preferred Form of Compensation*, 33 SOUTHERN ECON. J. 488 (1967). *See Singed Fringe*, *supra* note 232, at 1 (health insurance secured for rubber industry workers by the C.I.O).

255 Lester, *supra* note 254, at 488.

256 Id.

257 *See* H. Ellsworth Steele & Homer Fisher, Jr., *A Study of the Effects of Unionism in Southern Plants*, 87 MONTHLY LAB. REV. 258, 268 (1964).

258 *Union Official Raps Management's Waste*, BUFFALO COURIER EXPRESS, May 19, 1960, at 5.

259 Guttentag, Leonard & Rodewald, *supra* note 226, at 250–51 (quoting Murdoch, *Compensation Other Than Cash*, Paper presented before the Taxation Section of the American Bar Association, Sept. 18, 1951).

260 Id.; Edwin Nichols, *Tax Can Complicate Executive Pay Plans*, CHI. DAILY TRIB., Jan. 27, 1963, at A3.

As tax rates continued to rise, fringe benefits offerings and usage soared. Although this phenomenon was not limited to the US,[261] American companies seemed to be at the forefront. A speaker at the Internal Cost Conference in Salt Lake City in 1953 reported that a large number of fringe benefits were "coming into general use," including "group insurance, hospitalization, retirement" and many others such as "physical examinations . . . all forms of recreation, credit unions etc."[262] That same year, the US Chamber of Commerce commissioned a study of 940 companies, finding that the average annual expense for fringe benefits was $720 per employee.[263] Companies that spent 15.2 percent of payroll on fringe benefits in 1947 were spending 20.2 percent of payroll only six years later.[264] In 1951 alone, employers were estimated to have contributed $900 million to group insurance plans and $373 million to health and welfare plans, which reflected an increase of 200 percent and 340 percent, respectively, since 1946.[265] In 1954, Austin Fisher and John Chapman placed the growth in fringe benefits in context by noting that "fringe payments alone have soared to a point where their cost (now more than 40 cents per hour) exceeds the whole of that very controversial minimum wage which the New Deal put through."[266]

***

By demanding that corporations structure their pay to enable them to dodge as much of the tax burden as possible, executives effectively helped to legitimize tax dodging and spread it throughout the country. Between statutory antidiscrimination requirements, union pressure, and the copycat process of compensation in a tight labor market, there were both direct and indirect pressures to make the various techniques employed by executives more widely available. Moreover, it was in the executives' interests to normalize many of their so-called perks to better insulate them from legislative pressure. Not surprisingly, therefore, many of the techniques executives pushed to allow them to

261 Melvin Lurie, *The Growth of Fringe Benefits and the Meaning of Wage Setting by Wage Comparisons*, 15 J. Indus. Econ. 16, 20 (1966).
262 *Fringe Pay Climbs to 20% of Payroll*, N.Y. Times, June 19, 1953, at 35.
263 Landman, *supra* note 213, at 175.
264 Id.; Arthur M. Ross, *Fringe Benefits Today and Tomorrow*, 7 Labor L.J. 476, 478 (1956).
265 Guttentag, Leonard & Rodewald, *supra* note 226, at 251, n.6.
266 Fisher & Chapman, *supra* note 205, at 35.

dodge the high marginal rates became standard and were routinely touted in personal finance columns at the time with specific references to the tax advantages for the average worker.[267] The fact that most of these 1950s and 1960s-era compensation techniques are rarely mentioned today in articles discussing tax dodging is a testament to how deeply they became embedded in the modern American workplace.

[267] *You and Your Taxes*, N.Y. HERALD TRIB., Oct. 26, 1959, at 33; Eugene Miller, *Fringe Benefits Merit Study*, NEWSDAY, July 7, 1964, at 15C.

# PART II

## The Democratization of Tax Dodging

# 4

## The Rise of Tax Advice

### Professionals, Charlatans, Ideologues, and "Anybody with a Card Table and a Sign"[1]

With the rise in top rates and the increase in people required to file income taxes, the demand for tax planning services grew tremendously. As early as the 1930s, commentators noted that "[t]he combination of higher taxes and higher incomes has given powerful incentives to try every new-fangled tax-dodging scheme that lawyers can cook up."[2] Because the number of individuals subject to the income tax was still relatively small, though, few people could sympathize with the plight of those paying high rates and even fewer could possibly benefit from the services of tax planners. As a result, tax dodging during this period was the exclusive province of the wealthy, where tax advice on how to do it was reportedly "a favorite topic of conversation at the best clubs,"[3] but there was little need to advertise it publicly. During the 1930s, observers suggested that "fewer than a dozen of the eminent law firms of New York and Washington" were responsible for most of the tax dodging schemes then in circulation.[4]

By the 1950s, "the tax-avoidance business, dampened by the government which had zealously pursued every tax dollar during the depression, returned and boomed."[5] For the uber wealthy, the rationale for tax

1 Harry Anderson, *Just What Should be Done with Tax Return Preparers?* AUSTIN STATESMAN, July 26, 1972, at 20 (quoting an IRS official complaining about unregulated tax preparers).

2 Ernest K. Lindley, *Tax-Dodgers on Parade*, THE NATION, June 12, 1937, at 667.

3 Randolph E. Paul, *Restatement of the Law of Tax Avoidance*, in STUDIES IN FEDERAL TAXATION: TAXATION WITHOUT MISREPRESENTATION 9, 77 (1937). *See The Rich Get Richer*, NEW REPUBLIC, Aug. 28, 1935, at 68, 71 (noting that many "evasion devices to reduce the effective tax rate . . . are available only to substantial taxpayers purely because of the cost of lawyers and machinery.").

4 FERDINAND LUNDBERG, AMERICA'S 60 FAMILIES 471 (1937). Morgenthau had identified several prominent New York and Washington law firms as central to the proliferation of tax avoidance schemes during the 1930s. JOSEPH J. THORNDIKE, THEIR FAIR SHARE: TAXING THE RICH IN THE AGE OF FDR 202 (2013).

5 Richard M. Cooperman, *The Tax Thieves of 1951, Part VI. The True Villains*, NEW REPUBLIC, Dec. 24, 1951, at 10, 11. *See Tax Angles: Federal Levies Push More Americans*

dodging was obvious. As William J. Casey and J. K. Lasser explained in their 1952 book entitled *Tax Sheltered Investments*:

> It is unnecessary to stress the increasing degree to which taxes are biting into both yield and safety of investments, slicing away both income and capital. As this is written, Congress has evidenced an intention to take away as much as 82¢ out of a dollar of corporate income, and as much as 92¢ out of a dollar of individual income. The appalling fact is that a dollar of corporate income can shrivel down to less than a penny by the time it has passed through the wringer of the corporate income tax, the individual tax on dividends and the estate tax payable on passing savings on to one's family.[6]

When the top rate was 91 percent, "the impetus for tax sheltering was enormous, since a dollar saved in taxes was the equivalent of earning $11 before taxes."[7] As future IRS Commissioner Mortimer Caplin, explained, the high rates "led to increased interest in tax planning, in means for arranging one's affairs to minimize taxation, in tax avoidance."[8]

What changed in the post–World War II period is that the upper and middle class also began to seek out tax advice. Taxpayers who might have deemed the costs too high previously – both in terms of the fees charged by lawyers and accountants to perform such services and the potential penalties that could be imposed for engaging in questionable schemes – could now reasonably conclude that the benefits (in terms of the money saved on their taxes) exceeded the costs.[9]

Not only did they want access to tax advice just like the wealthy had, but they wanted access to the tax dodging tips provided to the wealthy. In House hearings held in 1972, Representative Richard Hanna, a Democrat from California, conceded that "taxpayers seek professional help with the hope of finding someone who 'knows the loopholes.'"[10] According to

*into Unusual Decisions*, WALL ST. J., Jan. 5, 1956, at 1 ("more and more individuals are seeking professional tax advice").

6 WILLIAM J. CASEY & J. K. LASSER, TAX SHELTERED INVESTMENTS 1 (1952).

7 Robert C. McIntyre, *Tax Cheats and their Enablers*, Economic Institute Tax Enforcement Forum, April 12, 2005, at 5.

8 Mortimer M. Caplin, *Threats to the Integrity of our Tax System*, 44 VA. L. REV. 839, 840 (1958). *See* Roswell Magill, *The Impact of Income Tax Leakages: A Postscript to Randolph Paul*, 12 TAX L. REV. 1, 1 (1956) ("high rates foster methods and plans for tax reduction and avoidance.").

9 Anthony M. Verana, *Tax Planning for the Not-So-Rich. Variable and Private Annuities*, 11 WM. & MARY L. REV. 1, 4 (1969).

10 Regulation of Income Tax Preparers. Hearings before a Subcommittee of the Committee on Government Operations, House of Representatives, 92nd Cong., 2d Sess. on H.R. 7590 77 (April 13, 1972) (prepared testimony of Richard Hanna, D-OH).

Hanna, "we have created the situation where limiting tax payments has become legal tax avoidance for the rich, but illegal tax evasion for the middle class and the poor. When the average taxpayer hears of millionaires paying no income tax, is it any wonder he thinks to himself 'why shouldn't some of those loopholes work for me?'"[11]

It was no surprise that there was a ready supply of people willing to meet the middle-class demand for tax advice. While these new tax advisors may not have recommended illegal activity, "practitioners often challenge the tax agency's interpretation and application of tax laws," which may lead them to "induce their clients to adopt more aggressive tax avoidance strategies than they would use on their own."[12] Moreover, not all tax advice was created equal. Some of it came from professionals such as lawyers and accountants, but much of it, especially for the middle and lower bracket taxpayers, came from less reputable sources, such as "retail" tax advisers, self-help materials, and tax protesters.

## Professionals

Accountants dominated the income tax field when the first post–Sixteenth Amendment income tax statute was enacted in 1913.[13] Companies and wealthy individuals already relied upon accountants to keep track of their financial affairs and handle tax payments of various kinds, so it was natural for them to prepare their tax returns too.[14] They were therefore the first set of professionals to familiarize themselves with the tax statutes and regulations.[15] As a result, "the enactment of a federal excise tax in 1911 and the federal income tax in 1913 . . . swelled the ranks of accountants in the U.S. and gave the profession a more powerful voice."[16] Mark Eisner,

11 Id.

12 Jennifer Reinganum & Louis L. Wilde, *Tax Practitioners and Tax Compliance*, California Institute of Technology Social Science Working Paper 666 1 (March 1988) (partially quoting Karyl A. Kinsey, *Advocacy and Perception: The Structure of Tax Practice*, American Bar Foundation 2 (1987)).

13 John L. Carey, *Ethics, "Unauthorized Practice," and Federal Income Taxation - An Accountant's Viewpoint*, 25 Rocky Mt. L. Rev. 435, 443 (1952).

14 J. Paul Jackson, *The Practice of Tax Law: The Lawyer-Accountant Controversy*, 9 Ark. L. Rev. 279, 280 (1955).

15 Robert Harris Aland, *Relations Between Lawyers and Certified Public Accountants in Federal Tax Practice*, 15 Ala. L. Rev. 517, 517–18 (1963).

16 Michael E. Doron, The End of the Disinterested Profession: American Public Accountancy, 1927–1962 37 (Ph.D. Dissertation, 2009); Jackson, *supra* note 14, at 280.

the former collector of internal revenue for Manhattan, even went so far as to declare in a speech to the Brooklyn Bar Association in 1921 that "the whole system of income taxation as it exists today is the plan of accountants."[17]

By contrast, for years lawyers "paid little attention to taxation" in their practices.[18] It was not until the 1930s that some attorneys and other professionals soon began to recognize the "lucrative professional opportunities" that might be had by offering their services in the area of "additional assessments, abatements, credits, and refunds."[19] In 1933, the former president of the New York Bar exhorted his fellow lawyers in a speech before the New York County Lawyers' Associations to pursue work in tax law,[20] although William Raymond Green, a Judge on the Court of Claims and former Chair of the House Ways and Means Committee, thought this was unnecessary, writing that same year that "there is a large body of very able lawyers who specialize in income tax law."[21] Regardless of who was right, there eventually was a large contingent of professionals working in the area of taxation. By 1937, Treasury estimated that more than 45,000 lawyers and accountants operated in the tax field, literally dwarfing the 2,800 field agents employed by the Bureau of Internal Revenue.[22]

Politicians and Treasury officials were not thrilled with this development, believing that lawyers, accountants, and other professionals were responsible for the rise in tax dodging. In 1934, Robert H. Jackson, at the time the Assistant General Counsel of the US Treasury Department, blamed "clever lawyers in aid of powerful clients" for many of "the holes poked in the [tax] law."[23] Jackson went on to describe these lawyers as "shyster tax lawyer[s]," noting that the description extended to a "mixed bar of lawyers, accountants, and agents" employed to aid taxpayers.[24] He

[17] Editorial, *As We Advance*, 32 J. of Accountancy 203 (1921).
[18] Aland, *supra* note 15, at 518.
[19] Joseph J. Klein, *The Lawyer and the Income Tax*, 11 Tax Mag. 52 (1933).
[20] Id. at 55, 75.
[21] William Raymond Green, The Theory and Practice of Modern Taxation 109 (1933).
[22] *Hearings on Tax Evasion and Avoidance*, Joint Committee on Tax Evasions and Avoidance, 75th Cong., 1st Sess. (1937), Pt. 1, at 10 (statement of Treasury Secretary Henry Morgenthau).
[23] Robert H. Jackson, *Changes in Treasury Tax Policy*, Tax Mag. 342, 343 (July 1934) (an address originally delivered before the Ninth Annual Meeting of the Federation of Bar Associations of Western New York at Niagara Falls, N.Y., June 30, 1934).
[24] Id. at 382.

went on to lament the fact that "conservative and honorable lawyers, whose habit has been to advise clients against tricks and deception to evade taxes, have seen their clients taken away by the solicitation of sharp practitioners who claimed to have safe schemes of evasion."[25] In testimony before a Joint Committee on Tax Evasion and Avoidance in 1937, Treasury Secretary Henry Morgenthau and Undersecretary Roswell Magill cited "the development of a group of clever attorneys and accountants who exercised every ingenuity in circumventing the law."[26] Similarly, during the House deliberations on what became the Revenue Act of 1937, Representative Henry Ellenbogen, a Democrat from Pennsylvania, complained that "a few extremely wealthy individuals have resorted to every trick and every device which their lawyers could conceive to avoid the payment of taxes justly due by them."[27] During the same Congressional debates, Representative Kent Keller, a Democrat from Illinois, referenced tax dodging by accountants as well, claiming that "the American people had been cheated and chiseled" out of $2.5 billion over a ten-year period through schemes organized by accountants involving personal holding companies located in Canada.[28]

After World War II, the growth of tax professionals, and the need to use them, continued unabated. Although Randolph Paul proclaimed in 1952 that "tax law as a specialized field of practice is still in its comparative infancy,"[29] the field had advanced significantly. The Bureau of Internal Revenue employed more than 57,000 individuals to examine the 52,000,000 individual returns and over 500,000 corporate tax returns filed each year.[30] In 1963, Jerome Hellerstein remarked that "the income tax has become a major factor in business and in the lives, not only of men of property, but also of millions of Americans of modest and middle incomes."[31] Perhaps more significantly, Hellerstein explained, "the tax law has grown into one of the most complex and refined statutes on the books, understood, if at all, only by those who devote most of

25 Id. *See* Robert H. Jackson, *Problems of the Federal Tax Bar*, TAX MAG. 466, 502 (Sept. 1934) (making a similar claim before the Tax Conference at the American Bar Association Meeting in Milwaukee on August 28, 1934 about "lawyers who give conservative and upright advice" seeing "their clients weaned away" by practitioners claiming to have "safe schemes to outwit the Treasury.")

26 Id.; ROY G. BLAKEY & GLADYS C. BLAKEY, THE FEDERAL INCOME TAX 429 (1940).

27 81 CONG. REC. 5459 (June 8, 1937).

28 Id. at 5461.

29 Randolph E. Paul, *The Lawyer as a Tax Adviser*, 25 ROCKY MTN L. REV. 412, 412 (1952).

30 HUGH C. BICKFORD, SUCCESSFUL TAX PRACTICE 1 (1950).

31 JEROME R. HELLERSTEIN, TAXES, LOOPHOLES AND MORALS 2 (1963).

their professional lives to studying its ramifications."[32] The result was that "[n]o sophisticated business man these days will make a move without consulting his tax man."[33] This increased demand meant that "there has grown up at the bar a considerable number of lawyers who specialize in taxation."[34]

This expansion of the profession exacerbated the spread of tax dodging schemes. Amid the prosperity that followed World War II and the rapid increase in tax rates in the Revenue Act of 1942, Randolph Paul noted that "the market had never buzzed with so many schemes as in 1943 . . . Never had the schemes been so bold."[35] A few years later, Paul wrote that the postwar fervor for tax dodging had not died down and included professionals advocating for reform: "The high rates and heavy burden also activated the imagination of many who were interested in reducing taxes or transferring the impact of taxes to others."[36] One member of the Boston University graduate tax faculty noted that tax lawyers spend the greatest part of their professional time engaged in what is generally known as "tax planning," which he acknowledged "is merely a euphemism for tax avoidance."[37] Both tax lawyers and accountants advocated teaching tax planning and avoidance as part of their regular coursework.[38]

The government deserved some of the blame for the growing sophistication of tax professionals. As far back as 1937, Senator Robert La Follette, a Progressive from Wisconsin, complained that the revolving door of Bureau of Internal Revenue officials seeking to "cash[] in" on their specialized knowledge was one of the "real problems in the struggle of the Government to collect its taxes."[39] Morgenthau conceded that "[t]he government [has] become[] a training school for many of its opponents."[40] According to the *Washington Post*, "[q]uite a number of former bureau employees have made fortunes advising clients how they may safely escape payment of income taxes by taking advantages of

32 Id.
33 Id.
34 Id.
35 RANDOLPH E. PAUL, TAXATION FOR PROSPERITY 279 (1947).
36 RANDOLPH E. PAUL, TAXATION IN THE UNITED STATES 438 (1954).
37 Frederic G. Corneel, *Tax Planning: Teaching and Practice*, 22 TAX L. REV. 221, 222 (1967).
38 Id. at 221; W. E. Dickerson, *Tax Planning and Tax Research in the Tax Accounting Courses*, 32 THE ACCT'G REV. 98 (1957).
39 *The Tax Expert Problem*, WASH. POST, June 28, 1937, at 6.
40 THORNDIKE, THEIR FAIR SHARE, *supra* note 4, at 203.

technicalities and loopholes in the law."[41] Nationally syndicated anti-New Deal columnist Westbrook Pegler, after calling Bureau tax agents "the best income tax and loophole experts in the country," advised that "any big taxpayer, corporate or individual, who wants the best advice on evading taxes and avoiding the traps set by the Treasury Department can save money by hiring an agent out of the Bureau of Internal Revenue to come and point out how."[42]

The rise in tax professionals helped contribute to the growth in the number and creativity of tax schemes, but the professional networks they developed helped to spread those schemes. For instance, the Tax Section of the American Bar Association (ABA), which was founded in 1939 with a few hundred members primarily from the east coast,[43] grew to 3,500 members by 1952 and to 4,000 two years later.[44] The development of this kind of an association, and many similar ones at the state and local level, may have helped to create what attorney Howe Cochran, the author of a treatise on tax practice,[45] marveled at the "incredible ... circulation among wealthy people and their counsel of tax avoidance schemes."[46] According to Cochran, "[a] clever scheme may be devised by a hungry lawyer in New York, and, within ten days, law offices in St. Louis and San Francisco are working nights applying the scheme for some of their avid clients."[47] These professional networks could just as easily help shut down schemes as support them, as the ABA once tried to do when it testified before Congress in 1954 about certain "unintentional loopholes" in proposed tax legislation, but it did not oppose "intentionally

41 *The Tax Expert Problem*, *supra* note 39, at 6.

42 Westbrook Pegler, *Fair Enough: Loophole Experts*, WASH. POST, June 9, 1937, at 8. For more on Pegler, *see* William F. Buckley, Jr., *Rabble-Rouser*, THE NEW YORKER, March 1, 2004.

43 Philip L. Mann, *A Brief History of the Tax Section, 1939–2014*, 68 TAX LAW. 13 (2014). There were predecessors of the Section on Taxation – the Standing Committee on Taxation (1906) and the Special Committee on Internal Revenue and its Means of Collection (1921) – but neither was long-lived. It took twenty-six years after the first modern federal income tax was enacted for tax lawyers to receive their own ABA section. Joseph J. Thorndike & Ajay K. Mehrotra, *Who Speaks for Tax Equity and Fairness? The Emergence of the Organized Tax Bar and the Dilemmas of Professional Responsibility*, 81 LAW & CONTEMP. PROBS. 203, 210 (2018).

44 Carey, *supra* note 13, at 443; Robert N. Miller, *History of Section of Taxation*, 8 BULL. SECTION OF TAX'N 12 (1954).

45 HOWE PRESTON COCHRAN, TAX PRACTICE AND PROCEDURE (1946).

46 Howe P. Cochran, *Tax Avoidance Schemes End in Disaster*, 5 MIAMI L.Q. 435, 437 (1950).

47 Id.

preferential provisions," possibly because its members may have been the one advocating for those provisions on behalf of their clients.[48]

In some cases, it was the clients, not the professionals, who were pushing the aggressive tax schemes. Randolph Paul wrote that "it is no trade secret that the emotions of tax clients sometimes make them 'keen for lawsuits and the reckless fray.'"[49] "Some [clients,]" Paul continued, "will pressure their advisers; others adopt the more subtle tactic of misstatement."[50] By the 1960s, they "started to bring marketed tax shelter offerings to their legal and accounting representatives for review."[51] A tax lawyer who "gained a reputation for squelching deals rather than facilitating them" might lose clients in tax practices that had grown more competitive than in prior years.[52] As a practical matter, so-called white shoe or "silk stocking" law firms effectively ceded tax practice to smaller firms that were willing to engage in more aggressive tax planning.[53]

Government officials spoke at professional association meetings to try to persuade tax advisers to clamp down on abuse. Mortimer Caplin, the IRS Commissioner, pleaded with participants at a University of Chicago Federal Tax Conference in 1962 to maintain "high standards of conduct among tax lawyers and advisers in the 'two-way street' of reasonable tax administration."[54] Other lawyers resorted to service in the American Bar Association, which was reportedly "replete with energetic ideologists."[55] As Louis Eisenstein noted, however, although "when they speak for the Association in tax matters, they usually do so through principle," the organization was as much a cover for their clients' tax dodging as it was a vehicle to fight against it.[56]

Most professionals resisted taxpayer pressure to stretch the truth. As Merle Miller, a tax lawyer and former head of the Interpretative Division of the Service's Office of Chief counsel, reported in 1952, "the tax practitioner today spends nine tenths of his time killing schemes believed

48 Eugene Neil Feingold, The Internal Revenue Act of 1954: Policy and Politics 285 (1960) (unpublished Ph.D. dissertation, Princeton University).

49 Randolph E. Paul, *The Responsibilities of the Tax Adviser*, 63 HARV. L. REV. 377, 379 (1950).

50 Id. at 383.

51 Henry Ordower, *The Culture of Tax Avoidance*, 55 ST. LOUIS U. L.J. 47, 88 (2010).

52 Id.

53 Id.

54 *Income Tax Laws Branded "Monster of Inequalities,"* CHICAGO DAILY TRIBUNE, Oct. 27, 1962, at F6.

55 LOUIS EISENSTEIN, THE IDEOLOGIES OF TAXATION 15 (1961).

56 Id.

by the proponents to be new, but which were actually dead and buried many Revenue Acts and decades ago."[57] Similarly, the Washington, DC accounting firm of Bobys, Switkes, Noble, and Brotman wrote to their clients to advise them that expense account claims must be "supported by canceled checks, vouchers, or other substantiating documents," noting that the firm would not "participate in the 'sport'" of padding expense accounts to disguise the tax-free transfer of what would otherwise be taxable compensation.[58]

Nevertheless, as one accountant admitted in a candid newspaper interview, "the entire system of the income tax leaves so many loopholes that most people have long since lost any sense of morality about trying to beat it."[59] He went on to say that "the vast majority of accountants save their clients money by utilizing all the legal machinery at their disposal," but "when that fails, some of them may have to resort to other methods – and only because that is the system and that is the way the game is played."[60] Louis Eisenstein confirmed that this process was the same for tax lawyers:

> A lawyer is not a competent tax advisor unless he is familiar with the highways and byways of avoidance . . . In the process of selling their skills, they soon become the mental captives of those they serve. Before long they either believe what they are paid to say or they hesitate to say what they believe. Dean Griswold has suggested that tax lawyers should "sell their services," not "their souls." While there are singular attorneys who have eluded spiritual captivity, they are only the exceptions which prove the general rule.[61]

As Hugh Bickford wrote in his highly acclaimed training guide for the practice of tax law,[62] "there is probably no better method of building a successful clientele than by keeping constantly abreast of the possibilities of tax savings and making them available to your clients. There is nothing that impresses clients more than a suggestion that saves them

57 Merle H. Miller, *Morality in Tax Planning*, 10 N.Y.U. Ann. Inst. on Fed. Tax'n 1067 (1952) in Ethical Duties to the Tax System: A Handbook 341, 348 (Scott A. Schumacher & Michael Hatfield, eds., 2015).

58 Philip M. Stern, The Great Treasury Raid 120 (1964).

59 Jack Altshul, *Secrets of a High Bracket Accountant*, Newsday, March 27, 1965, at 3, 37.

60 Id.

61 Eisenstein, *supra* note 55, at 205.

62 Hugh C. Bickford, Successful Tax Practice (1950). *See* John W. Reed, *Review of* Successful Tax Practice, *by H. C. Bickford*, 3 Okla. L. Rev. 484 (1950) (praising it for providing "essential, practical information about tax practice").

money."[63] It would have been hard, indeed, for a tax professional to remain above the fray during this period and still make an honest living.

The result was that many observers blamed tax lawyers and accountants for the rise in tax dodging schemes. Senator Paul Douglas, a Democrat from Illinois, lamented that "two highly profitable new professions have developed – those of tax lawyers and accountants – which assist men of means to avoid, and in some cases, to evade what would seem to be their moral and legal obligations."[64] Douglas identified as one of the main barriers to reform "the concentration of knowledge about our tax structure in the person of the avoiders and evaders and their professional retainers."[65] Norris Darrell, President of the American Law Institute and a long-time partner at the law firm of Sullivan & Cromwell, admitted that "there is much still to be desired," noting that "in most taxpayers, ourselves included, there is a tendency toward a little larceny when it comes to taxation."[66] Nevertheless, Darrell meekly protested that "I have the impression that during recent years there has been a considerable improvement in the tax practitioner's sense of public responsibility," citing "the increased attention at tax practitioner's gatherings to ethical problems in tax practice."[67]

If Darrell was right in his optimistic assessment, the profession's ability to hold the line did not last long. By the 1980s, tax shelter promoters, who rose to prominence in the 1970s as mass-marketed tax dodging investment deals became common,[68] recruited tax lawyers and accountants to help peddle their schemes by promising them so-called "review fees." Although it would not be unreasonable for an attorney or accountant to accept cash payments from promoters to compensate them for their work in confirming the promised tax consequences of the schemes, these fees were also reportedly paid "in exchange for the attorney's or accountant's cooperation in circulating the real-estate tax shelter documents to prospective investors."[69] That would be unethical because the adviser's

[63] BICKFORD, *supra* note 62, at 145.
[64] Paul H. Douglas, *After Taxes, the Deluge?* WASH. POST TIMES HERALD, Jan. 28, 1962, at E6.
[65] Id.
[66] Norris Darrell, *The Tax Practitioner's Duty to his Client and his Government*, 7 PRAC. LAW. 23 (1961) in ETHICAL DUTIES TO THE TAX SYSTEM, *supra* note 57, at 355, 367.
[67] Id.
[68] Tanina Rostain, *The Organized Tax Bar and the Tax Shelter Industry*, 23 YALE J. ON REG. 77, 83 (2006).
[69] Kenneth R. Haney, *Beware of "Irresistible" Tax Shelters*, WASH. POST, Nov. 6, 1982, at E31.

guidance on the appropriateness of the tax shelter for the client might be influenced by fees paid to them by the promoter that were reported to "run well into the thousands of dollars."[70] Particularly troubling was that there was some evidence that this practice, although not widespread, was not rare either. According to a 1986 Treasury Department survey, tax practitioners self-reported that they received a commission on 6.7 percent of the tax shelters they recommended and 3.2 percent of all the shelters they discussed with their clients.[71] Nevertheless, such commission arrangements were not easy to eliminate at the federal level. Congress enacted penalties for knowingly aiding individuals in understating their income tax liabilities,[72] which was designed in part to counteract some of these financial incentives for pushing truly fraudulent investment schemes, but the intent requirement still left tax advisers a fairly wide berth.[73]

## Retail Tax Advisors

High bracket taxpayers may have been uniquely motivated to seek out professional tax advice, but as the Tax Code grew in complexity, many of what one observer called "the largely unrepresented and heavily taxed middle and lower income taxpayer" needed help themselves.[74] When the income tax first expanded to cover these groups during World War II, the then-Internal Revenue Bureau trained thousands of government tax advisers to help taxpayers prepare their returns.[75] Initially, the government provided these services without cost, but eventually, they charged a modest fee.[76] In 1954, the newly renamed

70 Id.

71 U.S. Dept of Treasury, Internal Revenue Service, Research Division, Survey of Tax Practitioners and Advisers (1986) (Questions 35(a) and (b)).

72 I.R.C. § 6701.

73 Mortimer Caplin, *Handling Tax Shelter Disputes and Litigation with the IRS*, William & Mary Annual Tax Conference 155, 158 (1985).

74 Anthony M. Vernava, *Tax Planning for the Not-So-Rich. Variable and Private Annuities*, 11 Wm. & Mary L. Rev. 1, 64 (1969).

75 *Millions Suffering from Form-Phobia Ask Aid of Revenue Bureau*, Wall St. J., Feb. 25, 1944, at 1; *10,000 Here Request Aid on Tax Return*, Wash. Post, March 13, 1945, at 4; *Storefront Tax Service Earns a Good Return*, Bus. Week, March 25, 1967, at 196,197.

76 *Your Income Tax*, Christian Science Monitor, Feb. 5, 1947, at 15; *Revenue Office Ready to Aid Travis Taxpayers*, Austin American, March 12, 1944, at 4. By 1950, one taxpayer reported waiting in line 2.5 hours for a brief interview with the Tax Collectors, for which he paid $1.20, but it was considered better than paying a private service, which could cost $5 or more. *Taxpayers Besiege Income Tax Office*, Wash. Post, March 14, 1950, at 5.

Internal Revenue Service was forced to abandon the service because it did not have the personnel to keep up with the expanding tax base.[77] As a result, the *Wall Street Journal* reported in 1956 that "[m]ore and more individuals are seeking professional tax advice," but as one New York tax attorney lamented, "[u]nfortunately, it is only the wealthy taxpayer who can avail himself of this advice."[78]

To fill this gap in the market, a new industry developed in the field of tax planning and preparation. Some estimates suggested as many as 50 percent of filers were using tax preparers by the early 1970s, plus as many as 20 or 30 percent more who used preparers who refused to sign the returns.[79] A large percentage of these potential customers were low-income taxpayers whose income was too small for regular tax professionals, but often needed the most help in preparing even their simple returns.[80] The Internal Revenue Services' decision to eliminate the 1040A short form card-sized tax return that was used by many low bracket taxpayers in the late 1960s in favor of a larger form return "opened the gates," with the result that the market for tax return preparation services was "flooded with 21 million more customers."[81]

A wave of what might be called "retail tax advisers" took advantage of this new demand by advertising themselves as experts, even though they lacked any obvious credentials to justify such claims. H. F. Millikin, the pseudonym for journalist and author Joachim Joesten, explained in 1963 that

> in this country anybody who can read and write has a perfect right to set himself up as a tax expert and is likely to do so at one time or another, for want of anything better. You don't need a license, or a diploma, nor even experience to hang out a shingle: "Joe Smith – Tax Returns Expertly Prepared" or something like that.[82]

[77] Joel Forster, *Taxpayer Assistance and the Tax Practitioner*, J. ACCOUNTANCY 79, 80 (Feb. 1973) (reproducing an edited version of a speech by Raymond F. Harless, deputy commission of Internal Revenue, delivered at the Fall meeting of the American Institute of CPA's division of federal taxation in San Francisco on December 4, 1972); Patricia A. Ryan, *Tax Preparation Agencies: What is Needed for the Public's Protection*, 13 B.C. INDUS. & COMM. L. REV. 895, 895 (1972).

[78] *Tax Angles: Federal Levies Push More Americans into Unusual Decisions*, WALL ST. J., Jan. 5, 1956, at 1.

[79] *The War on Refund Mills*, TIME, March 12, 1973, at 93; Gerald A. Kafka, *Regulation of Income Tax Return Preparers: The Need for a Systematic Program*, 43 U. CIN. L. REV. 863, n.6, and 864 (1974).

[80] Kafka, *supra* note 79, at 863 and n.6.

[81] *Taxes: Happier Returns*, NEWSWEEK, Feb. 23, 1970, at 74.

[82] H.F. MILLIKIN, THE PRUDENT MAN: TAX DODGING AS AN ART 153 (1963) (pen name for Joachim Joesten).

The quintessential example of this new wave of retail tax advisers was H&R Block, which was founded in 1955 in a storefront in Kansas City, Missouri by two brothers, Henry and Richard Bloch.[83] As Henry Bloch recalled, a tax preparation service that they previously used to throw in for free to clients of their bookkeeping company suddenly became a full-time business when the IRS stopped preparing returns.[84] It quickly spread all over the country through franchising and opening branches they themselves owned,[85] with over 5,000 locations in operation in the United States (and eventually Canada) by the early 1970s.[86] As a result, annual revenues increased dramatically, growing from $960,000 in 1962 to $54 million by 1970.[87] By that time, H&R Block prepared approximately 7.2 million returns,[88] which was nearly 10 percent of all individual income tax returns filed in the United States, and employed 20,000 individuals, 12,000 of whom were engaged in tax preparation services.[89] Additionally, former H&R Block franchisees often continued their business under different names after their franchise contracts expired.

Few H&R Block employees were tax professionals in the traditional sense of the word. As Harry Bloch later recalled, "the problem of getting trained personnel was bigger than that of getting customers."[90] Part of this may have been because the company's business model was not geared toward hiring people full-time. Indeed, most of their employees were seasonal. Consequently, H&R Block tax preparers included people from many walks of life. According to one report, "some are housewives, some are moonlighting policemen and firemen, [and] some are proprietors or own off-season businesses of their own."[91] To train their tax preparers, they established "tax schools" and charged people to take a seventy-two-hour course over eight weeks.[92] If the trainees worked

[83] *Storefront Tax Service*, *supra* note 75, at 197; *Paper Empire?* FORBES, Nov. 15, 1970, at 19. They used the phonetic spelling of their surname to make it simpler for customers. Id.

[84] *Storefront Tax Service*, *supra* note 75, at 197.

[85] Id.

[86] Ryan, *supra* note 77, at 895.

[87] *The Troubles that are Taxing H&R Block*, BUS. WEEK, Dec. 8, 1973, at 112.

[88] James J. Gadarowski, *Regulation of Tax Preparers: Bone or Bane*, 55 TAXES 532, 534 (1977).

[89] *Paper Empire*, *supra* note 83, at 19; *Storefront Tax Service*, *supra* note 75, at 197.

[90] *Storefront Tax Service*, *supra* note 75, at 198.

[91] Id. at 197.

[92] Id. at 198.

a full tax season, they reimbursed the tuition and paid them $1 an hour for the time spent in the school.[93]

Several competitors sprung up to challenge H&R Block in the retail tax adviser market. For example, department stores like Sears, Roebuck, J. C. Penney, and Montgomery Ward started tax preparation services, as did banks and financial services companies.[94] They copied H&R Block's business model of using personal interviews and tried to lure in customers with extensive television advertising and "savings-and-loan-style giveaways," such as TVs and tape recorders.[95] With "no legal bar to using the information for sales leads or selling it to insurance companies, real-estate firms and the like," the incentives to get in the business went beyond the fees they received from customers.[96]

Officially, most of these multi-office retail tax advisers were not particularly aggressive in the tax positions they took for their clients. H&R Block, for example, insisted that it "scrupulously avoids getting into tax law. When a customer insists on claiming a clearly questionable item, the company refers him to his attorney."[97] The way they compensated their employees supported that position. Tax preparers were paid on commission, but it was based upon the volume of work, rather than the size of refund or the amount of deductions secured for their customers.[98] That said, these types of retail tax advisers did tend to be a bit looser in their advice to customers. For example, when dividend and interest payers became subject to information reporting under the Revenue Act of 1962, the *Wall Street Journal* reported that a "major tax preparation service" advised customers "to forget any oversights in reporting past income from dividends and interest."[99] The president of the tax preparation service insisted that as long as "the average guy keeps current, that's all the Government is interested in."[100] By contrast, an official from the accounting firm of J. K. Lasser & Co. reported that "if we found that a client of ours had ignored

[93] Id.

[94] *Paper Empire, supra* note 83, at 19; Ryan, *supra* note 77, at 895, n.1; *Taxes: Happier Returns, supra* note 81, at 74.

[95] *Taxes: Happier Returns, supra* note 81, at 74.

[96] Id.

[97] Id.

[98] *Storefront Tax Service, supra* note 75, at 200.

[99] Lee Silberman, *Tips for Taxpayers: Business of Advisers Grows as More People Struggle to Trim Taxes*, WALL ST. J., April 1, 1963, at 1.

[100] Id.

interest or dividends, we'd insist he file amended returns. If he refused, we'd throw him out."[101]

If national tax preparation chains at least publicly claimed that they were conservative in preparing returns for their customers, many smaller preparers took the opposite approach. To compete with the national firms, these "fly-by-night operators who set up shops in vacant stores when there's open season on taxpayers" promised larger refunds than the more established retail tax preparation services could deliver.[102] Some even used names to advertise their tax dodging prowess. For example, one classified advertisement was for an outfit called "Income Tax Avoidance Service, Inc." It warned taxpayers that they should "plan now or pay later."[103] According to a report of an official in the Los Angeles field office of the IRS, many of these "phony tax advisers ... 'guarantee' to save their clients money. And often the only way they can fulfill their promise is to recommend outright tax fraud."[104] Millikin warned that "come Spring, they'll blossom out all over again in the store windows of barber shops, delicatessens, real-estate agencies, drugstores and the like, these bogus tax experts who take your dollar and play – or rather make you play – Russian roulette with it."[105]

Over this period, there was "a rapid proliferation of commercial tax specialists, including many 'refund mills' that pop up like crocuses in March, making a killing helping taxpayers cheat the Government, then fade away on April 16."[106] They placed signs announcing "Income Tax Forms Filled Out Here" in "candy stores, dry-cleaning establishments, drug stores, luncheonettes, office buildings – almost any available space."[107] When Tax Day passes, these retail tax preparers would close up shop without providing a forwarding address, leaving landlords to field calls from irate former clients who later discovered issues with the returns they had filed.[108] The retail tax advisers were so successful in attracting customers with outlandish promises of big refunds that they attracted the attention of government officials. H. Alan Long, the

101 Id.
102 Anthony Marcin & Marietta Marcin, *Pick a "Tax Expert" with Care!* CHICAGO DAILY TRIBUNE, March 1, 1959, at H41; *The War on Refund Mills*, *supra* note 79, at 93.
103 *Classified Ads 17*, WASH. POST, Nov. 21, 1965, at D1.
104 *Tax Dodgers: Stiffer Enforcement Deters Some Cheaters, But Many Persevere*, WALL ST. J., April 11, 1957, at 1.
105 Millikin, *supra* note 82, at 154–55.
106 *The War on Refund Mills*, TIME, March 12, 1973, at 93.
107 *Quickie Tax Men Faze Landlords*, N.Y. TIMES, Feb. 14, 1965, at R1.
108 Id. at R1.

Director of Internal Revenue for the Chicago District, advised taxpayers to "be careful of the 'expert' who will no longer be around to help answer questions Internal Revenue might ask about your return after the filing period."[109]

More legitimate tax advisers, such as licensed accountants, attempted to counter these shadier practitioners. They emphasized their credentials and their permanence. One accountant in Southern California ran an advertisement in the *Los Angeles Times* in 1961 that included a reproduction of his license from the State Board of Accountancy.[110] The advertisement advised taxpayers "Don't risk the disservice of unqualified fly-by-night 'tax experts' who come to your home or set themselves up in temporary or permanent offices to appear legitimate."[111] It suggested you'll be sorry "if you let some illegitimate fool you with a real estate, notary, or electrician's license,"[112] concluding by warning taxpayers "don't be high-pressured by the assertion: 'I haven't got a license but I've been making out tax returns for 10 years,' This is the surest sign of a petty racket."[113]

The IRS "suspect[ed] that vast amounts of revenue are being lost because of the activities of cheating or inept smaller tax preparers."[114] Such "unscrupulous" tax preparers "urge their not-always-unwilling clients to inflate claims for property damage, write off the value of items lost in a robbery that never occurred, or deduct interest paid on nonexistent loans."[115] In one example, a Texas tax preparer was convicted of fraud after he "encouraged clients who owned dogs or parakeets to classify themselves as farmers and claim depreciation allowances."[116] In another more extreme example, preparers reportedly got their customers to sign a blank return for a flat fee and then they would claim fraudulent deductions and retain the refund for themselves.[117]

The people in the IRS national office were not the only ones worried about these unscrupulous tax preparers. The *Wall Street Journal* reported in 1957 that many enforcement agents in regional IRS offices "express[ed] concern over the growing number of self-styled 'tax experts' who have set

109 Marcin & Marcin, *supra* note 102, at H41.
110 *Need Help with Tax Problems*? L.A. Times, April 7, 1961, at B8.
111 Id.
112 Id.
113 Id.
114 *The War on Refund Mills*, *supra* note 79, at 92.
115 Id.
116 Id.
117 Id.

up offices."[118] As one newspaper observed around tax time, "this time of year you can walk down almost any street and spot 'INCOME TAX EXPERT' signs – many of them in glowing neon" or find "a person [who] is among the 142 listed under 'tax return preparation' of the yellow pages," but in neither case does it guarantee they are honest, dependable, or reliable.[119] Another pointed out that "anyone can become a tax consultant simply by calling himself one ... there is no central clearing agency to verify the qualifications of tax experts."[120] "Anybody with a card table and a sign," an IRS official complained, "can do tax returns for money as long as he has a local business license."[121]

Treasury officials tried to crack down on those tax preparers who participated in fraudulent activity, but it was an uphill battle it had been losing for years. As far back as 1934, long before tax dodging had become a mass market phenomenon, Treasury Secretary Henry Morgenthau, told attendees at the American Bar Association annual convention that he planned to appoint a special committee "to scrutinize the morals of lawyers, accountants and special agents who argue cases before the Treasury Bar."[122] Morgenthau "advised the conventionites to oust voluntarily from their association out-and-out crooks, over-sharp connivers, and boasters of special influence."[123] This appeal to trade associations may have worked to some extent in getting them to police their own members, but it was the nonprofessionals not even eligible for membership in trade associations that appeared to pose the greatest risks.

There was a question about whether it was worth the effort to go after commercial preparers. Over the years, many proposals had been discussed to regulate them. A 1972 IRS field study in which agents had posed as taxpayers and sought preparation from assistance of certain "suspect preparers" had found that 60 percent of the returns prepared were "potentially fraudulent."[124] This led the House to initiate hearings on

118 *Tax Dodgers: Stiffer Enforcement Deters Some Cheaters, But Many Persevere*, WALL ST. J., April 11, 1957, at 1.

119 Marcin & Marcin, *supra* note 102, at H41.

120 Id.

121 Harry Anderson, *Just What Should Be Done with Tax Return Preparers?* AUSTIN STATESMAN, July 26, 1972, at 20.

122 *Morals in Milwaukee*, TIME, Sept. 10, 1934, at 27.

123 Id.

124 Comptroller General of the United States, Report to the Joint Committee on Internal Revenue Taxation, Congress of the United States, No Apparent Need to Regulate Commercial Preparers of Income Tax Returns, GGD-76-8 2 (Dec. 8, 1975) ("GAO Report").

the largely unregulated "mushrooming tax return preparation industry," but no action was taken.[125] A 1975 report of the Comptroller General of the United States prepared for the Joint Committee on Taxation once again found that "there are no restrictions on anyone entering the field," noting that "the 200,000 to 250,000 individuals comprising the tax preparer industry have widely varying training, experience, and ethics."[126] Although the report conceded that "some preparers have been guilty of fraud and misconduct," it concluded that "commercial preparers, as a group, are not a special problem."[127] According to the report, "a comparison of the returns prepared by commercial preparers with those prepared by professional preparers, a generally respected group, showed that the percentage of error in reported tax found by IRS were about equal."[128]

## Tax Dodging "Schools"

Upper middle-income individuals, such as professionals like doctors and lawyers, as well as small businessmen, had incomes high enough that it was well worth it for them to pay for professional assistance in reducing their tax burden, but not so high that they could afford the custom solutions devised for the wealthiest taxpayers. Organizations were formed to fill that market gap by claiming that they would teach members tax dodging techniques used by millionaires. In effect, these were off-the-rack techniques, but at a level of sophistication that the users still needed professional help to implement them.

An example of such an organization was a group called "Americans Building Constitutionally," or "ABC,"[129] whose motto was "to help citizens of the United States make full use of the rights guaranteed them under the Constitution."[130] Representative Wright Patman, a Democrat from Texas, described ABC as "a school for tax dodging,"[131] while Representative Silvio

125 Regulation of income tax return preparers. Hearings before a subcommittee of the Committee on Government Operations, House of Representatives, Ninety-second Congress, second session, on H.R. 7590, April 13, 18; and August 15, 1972, at 1.

126 GAO Report, *supra* note 124, at 2.

127 Id. at i, 20.

128 Id. at 20.

129 Morton Mintz, *School on Tax Avoidance Facing Contempt of Congress Resolution*, WASH. POST, TIMES-HERALD, Oct. 31, 1967, at A4.

130 Id.

131 *"Tax-Avoidance" Adviser Refuses to Produce Records for Congress*, WALL ST. J., Oct. 31, 1967, at 15.

Conte, a Republican from Massachusetts, suggested the acronym should read "A Better Chance – to beat the income tax."[132] The group provided the "physicians, dentists, and other wealthy professionals" who became members "do-it-yourself seminars" on how to evade taxes through the creation of private foundations, charitable trusts, or other means.[133] These schemes were "purportedly modeled after those set up by millionaires," while being made available to "the 'average well-off citizen'" through what Patman described as "a mammoth assembly line for turning out foundations."[134] As *Time Magazine* wrote in 1968 about the foundations ABC helped to set up, "if such big shots as the Kennedys and the Johnsons could set up tax-free trusts and foundations, why couldn't the middle shots?"[135]

The goal was to effectively allow taxpayers to shift a large portion of their regular living expenses to a nominally educational or charitable foundation. Generally, the tax-exempt foundation would take over the taxpayer's business and hire the taxpayer to run it, shielding all the profits from taxation.[136] As ABC told students in their seminars, "A foundation may, under most state laws, own anything and everything that is ownable in the world,"[137] which, under this logic, included both business and professional property. Not only would profits from a taxpayer's business or profession be shielded from taxation by running their business through the foundation, but the foundation would pay or reimburse the taxpayer, as the head of the foundation, for the expenses associated with their house, office, car, and insurance. Furthermore, if the individual was self-employed, such as a physician, the foundation would become the service provider and the individual a mere employee paid at a minimal salary.[138] That would permit all fees for work performed to be paid tax-free to the foundation rather than the individual with taxes due only upon the small salary.[139]

[132] *Tax-Exempt Foundations: Their Impact on Small Businesses*, Hearings before Subcommittee No. 1 of the Select Committee on Small Business, U.S. House of Reps., 90th Cong., 1st Sess. 56 (1967) ("1967 Subcommittee Hearings").

[133] Ovid Demaris, Dirty Business: The Corporate-Political Money-Power Game 281 (1974).

[134] Mintz, *supra* note 129, at A4; 113 Cong. Rec. 28492 (1967) (statement of Rep. Wright Patman); 114 Cong. Rec. 3015 (1968) (statement of Rep. Wright Patman, quoting from Lawrence R. Gustin, *How to Organize Your Own Foundation*, Lansing, Mich. State J. (Jan. 24, 1968)).

[135] *Foundations as Easy as ABC*, 91 Time 46 (1968).

[136] *Tax Avoidance Adviser, supra* note 131, at 15; Demaris, *supra* note 133, at 282.

[137] Demaris, *supra* note 133, at 281–82.

[138] *Foundations as Easy as ABC, supra* note 135, at 46; 114 Cong. Rec. at 3015 (quoting Gustin).

[139] *Id.*

In a pitch to a group of life insurance executives in January 1967, an ABC representative reportedly described just how extensive these reimbursements could become under their proposals:

> They stated that the home, as well as his transportation, his vacation – along with his family – and all of his other major needs are supplied in the form of fringe benefits from this Foundation. Further, they stated that he would have the right, as Executive Director of the Foundation, to endow his children's college education. In fact, they stated that the Foundation would supply all the needs of himself and his family, excluding only the most personal items, such as food, clothing, cigarettes and liquor.[140]

Presumably, ABC thought it had exhibited admirable restraint by excluding "the most personal items" from expenses covered by the foundation.

Some of these ABC-guided foundations apparently did not adhere to ABC's recommended level of restraint. In one example involving a tax-exempt foundation created by physician Michael Saxton of Aurora, Illinois, his Saxton Foundation paid educational grants for his four children to go to college and paid Saxon's wife to be the "assistant medical administrator."[141] In a similar case, the D. W. Anderson Foundation, set up for a physician with the help of ABC, not only hired the physician to work as medical director and president of the foundation, but also employed his wife as vice-president, and his twenty-one-year-old daughter as secretary.[142] In another involving the St. Genevieve Foundation created by Spencer R. Collins, an accountant in Eugene, Oregon, the Foundation supported twin sisters with approximately $100,000 for serving as Collins' "companions" and, at least in the case of one of the twins, for being a caretaker of a five-bedroom mansion on Lake Oswego.[143]

The key to ABC's scheme was its contention that these foundations were charitable or educational and therefore exempt from taxation. The

[140] Letters from L. A. Krupnick to H. S. Redeker, January 10, 1967 and from H. S. Redeker to John Shannon, February 17, 1967, in Box 1557A, folder untitled, in Wright Patman Papers, Lyndon B. Johnson Library, University of Texas, quoted in JOHN A. ANDREW III, POWER TO DESTROY: THE POLITICAL USES OF THE IRS FROM KENNEDY TO NIXON 120 (2002).

[141] DEMARIS, *supra* note 133, at 282; F. EMERSON ANDREWS, PATMAN AND FOUNDATIONS: REVIEW AND ASSESSMENT 42 (1968).

[142] Leslie H. Whitten, *House Probes Seek Details: Doctor Says Foundation Slashes Taxes in Half*, BALTIMORE NEWS AMERICAN, Nov. 1, 1967, in 1967 Subcommittee Hearings, *supra* note 132, at 87.

[143] Id.; Martin A. Larson, *The Great Tax Fraud*, in 115 CONG. REC. 2838, 2842 (Feb. 5, 1969).

problem, as California Deputy Attorney General H. Warren Siegel explained in 1969, was that they "never really intended it to be set up exclusively for charitable purposes."[144] For example, the Robert O. Hayes Foundation of Grand Blanc, Michigan, which was set up by one of the founders of ABC, Robert D. Hayes, made charitable contributions in one year of $2 each to the Easter Seals, the American Cancer Society, and the Muscular Dystrophy Association.[145] All recognized charities, to be sure, but seemingly a paltry exchange for the tax dodging the scheme permitted.[146]

While ABC's claims may have seemed too good to be true, its methods still attracted plenty of interest. In 1966–1967 alone, ABC reportedly had 800 members.[147] Given the cost structure, this was not an insignificant commitment for these individuals. There were apparently three levels of membership. There was what was called an "educational membership" for individuals that charged $1,050 and entitled the educational members to attend a thirty-hour seminar on foundations.[148] If the educational members wanted actual instruction on the legal procedures and documents necessary to set up the foundations ABC discussed in its seminars, that cost an additional $4,200. Most people who took advantage of this second level of membership sent their lawyers for that additional training on how to set up their own foundations.[149] If a member then paid an additional $5,250, for a total cost of $10,500, they would be a full member, which would entitle them to information on more complex transactions, such as setting up ownership trusts.[150] According to IRS Commissioner Sheldon Cohen, the membership numbers may have been inflated,[151] but even half that number would have been high for a single tax dodging scheme. Moreover, ABC's program not only attracted

144 *A Taxing Experience*, 94 TIME 57 (1969).

145 *Foundations as Easy as ABC*, *supra* note 135, at 46.

146 When asked about the size of the donations, Hayes explained, perhaps tongue-in-cheek, "when somebody comes around to the door for a donation, most people will give a buck. With the foundation approach, we can do a little better." 114 CONG. REC. at 3015 (quoting Gustin, *supra* note 134).

147 House of Representatives, *Final Report of the Select Committee on Small Business pursuant to H. Res. 53: A Resolution Creating a Select Committee to Conduct Studies and Investigations of the Problems of Small Business*, 90th Cong., 2nd Sess. 74 (Dec. 31, 1968) ("1968 Subcommittee Report"); Demaris, *supra* note 133, at 282.

148 ANDREWS, *supra* note 141, at 41; 1967 Subcommittee Hearings, *supra* note 132, at 99 (Testimony of Robert D. Hayes).

149 Id.

150 Id.

151 ANDREWS, *supra* note 141, at 45.

laymen interested in dodging taxes, but it also got the attention of tax professionals. The Practicing Law Institute held a session in its conferences for tax lawyers on private foundations entitled "The 'ABC' Foundation Plan: Magic Formula or Sham?"[152] It is possible that some in attendance answered the conference session's question with the former and used that formula for their own clients without involving ABC.

ABC's methods soon came under attack. In October of 1967, the House Small Business Subcommittee on foundations convened hearings to investigate charges that ABC was involved in the "mass production of tax-dodging foundations."[153] According to the Subcommittee, one trustee of ABC explained that

> the purpose of ABC . . . is to "Henry Fordize" the tax-dodging specialties that were once associated only with millionaires. If a Rockefeller, Ford, or Mellon can avoid taxes under the guise of "charity," why shouldn't every doctor, lawyer, and other professional in the land who can afford the rather stiff tuition (at least $10,500) for the tax-ducking school? It is a harsh but logical question.[154]

Early the next year, the House Ways and Means Committee also investigated ABC and other foundations as part of Representative Wright Patman's "seven-year personal crusade to make foundations accountable."[155] From Patman's perspective, the concern was not just with ABC and its attempt "to mass-produce the tax-dodging specialties that were once associated only with millionaires,"[156] but that its tactics would inspire imitators. As Patman warned, "if ABC continues to operate, and, if its success is what I think it could be, other groups will undoubtedly go into the same business."[157] This focus on the risks of ABC, however, had the side effect of ensnaring less extreme attempts to use the tax-exempt foundation as a home for businesses with charitable aims. For example, tax professionals such as the accounting firm Touche Ross, which had developed a research and charitable fund for physicians

152 Bryon F. Calame, *Nine Tied to Group Fostering Tax-Sidestep Foundations Indicted for Theft and Fraud*, WALL ST. J., July 25, 1968, in 1968 Subcommittee Report, *supra* note 147, at 76, 78.

153 113 CONG. REC. 28491 (Oct. 10, 1967) (title of section in which Rep. Patman announced the start of the hearings).

154 1968 Subcommittee Report, *supra* note 147, at 74–75.

155 Peter Frumkin, *Strangled Freedom*, 64 AM. SCHOLAR 590, 591 (1995); *2 Tax Avoidance School Officials Invoke 5th Amendment at Hearing*, WASH. POST TIMES HERALD, Nov. 15, 1967, at A2; Mintz, *supra* note 129, at A4.

156 113 CONG. REC. at 28492 (statement of Rep. Patman).

157 Id.

volunteering their time at Chicago's Cook County Hospital, had their application for a private letter ruling on the proposed organization held up because of the Congressional spotlight on the abuses associated with the use of tax-exempt organizations.[158]

In response to the hearings and a "barrage" of inquiries from Patman, the Internal Revenue Service also began investigations into ABC and its abuse of tax-exempt private foundations.[159] Commissioner Cohen reported that the Service could not find any evidence that ABC itself had applied for exempt status or that any foundation established under ABC's program was properly registered with the Service.[160] State attorneys general in California, Illinois, and Michigan also commenced investigations of whether members of ABC were using their state-chartered trusts and foundations improperly,[161] with three of the ABC trustees indicted in the California case and eventually found guilty of grand theft.[162]

The revelations about ABC may have been the catalyst for legislative action on the question of reforming the tax treatment of private foundations more broadly.[163] The Subcommittee on Small Business warned in its report that "this tax-dodging scheme will snowball among professional and upper middle income groups, unless meaningful reforms are instituted in the foundation field very soon," while Patman warned that "tax-exemption foundations would be as 'commonplace in this country as bath-tub distilleries were during the Prohibition Era.'"[164] The Subcommittee concluded that "if reforms are ignored, the Nation may be faced with a 'revolt' among those taxpayers who are unable to take advantage of such contrivances." Heeding these warnings, Congress enacted a variety of reforms designed to shut down the specific tactics by the ABC organization as part of the Tax Reform Act of 1969.[165]

158 William G. McMillan, *Double Return on Volunteer Medical Services*, 14 TEMPO 24, 25 (1968) in the Deloitte Collection at the University of Mississippi.

159 ANDREW III, *supra* note 140, at 120; Frumkin, *Strangled Freedom*, *supra* note 155, at 591; *2 Tax Avoidance School Officials Invoke 5th Amendment at Hearing*, WASH. POST TIMES HERALD, Nov. 15, 1967, at A2; Mintz, *supra* note 129, at A4.

160 ANDREW III, *supra* note 140, at 120.

161 *Michigan Investigates 15 Charitable Trusts that are Unregistered*, WALL ST. J., Nov. 6, 1967, at 8.

162 1968 Subcommittee Report, *supra* note 147, at 76; NANCY BECK YOUNG, WRIGHT PATMAN: POPULISM, LIBERALISM, & THE AMERICAN DREAM 211 (2000).

163 ANDREW III, *supra* note 140, at 120.

164 1968 Subcommittee Report, *supra* note 147, at 81; 113 CONG. REC. 28492 (1967) (statement of Rep. Patman).

165 Frumkin, *supra* note 155, at 590–91.

Nevertheless, little was done to regulate "tax dodging schools" as a means of marketing tax schemes directly to individuals, which persists even to this day.[166]

## Tax Dodging "Textbooks"

Lawyers and their clients did not have to shell out over $10,000 to learn how to dodge taxes. Publishers were eager to capture a share of the market for tax advice and they did not hide the nature of the books they published in this area. In 1958, attorneys Sydney Gutkin and David Beck published the book, *Tax Avoidance v. Tax Evasion.*[167] The book, which the *Wall Street Journal* featured in a column on recommended reading for businessmen,[168] reviewed and categorized 250 litigated tax cases to help identify the "criteria for distinction" between legal tax avoidance and illegal tax evasion and what would be likely to result in civil fraud penalties or criminal prosecution.[169] The *Journal* highlighted the fact that the book offered "various steps to avoid corporate and individual taxes," in what it called the endless "cat-and-mouse game" between taxpayers and the government.[170] Duquesne University accounting professor Albert Raizman said it was "refreshing to find a source of information that completely covers the realm of what has been done to reduce taxes and at the same time gives proper methods that practitioners may follow to achieve those ends."[171] Raizman characterized it as a "How to Solve it Book," which provided taxpayers and their counsel a step-by-step presentation of a "complete tax avoidance plan."[172]

For a book that appeared to go beyond a "complete tax avoidance plan," a reader could consult Prentice-Hall's *Encyclopedia of Tax Shelter*

[166] *See, e.g.*, Anna Scott Farrell, *Tax Avoidance School Operators Owe $93K, 9th Cir. Says*, LAW360.COM, April 21, 2023 (discussing a case involving the non-payment of taxes by the operators of a business called the "Freedom Law School," which taught individuals tax avoidance techniques through conferences and multi-level marketing schemes).

[167] SYDNEY A. GUTKIN & DAVID BECK, TAX AVOIDANCE V. TAX EVASION (1958).

[168] *Reading for Business: Deep in the Heart of Taxes*, WALL ST. J., Dec. 16, 1958, at 13 (reviewing SYDNEY A. GUTKIN & DAVID BECK, TAX AVOIDANCE V. TAX EVASION (1958)).

[169] Id.

[170] Id.

[171] Albert I. Raizman, *Book Review*, SIDNEY A. GUTKIN & DAVID BECK, TAX AVOIDANCE V. TAX EVASION (1958), 20 U. PITT. L. REV. 722 (1959).

[172] Id. at 723.

*Practices*, which was published in 1963.[173] One reviewer, Arthur Custy, a law professor at the University of Mississippi, called it "the first all-inclusive omnibus of tax shelter methods and techniques contained in one volume."[174] Another reviewer wrote that "the book goes into considerable detail to explain the nearly infinite variety of tax strategies that have been successfully used 'by taxpayers in all walks of life to slash their tax bills.'"[175] As the review continued, "it contains something for everyone. Tax shelters are described for the businessman, executive, investor, individual wage earner, and the family."[176] The encyclopedic nature of the book was "designed to offer the attorney a carefully treated and detailed analysis of suggested alternatives which," it claimed, "will assist him in implementing the plans of his clients in reducing their tax bill."[177] According to Professor Custy, the book even offered attorneys a "methodology to assist him" in taking a "calculated risk approach" in making a decision about which alternative to pursue.[178]

## Self-Help Resources

For taxpayers who were interested in a less expensive and more accessible source of tax advice, an industry developed to provide do-it-yourself resources. In 1936, publisher Simon & Schuster, published a book for taxpayers who sought to prepare their tax returns on their own, authored by tax lawyer Hugh Satterlee and attorney and accountant I. Herman Sher, titled *Your Income Tax*.[179] By 1939, accountant J. K. Lasser took over the book and established its brand.[180] With the expansion of the tax base during World War II, demand soared. Millions of copies of Lasser's book were sold to the taxpaying public and it quickly rose to the top of the bestseller lists.[181] After the Revenue Act of 1941 was enacted, which

173 Prentice-Hall Editorial Staff, Encyclopedia of Tax Shelter Practices (1963).
174 Arthur B. Custy, *Recent Books: Encyclopedia of Tax Shelter Practices*, 35 Miss. L.J. 337 (1964).
175 John O. Dyrud, Jr., *Book Notes: Encyclopedia of Tax Shelter Practices*, 21 Bar Bulletin (New York) 136, 137 (1963).
176 Id.
177 Custy, *supra* note 174, at 338.
178 Id. at 340.
179 Hugh Satterlee & I. Herman Sher, Your Income Tax (1936).
180 Mark Murray et al., *Pioneer Specialists*, J. Accountancy, May 31, 2012.
181 Id.; *Books on Income Taxes Being Read These Days*, Chi. Daily Trib., Jan. 22, 1941, at 14.

lowered exemptions and added as many as five million new taxpayers to the income tax,[182] the book sold 150,000 copies in less than a month.[183] It was not only popular, but the book received critical acclaim. The *Washington Post* wrote that "of all the 'self-help" books published in America, 'Your Income Tax" by J.K. Lasser is undoubtedly the most useful."[184] By the middle of the 1940s, the annually updated *Your Income Tax* had sold seven million copies and it has remained popular to this day.[185] Even after Lasser's premature death in 1954,[186] his J. K. Lasser Tax Institute continued producing new books to meet the popular demand for tax dodging assistance. In 1957, for instance, the Lasser Tax Institute published special reports entitled *How to Build Tax Sheltered Income and Capital: 58 Valuable Tax Saving Ideas in the Fields of Investment, Pay, Business, and Interfamily Arrangements* and *How Trusts Can Save You Income, Estate, and Gift Taxes,*[187] which the *Wall Street Journal* identified as books of special interest to its readers.[188]

These self-help guides were promoted as life preservers for the average taxpayers. Lasser and his publisher Simon & Schuster heavily promoted the book in newspapers and other publications around tax time. As Lasser explained, while the "phantasmagoria of exemptions, deductions, graduated surtax brackets, computations of capital gains and losses, percentages piled on nets and all those other minutiae … are designed to make sure the distribution of the tax burden is equitable," in most cases they result in the reverse with "most of these inequities fall[ing] upon the lower-bracket taxpayers."[189] "Year after year," Lasser lamented, "the inequities have mounted – inequities most often in favor of the well-off and against the poor."[190] As Lasser explained, "too many people don't know what deductions they are allowed on their taxes. Or, very often, they are too timid for

[182] STEVEN A. BANK, KIRK J. STARK, AND JOSEPH J. THORNDIKE, WAR AND TAXES 91–92 (2008).

[183] *Tax Guide Sales Heavy*, N.Y. TIMES, Nov. 6, 1941, at 21.

[184] S.N., *Why Tax Your Arithmetic Too?* WASH. POST, Dec. 26, 1948, at B7.

[185] Robert J. Cole, *Personal Finance: The Tax Preparers*, N.Y. TIMES, Feb. 4, 1974, at 41. The book continues to be published today. J. K. LASSER'S YOUR INCOME TAX 2025: FOR PREPARING YOUR 2024 TAX RETURN (2024).

[186] *J.K. Lasser Dies; Expert on Taxes*, N.Y. TIMES, May 12, 1954, at 31.

[187] J.K. LASSER TAX INSTITUTE, HOW TO BUILD TAX SHELTERED INCOME AND CAPITAL (Business Reports, 1957); J.K. LASSER TAX INSTITUTE, HOW TRUSTS CAN SAVE YOU INCOME, ESTATE, AND GIFT TAXES (Business Reports, 1957).

[188] William Peterson, *Reading for Business*, WALL ST. J., Dec. 26, 1957, at 4.

[189] J. K. Lasser, *A Plea for the Small Taxpayer*, N.Y. TIMES, March 2, 1947, at 128.

[190] Id.

their own good."[191] Not surprisingly, Lasser was called "a guardian angel to thousands who are bewildered by the income tax."[192]

While Lasser poked fun at individual taxpayers who took the call for tax equity to excess, he also inadvertently publicized how prevalent tax dodging had become. In one column for the *New York Herald Tribune*, Lasser recounted the tales of taxpayers who claimed questionable deductions, such as (1) "the bigamist who listed all three of his wives as dependents," (2) a businessman who was caught by a hotel detective in a late night dalliance with someone he claimed to be his secretary, but who was really his wife, or (3) the wife who pretended to be a secretary at her husband's business until, as Lasser explained, "the illusion crumbled when the wife interrupted a discussion between her husband and the revenue agent to inquire, 'Dear, where is the ladies' room?'"[193] Lasser advised taxpayers not to try these moves themselves, but only after noting that "the only bright spot" at income tax time "is those blessed deductions."[194]

For taxpayers who wanted their tax planning tips in more bite-sized portions, there were plenty of options. Magazines emerged in the postwar period to serve the broad new market in personal finance. One of the first was *Kiplinger Magazine: The Changing Times*, which began publication in 1947.[195] It ran regular columns, offering tax advice, often in response to reader questions.[196] Although most of its responses hewed closely to the statute and administrative guidance, it sometimes offered more aggressive tax dodging tips, such as in one column where it recommended that you should "make your child a partner in your business" in order to "shift part of the business income into your child's lower tax bracket."[197]

191 J. K. Lasser, *Watch Your Tax Deductions*, L.A. TIMES, Feb. 29, 1948, at G8.

192 *Books to Help You on Income Tax Return*, CHI. DAILY TRIB., March 3, 1946, at B4.

193 J. K. Lasser, *Fun on March 15th*, NEW YORK TRIBUNE/HERALD TRIBUNE, March 5, 1950, at SM19.

194 Id.

195 PAUL CROSTHWAITE, PETER KNIGHT, NICKY MARSH, HELEN PAUL and JAMES TAYLOR, INVESTED: HOW THREE CENTURIES OF STOCK MARKET ADVICE RESHAPED OUR MONEY, MARKETS & MINDS 208 (2022).

196 *See, e.g., Your Income Tax*, CHANGING TIMES: THE KIPLINGER MAGAZINE, April 1961, at 16; *It's Income Tax Time*, CHANGING TIMES: THE KIPLINGER MAGAZINE, Feb. 1959, at 7.

197 *Start Now to Save on Taxes*, CHANGING TIMES: THE KIPLINGER MAGAZINE, Aug. 1960, at 33, 34.

Newspapers began running regular columns or series on tax tips, either separately or as part of a general personal finance section.[198] For example, in the tax help installment of a series entitled "Your Money Problems," which ran in the *Cincinnati Enquirer* in 1954, economist Merryle Rukeyser started by reminding readers that "while tax evasion is illegal, 'tax avoidance' – properly done – is every man's privilege," before proceeding to offer tips on capital gains, home offices, tax-exempt bonds, and expense accounts.[199] Similarly, in a regular column entitled "Money Talks" in the *Philadelphia Tribune*, Mark Dungee of the investment firm King, Merritt & Co. informed readers about a conference his employer had held where a "nationally known tax savings authority" spoke about the tax advantages of living trusts.[200] In another column, Dungee explained that "we are greeted with innumerable ideas from practically every quarter as to how tax savings may be achieved," noting that because of this newfound tax literacy "the typewriter salesman ... inquires whether you have fully depreciated your old equipment" and "an automobile man may recommend that you lease rather than buy your car for tax reasons."[201] The *Chicago Tribune* offered a similar column described as an "Investors' Guide," but many of its tips involved tax dodging strategies, such as selling stocks with an eye to matching gains against losses and keeping track of short-term and long-term holdings.[202] In 1969, this column was used to explain the type of loopholes relied upon by the 154 millionaires who reportedly escaped income tax altogether that year, helping to lead to the creation of the alternative minimum tax.[203] Finally, accountant N. R. Caine, a New York-based accountant and tax advisor, wrote a column for the *Los Angeles Times*

[198] The *Wall Street Journal's* "Tax Report" first appeared in the spring of 1941, but this was focused primarily on legislative and regulatory developments, rather than tax dodging tips. *Tax Report: A Special Summary and Forecast of Federal and State Tax Developments*, WALL ST. J., Apr. 2, 1941 at 1. *See* Richard J. Tofel, *The Man behind the Wall Street Journal*, WALL ST. J., Nov. 10, 2008, at A19 (crediting Barney Kilgore with inventing the new Tax Report column as part of a series of changes to remake the paper during "11 whirlwind months in 1941.").

[199] Merryle S. Rukeyser, *Your Money Problems: Keep Books, Trim Taxes*, CINCINNATI ENQUIRER, Dec. 8, 1954, at 33.

[200] Mark A. Dungee, Jr., *Money Talks*, PHILA. TRIB., Aug. 25, 1959, at 5.

[201] Mark A. Dungee, Jr., *Money Talks: Does the Idea Fit?*, PHILA. TRIB., Oct. 17, 1959, at 5.

[202] William Bromage, *Income Tax Savings Can Be Effected through Stock Switching: Investors' Guide*, CHI. TRIB., Nov. 13, 1967, at E10; *Year-End Tax Policy*, CHI. TRIB., Nov. 1, 1947, at 23.

[203] William Bromage, *Tax "Loopholes": Investors' Guide*, Chi. Trib., Aug. 31, 1969, at B7.

that specifically focused on tax planning.[204] In one example from 1953, Caine advised readers to "try to conform any transaction in which [a taxpayer] expects to realize taxable income to the shape of a sale of a long-term capital asset," which Caine noted, "will reap the benefit of the 'ceiling' tax rate on long-term capital gains."[205] In describing what underlay most tax dodging schemes of this era, Caine noted that "in contrast to ordinary income tax rates which may range to astronomical heights (92% in the top bracket), the rate of tax on the profit from the sale of a long-term capital asset may never exceed 26%."[206] In another column, Caine advised readers with rental property to "consider the possible tax and estate planning advantages that he would gain by incorporating the property" in exchange for "stocks and interest-bearing bonds."[207] Caine went on to provide fairly sophisticated advice as to how the corporation could purchase insurance on the life of the taxpayer, use a reverter trust to accumulate interest on the bonds to pay for a child's education "under extremely low tax rates," and use the corporation to hold dividend-paying stock and take advantage of the dividends-received deduction.[208]

Perhaps as evidence of the penetration of tax advice columns throughout the country, they appeared in so-called "Black newspapers," which had "had a monopoly on minority news" for over a century.[209] In 1951, for example, the *Philadelphia Tribune*, "the oldest continuously circulating black newspaper in the United States ... in one of the largest urban black communities in the country,"[210] invited Lasser to write a series of columns with tax savings advice. Over the course of ten articles, Lasser wrote columns entitled "Save Money Legally on Your Income Tax," with individual columns subtitled to cover topics such as the deduction of interest, joint returns,

204 Caine was apparently so successful in publicizing his services indirectly through his column that he opened a branch office in Los Angeles in 1953. *Caine Opens L.A. Office*, L.A. TIMES, Dec. 2, 1953, at A12.

205 N.R. Caine, *High Premium Placed upon Transaction Tax Planning*, L.A. TIMES, Feb. 1, 1953, at A18.

206 Id.

207 N. R. Caine, *Tax Advantages for Who Incorporates Told*, L.A. TIMES, Sept. 21, 1958, at A15.

208 Id.

209 Henk La Brie III, *Black newspapers: The Roots are 150 Years Deep*, 4 JOURNALISM HIST. 111 (1977).

210 V.P. Franklin, *"Voice of the Black Community:"* The Philadelphia Tribune, *1912–1941*, 51 PA HIST: A J OF MID-ATLANTIC STUD. 261, 261 (1984).

storm losses, the timing of reporting interest, deductions for uniforms and work clothes, and the medical expense deduction.[211] These were practical advice columns drawing upon Lasser's book, *Your Personal Income Tax*, and designed to induce the readers of the paper to purchase the book.

Other newspapers targeting the black community ran tax advice columns like the ones written by Lasser, but they were authored by local tax experts from the black community. For example, the *Baltimore Afro-American* ran a column authored by Jay McRae and George Russell.[212] The authors were described as "tax consultants," which may have meant that they were tax preparers or that they did not want to list their professional qualifications and run afoul of professional advertising restrictions.[213] Notably, unlike in Lasser's columns for the *Philadelphia Tribune*, McRae and Russell's column was accompanied by a picture of the authors.[214] This may have been to establish that they were members of the community and therefore could be trusted. In that sense, there may have been a shared desire to dodge taxes in both the white and nonwhite communities, but not a shared trust of the experts dispensing that advice in each community.

Not surprisingly, the turn to self-help guides led to self-help tax dodging. While the wealthy were availing themselves of the technically legal methods crafted by sophisticated tax lawyers and accountants to

211 *See e.g.*, J. K. Lasser, *Save Money Legally on Your Income Tax: How You Can Increase Your Medical Expense Deduction*, PHIL. TRIB., Feb. 10, 1951, at 4; J. K. Lasser, *Save Money Legally on Your Income Tax: You Can Usually Deduct Your Uniform and Work Clothes Expenses*, PHIL. TRIB., Feb. 17, 1951, at 4; J. K. Lasser, *Save Money Legally on Your Income Tax: Donations in Property You Can Deduct*, PHIL. TRIB., Feb. 20, 1951, at 4; J. K. Lasser, *Save Money Legally on Your Income Tax: How You Can Estimate Your Deductible Taxes*, PHIL. TRIB., Feb. 24, 1951, at 4; J. K. Lasser, *Save Money Legally on Your Income Tax: When You Can Claim That You Support a Dependent*, PHIL. TRIB., Feb. 27, 1951, at 4; J. K. Lasser, *Save Money Legally on Your Income Tax: Your Stom Losses are Deductible*, PHIL. TRIB., March 3, 1951, at 4; J. K. Lasser, *Save Money Legally on Your Income Tax: You Get Some Deductions in Addition to the Standard Deduction*, PHIL. TRIB., March 6, 1951, at 4; J. K. Lasser, *Save Money Legally on Your Income Tax: You Can Deduct Interest That You Paid*, PHIL. TRIB., March 10, 1951, at 4; J. K. Lasser, *Save Money Legally on Your Income Tax: You Can Choose the Year to Report U.S. Savings Bond Interest*, PHIL. TRIB., March 13, 1951, at 4; J. K. Lasser, *Save Money Legally on Your Income Tax: What You Should Know About Joint Returns*, PHIL. TRIB., March 17, 1951, at 4.

212 *See, e.g.*, Jay G. McRae & George L. Russell, *Timely Advice for Taxpayers: If You Pay Too Much It's Your Own Fault*, BALTIMORE AFRO-AMERICAN, March 1, 1952, at 22K.

213 Id.

214 Id.

dodge taxes, the less well-to-do, according to former New Deal advisor Raymond Moley, "fashion do-it-yourself methods of cheating."[215] William Hoffman, a professor at the University of Texas, observed that "the unhappy part about so much of the so-called tax planning is that it is carried out by the taxpayer alone and without professional guidance. Sometimes it is the product of some high sounding 'do-it-yourself' tax pamphlet that makes every taxpayer a self-styled expert in return for the publisher's list price."[216] This sometimes resulted in what Hoffman described as "second-hand" tax advice where "tax planning may consist of an attempt on the part of the taxpayer to apply to himself the 'gimmicks' that work so well for his neighbor."[217]

Moreover, even those who did seek out professional help had become sophisticated enough to shop around for what they wanted to hear. Moley recounted the story of a lawyer in a rural farming area who explained that "he lost many clients because he prepared for them what he considered honest returns."[218] Apparently not liking what he was planning to file on their behalf, "the clients marched over to another lawyer whose morality rested on another plane."[219]

The Internal Revenue Service offered do-it-yourselfers advice to undercut some of the tax planning advice offered by the unscrupulous. One method was to have area officials speak to the community about legitimate means of reducing their tax burden. In an example of this, Thomas McHugh, chief of the audit division of the Louisville, Kentucky division of the IRS, assured the local Real Estate Board that the government recognized that "everyone is interested in saving on taxes."[220] McHugh then pointed to a few ways of "legitimately reducing tax liability," such as selling capital assets instead of ordinary income-producing assets to lower the applicable tax rate and selling on an installment basis to defer income.[221]

215 Raymond Moley, *Tax Burden Causing Morality Breakdown*, L.A. TIMES, Feb. 25, 1959, at B4.

216 William H. Hoffman, *The Theory of Tax Planning*, 36 THE ACCT'G REV. 274, 277 (1961).

217 Id. at 277.

218 Moley, *supra* note 215, at B4.

219 Id.

220 Morgan Lawson, *Don't Overpay Taxes, I.R.S. Auditor Advises*, COURIER-JOURNAL, Feb. 7, 1960, at 5.

221 Id.

## Tax Protesters

A final source of tax advice was more pernicious and potentially subversive than the fly-by-night retail tax preparers or the without-a-net self-help columns or books. Tax protestors in America have been around since the founding,[222] but "organized tax resistance" at the local level "grew astronomically" in the early years of the Great Depression.[223] At the federal level, however, the tax protestor movement grew to be more organized and influential in the 1950s alongside the growth in the tax base and the decline in the support for the continuing high wartime rates.[224] By taking advantage of the general disquiet about the new, and growing, tax burden, tax protestors spread their general anti-tax philosophies and may thereby have encouraged blatant tax dodging.

Prior to World War II, the tax protestor movement sought unsuccessfully to repeal the Sixteenth Amendment.[225] In the years that followed, however, many tax protestors had moved on from that crusade to one that sought to limit the reach of federal taxes by pushing for constitutional limits on taxation and arguing why individuals were not obligated to pay income taxes.[226] Activists pushed state legislatures to pass resolutions in favor of the proposed federal constitutional limit on taxation and support for such resolutions "swelled" during this period, with eight state legislatures endorsing the resolution in 1952 alone and mainstream groups such as the US Chamber of Commerce, the American Legion, the National

[222] Michael J. Graetz , The Power to Destroy: How the Antitax Movement Hijacked America 2 (2024).

[223] Martha B. Brissette, *Tax Protest and Tax Reform: A Chapter in the History of the American Political Process*, 187 J. L. & Pol. 187 (1988); Linda Upham-Bornstein, "Mr. Taxpayer versus Mr. Tax Spender": Taxpayers' Associations, Pocketbook Politics, and the law During the Great Depression 35 (2023).

[224] Lawrence Zelenak, Learning to Love Form 1040: Two Cheers for the Return-Based Mass Income Tax 41 (2013). *See* Arthur Acevedo, *Abusive Tax Practices: The 100-Year Onslaught on the Tax Code*, 17 Barry L. Rev. 179, 187 (2012) (describing the increasing number and sophistication of tax protester cases).

[225] Isaac William Martin, Rich People's Movements: Grassroots Campaigns to Untax the One Percent 68–89 (2013); Nathan J. Hochman, *Tax Defiers and the Tax Gap: Stopping "Frivolous Squared" Before it Spreads*, 20 Stan. L. & Pol'y Rev. 69, 71 (2009). *See, e.g.*, Porth v. Broderick, 214 F.2d 925 (10th Cir. 1954) (rejecting the argument that the 16th Amendment was unconstitutional because it subjected individuals to involuntary servitude in violation of the 13th Amendment).

[226] Martin, *supra* note 225, at 102–03; *Tax Protest Movement*, Anti-Defamation League.

Association of Manufacturers, and the American Bar Association all offering their voices in support of it as well.[227]

Tax protesters engaged in misinformation campaigns, using pamphlets and town meetings to spread their antitax gospel.[228] During the war, Robert Dresser and the Committee for Constitutional Government fought against the progressive income tax by drafting a pamphlet that they intended to "have the country seeded" with one million copies.[229] Vivien Kellems, who publicly announced that she had refused to pay her taxes, engaged in what amounted to a speaking tour in what she called her "one-woman Westport tea party" to encourage people to similarly resist the income tax by sending teabags to their representatives in Congress instead, appearing before civic groups in places ranging from small towns such as Marshall, Texas, to bigger cities such as Kansas City and Los Angeles.[230] This use of pamphlets and town meetings evolved into CDs and, eventually, social media as the tax protest movement sought to teach others how to avoid paying income taxes.[231] Historian Romain Huret observed that "tax resisters ... drew inspiration from tapping into a popular antitax literature comprised of newsletters, popular books, and conservative pamphlets."[232] "All these publications," Huret continued, "helped [tax resisters] formulate their opposition to progressive taxation in a moralistic way."[233]

Although tax protesters or resisters were in the minority,[234] some of the half-truths and general sentiments of the tax protester movement may have seeped into the popular consciousness of a public eager to find methods and a legitimate basis for not paying taxes. Even the nonpayment of taxes by a small minority of people can break down social norms in favor of payment. As Professor Richard Lavoie observed in discussing the growing appeal of the Tea Party movement in the early 2000s, "a societal belief in the existence of a taxpaying norm can be undermined ... by the

227 MARTIN, *supra* note 225, at 102–03, Figure 4.1.

228 Hochman, *supra* note 225, at 70.

229 MARTIN, *supra* note 225, at 98 (quoting Dresser, *Brief in Support of Proposed Constitutional Amendment*, 9 15; Committee for Constitutional Government, *A Ceiling on the Power to Destroy You by Taxation*).

230 MARTIN, *supra* note 225, at 114–16; GRAETZ, *supra* note 222, at 13.

231 Donald J. Furman et al., *Tax Resistance: How the Internet has Impacted Tax Resistance and the Tax Gap*, 8 J. THEORETICAL ACCT'G RES. 1, 7 ((2013).

232 ROMAIN D. HURET, AMERICAN TAX RESISTERS 7 (2014).

233 Id. at 196.

234 Id. at 207.

non-taxpaying norm of a subgroup gaining wider acceptance."[235] Indeed, Vivien Kellems' public transformation from someone accused of disloyalty during World War II to a great patriot by the early 1970s reflected the extent to which her brand of tax resistance, and the tax dodging generally, had gone mainstream over this period.[236]

235 Richard Lavoie, *Patriotism and Taxation: The Tax Compliance Implications of the Tea Party Movement*, 45 Loy. L.A. L. Rev. 39, 51 (2011).

236 Olivier Burtin, *"A One-Woman Tea Party": Tax Resistance, Feminism, and Conservatism in the Life of Vivien Kellems*, 28 J. Pol'y Hist. 162, 163–64 (2016).

# 5

## Advertising Tax Dodging

Tax advisors may have helped a meaningful percentage of taxpayers to dodge their taxes, but advertising was a far more powerful medium in mid-century America for signaling the rising respectability of tax dodging. Publicity and advertising provided exposure and exposure helped to demystify, destigmatize, and normalize tax dodging. Although stories about the high-profile tax dodging described in the previous section provided exposure too, advertising suggested that it was not something only available to the rich and famous. Advertising alone may not have changed attitudes toward tax dodging, but it mirrored and reinforced changes in social attitudes toward the practice.

This chapter examines both display and classified advertisements in five large circulation newspapers from 1935 through 1970 – the *Chicago Tribune*, *Los Angeles Times*, *New York Times*, *Wall Street Journal*, and *Washington Post* – to identify advertisements for the kinds of tax dodging services or products described in the previous chapter or that were provided in connection with the sale of other services or products, such as an investment advice. The newspapers are all national in scope, while still allowing for regional differentiation. A separate study was conducted over the same period for newspapers in the ProQuest Historical Black Newspapers database. This offered a check on whether the trends observed in the first sample extended to a set of newspapers where national advertising was less common and where the penetration of tax advisers and attitudes toward tax dodging may have been different. In both cases, the period was designed to provide perspective on the difference between advertisements before and after World War II, which is a critical dividing line in the scope and reach of the income tax.

One difficulty is defining what counts as a "tax dodging" advertisement. Advertising tax return preparation services alone, especially after World War II when so many people were required to file income tax returns for the first time, is not enough even if that tax return preparation might have included some discussion of methods to reduce your tax bill.

Therefore, this chapter examined advertisements that went beyond tax return preparation to include services or promises such as offering guidance in "shaping your affairs to incur the least possible taxes,"[1] or offering to help you make "adjustments in your portfolio" to reduce your tax burden.[2] As in the discussion of the concept of "tax dodging," the focus is on advertisements encouraging individuals to engage in tax planning to minimize, avoid, or maybe even evade, their tax liabilities, or offering to help them "find" deductions they may not have realized existed, rather than merely to report their income. It is not an exact science, but the point is less to demonstrate precisely the amount of the increase, but more to demonstrate the trend and to examine how the nature of the advertisements, including what they offered and claimed, changed over the time period.

As this chapter will demonstrate, tax advisers found ways to get the word out about tax dodging opportunities before World War II, but advertising itself was controversial and the smaller base of taxpayers, the limited circle of tax advisors they consulted, and the political attacks on tax dodging made it an unwise strategy to advertise more publicly. In the post–World War II period, however, as more people were made subject to taxation and tax advisors proliferated, advertising for tax dodging services and opportunities exploded. This both increased tax dodging's exposure beyond what the public saw in the news stories and associated it with planning ahead rather than with scandal and Treasury enforcement actions.

## Pre–World War II

As seen in Figure 5.1, tax planning advertisements before World War II were rare, only increasing slightly during the War itself. The annual number of advertisements for tax planning services posted in national newspapers between 1935 and 1945 was in the single digits. In most years, there were no more than three in any newspaper in an individual year and in 1937, when President Franklin D. Roosevelt's bill to address tax dodging was under consideration, there were none at all. Given the public reactions to some of the fairly mundane types of tax planning exposed in the Pecora Hearings in 1934 and the expansive definition of tax evasion held by political leaders such as Roosevelt and Morgenthau, it

[1] Display Ad 29, N.Y. Times, Dec. 28, 1936, at 34.

[2] Display Ad 10, *Can you make a 1951 Tax Savings?*, Wash. Post, Dec. 11, 1951, at 12.

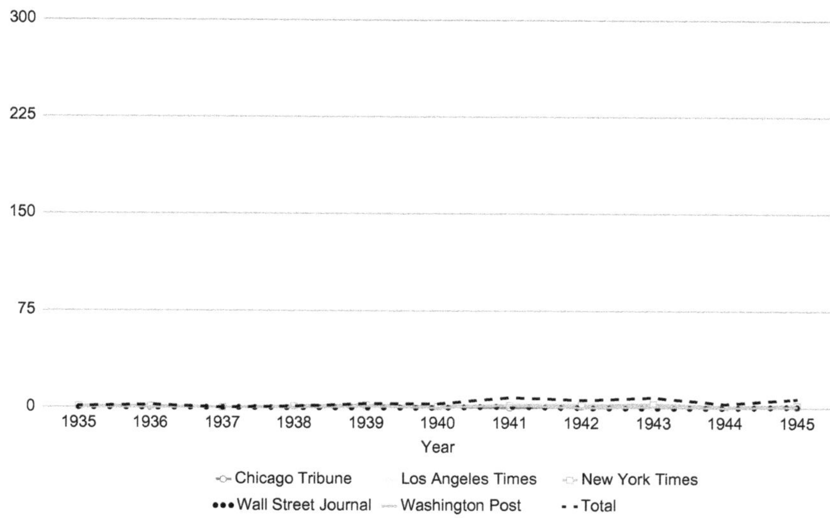


**Figure 5.1** Tax planning advertisements by year 1935–1945

was not surprising that advisers were not publicly advertising their tax planning prowess.

Part of the reason that advertisements for tax planning services were so rare prior to World War II is that advertising itself was disfavored in respectable circles. Critics argued that advertising was designed to deceive, to mislead, and to prompt unnecessary consumption.[3] Some even went so far to call it a "social evil" in light of the many "patent medicines, frauds, and quack doctors" peddling fake cures in the newspapers and elsewhere.[4] In the 1920s, Herbert Hoover reportedly declared in his response to a proposed bill to regulate the commercial use of broadcasting that "the American people would not stand for advertising on the air."[5]

Academics were equally skeptical about the benefits of advertising. This was especially true during wartime. Indeed, Amherst professor Colston E. Warner, in his capacity as president of the Consumer's Union,

[3] Harold Chapman Brown, *Advertising and Propaganda: A Study in the Ethics of Social Control*, 40 INT'L J. OF ETHICS 39, 40 (1929).

[4] Maurice I. Mandell, A History of the Advertising Council 15 (1953) (unpublished Ph.D. dissertation, Indiana University).

[5] Erwin W. Fellows, *"Propaganda:" History of a Word*, 34 AM. SPEECH 182, 186 n. 23 (1959) (quoting Hoover).

submitted a petition signed by two hundred professors calling for government to end advertising altogether, ostensibly on the grounds that it used energy, newsprint, and manpower as well as "stimulating buying" that could create inflation.[6] Classical and neoclassical economists only saw a need for so-called "constructive" advertising, which told consumers where to find goods, rather than "competitive" advertising that tried to convince consumers to buy some product or service, which they viewed as a "social waste."[7] As University of Oklahoma Economics Professor Floyd Vaughan wrote in 1928, "some of the results of advertising, such as crudity of advertisements themselves, creation of disutility, goods v. leisure, harmful consumption, sale of competitive goods regardless of intrinsic merits, sale of a less desirable class of goods, and excessive stimulation of consumption, have caused a poorer satisfaction of wants."[8] With advertisers primarily focused on enriching themselves without much care about consumer welfare, it was characterized as being subject to "flagrant abuses," including "a great deal of advertisement which falls short of economic justification because of the dishonest use or inefficiency so gross as to constitute grounds for indictment on sheer waste."[9]

If advertising was controversial generally, it was particularly controversial for professionals in the legal and accounting fields. Although lawyer advertising was accepted, if not fully embraced, in the nineteenth century,[10] by the turn of the century it had become heavily disfavored. In the American Bar Association's original Canon of Ethics, adopted in 1908, Canon 27 stated that "solicitation of business by circulars or advertisements, or by personal communications, or interviews, not warranted by personal relations, is unprofessional."[11] State bar ethics committees and

[6] Philip Salisbury, *Has Advertising Come of Age?* 8 J. of Marketing 25 (1943).

[7] Hector Lazo, *What Shall We Do About Advertising?* 25 J. of Marketing 22 (1961).

[8] Floyd L. Vaughan, Marketing and Advertising: An Economic Appraisal 17 (1928). *Compare* Fred E. Clark, *An Appraisal of Certain Criticisms of Advertising*, 15 Am. Econ. Rev. 5, 5–7 (1925) (discussing and rejecting this and other criticisms from economists).

[9] W. D. Moriarity, *An Appraisal of the Present Status of Advertising*, 15 Am. Econ. Rev. Supp. 23, 25 (1925).

[10] Geoffrey C. Hazard, Jr., Russell G. Pearce, & Jeffrey W. Stempel, *Why Lawyers Should Be Allowed to Advertise:" A Market Analysis of Legal Services*, 58 N.Y.U. L. Rev. 1084, 1084–85, n. 2 (1983). This was a bit of a reversal from the colonial period when lawyers brought over the English legal tradition against advertising. Catherine M. Harris, *Note, Solicitors' Right to Advertise: A Historical and Comparative Analysis*, 15 Ga. J. Int'l & Comp. L. 317, 332 (1985).

[11] American Bar Association, *Canons of Professional Ethics* 27 (adopted Aug. 27, 1908), *reprinted in* 33 A.B.A. Rep. 566, 569 (1908).

their professional canons also came out against lawyer advertising. In 1914, for example, the Committee on Legal Ethics and Grievances of the State Bar of Georgia, reporting on some "very reprehensible" practices among some lawyers seeking business in the bankruptcy courts, quoted its former chair, Judge Samuel B. Adams, stating that "there is no room for debate on the proposition that a lawyer cannot seek business or employment. ... A lawyer who seeks business is therefore a forsworn man – is a lawbreak – and publishes the fact that he is a proper subject of disbarment. We cannot exaggerate the unworthiness and perniciousness of this evil."[12]

Given such attitudes, it was not surprising that advertising and its close cousin of solicitation were rejected by the legal community. Julius Henry Cohen, Chairman of the Committee on Unlawful Practice of Law of the New York County Lawyers' Association, noted in 1916 that advertising "is condemned by the professional canons of ethics, penal codes, Bar associations and the courts, and the lawyer who indulges in such practices subjects himself at once to professional discipline and advertises by his conduct not his worth and character, but his complete failure in both."[13]

By 1924, almost all state bar associations and their legal ethics committees had either adopted the ABA's Canon of Ethics, and therefore its Canon against lawyer advertising, or had adopted their own version of a ban on lawyer advertising.[14] The Canon did permit lawyers to use business cards and identify if they specialized in certain traditionally distinct practice areas, but taxation was not one of the identified specialties, which John Maguire, a long-time Harvard law professor, called "distinctly questionable," noting that "in no other field of the law can fumbling cause more grief to clients or, it may be added, to governmental authorities."[15] The ban on lawyer advertising at the national level continued when the American Bar Association reaffirmed the canons and adopted a Code of Profession Responsibility in 1969.[16] It was not until 1977, when the Supreme Court struck down the ban in *Bates v. Arizona State Bar* that lawyer advertising

[12] Julius Henry Cohen, The Law: Business or Profession? 177 (1916) (quoting Report, State Bar Association of Georgia 269 (1914)).

[13] Id. at 190.

[14] James M. Altman, *Considering the ABA's 1908 Canons of Ethics*, J. Prof. Law. Symp. 235, 236 (2008).

[15] John Maguire, *Conscience and Propriety in Lawyer's Tax Practice*, 13 Tax L. Rev. 27, 34 (1957). Even lawyers who also held CPA licenses were prohibited from identifying that qualification on their business card, which Maguire called "highly formalistic" given "the intermingling practices of accountancy and law in matters of taxation." Id.

[16] Altman, *supra* note 14, at 235, n.2.

was permitted.[17] Even years later, state restrictions on certain kinds of lawyer advertising remained on the books.[18]

Unlike in the legal profession, advertising was more accepted in accounting, although it remained controversial. In 1914, the *Journal of Accountancy* asked the question "Should Accountants Advertise?"[19] The Journal's editor explained that "one of the most frequently discussed topics before the public accountants of the country is the extent to which it is ethical or desirable to advertise."[20] It invited several prominent accountants to present their views on the question.[21] All were to some degree sympathetic with the need to advertise, with E. G. Shorrock noting that "unless and until it is dealt with in a broad and intelligent way by state societies or the American Association, separately or in conjunction, individual advertising, with whatever evils may attend it, will continue."[22] Nevertheless, they acknowledged the problems advertising posed if accountants wanted to establish themselves as a profession. John Alexander Cooper warned accountants not to act like "a class of unscrupulous, scheming, self-laudatory, pettifogging, barratrous, customseeking, money-making advertising lawyers who cause the blush of shame to rise to the face of those exalted characters who are ever conscious of the dignity and ethical demands of their profession."[23]

In the early 1920s, two then-rival accounting organizations – the American Society of Certified Public Accountants (ASCPA), primarily comprised of local and regional accountants from the Midwest, and the American Institute of Accountants (AIA), which was controlled by accountants for the larger, more established, elite accounting firms in the big cities on the East Coast – were involved in a "harsh fight" over, among other things, the AIA's Code of Ethics' restriction on the ability of its members to engaged in advertising of their services.[24] The AIA's ban

[17] Bates v. Arizona State Bar, 433 U.S. 350 (1977).

[18] Nat Stern, *Commercial Speech, "Irrational" Clients, and the Persistence of Bans on Subjective Lawyer Advertising*, 2009 B.Y.U. L. Rev. 1221 (2009).

[19] *Should Accountants Advertise?* 18 J. of Accountancy 85 (1914).

[20] Id.

[21] Id. (the accountants asked to write columns in answer to the question posed by the journal were John Alexander Cooper, Edward E. Gore, and E. G. Shorrock)

[22] *Should Accountants Advertise?*, *supra* note 19, at 100, 108 (guest column of E. G. Shorrock).

[23] *Should Accountants Advertise?*, *supra* note 19, at 89 (guest column of John Alexander Cooper).

[24] Mindy Herzfeld, *The Role of Professional Organizations in Practice and Policy: How Lawyers Overtook Accountants and Economists in the Early 20th Century Tax Field*, 75

on advertising was prompted as an immediate matter by a desire to pre-empt Treasury from enacting its own, likely more stringent, prohibition on advertising.[25] More broadly, however, it was motivated by a general desire to professionalize accounting, which meant in part following the example of the American Bar Association, which had codified "the custom of members of the legal . . . profession of refraining from advertising their services" by adopting a ban on advertising by lawyers in its membership.[26]

Small town midwestern accountants viewed the AIA's decision to ban advertising by individual accountants "as deliberate constraints on the expansion of their practices" to protect the larger firms against competition.[27] The objection was that the ban still permitted the kind of institutional advertising engaged in by the large firms to which many of its individual members were associated. Under the AIA rules, members could "advertise accountancy without reference to the accountant."[28] This allowed the large elite accounting firms to advertise their firms as long as they did not "promot[e] personal attainments" of individual accountants associated with the firm.[29] Meanwhile, AIA leaders cast aspersions at the objections, with A. P. Richardson, the secretary of the AIA, criticizing "the little fellows starting out in the world" who "yearn to see their names in print, even at so much a word or an agate line, and they are fond of saying that they should be allowed to advertise because they are not well known."[30]

Although the ban remained in effect despite these objections, accountants did find ways to get some publicity. Under the original AIA Code enacted in 1917 and subsequent iterations enacted in the following few years, accountants were permitted to post a small

TAX LAW. 79, 100 (2021); Diane Roberts, *Socialization of U.S. Novice Accounting Professionals Through Ethical Discourse 1931*, 42 ACC'T HISTORIANS J. 63, 64, 69 (2015).

25 Roberts, *supra* note 24, at 69; GARY JOHN PREVITS & BARBARA DUBIS MERINO, A HISTORY OF ACCOUNTANCY IN THE UNITED STATES 248 (1998).

26 *Should Accountants Advertise?*, *supra* note 19, at 94 (guest column of Edward E. Gore). This was motivated by a desire to become more accepted as a "profession," rather than a mere "occupation." As one accounting professor explained in a conference on the subject, "contempt" for accounting was "well-nigh universal." *Respectable Occupations*, SATURDAY EVENING POST, April 16, 1927, at 30.

27 Ram S. Siriam & Gloria Vollmers, *Reexamination of the Development of the Accounting Profession – Critical Events from 1912–1940*, 24 ACC'T HISTORIANS J. 65, 74 (1997).

28 Roberts, *supra* note 24, at 78.

29 Id.

30 A. P. RICHARDSON, THE ETHICS OF A PROFESSION 66 (1931) (published under the auspices of the American Institute of Accountants). Richardson was the secretary of the American Institute of Accountants.

advertisement, known as a "card," with "name, title, and address."[31] The AIA's Committee on Professional Ethics routinely investigated complaints about infractions involving the ban on advertising, but, as the Committee stated in its 1929 Annual Report, most instances were not found to involve a willful evasion and the punishment was limited to asking the offending party to conform with the rules in the future.[32] By 1931, however, after ridicule and defections from the association over the ban,[33] the AIA had loosened its rules and accountants were permitted to print advertisements in newspapers or magazines as long as limited to contact information, professional affiliation, and practice areas.[34]

Perhaps more significantly, accountants managed to evade the restrictions on newspaper advertisements with other methods that may have been more effective substitutes for advertising. Under the AIA rules, they were permitted to mail letters that contained "self-laudatory" language.[35] The assumption was that these types of letters were primarily being sent to personal friends and clients, but it became the "greatest area of abuse" of the advertising restrictions because accountants ended up mass-producing circular letters that were "sent indiscriminately through the mails."[36] Making matters worse, the circulars often solicited business "based wholly or partly upon contingent fees" according to a Report of the AIA's Special Committee on Professional Advancement.[37] Richardson compared "the circulars with which every morning mail is burdened" to "poison gas" that was expected to wander around and "penetrate where the personal solicitor or even the newspaper advertisement might not be heard or seen."[38]

In one circular, the accountant suggested that he could cut a company's tax liability in half.[39]

31 Id. at 61.

32 *Report of the Committee on Professional Ethics*, in 1929 YEARBOOK OF THE AMERICAN INSTITUTE OF ACCOUNTANTS 165, 166 (1929).

33 PREVITS & MERINO, *supra* note 25, at 248.

34 Roberts, *supra* note 24, at 78.

35 Id.

36 Id.

37 American Institute of Accountants, Report of Special Committee on Professional Advancement 4 (1921), in Deloitte Collection, University of Mississippi ("AIA Special Committee Report").

38 RICHARDSON, *supra* note 30, at 71.

39 AIA Special Committee Report, *supra* note 37, at 6

Dear Sir:

A prominent —— manufacturer in your district has requested us to bring our service to your attention. He believes the reason we have not closed a contract with your concern is due to the fact that you do not know what we can accomplish for you.

Why does this executive speak so frankly? He knows that we have canceled 50% of his tax, amounting to many thousands of dollars, at a minimum expense of about 25%. The system that we installed for him protects his interests – decreases his clerical expense nearly 25% – has obtained twice the information as given by his former methods. He knows the profit that he is making monthly and thru charted comparisons he knows more about his plant than ever before. There's a reason we have produced results, i.e., DOLLARS.

Our special proposition will do the same for you. Let us show you a few of the many letters received from clients proving our statement. It matters but little whether or not you have filed your Federal Tax Returns for the past year and have perhaps paid the first installment. If we find conditions warrant, it may be possible for us to cancel the other installments as they come due.

Our policy of rendering accounting to a selected clientele enables us to give special attention to each client. Your name has been recommended by the executive referred to in the first part of this letter, and if you will advise office just when you will be ready for an interview, the writer will call personally to present our proposition in definite form. Yours very truly,

This led the AIA Special Committee to suggest "the writer seems to have lost all sense of decency and wanders in a world of imagination."[40] The mention of being referred to the recipient by another company made it appear that this was not a widespread "cold call"-type solicitation, but for all intents and purposes it was exactly that.

By the 1930s, circulars were a common way for both accountants and lawyers to "privately" advertise tax dodging methods to each other without running afoul of either the bans on professionals advertising in newspapers or the bias against advertising generally. According to accountant William Layman, the Revenue Act of 1936 and its undistributed profits tax reportedly promoted "increasing numbers of circulars in the mail of attorneys, accountants, and corporation executives purporting to show many ways of

[40] Id.

effecting reduced tax liability under the revenue laws."[41] In 1937, lawyer Randolph Paul reported in his *Restatement of the Law of Tax Avoidance* that "the mills bring each week circulars," containing "[n]otices of lawyers, accountants, and tax consultants [who] speak luringly of reducing taxes and procuring refunds.[42] In one example, Paul described "a recent advertising circular [that] speaks of nearly 50 tax avoidance methods, covering practically the entire field of the income tax."[43]

It was not just lawyers and accountants who authored such circulars. Nor were they any more professional because of their targeted distribution. According to Paul, "Banks are constantly distributing for the benefit of their clients, pamphlets on the minimization of taxes."[44] "One recent pamphlet," Paul explained, "states that the 'attitude of the courts is traditionally favorable to the taxpayers and that the courts impose no penalty on a taxpayer who seeks to avoid a tax rather than evade it.'"[45] Paul remarked on this statement in understated fashion, suggesting that "the taxpayer who relies upon such a summary of the law on this subject courts trouble."[46] This deluge of circulars continued throughout the decade. In 1940, NYU Law Professor Harry Rudnick wrote that "the mails are flooded with circulars advertising books and services telling them how to save income taxes."[47]

One way that lawyers and accountants were able to get their names in the newspaper in advertisements for their tax prowess before World War II was by publishing an income tax guide. For example, as discussed in the previous chapter, advertisements for the income tax guide entitled *Your Income Tax* started appearing in the late 1930s.[48] The advertisements for the original edition written by attorney Hugh Satterlee and attorney and accountant I. Herman Sher sometimes included their biographies, which recounted their credentials with the N.Y. Bar and associated tax committees, as well as their past experience and writings.[49] Sometimes, however, the advertisements for

41 William N. Layman, *Some Suggestions for Reducing Income Tax Liability*, 14 TAX MAG. 575 (1936).
42 Randolph E. Paul, *Restatement of the Law of Tax Avoidance*, in STUDIES IN FEDERAL TAXATION: TAXATION WITHOUT MISREPRESENTATION 9, 77, n. 261 (1937).
43 Id. at n. 261.
44 Id.
45 Id.
46 Id.
47 Harry J. Rudnick, *The Problem of Personal Income Tax Avoidance*, 7 L. & CONTEMP. PROBS. 243 (1940).
48 *See Display Ad 8*, CHI. TRIB., Feb. 17, 1936, at 9.
49 Id.

this book were done in such a way as to omit the author information and biographies entirely, such one from the department store Marshall Field & Company.[50] The book, which was only published under Satterlee and Sher's names in 1936 and revised by Sher in 1937,[51] was revived by accountant J. K. Lasser in 1939, but advertisements for this new edition omitted his biography and sometimes his name altogether.[52]

Outside of these circulars and income tax guides authored by lawyers and accountants, most tax planning-related advertisements that were published during this earlier period were issued by investment firms or the first wave of tax preparers under the new wartime tax measure. They were relatively modest in their claims. One example was an advertisement from Clinton Gilbert & Co., an investment firm and a member of the New York Stock Exchange, which appeared in the *New York Times* in 1939.[53] This advertisement did put "Income Tax Savings" in bold and at the top, so there was no doubt that it was trying to attract the attention of readers by appealing to their interest in dodging taxes. Nevertheless, the actual content of the advertisement was fairly tame, merely pointing out that taxpayers could change their mix of investments to reduce their taxes, presumably to take advantage of the different tax treatment of investment assets held for more or less than eighteen months and between eighteen months and two years or over two years under a law that went into effect in 1938.[54] Moreover, although the advertisement offered to provide tax planning advice through some materials it had prepared, it was using tax advice as a means of inducing individuals to trade in securities, rather than attempting to profit from tax advice directly.

In another, perhaps bolder, advertisement from 1936, a Chicago investment firm promised readers a "Profit Opportunity . . . on how to minimize your 1936 income tax by stock or bond 'Tax-Loss' sales."[55] Even this, however, was published as a classified advertisement, making it both smaller and less noticeable than a display advertisement.

Most advertisements were more conservative in their promises, such as one from an investment firm offering to help customers "obtain the tax

[50] *Display Ad 5*, CHI. TRIB., March 10, 1936, at 6.

[51] *Books: Bugaboos Laid*, TIME MAG., Feb. 20, 1939; *Paperbacks: Dingbats*, N.Y. TIMES, March 23, 1975, at 259; *Display Ad 69*, N.Y. TIMES, March 1, 1937, at 38.

[52] *Display Ad 4*, CHI. TRIB., Feb. 19, 1939, at 4; *Display Ad 66*, N.Y. TIMES, Sept. 21, 1941, at E8.

[53] *Display Ad 170*, N.Y. TIMES, Nov. 5, 1939, at 64.

[54] *See* R. S. Jessup, *Capital Gains and Losses Since 1922*, 17 TAXES 333 (1939) (explaining the new scheme).

[55] *Classified Ad 11*, CHI. TRIB., Dec. 9, 1936, at 34.

savings allowed by the law,"[56] and another from a tax preparer advising readers "pay what you should, no more. Don't evade the law. Chances are we can help you save."[57] Others were simply advertisements for tax guides,[58] with some focused on estate taxes, which would have been of more interest to clients of investment firms than ordinary taxpayers,[59] or corporate taxes, which would have been of more interest to businesses.[60]

## Post–World War II

As seen in Figure 5.2, the total number of tax planning advertisements took off during the postwar period, increasing more than fiftyfold in less than a decade and rising another five times over that through the 1960s. Although the increase was more pronounced in the *New York Times* and the *Los Angeles Times*, perhaps reflecting the size of their respective tax advising communities and investment industries, the trend is evident in all five newspapers.

The rise in tax dodging advertisements was not because advertising had suddenly become more acceptable after World War II. Indeed, there was renewed criticism of it. A 1947 study by Harvard Professor Neil Borden on *The Economic Effects of Advertising* highlighted this in its opening:

> Advertising is under fire. Its adverse critics come from many camps and their complaints tend to become increasingly vehement. Certain economists complain that its extensive use involves undue costs and is a bar to

56 *Display Ad 71*, N.Y. Times, Nov. 14, 1943, at S7. *Compare Display Ad 90*, Wall St. J., Oct. 18, 1945, at 15 (offering "a selected list of security exchanges for those who wish to establish tax profits or losses.").

57 *Display Ad 22*, Atl. Const., Jan. 13, 1943, at 9.

58 *See, e.g.*, Display Ad 21, Wall St. J., Sept. 2, 1937, at 9 (Minimizing Taxes on Incomes and Estates, by Lowe and Wright).

59 *Display Ad 88*, N.Y. Times, Jan. 12, 1936, SM22 (advertising the book Federal Taxes, on Estates, Gifts, and Trusts, 1935–36); *Display Ad 30*, L.A. Times, June 2, 1937, at A20 (headline was "Minimizing Your Taxes – Your Will – or the Tax Collector's," but the advertisement only offered to supply inquirers with two articles from Barron's about estate taxes); *Display Ad 29*, L.A. Times, June 2, 1937, at A19 (same, but offering two provide all eight articles from the Barron's series, including those about income taxation); *Display Ad 23*, L.A. Times, Mar. 3, 1938, at A14 (offering to help with "planning estates for tax savings").

60 *Display Ad 43*, N.Y. Times, Nov. 5, 1936, at 47 ("What to do about . . . the new surtax on corporations"); *Display Ad 12*, N.Y. Times, Nov. 19, 1936, at 13 (advertising a new book by Sher on the new corporation tax).

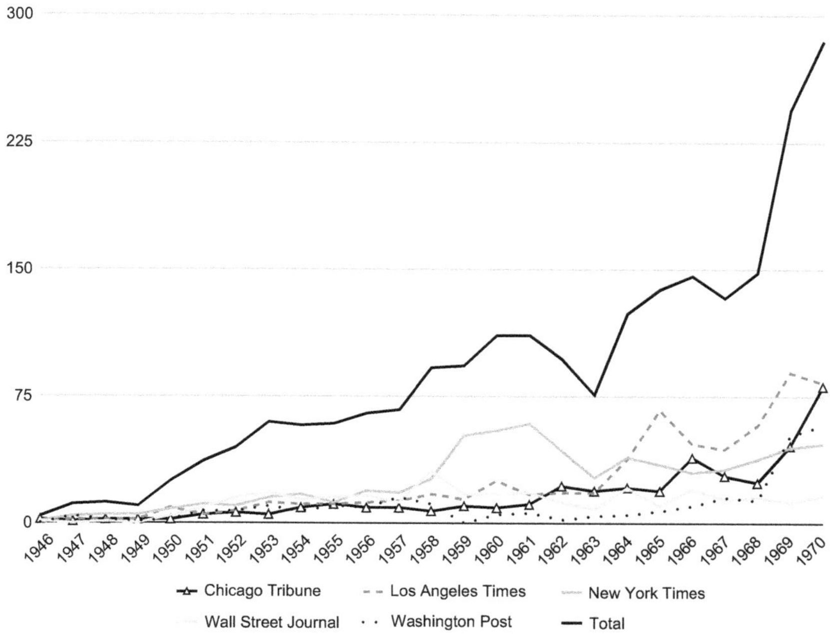


**Figure 5.2** Tax planning advertisements by year 1946–1970

> free competition, with a resultant adverse effect on the operation of the free price system. Home economics teachers charge it with being a poor guide to consumption. Students of ethics accuse it of showing frequent display of poor taste and misrepresentation. Businessmen themselves have not infrequently doubted its effectiveness for business purposes.[61]

This was not mere idle criticism. Advertising was "facing very stern scrutiny by the various federal regulatory and judicial bodies and an ominous storm of public criticism because of certain abuses."[62] In 1951 alone, the Federal Trade Commission had issued orders against "such major advertisers as Sterling Drug, Bristol-Meyers, Emerson Drug, P. Lorillard Company, Reynolds Tobacco Company, Miles Laboratories, American Tobacco Company, and many others" for deceptive trade practices.[63] One contemporary observer wrote that "seldom has

[61] NEIL H. BORDEN, THE ECONOMIC EFFECTS OF ADVERTISING 3 (1947).

[62] Arthur Kroeger, *Book Review, Advertising at the Crossroads*, 17 J. OF MARKETING 331 (1953).

[63] MAX A. GELLER, ADVERTISING AT THE CROSSROADS: FEDERAL REGULATION VS. VOLUNTARY CONTROLS 258 (1952). The regulatory attention on pharmaceutical

a major area of marketing been subject to so much criticism, self-abasement, and general condemnation as has advertising in recent years."[64]

The rise in tax dodging advertisements cannot be attributed to a rapid increase in newspaper advertising expenditures at the end of the war. Although there was a steady growth in advertising expenditures in the second half of the twentieth century, the growth during the 1950s and 1960s was comparatively modest.[65] For professionals, advertising largely continued to be disfavored. Some certified public accountants were "engaged in public relations, advertising, and lobbying" by the 1950s to the consternation of senior leaders in the field,[66] but the same was not true for lawyers. Advertising bans remained in place under most state bar rules.

Notwithstanding such advertising bans, lawyers found alternative ways to promote tax shelters and other tax dodging devices. Typically, this involved helping to legitimize tax dodging schemes developed by others or developing schemes themselves for the use of taxpayers who were not their clients. In 1958, Mortimer Caplin explained that many tax dodging schemes were promoted by a "tax broker," or "a person who, for a commission, solicits sales and deals which depend upon a tax quirk for their validity."[67] Although tax brokers were generally not an individual taxpayer's advisor in a legal sense, they often were lawyers or consulted with lawyers who contributed to the promotional material. The tax brokers tried to convince wealthy individuals and their professional advisors to invest in their tax dodging schemes "through personal contacts, paid advertisements, and repetition of many of their plans in publications and in the press."[68]

In one example, columnist George Sokolsky wrote about a pamphlet he received entitled "Tax and Business Benefits Offered by the Bahamas," which was authored by an attorney from New York and another attorney

companies, in particular, reflected an inter-agency battle between the Federal Trade Commission and the Food and Drug Administration on the question of jurisdiction over advertising. Vince A. Kleinfeld, *Applicability of the Federal Food, Drug, and Cosmetic Act to Drug Advertising*, 5 FOOD DRUG COSMETIC L. J. 45, 46 (1950).

64 Lazo, *supra* note 7, at 22.

65 Robert G. Picard, *Shifts in Newspaper Advertising Expenditures and their Implications for the Future of Newspapers*, 9 JOURNALISM STUD. 704, 713 (Fig. 16) (2008).

66 Michael E. Doron, The End of the Disinterested Profession: American Public Accountancy 1927–1962 96 (Ph.D. dissertation 2009).

67 Mortimer M. Caplin, *Symposium: Federal Taxation, 1958: Threats to the Integrity of our Tax System*, 44 VA. L. REV. 839, 842 (1958).

68 Id.

from the Bahamas.[69] As Sokolsky points out, the attorneys who authored the pamphlet were not actually providing legal advice for any individual: "The Pamphlet tells you that your tax avoidance must be bona fide, which your lawyer, I'm sure, will show you how to do."[70] Caplin had a similar observation: "the public seems to be barraged with information about new 'tax shelters' or 'tax havens' designed primarily for tax avoidance" and tax brokers seemed to be at the root of that publicity campaign.[71]

While lawyers and accountants had to navigate their ethics rules to find ways to advertise their services, the retail tax preparation industry was largely unregulated.[72] This was one source for the expansion in advertisements. With the drop in the World War II-era exemption amount and the advent of retail tax advisers like H&R Block, taxpayers were annually "inundated with advertisements urging them to utilize various tax preparation services."[73] Many of these tax preparation service advertisements, however, made claims or promises that were arguably misleading or concerning. The Federal Trade Commission prosecuted a complaint against H&R Block for false or deceptive advertising related to a series of radio, television, newspaper, and periodical advertisements that promised to pay any penalty or interest resulting from an error in the preparation of a tax return.[74] The FTC's concern was that the advertisements may have misled consumers into thinking that H&R Block would pay the cost of the higher tax due as well. Consider the text of the following television commercial cited in the FTC complaint:

> We guarantee accurate preparation of every tax return. If we make any errors which cost you penalty or interest, we will pay that penalty or interest.
>
> That's the H &R Block guarantee.
>
> I'm John Cameron Swayze with some plain talk about H & R Block.
>
> They feel when you pay for their service, you are entitled to complete satisfaction.
>
> If Block's service falls short through no fault of yours, they must accept that responsibility at no additional cost to you.
>
> So, it's little wonder over 8 million Americans will trust their tax returns to

[69] George Sokolsky, *How to Get Rich*, WASH. POST & TIMES HERALD, Oct. 15, 1957, at A13.

[70] Id.

[71] Caplin, *supra* note 67, at 842.

[72] Patricia A. Ryan, *Tax Preparation Agencies: What is Needed for the Public's Protection?* 13 B.C. INDUS. & COMM. L. REV. 895 (1972); PREVITS & MERTINO, *supra* note 25, at 329.

[73] Ryan, *supra* note 72, at 895.

[74] In the Matter of H&R Block, Inc., 80 F.T.C. Decisions 304 (1972).

H & R Block this year. You should, too.
H & R Block – A good place to place your confidence.[75]

The FTC concluded that H&R Block "directly or by implication" represented that it would "reimburse the taxpayer for any payments the taxpayer may be required to make in addition to his initial tax payment, if such additional payment results from an error . . . in the preparation of the tax return."[76] This and other questionable "industry solicitation practices" led observers to conclude that "taxpayers need protection from . . . misleading advertising practices" in the tax return preparation industry.[77]

Tax advisers and promoters were not the only ones to advertise, and thereby publicize, tax dodging. In some cases, those seeking tax dodging opportunities placed advertisements themselves. For example, businesses with taxable income often sought to find a way to generate losses to offset that income. One quick way to do that, which was permitted at the time, was to acquire a corporation that had large net operating loss carryforwards and no income against which to take a deduction from those losses or to find a corporation where the investment in its assets far exceeded the current values of those assets.[78] In the former case, the acquired business' losses could be used to offset the acquiring business' income, while in the latter case the acquirer could sell off the acquired business' assets to generate a capital loss that it could use to offset its own capital gains.

The problem was finding a business to acquire that possessed the necessary tax attributes. In the post–World War II era, some businesses solved that problem by taking a page from the personal ads section and simply placing a classified advertisement in the newspaper. In one example, an advertisement in the *Wall Street Journal* read "WANTED: Loss Corporation," and specified that the losses must amount to a "minimum carry-over [of] one million dollars."[79] According to one report from 1943, "the going rate for loss carry-over corporations was 25 per cent of the amount of the loss,"[80] suggesting that if that rate had

[75] Id. at 306.
[76] Id. at 307. H&R Block entered into a consent decree with the FTC as a result of the complaint, agreeing to cease and desist from such practices. Id. at 310–11.
[77] Ryan, *supra* note 72, at 908–09. *See* John D. Morris, *False Advertising Laid to H&R Block*, N.Y. TIMES, July 1, 1971, at 1.
[78] Harry J. Rudick, *Acquisitions to Avoid Income or Excess Profits Tax: Section 129 of the Internal Revenue Code*, 58 HARV. L. REV. 196, 197 (1944).
[79] *Classified Ad 24*, WALL ST. J., March 20, 1957, at 19.
[80] Rudick, *supra* note 78, at 197.

continued throughout the period then the business that placed this advertisement was willing to pay at least $250,000 for the acquisition. The only attempt at subtlety was that the advertisement asked that responses be provided "in confidence" to a mail box in care of the *Journal*.[81] There were similar advertisements placed throughout the mid-century period, often specifying the industry to help ensure that a court would allow the losses to be used by the acquirer,[82] but expressing indifference as to whether it was operating.[83]

The advertisements also went in the opposite direction, with the owners of corporations that held losses or other useful tax attributes advertising for a potential acquirer who could use its tax benefits. In one example, the owner of a motion picture production company located in a tax haven jurisdiction placed a classified advertisement seeking a buyer. "TAX FREEDOM GUARANTEED," the advertisement claimed for the company that had "no assets, no liabilities, no trading."[84] Presumably, the owner had formed the corporation and secured tax protection for twenty-five or thirty years, making the corporate shell valuable for someone seeking to move their film business there.

During World War II, after Congress' adoption of an excess profits tax,[85] advertisements started to appear for businesses interested in transactions that would reduce their liability for the new tax. Under the tax, one of the methods taxpayers could choose to segregate the "normal" from the "excess" profit was called the invested capital method, which was triggered at a rate of return on a certain amount of invested capital.[86] Therefore, acquiring a corporation that had a large amount of invested capital was valuable for its ability to increase the amount of profits the corporation could earn without incurring excess profits tax liability. In one example, an advertisement was placed in the *Wall Street Journal* seeking to acquire the stock of another corporation.[87] The text did not mention anything about the tax benefits of the acquisition, but it specified that the desired corporation should have "original invested capital of

81 *Classified Ad 24*, *supra* note 79, at 19.

82 *See, e.g.*, *Classified Ad 65*, N.Y. TIMES, July 8, 1957, at 31 ("WANTED! Loss corporation: woodworking field").

83 *See, e.g.*, *Classified Ad 99*, N.Y. TIMES, Feb. 27, 1956, at 43 ("WANTED: Loss corporation in Glass or Allied field; active or inactive").

84 *Classified Ad 103*, WALL ST. J., Jan. 23, 1970, at 15.

85 See STEVEN A. BANK, KIRK J. STARK, & JOSEPH J. THORNDIKE, WAR AND TAXES 87–90 (2008) (discussing the adoption of the excess profits tax).

86 Id. at 87–88.

87 *Display Ad 41*, WALL ST. J., July 15, 1943, at 11.

several hundred thousand dollars with present assets at nominal values."[88] That was considered a dead giveaway that this acquisition was motivated by the desire to dodge excess profits tax liability.[89] The desired target corporation could provide the invested capital to help reduce the proportion of profits subject to excess profits tax and potentially the high asset basis and low value that would allow the acquirer to buy it for a low price and then sell or liquidate it to generate tax losses it could use to offset its taxable income. In another example from the *New York Times*, a corporation with high unused losses sought to find an acquirer, marketing itself not by its future prospects, but by the potential to use its losses to reduce its excess profits tax liability.[90] The advertisement was headlined with the words "EXCESS PROFITS TAX SAVINGS OPPORTUNITY," and indicated it was selling "stock of corporation having 1943 tax loss deduction of $120,000" and its "sole assets are $80,000 in cash and equivalent."[91]

With Congress' adoption of the Excess Profits Tax Act of 1950, advertisements for businesses related to the excess profits tax reappeared. In one such example from 1952, someone advertised the sale of a Tennessee manufacturing plant.[92] Although the advertisement did mention that its square footage and other attributes that were presumably positive for business reasons, it put in bold capital letters that it had "GOOD EXCESS PROFITS TAX BASE" and added that the plant had a "$100,000 loss carry over for year ending June 30, 1952."[93] In another example, an investment firm advertised a special report recommending the purchase of railroad corporation stock because "large invested capital affords good excess profits tax shelters."[94]

Not only did the number of advertisements hawking tax dodging opportunities grow, but they became increasingly bolder. For example, although advertisements for J. K. Lasser's *Your Income Tax* appeared before World War II, they followed the pattern of the tax advertisements of the time, such as one from 1940 that promised only to "make sure you overlook nothing to which you are justly entitled."[95] By the 1950s, Lasser

88 Id.
89 Rudick, *supra* note 78, at 196.
90 *Classified Ad 3*, N.Y. Times, Oct. 31, 1943, at S11.
91 Id.
92 *Classified Ad 24*, Wall St. J., April 11, 1952, at 9.
93 Id.
94 *Display Ad 194*, N.Y. Herald Trib., Dec. 3, 1950, at A8.
95 *See, e.g.*, *Display Ad 4*, Chi. Trib., Feb. 19, 1940, at 4.

had branched into much more explicit books on tax dodging and the advertisements for the books made no attempt to hide this. In 1954, Lasser's book *Tax Shelter for the Family* claimed to provide the "new methods of providing 'tax shelter' – many of which have just been opened up by the big new Eisenhower tax law."[96] In 1956, an advertisement for Lasser's new book called *Treasury of Tax Saving Ideas* identified "the four cornerstones of tax shelter upon which your financial success depends," including tax shelters for business, for pay, for investments, and for family."[97]

Moreover, unlike the prewar years, more of the advertisers appeared to be selling tax-beneficial investments rather than using tax advice to sell the underlying investments. An advertisement for a guide called *Tax Sheltered Investments* highlighted "Oil Investments for Tax Shelter," while also promoting tax shelters in a wide variety of areas such as real estate, cattle, timber, citrus, and mining.[98] It promised high after-tax returns "even in drilling on wildcat" land,[99] which generally refers to land where the risk of finding nothing is great because the well is merely exploratory.[100] The advertisement promised that the tax savings will drive the promised return of "27% of gross receipts TAX FREE, year after year."[101] And if that was not clear enough, the advertisement claimed that the guide would provide "full details of all of these unusual and successful methods of building your personal assets WITHOUT suffering high taxes on ordinary income."[102]

Tax dodging advertisements also spread beyond the financial sections of the largest newspapers. There was an advertisement in the *Baltimore Sun* for investments in real estate syndications claiming to be an "excellent tax shelter" that was sandwiched between advertisements for a 1960 Plymouth Valiant and another for "Free Fill Dirt."[103] *The Austin Statesmen* included a classified advertisement titled "TAX SHELTER" for one-bedroom apartments in the university area next to an

96 *Display Ad 179*, N.Y. TIMES, Nov. 21, 1954, at F8.
97 *Display Ad 596*, N.Y. TIMES, May 13, 1956, at 152.
98 *Display Ad 76*, WALL ST. J., March 13, 1956, at 22.
99 Id.
100 Rachel Curtis, *What is the Difference between an Exploratory Well and a Production Well?* THE INST. FOR ENERGY AND ENVIRONMENTAL RESEARCH OF NORTHEASTERN PENNSYLVANIA, March 25, 2011. *See* WILLIAM J. CASEY & J. K. LASSER, TAX SHELTERED INVESTMENTS 90 (1952) ("one out of 9 wildcat holes hit oil or gas").
101 *Display Ad 76*, *supra* note 98, at 22.
102 Id.
103 *Display Ad 65*, THE BALTIMORE SUN, Aug. 12, 1960, at 38.

advertisement from someone wanting to trade a $500 house trailer for a small Lake Austin lot.[104]

Perhaps as further evidence of the democratization of tax dodging that characterized this era, the new wave of advertisements offered to let regular folks in on the "secrets" wealthy people used to dodge taxes. In the advertisement for the *Treasury of Tax Saving Ideas*, for example, the book promised that it would teach readers about "converting income to capital gain," "tax-sheltered investments in real estate, citrus, oil, timber, cattle, uranium and other strategic minerals," and "shifting income to decrease taxes, using family trusts."[105] Around the same time, an advertisement for Lasser and Francis Durand's new book *How to Get Tax Protected Income from Oil and Gas Investments*, explained that "now you need not be an 'insider' to share in the tremendous returns (as high as 50%)" of oil and gas tax shelters "which produce maximum net-after-tax-returns."[106] Similarly, an advertisement for the book, *Encyclopedia of Tax Shelter Practices*,[107] promised to deliver to the ordinary man information on "how the 'insiders' get rich on tax-wise real estate deals,"[108] while an advertisement for a book by William Casey entitled *Tax Shelter in Real Estate* claimed that it would explain "how 'big' operators like Hilton, Sheraton, and Zeckendorf use 'financial magic' to set up real estate deal which provide different tax positions."[109]

These advertisements pushed the narrative that everyone was dodging taxes. In 1971, the book *Tax Tips and Tax Dodges* offered to provide to the public what others get from the professional advisors.[110] As an advertisement for the book explained,

> An essential part of this system is the willingness of the people of the United States to pay income taxes. At the same time, however, thousands of highly trained attorneys, accountants, and tax advisors make a handsome living counselling clients on how to avoid – and at times, evade – the tax bite. That, too, is part of the system. And that's why this book is so unique. It provides an enormous number of tax tips . . . to help you avoid the tax bite.[111]

[104] *Classified Ad 5*, The Austin Statesman, Oct. 26, 1959, at 21.
[105] *Display Ad* 46, Wall St. J., Feb. 16, 1956, at 15.
[106] *Display Ad 83*, Wall St. J., March 12, 1958, at 20.
[107] *Display Ad 49*, Wall St. J., July 9, 1964, at 11.
[108] Id.
[109] *Display Ad 148*, N.Y. Times, Jan. 26, 1958, at F8.
[110] Frederick Andrews, Tax Tips and Tax Dodges (1971).
[111] *Display Ad 6*, Wall St. J., Feb. 14, 1972, at 2.

The advertising concluded by saying "Other people cut their taxes ... This book proves it. Why shouldn't you?," with the ellipses included presumably to allow the point to sink in that tax dodging was widespread and you might be a sucker if you didn't join in.[112]

## Tax Dodging Advertisements in Black Newspapers

To assess whether the tax dodging advertisement was truly a national phenomenon and cut across communities and groups, the study was re-run with a sample of newspapers from the ProQuest Historical Black Newspapers database, which contained ten newspapers that were targeted toward a city's Black community.[113]

As Figure 5.3 below demonstrates, the rise in tax planning advertisements in the Black Newspapers database did largely track the trend in the five national newspapers, even if the rise lagged somewhat beyond the rise in advertisements in the national newspapers.

Notwithstanding the similar trend line, most of the tax dodging advertisements in Black newspapers were distinctly local. This was a general phenomenon, though, that was not limited to tax dodging advertisements. National advertisers had long ignored the Black community, with Black newspapers relying primarily upon circulation revenue and local advertisers.[114] National advertising in black newspapers modestly grew in the 1940s, spurred by the adoption of an excess profits tax during World War II that lessened the after-tax cost of advertising, but even that modest gain disappeared during the postwar years.[115] After a promotional effort by the National Newspaper Publishers Association (NNPA), which was founded to coordinate the campaign, and consumer research that demonstrated the degree to which many businesses depended upon purchasers from the Black community, this slowly started to change.[116] Businesses eventually began to take a more active

[112] Id.

[113] ProQuest Historical Newspapers Black Newspapers. The Black Newspapers in the database during the period at the time this study was conducted were Atlanta Daily World, Baltimore Afro-American, Chicago Defender, Cleveland Call & Post, Los Angeles Sentinel, Michigan Chronicle, New York Amsterdam News, Norfolk Journal & Guide, Philadelphia Tribune, and Pittsburgh Courier.

[114] Henk La Brie III, *Black Newspapers: The Roots are 150 Years Deep*, 4 JOURNALISM HIST. 111, 112 (1977).

[115] Mary Alice Sentman & Patrick S. Washburn, *How Excess Profits Tax Brought Ads to Black Newspapers in World War II*, 64 JOURNALISM Q. 769, 770–71, 774–75 (1987).

[116] Id. at 113.

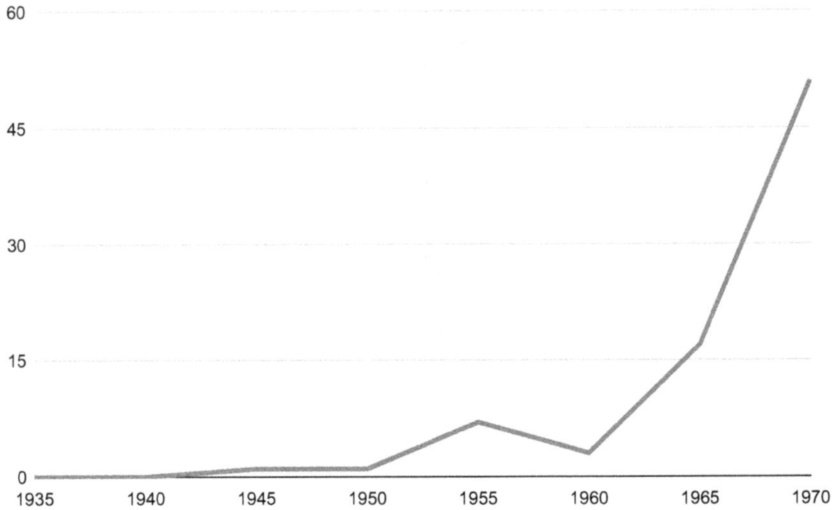


**Figure 5.3** Tax planning advertisements in ProQuest Black Newspaper Group by year 1935–1970

interest in "nonwhite consumers as a distinct marketing entity."[117] By 1973, Sherman Briscoe, the director of the NNPA, claimed that Black newspapers "have more national advertising than ever."[118]

Nevertheless, the absence of national advertisements in the 1950s and 1960s does not appear to be evidence that the Black community was any less interested in tax dodging or more afraid of detection than any other community, at least based on the activities of local advertisers. In areas such as income tax preparation and real estate investment, local advertisers openly embraced tax dodging. For example, in the tax preparation context, one advertisement for a former Internal Revenue Service employee in Los Angeles who provided income tax preparation, tax counseling, and audit defense services, called itself "Shewag Tax Shelter."[119] Another advertisement for a local income tax service advised readers "DON'T Over-

[117] Marcus Alexis, *Book Review: D. Parke Gibson, The $30 Billion Negro (1969)*, 4 J. of Consumer Affairs 135 (1970).

[118] Francis B. Ward, *The Black Press in Crisis*, 5 J. Black Stud. & Research 34, 35 (1973).

[119] *Display Ad 157*, L.A. Sentinel, Feb. 17, 1966, at D1.

Pay Your Taxes!," claiming that they could provide customers with "MANY tax-saving angles."[120]

Advertisements for real estate commonly invoked the typical tax dodging phrases to sell their properties. One advertisement for a real estate brokerage described several of its listings as a "Good Tax Shelter!," without any attempt to explain how the buyer could use them to obtain tax shelter-like benefits,[121] while another broker advertisement asked "High Tax Bracket? Tax Laws Work for You Too!," suggesting that real estate was an entry point for getting the type of tax breaks other people enjoyed.[122] A classified advertisement for office space in a medical building was headlined as a "Doctor's Tax Shelter," explaining that prospective buyers could "investigate for income tax shelter under leaseback arrangement," while others described apartment buildings as "tax shelter" properties.[123] One claimed that the building it was selling offered both "Pride of Ownership" and a "Tax Shelter," as if the two could be easily equated.[124] An advertisement for an investment firm similarly used the phrase "Tax Shelter" to persuade its readers to invest in a real estate syndication.[125]

The one group of national advertisers that did publish advertisements for tax dodging products in Black newspapers was publishers of national tax guides and do-it-yourself books. Studies have shown that members of the Black community often felt more positively about information and stories in Black newspapers than in mainstream newspapers and publishers may have hoped to take advantage of those attitudes.[126] It is also possible that they saw the market as one more likely to do their own tax planning and therefore to be interested in the resources that they provided. Regardless of the reason, it was a strategy employed by several of the largest publishers. For example, Prentice-Hall posted a full-page advertisement in the *Los Angeles Sentinel* for its book promising "Immediate Savings in Personal, Estate and Company Taxes" with

120 *Display Ad 14*, PHIL. TRIB., March 16, 1963, at 6.

121 *Display Ad 168*, L.A. SENTINEL, Jan. 11, 1970, at D8.

122 *Display Ad 60*, CHI. DEFENDER, Nov. 12, 1970, at B2. *See Classified Ad 27*, L.A. SENTINEL, Dec. 3, 1970, at D12 (claiming it was the "best bread and butter tax shelter on today's market.").

123 *Classified Ad 10*, L.A. SENTINEL, Dec. 15, 1960, at D10; *Classified Ad 11*, L.A. SENTINEL, July 30, 1964, at E6; *Classified A 9*, L.A. SENTINEL, July 17, 1969, at D5.

124 *Classified Ad 12*, L.A. SENTINEL, Feb. 22, 1968.

125 *Display Ad 1*, PITT. COURIER, April 28, 1962, at 4.

126 Timothy Vercellotti & Paul R. Brewer, *"To Plead Our Own Cause" Public Opinion Toward Black and Mainstream News Media Among African-Americans*, 37 J. BLACK STUD. 231, 238 (2006).

a full year's subscription to its weekly "What's Happening" report.[127] The Research Institute of America also placed advertisements in the *Sentinel* for its tax guide materials, but it went the extra step of quoting Judge Learned Hand's famous statement that "any one may so arrange his affairs that his taxes shall be as low as possible" from the *Helvering v. Gregory* case just in case anyone was leery of the legality of their methods.[128] Similarly, Simon and Schuster purchased a full advertisement for the 1950 edition of J. K. Lasser's *Business Tax Handbook*, which offered to "show you how to cut your business taxes to the bone in 1950."[129] An advertisement was published for Lasser's book, *Your Personal Income Tax*, which claimed to be an exclusive offer in the *Philadelphia Tribune*, for which he was also writing a series of twelve articles,[130] although Lasser placed other advertisements in Black newspapers for his books as well.[131]

## The Influence of Advertising

The question is whether this rise in advertisements affected the perception and perhaps the practice of tax dodging in mid-century America. That requires some examination of the purpose of advertising at the time. In a 1932 contest, the broadsheet trade publication newspaper *Advertising Age* asked readers to define the term "advertising." The winning entry defined it as the "dissemination of information concerning an idea, service, or product to compel action in accordance with the intent of the advertiser."[132] A judge in the contest decided to take the best parts of several of the contenders, coming up with an alternative definition of advertising as "the printed, written, spoken, or pictured representation of a person, product, service, or movement, openly sponsored by the advertiser and at his expense for the purpose of influencing sales, use, votes or endorsement."[133] In both cases, the definition emphasized that advertising was supposed to push the reader, to "compel" them to act or to "influence" them to do something.

127 *Display Ad 34*, L.A. SENTINEL, Nov. 1, 1942, at B12.
128 *Display Ad 129*, L.A. SENTINEL, Aug. 8, 1954, at F7 (*quoting* Helvering v. Evelyn F. Gregory, 69 F.2d 809, aff'd 293 U.S. 465).
129 *Display Ad 738*, L.A. SENTINEL, Jan. 8, 1950, at 132.
130 *Display Ad 8*, PHIL. TRIB., Feb. 17, 1951, at 8.
131 *Display Ad 21*, L.A. SENTINEL, Jan. 10, 1952, at 5.
132 *Definition of Brooklyn Man Held Best*, ADVERTISING AGE, July 28, 1932, p. 1.
133 Id. at 1.

In some cases, advertising was designed to influence the public to embrace or accept a certain way of thinking. In its most direct form, this was known as "institutional advertising" or "public interest advertising."[134] This form of advertising, which began during the New Deal and continued into World War II and beyond, was designed not so much to promote a product or sell a service, but to do something more akin to promoting "the sale of an ideology," often involving techniques associated with wartime propaganda.[135] As one contemporary observer of advertising noted:

> The impact which advertising has exerted in the past has been largely economic in character. While the application of advertising to material things is not diminishing, its use in the promotion of ideas is increasing rapidly. Political parties, governments, churches, business institutions and labor groups are making greater and greater use of advertising as a means of informing people and persuading them toward a particular philosophy or point of view.[136]

Some versions of this new form of advertising were explicitly directed at specific policies, such as a 1953 advertisement by Warner & Swasey Precision Machinery that attacked the welfare state, calling it the same as jail, socialism, and communism.[137] Other versions, however, were directed toward particular values or concepts that generally had widespread support, at least as goals if not as to the method of implementing them. For example, the Advertising Council, a group formed during World War II to help the government sell tangible products such as war bonds or recruit soldiers for the war effort, remained after the war to "promot[e], through advertising, ideas which seem to be in the public interest ... [such as to] reduce accidents ... improve public health, develop a better understanding of the meaning of democracy, increase human tolerance, improve the status of the education profession, and help hospitals recruit more nurses."[138] The Advertising Council

[134] Leonard I. Pearlin & Morris Rosenberg, *Propaganda Techniques in Institutional Advertising*, 16 PUB OPINION Q. 5 (1952); James W. Prothro, *Public Interest Advertising – Hucksterism or Conservatism?*, 45 SOC. STUD. 172 (1954).

[135] Pearlin & Rosenberg, *supra* note 134, at 5.

[136] C. H. Sandage, *The Role of Advertising in Modern Society* 28 JOURNALISM QUARTERLY 31, 37–38 (1951).

[137] *Warner & Swasey, advertisement*, U.S. NEWS & WORLD REPORT, March 13, 1953, at 1.

[138] Sandage, *supra* note 136, at 38. Formation of the group was reportedly motivated by a general desire of several advertising organizations to benefit from using mass communication techniques for social good, although the proximate cause for the group to ramp up was the U.S. entry into World War II after the bombing of Pearl Harbor. *See* Maurice I. Mandell,

voluntarily provided the public service content and the periodical publishing industry contributed the newspaper and magazine space, while many national advertisers contributed time on the radio shows they sponsored.[139]

Not only did these efforts help to rehabilitate the public, if not the academic, image of advertising,[140] but advertising theorists believed that they laid the groundwork to make advertising more effective and powerful as a tool to mold consumer attitudes. As marketing professor Edmund McGarry wrote in 1958, "advertising as used today is primarily a type of propaganda."[141] It "is so prevalent, so pervasive, so extensive, and so conspicuous," McGarry contended, "that it would be absurd to argue that it does not affect our attitudes."[142] The rise in advertisements, McGarry explained, can have "a barrage effect" similar to other kinds of propaganda.[143] "It creates a pattern of thought in a much larger population" he continued, by reaching not just those who hear or see the advertisement, but "many others who do not see or hear the message directly, learn of it from others by word of mouth."[144] Moreover, as advertising increases for a particular type of service or even a belief or ideology, McGarry argued that it could have a "spill-over" effect.[145] The notion is that an advertisement for a particular service, or provider of that type of service, can lead to increased demand for other services promising something similar. In effect, the advertisement inferentially promotes the need for that service, and not just the advertisement's particular method of providing that service or the benefits of using that particular provider.[146]

Notwithstanding his arguments for advertising's influence, McGarry recognized that was only one side of the picture. Advertising's power was not unlimited. As he pointed out, "its influence is tangential rather than direct . . . it tends to fit in with and supplement other motivational influences rather

A History of the Advertising Council 5 (Ph.D. dissertation 1953); Theodore S. Repplier, *Advertising Dons Long Pants*, 9 Pub. Opinion Q. 269, 269–70 (1945).

139 Drew Dudley, *Molding Public Opinion through Advertising*, 250 Annals of the American Academy of Political and Social Science 105, 108 (1947).

140 Salisbury, *supra* note 6, at 26–27.

141 Edmund D. McGarry, *The Propaganda Function in Marketing*, 23 J. of Marketing 131 (1958).

142 Id. at 138.

143 Id. at 132.

144 Id.

145 Id.at 132–33.

146 Id.

than act as an independent force."[147] In that sense, it may be more accurate, as a modern observer of studies in this area concluded, to say that "advertising is both a driver and reflective of social change,"[148] or, as another put it, "advertisers influence society and changes in society influence advertisers."[149]

In the context of tax dodging, the flurry of advertisements appeared to reflect these theoretical insights. As tax dodging schemes moved from individually targeted circulars and the cloistered rooms of exclusive clubs to the pages of national newspapers and magazines, more people were exposed to and became comfortable with the concept of tax dodging, even if they did not have the income or tax exposure to dodge taxes themselves. Others may have heard about tax dodging from those who had seen the advertisements or who knew someone who had taken advantage of some of the tax savings ideas mentioned there.

If the public had considered tax dodging to be offensive or immoral, it is likely that the advertising would not have been well received.[150] Since the number and boldness of such advertisements increased over the period, however, the implication is that the public was not offended by the advertisements and, indeed, patronized those that placed the advertisements. That may have been because the pre–World War II disapproval of tax dodging was weakening due to the disappearing consensus for the high marginal income tax rates enacted during the war. Alternatively, there may have been a declining fear of detection or of the kind of legislative action designed to shut down the schemes such as when Congress passed the Revenue Act in 1937.[151] Moreover, the flood of advertisements may have conquered any lingering doubts of those still

[147] Id.

[148] Harry A. Taute, Vaidotas Lukosius, & Andreas W. Stratemeyer, *The Changing Nature of Controversial Advertising: A Content Study*, in PROC. OF THE ANN. MEETING OF THE ASSOCIATION OF COLLEGIATE MARKETING EDUCATORS, 13, 15 (2008).

[149] Robert E. McDonald, Debra A. Leverie, & Kerry T. Manis, *The Interplay between Advertising and Society: An Historical Analysis*, 41 J. MACROMARKETING 585 (2021).

[150] *See* D. KIRK DAVIDSON, SELLING SIN: THE MARKETING OF SOCIALLY UNACCEPTABLE PRODUCTS 1 (2003) (explaining that certain products or services can be legal, but the public may be hostile toward the marketing of them because "certain segments of the public find them offensive, inappropriate, or harmful for a variety of reasons.")

[151] This also occurred in the 1920s and 1930s in Britain where "the promotion of some of the more blatant schemes in the popular press" was ultimately the provocation that "spurred the Revenue into some sort of action." Edward Troup, *Unacceptable Discretion: Countering Tax Avoidance and Preserving the Rights of the Individual*, 13 FISC. STUD. 128, 130 (1992).

holding out. Indeed, the fact that tax dodging was pitched to people of all income levels in these advertisements may have helped to unite the public in support of broadening tax dodging, rather than marginalizing the rich for dodging taxes. After all, when a classified advertisement is headlined with the question "Who is Handling Your Tax Avoidance?," it would be quite natural to think you must need a "tax avoidance specialist" like the one offered in the advertisement.[152]

Perhaps one piece of evidence of advertising's aid in the cultural immersion of tax dodging was that the commonly used phrases to describe tax dodging expanded beyond tax dodging advertisements. For example, as described in previous chapters, sellers of real estate often used the terms "tax haven" or "tax shelter" even when the advertisements made little to no attempt to explain the connection to taxation or tax dodging. Their use of the terms may have referred more to the "shelter" or "haven" aspect of the real estate than the tax benefits, but the association was considered a positive one by the seller and, presumably because of the seller's choice to invoke the association, by the buyer as well. In some cases, however, advertisers made clear that the tax terms were being used humorously or ironically. In one such instance, the well-known Chalfonte-Haddon Hall hotel in Atlantic City posted an advertisement on February 24 titled "Tax Evasion" over a sketching of the hotel.[153] The advertisement explained that, "it's only a temporary injunction but while you're here March 15th will seem months away."[154] The message was that a relaxing vacation by the sea shore was a great way to evade those pesky tax returns that were due a few weeks later, but the underlying implication was that "tax evasion" was a harmless, and even enjoyable, way to avoid something unpleasant. In another example, a classified advertisement was titled "VOYAGE OF $ DISCOVERY," and promised an "exotic ecological escape from taxes, inflation & pollution" in "tax & retirement havens by multi-lingual syndicate."[155] It was not clear whether the voyage was a vacation, a tax dodge, or some combination of the two. In perhaps the most humorous example, an advertisement for a church's Sunday services promoted its sermon, entitled "Divine Tax Evasion."[156] The following year, however, when that church advertised the same Sunday sermon, it altered the title to

[152] *Classified Ad 59*, WALL ST. J., Jan. 25, 1979, at 28.
[153] *Display Ad 42*, WASH. POST, Feb. 24, 1952, at S15.
[154] Id.
[155] *Classified Ad 154*, L.A. TIMES, Nov. 8, 1970, at P20.
[156] *Display Ad 72*, L.A. SENTINEL, Nov. 6, 1958, at B9.

read "The Tragedy of Divine Tax Evasion,"[157] leading one to wonder if the previous year churchgoers had come in droves expecting to get some heavenly secrets for dodging their own taxes and the pastor had to revise the title once he realized that everyone was so convinced that "tax evasion" was a good thing that they had failed to understand the message of his sermon.

[157] Id. The author of the sermon, Dr. Earl C. Cotton, was eventually honored for his long ministry at the church, with the City of Los Angeles establishing Dr. Earl C. Cotton Square and erecting a monument in his honor at the site. Cora Jackson-Fossett, *Liberty Baptist Dedicates Cotton Square*, L.A. SENTINEL, July 14, 2011, at C4.

# 6

## "His Expense Accounts Are Padded . . . with Danger and Romance!"[1]

In 1949, the show, *Yours Truly, Johnny Dollar*, the "private insurance investigator with the action-packed expense account," began a thirteen-year run on CBS Radio.[2] The show's gimmick was that the protagonist, Johnny Dollar, recounted his investigative adventures by reading his expense account, which triggered flashbacks to the events that led him to incur those purportedly business expenses.[3] The opening dialogue from the 1949 episode "Murder is a Merry-Go-Round" illustrates the prominence of the expense account in these shows.[4]

| | |
|---|---|
| ANNOUNCER: | The next half hour has its baggage packed to take a trip with America's fabulous freelance insurance investigator, Johnny Dollar. [X] At insurance investigation, he's just an expert – at making out his expense account, he is an absolute genius. |
| DOLLAR: | (NARRATES) Expense Account, submitted by Special Investigator Johnny Dollar, to Home Office, Nutmeg State Casualty and Bonding Company, Hartford, Connecticut. The following is an accounting of my expenditures during investigation of a series of accidents affecting your policy holder, The Fun Fair and Weatherly Carnival Shows, or how I went for a spin on a case we might refer to as "Murder Is a Merry-Go-Round." |

1 The Roanoke Times (Roanoke, Virginia), May 5, 1953, at 26 (advertisement for the CBS radio show, "Yours Truly, Johnny Dollar")

2 Jim Cox, AMERICAN RADIO NETWORKS: A HISTORY 164 (2009); John Dunning, *Yours Truly, Johnny Dollar*, in ON THE AIR: THE ENCYCLOPEDIA OF OLD-TIME RADIO 741–43 (1998).

3 Jeff Ousborne, "*Something Different That Still Spells Law*": Yours Truly, Johnny Dollar *and the Fate of the Radio Detective*, 37 STUD. POPULAR CULTURE 1 (2015).

4 CBS Radio, Yours Truly, Johnny Dollar, *Murder is a Merry-Go-Round*, March 11, 1949, Generic Radio Workshop, Script Library.

DOLLAR: (NARRATES) Expense Account Item One – twenty-five cents. Purchase of Billboard, theatrical magazine, to check the route of Fun Fair and Weatherly Carnival Shows.

Expense Account Item Two – sixty-eight dollars. Air and train fares to Talladega, Alabama.

Expense Account Item Three – a dollar ten. Cab fare in what was only a fair imitation of a cab, from Talladega Depot to the dusty vacant lot which had overnight found itself wearing theatrical make-up.

The show's signature feature was that Johnny Dollar not only solved the mystery, but he did so in style because he was a whiz with his expense account. Dollar was described as "an insurance investigator with a fondness for padding his expense account,"[5] a gag that was replayed in exchanges like the following from the 1956 episode, "Case of the Medium, Well Done."[6]

SARGE: Good, Johnny, just where you staying?
JOHNNY: Hi, you old reprobate, I'm at the Towers, East 52nd.
SARGE: The Tow . . . Eh, expense account, huh?
JOHNNY: How'd you guess. I want to see you.

Dollar was often hailed more for his "genius" in figuring how to write everything off on his expense account than for his investigative ability.[7] Dollar was generous too. As one account reported, "Dollar was a free-wheeling tipper who tossed silver dollars to busboys and doormen."[8]

At the conclusion of each show, Dollar tallied up his expenses for the home office.[9] Not everyone was impressed by the gimmick originally,[10] but it appeared to have worked because, despite having "little budget and only brief periods of sponsorship," the series aired for 886 episodes and

[5] *Investigator*, CINCINNATI ENQUIRER, March 11, 1949, at 16.

[6] CBS Radio, Your Truly, Johnny Dollar, The Case of the Medium, Well Done (Pt. 1), May 14, 1956, Generic Radio Workshop, Script Library.

[7] *Tough and Expensive*, THE MIRROR (Los Angeles, California), July 20, 1950, at 38.

[8] Dunning, *supra* note 1, at 742.

[9] Bob Greene, *You Didn't Nickel-and-Dime Johnny Dollar*, CHI. TRIB., April 24, 2001, at 5. Listeners let him know if his tally was incorrect too. *See Error in Dollar's High Finances*, DAILY BOSTON GLOBE, April 4, 1954, at A12.

[10] *See "Yours Truly, Johnny Dollar,"* KNX, 6–6:30, Sat., THE HOLLYWOOD REPORTER, Oct. 2, 1950, at 6 ("The only thing that distinguishes this show from some 46 others is the [expense account] gimmick. As gimmicks go, it's a perfectly normal one.")

literally "closed down the art of the dramatic network radio" when it went off the air in 1962.[11]

Johnny Dollar's run almost exactly matched the heyday of expense accounts in American society. The show's expense account gimmick was emblematic of a period when expense accounts, and their abuses, were highly salient for the average person. They were widely used, people were envious of the glamorous lifestyles they appeared to enable, and tales of their abuses were legendary.

Not only did the show illustrate the cultural penetration of the 1950s-era expense account at a time when they were only lightly regulated by tax authorities, but the show helped to grow the legend of expense account abuse. People used the phrase "a Johnny Dollar expense account" as a shorthand way of referring to the ability to travel and spend freely in expensive locales beyond what they could spend in their own humdrum lives.[12] Even if it did not normalize expense account padding on its own, it allowed the average listener to imagine it was widespread. One newspaper, previewing an episode, observed that "the Dollar-man . . . pads his expense account about as well as reporters."[13] Another included a review that jokingly complained that Dollar's expense accounts were not padded enough, making it tough on other detectives: "What's the idea of turning in an expense account of $356.72 for going to Ushuala, Argentina, and tracking down that dope peddler," the reviewer imagined the detective's boss asking. "Johnny Dollar solved 14 murders last Tuesday night for $8.75!"[14]

Although expense accounts were at least in part a solution to a logistical problem in business travel and entertainment, their use accelerated as one way to mitigate the post–World War II high tax rates on wage and salary income. As their use grew, they normalized tax dodging and inspired envy among those who did not have them. Congress ultimately enacted rules to limit their use, but they persisted as a symbol of tax-financed personal consumption.

11 Dunning, *supra* note 1, at 742.

12 *See, e.g.*, Dave Holland, *Actor Joined "Nina" cast in Australia*, VALLEY TIMES TODAY (North Hollywood, California), Jan. 14, 1963, at 8 (actor Myron Natwick, in an interview about his travels, described the night clubs in Tokyo as "Fabulous! Particularly if you've got a Johnny Dollar expense account.").

13 *Johnny Dollar*, SUNDAY JOURNAL AND STAR (Lincoln, Nebraska), Aug. 9, 1953, at 23.

14 Redford H. Dibble, *Dib's Diary*, TULARE ADVANCE-REGISTER (Tulare, California), Nov. 13, 1953, at 10.

## Business Origins

Businesses have long valued personal relationships, often nurtured in-person in casual settings such as over meals and at entertainment events. When businesses were owned and operated by the same small group of people, there was little need to police the boundaries between personal and business expenses since the funds came from the same pot. As the managerial economy grew, with the separation of ownership and control and the rise of large firms with many employees, firms began reimbursing or directly paying expenses employees incurred in meeting with and entertaining clients, while instituting safeguards to ensure the expenses were genuinely business-related. These reimbursement or direct payment arrangements often covered either all actual expenses supported by employee records or specific types of preapproved expenses.[15]

The problem with reimbursements and direct payments is they required advance planning or record keeping or they presumed that the employee could obtain an itemized receipt for their expenses, which may not have been possible for many types of expenditures. To deal with this, some executives negotiated increased salary either in lieu of reimbursement or in addition to it to cover expenses that were "not readily susceptible to the usual accounting."[16] This was problematic, however, unless their salary was grossed up for the tax associated with the extra compensation. They tried to avoid this by including a clause in their contracts stating that a portion of their salary was for business expenses, but that was a poor second-best for securing proper receipts and documentation.[17]

Expense accounts were created as a way around both the rigidity of reimbursements or direct payments and the tax risks of extra compensation. They were "designed to keep selected key employees from having to absorb losses on account of certain necessary expenditures, largely of a social character, incurred on behalf of the employer."[18] By setting a spending cap, rather than requiring reconciliation or accounting, the expense account was a "convenience device" for expenses that would have been reimbursable "had such a course of action been practical and timely."[19] This incentivized

[15] *Executive Expense Practices*, AM. BUS. MAG., Jan. 1957, at 29 (survey of companies).

[16] V. Henry Rothschild and Rudolf Sobernheim, *Expense Accounts for Executives*, 67 YALE L.J. 1363, 1368 (1958).

[17] Id.

[18] William H. Hoffman, Jr., *Control of the Corporate Executive's Expense Account*, 13 TAX EXECUTIVE 23, 24 (1960).

[19] Id.; *Executive Expense Practices*, *supra* note 14, at 29–30.

employees to be nimble and creative in entertaining clients, while creating a subtle expectation that they use their expense accounts.

Expense accounts had logistical advantages, but the lack of oversight opened the door to abuse for those seeking to finance personal consumption with business dollars. They instead came to be seen as an employment perquisite or supplemental compensation. Moreover, the more widely they were used, the more employees began to expect them. Although they were most famously used by traveling salesmen, most top executives in large firms had expense accounts.[20] Executives even negotiated for expense accounts of a certain size in their employment contracts through the insertion of what were called "expense clauses" with generous caps and limited oversight.[21]

The amount of money involved in expense accounts was large. By 1958, aggregate expense account spending was "conservatively" estimated to be around $5 billion annually,[22] with the upper range reaching as high as $10 billion.[23] Although the IRS estimated that only about 10 percent of individual taxpayers had expense accounts or charged expenses to employers,[24] the absolute value was still high with one estimate placing it in the neighborhood of twenty million people.[25] People used their expense accounts too. The US Commerce Department estimated in 1958 that as many as 4.3 million people attended business conventions on expense accounts and the use of the Diners Club card, which was created to allow its holders to better keep track of spending on meals, hotels, travel, and entertainment expenses, grew by almost 13 percent after the IRS required itemized receipts for expense accounts.[26]

## Tax Treatment

Business expenses for meals and entertainment were deductible when the first post–Sixteenth Amendment income tax was enacted in 1913.[27] At that time, deductions were allowed for "the necessary expenses actually

[20] Rothschild and Sobernheim, *supra* note 15, at 1364.
[21] Id. at 1366, 1368.
[22] Id. at 1363.
[23] Ernest L. Barcella, *New Accounting of Expense Accounts*, N.Y. Times Mag., April 20, 1958, at 48.
[24] Mortimer M. Caplin, *The Travel and Entertainment Expense Problem*, 39 Taxes 947, 952 (1961); Philip M. Stern, The Great Treasury Raid 111 (1964).
[25] Barcella, *supra* note 23, at 48.
[26] Id.
[27] Richard Schmalbeck & Jay A. Soled, *Elimination of the Deduction for Business Entertainment Expenses*, 123 Tax Notes 757, 757 (2009).

paid in carrying on any business."[28] Congress was careful even then, however, to make clear that the deduction for business expenses would not extend to "personal, living or family expenses."[29] Congress specifically permitted the deduction of travel expenses for business in the Revenue Act of 1921 and added membership in business and trade organizations and attendance at their meetings in the Revenue Act of 1928.[30] Treasury further reinforced the distinction between business and personal travel when it issued regulations defining deductible travel as "solely on business," leaving all other travel as "personal,"[31] although the "solely" language was generally interpreted so as to permit a deduction as long as the "primary purpose" was business.[32]

Despite the distinction between deductible business expenses and non-deductible personal expenses, there was little attempt to identify a method to keep track of the former and distinguish them from the latter. Indeed, the long-standing *Cohan* rule – which permitted taxpayers to deduct expense accounts without any detailed receipts or documentation until the early 1960s – derived from a 1930 case in which a Broadway producer had been "free-handed in entertaining actors, employees, and, as [the producer] naively adds, dramatic critics," in 1921 and 1922.[33] The taxpayer, though, "kept no account" of his expenses and the Board of Tax Appeals denied his deductions "on the ground that it was impossible to tell how much he had in fact spent, in the absence of any items or details."[34] The Second Circuit, however, overturned the decision, with Judge Learned Hand writing that "absolute certainty in such matters is usually impossible and is not necessary; the Board should make as close an approximation as it can."[35] Hand acknowledged that "we do not know how many trips Cohan made, nor

[28] Revenue Act of 1913, Pub. L. No. 63–16, 38 Stat. 167 (1913).

[29] Id.

[30] Revenue Act of 1921, Pub. L. No. 67–98, 42 Stat. 227 (1921); Revenue Act of 1928, Pub. L. No. 70–562, 45 Stat. 791 (1928). During this period, the primary concern was over travel and per diem expenses, rather than entertainment more broadly. Caplin, *supra* note 24, at 947.

[31] Treas. Reg. 101, §23(a)-2 (1939) ("if the trip is undertaken for other than business purposes, the railroad fares are personal expenses ... [but] if the trip is solely on business," the fares are deductible).

[32] William A. Klein, *The Deductibility of Transportation Expenses of a Combination Business and Pleasure Trip: a Conceptual Analysis*, 18 Stan. L. Rev. 1099, 1105 (1966).

[33] Cohan v. Commissioner of Internal Revenue, 39 F.2d 540, 543 (2d Cir. 1930).

[34] Id. at 543.

[35] Id. at 544.

how large his entertainments were," but concluded that "there was basis for some allowance, and it was wrong to refuse any."[36]

## Post–World War II

Although the expense account originated in the first half of the twentieth century, it was not until World War II that it truly took off.[37] Some of that was for nontax reasons. One contemporary observer explained

> [t]he expense account grew into a fat-cat fringe benefit during World War II, its growth triggered by the war-time wage freeze. Companies short of manpower and desperate to keep what they had, looked for special inducements and gimmicks to retain their help. . . . In lieu of the raise they couldn't give because of the freeze, they would increase an employee's take by adding an extra $10 or $100 to his expense account.[38]

Nevertheless, "soaring taxes were the most powerful propellant."[39] As Treasury Secretary Douglas Dillon testified in 1961, "much of [expense account abuse] is done in response to competitive pressure which has in large measure been created by tax law and not by the dictates of business."[40] Moreover, because of the way that it blurred the line between the professional and private sphere and reshaped in a visible way the dining, entertainment, and travel industry, it may have done more than anything else to create the impression that tax dodging was widespread.

In large part, "the great expense account charade" began with the enactment of an excess profits tax in World War II.[41] This tax, an add-on to the income tax already applied to corporate income, purported to capture the profits corporations were earning as a windfall from the

36 Id.

37 U.S. Treasury Department, Study on Entertainment Expenses in President's Tax Message along with Principal Statement, Detailed Explanation, and Supporting Exhibits and Documents submitted by Secretary of the Treasury Douglas Dillon in connection with the President's Recommendations Contained in his Message on Taxation at Hearings conducted by Committee on Ways and Means, House of Representatives (May 3, 1961), Exhibit V, at 243. ("Study on Entertainment Expenses").

38 Barcella, *supra* note 23, at 48.

39 Id.

40 See Hearings before House Committee on Ways and Means on the Tax Recommendations of the President Contained in his Message Transmitted to Congress, April 20, 1961, 87th Cong., 1st Sess. 42 (1961) (Statement of Treasury Secretary Dillon) ("Hearings on President Kennedy's Special Message").

41 Michael G. Emmanuel and Norman H. Lipoff, *Travel and Entertainment: The New World of Section 274*, 18 *Tax L. Rev.* 487, 487 (1963); John D. Pomfret, *"Expense Account Living" Coming Under Close Scrutiny*, N.Y. Times, Dec. 10, 1962, at 13.

government's mobilization of the economy for wartime production.[42] It levied a penalty upon the profits corporations made beyond a "normal" return, which Congress defined to be, at the election of the taxpayer, either the average of the earnings in the three prewar years or an amount of earnings on invested capital beyond 5 percent (or 8 percent for smaller businesses).[43] Although the World War II excess profits tax was repealed in 1945, it was revived in 1950 as the Korean conflict began.[44] By 1952, with the corporate income tax rate at 52 percent and the excess profits tax rate an additional 30 percent,[45] the burden on business was crushing and the temptation to look for additional deductions was overwhelming.

Under these corporate and excess profits tax rates, it was not surprising that the expense account flourished. As *Newsweek* explained, "[t]axes . . . have been largely responsible for the postwar boom in expense accounts; until 1954, the combined income and excess profits tax of 82 percent on the income of a big corporation meant that each expense account dollar cost the company only 18 cents."[46] This made it easy for employees to justify expenses that might otherwise have garnered greater scrutiny.[47] Moreover, these rates came at a time when many companies were flush with cash because of wartime profits. According to one Pennsylvania manufacturer, "expense account spending first reached a peak during World War II when the companies had more money than ever before and couldn't keep it because of taxes."[48] Because of this, "they had to throw it around, and they did it by advertising and entertaining."[49]

Expense accounts were costly for the government, with deductions resulting in a $1 to $2 billion loss of revenue.[50] A 1960 Internal Revenue Service study of 38,000 federal income tax returns provided a peek at where those expense accounts were being spent. It found that in this small universe of returns, $11 million was spent on business gifts, $5.7 million was spent on

[42] Steven A. Bank, Kirk J. Stark & Joseph J. Thorndike, War and Taxes 87–88 (2008).

[43] Id. at 88–89; Carl Shoup, *The Concept of Excess Profits Under the Revenue Acts of 1940–42*, 10 L. & Contemp. Probs. 28, n. 2 (1943).

[44] Bank, Stark & Thorndike *supra* note 42, at 117.

[45] Federal Corporate Income Tax Rates, Income Years 1909-2012, Tax Foundation, July 6, 2012.

[46] *See I'll Just Sign: Those Big-Figure Expense Accounts*, Newsweek, May 20, 1957, at 87.

[47] Ernest Havermann, *The Expense Account Aristocracy: Tax Deductions 'For Business Purposes' Make it Cheap to Live*, Life Mag., March 9, 1953, at 140.

[48] Richard Gehman, *Expense Accounts*, Cosmopolitan, March 1957, at 44, 45 (1957).

[49] Id.

[50] Jerome R. Hellerstein, Taxes, Loopholes, & Morals 125 (1963).

dues for private clubs, $2.6 million went toward yachts, $2 million was for theater tickets, and $1 million was for hunting lodges and fishing camps.[51]

Businesses were not shy about citing the high rates specifically as the justification for their generous expense accounts. During 1961 hearings on tax reform options, George Newman, a representative of the Iowa Manufacturers Association told the House Ways and Means Committee that "viewed in light of the present combined top corporate rate of tax on net profits, of 52 percent, and the steeply graduated of individual tax going up to 91 percent which apply to the net income of unincorporated businesses, erosion of the 'ordinary and necessary' rule would be economic folly."[52]

In addition to the lure of deductible expenses, companies were also motivated to use expenses accounts as a form of tax-exempt compensation. The *Wall Street Journal* explained that "the expense account has become, willy-nilly, an adjunct to salary."[53] In an era of high rates, converting taxable compensation to non-taxable benefits was a way to ease the burden on their employees and effectively gross up their after-tax pay. According to one report, "[m]any companies have built into their pay scales liberal and non-taxable expense allowances in place of heavily-taxed salaries as a device for attracting and holding executive talent."[54]

Expense accounts became status symbols. One commentator reported "[t]he measure of a man's business success today often isn't the size of his salary – it's how big an expense account he draws ... [it's] the passport into a golden world of free-spending splendor."[55] According to one holder of this golden ticket, "[a]n expense account beats a paycheck because you don't have to explain it to Uncle Sam."[56] Companies enhanced its value by providing top executives an "automobile, yacht, hunting or fishing lodge, country club membership, theater and sporting events tickets, and various other personal benefits."[57]

[51] Id.

[52] Hearings Before the Committee on Ways and Means, House of Representatives, 87th Cong., 1st Sess. on the Tax Recommendations of the President contained in his Message transmitted to Congress on April 21, 1961 at 1654 (1961) (statement of George Newman, Iowa Manufacturers Association) ("1961 House Hearings").

[53] *Expense Accounts: Firms Check Outlays Closer, Hunt Ways to Soften Tax Crackdown*, WALL ST. J., Feb. 14, 1958, at 1.

[54] STERN, *supra* note 24, at 113.

[55] *Hal Boyle Says*, THE POMONA PROGRESS BULLETIN (Pomona, California), March 6, 1953, at 4.

[56] Id.

[57] Norman H. Lipoff, *Entertainment and Related Expenses Under Legislative Attack*, 17 TAX L. REV. 183, 188 (1962).

It was difficult for companies to resist providing generous expense accounts. As Russell Lynes, the managing editor of *Harper's Magazine*, observed in the *New York Times*, an employee of such a company might "leave in a huff for another company that will give him more."[58] Companies fearful of losing their best workers therefore used entertainment expense-justified items to induce them to stay. "In some cases," Lynes continued, "he is supplied by the company with a house and garden and swimming pool, several cars and the service to maintain them."[59] The company rationalizes its deduction of the expenses by the fact that the employee "lives on company property and entertains for the company there" in what "is properly speaking, a dwelling maintained for what the company considers to be its business, or that part of it which goes by the name of 'public relations.'"[60]

There were countless colorful anecdotes involving companies that used expense accounts as a method of increasing after-tax compensation. In 1957, a former linoleum company executive noted that "an executive earning $50,000 a year today pays between $22,000 and $27,000 in taxes. If we gave him another $10,000 raise, he would pay still more. But if we give him $10,000 to spend on promoting our products and name, we've substantially rewarded him without penalizing him."[61] This exact scenario was described in one account in the *New York Times*. A "Midwestern executive," who was reportedly due to receive a $10,000 raise, negotiated to instead have his company pay his membership dues and $10,000 worth of expenses at a "swank local country club. . . . Immediately, the executive and his family all but moved into the club. They had most of their meals at the club, entertained their friends there, purchased the family supply of liquor at the club – all on the $10,000 expense account."[62] In another example involving a chemical company, one company lured away another company's executive with an offer that only matched his salary. The difference was that "the second company had some wholesalers and distributors up in Wisconsin. The man liked to fish. In his old job, he'd taken his vacation to do some fishing. Now he could visit the wholesalers for the company and nobody in the company minded if he went fishing with them. The company was delighted – and delighted to pay for his

58 Russell Lynes, *Visit to the World of Expense Accounts*, N.Y. Times, Feb. 24, 1957, at 201.
59 Id.
60 Id.
61 Gehman, *supra* note 48, at 45.
62 Barcella, *supra* note 23, at 48.

trips, too, and *still* give him a vacation."[63] This use of the expense account in lieu of extra compensation occurred among lower-paid employees as well. In one account, an oil company gave its top salesmen expense accounts of $700–$900 per week, as opposed to the $125 per week normally provided to salesman, with the larger amount effectively acting as a tax-free bonus.[64]

This practice of compensating employees with tax-free benefits was well known in government circles. Indeed, a House Ways and Means Subcommittee on Administration of the Internal Revenue Laws called for an investigation of "attempts by some business organizations to reward key personnel with tax-free personal benefits."[65] In January of 1953, the House Ways and Means Committee issued a report in which it acknowledged that "recent high tax rates have resulted in attempts by some business organizations to reward key personnel with tax-free personal benefits."[66] It specifically highlighted the way in which expense accounts fit into this practice, not just because they allowed personal consumption to be financed by tax-free dollars, but because the employers openly condoned the abuse of those expenses accounts to increase their incomes. The report condemned "the practice of allowing overly liberal expense accounts to employees whose duties involve travel or business entertainment" and "tolerat[ing] padding of the expense account by the employee as a way of giving him tax-free income."[67]

Expense account abuse was so rampant that expense account reports were known as "swindle sheets."[68] One observed that "it is not uncommon for a man, signing a tab in a restaurant where he is known, to put down an amount double the size of the check and take the remainder of the money for himself."[69] To demonstrate this, a writer related the story of "a well-known photographer, a gay, lively fellow with no sense

63 Gehman, *supra* note 48, at 45 (italics in original).

64 STERN, *supra* note 24, at 113.

65 S. Ralph Jacobs, *Glamorous Fringe Benefits*, B.U. L. REV. 151, 153 (1956).

66 Internal Revenue Investigation, Report of the Committee on Ways and Means, House of Representatives, 82d Cong., pursuant to H. Res. 78, 82d Cong., A Resolution Authorizing and Directing Certain Studies and Investigations to be Conducted by the Committee on Ways and Means 29 (Jan. 3, 1953).

67 Id.

68 H. F. MILLIKIN, THE PRUDENT MAN: TAX DODGING AS AN ART 24–25 (1963) (pen name for Joachim Joesten); Gehman, *supra* note 48, at 44.

69 Gehman, *supra* note 48, at 44, 47. *See* John D. Pomfret, *"Expense Account Living" Comes Under Close Scrutiny*, N.Y. TIMES, Dec. 19, 1962, at 13 ("Sometimes cruder types padded the expense account and pocketed the difference.").

whatever of personal finance, [who] once was asked how he managed to exist. 'I live on the change that waiters give me,' he said blithely."[70] Another pointed out that "there are countless varieties of how to rig a swindle sheet that will deflate a huge income like a pricked balloon, and new ones are constantly being dreamed up by executives and their high-priced tax experts."[71]

This was perhaps the most extreme version of the common phrase that people could "live off the expense account."[72] As *The Nation* reported, "the racket has reached such proportions that in some cases it is scarcely necessary for a business executive to earn a salary – he can live like a millionaire on his expense account."[73] Noted journalist Ferdinand Lundberg claimed that "many corporation executives derive most of their take-home pay from" (1) expense accounts and (2) cut-rate stock options, "insouciantly allowing the government to clip their direct-cash salaries up to 70 percent."[74] Lundberg described one example of an executive of a corporation who was paid a salary of $25,000 that was increased in value to $98,000 because "his company paid his apartment rent, club dues and expenses (meals and drinks), entertainment expenses and an occasional trip abroad 'to study business methods overseas and improve his firm's competitive position.'"[75]

The practice of padding the expense account spread beyond the C-suite to include more than just the top executives.[76] "The big spenders," one restaurateur reported, "are advertising men, public relations guys, manufacturers, motion picture people, brokers and auto salesmen."[77] Not only did businessmen deduct many of the daily costs of living, such as lunches, but they deducted the costs of special events too, including "weddings, debuts and other social occasions where customers and business contacts are among the invited guests."[78] As one commentator exclaimed, "many a man woos and weds a wife now on

70 Gehman, *supra* note 48, at 44, 47.
71 MILLIKIN, *supra* note 68, at 24–25.
72 Malcolm Reed, *Uncle Sam v. The Expense Account*, 39 TAXES 329, 331 (1961).
73 *High on the Hog*, THE NATION, Dec. 17, 1960, at 467.
74 FERDINAND LUNDBERG, THE RICH AND THE SUPER-RICH 430 (1968).
75 Id. at 434.
76 *See, e.g.*, William K. Zinsser, *There's No Business Like Lunch Business*, NEW YORK TIMES MAGAZINE, March 20, 1960, in Study on Entertainment Expenses, *supra* note 37, Exhibit V, at 243.
77 *Hal Boyle Says*, *supra* note 55, at 4 (quoting Toots Shor).
78 STERN, *supra* note 24, at 112.

expense account money, or gives his dear old mother a winter vacation in Florida, or sends his son to a college he couldn't otherwise afford."[79]

## Entrenchment of Expense Account Spending

If the tax rates had been the only reason for the boom in expense accounts, there should have been a marked decline in expense account spending as rates dropped. For example, the excess profits tax was repealed in 1954.[80] That raised a corporation's after-tax cost share of entertainment expenses because of the elimination of the additional 30 percent rate that had previously been levied on its excess income. Nevertheless, the change "made for little, if any, cutback in the overall spending."[81] Part of the reason was that the rates had already spurred cultural and institutional changes that were not so easy to reverse.

With the growth of the expense account came the development of businesses, restaurants, night clubs, and all forms of entertainment facilities designed to take advantage of government-financed consumption.

> Wartime businessmen, spending their twenty-cent dollars, fathered a large family of new facilities which grew and prospered as the result of the travel and entertainment practices of their progenitors. During the post-war years new hotels were built and old ones expanded and modernized; the boom in restaurants, night clubs and cocktail lounges reached the proportions of a population explosion – all supported by the organization man's expense account.[82]

Although there may have been "little real relation to business" between these facilities and others, including "yachts [and] gun clubs," they were all "put on the corporate tab and written off on the tax form."[83] As Treasury Secretary Douglas Dillon testified before the House Ways and Means Committee in 1961, "there are few of the luxuries of life, such as vacations at fancy resorts, club memberships, and cruises which a large number of taxpayers cannot in some way deduct on tax returns as business expenses."[84] There were sometimes "serious and extensive

[79] *Hal Boyle Says*, *supra* note 55, at 4.
[80] Jacquin D. Bierman, *Excess Profits Tax Termination*, 9 Tax L. Rev. 25 (1953).
[81] *See I'll Just Sign: Those Big-Figure Expense Accounts*, Newsweek, May 20, 1957, at 87.
[82] Emmanuel & Lipoff, *supra* note 41, at 487.
[83] John D. Pomfret, *"Expense Account Living" Coming Under Close Scrutiny*, N.Y. Times, Dec. 10, 1962, at 13.
[84] Hearings on President Kennedy's Special Message, *supra* note 39, at 42 (Statement of Treasury Secretary Douglas Dillon).

business meetings" held in such places, but "all too often ... the recreational activities predominate, and the business activities are so insubstantial as to constitute a sham."[85]

The expense account's influence was particularly evident in a city like New York that was both dominated by large businesses and was a destination for retail buyers for stores across the country. According to one estimate, in 1957 "some 80 per cent of luncheons served at top Manhattan restaurants like '21,' Le Pavilion and Chambord ... are expensed."[86] During the same year, Broadway theater representatives reportedly estimated that 30 to 40 percent of all ticket sales were bought on expense accounts.[87] A decade later, little had changed. Ferdinand Lundberg estimated that the entire "New York pleasure-belt, extending roughly from 34th to 59th Streets and First to Eighth Avenues, is largely supported by expense-account deductions."[88]

Conventions were the quintessential example of an industry that literally became an institution because of the expense account. Often located in exotic places that were once the exclusive province of the wealthy, conventions offered companies the chance to reward their employees with a fantasy vacation financed largely by the government's tax subsidy.[89] The Greenbriar, for example, a posh resort in White Sulphur Springs, West Virginia that had been the playland for presidents, diplomats, and power brokers since before the Civil War, had effectively become a convention center. *Business Week* reported that what drew the Magazine Publishers Association to the resort in May of 1959 – in addition to the organization's annual spring meeting – was "the golf, tennis, swimming, fine food, and secluded luxury that ever since the war had been luring an increasing share of conventioneering Americans to the resort hotels."[90] Expense accounts, according to the magazine, were largely responsible for this shift:

> The America penchant for conventions – increasingly bearing the more elegant label of conferences – has reached its de luxe flowering in these

[85] Henry Cassorte Smith, *Watch Your Expense Accounts*, 36 HARV. BUS. REV. 120, 121 (1958).

[86] Sanford Brown, *I'll Just Sign: Those Big-Figure Expense Accounts*, NEWSWEEK, May 20, 1957, at 87.

[87] *Expense Accounts: A $5 Billion Tax Deduction, and Growing*, U.S. NEWS & WORLD REPORT, Aug. 16, 1957, at 83, 86.

[88] LUNDBERG, *supra* note 74, at 436.

[89] Id. at 431.

[90] *The Conventions – Hard Work, Hard Play*, BUS. WEEK, May 16, 1959, at 176.

> rural spas that once were the exclusive domain of wealthy families and dowagers who are moving over for the growing number of expense account guests.[91]

Unlike the compensation perquisites like stock options and deferred compensation, which were primarily the exclusive province of a company's executives, conventions were a benefit available to "just about everyone in the U.S. . . . be he hod carrier, teacher, banker, or top industrialist."[92]

Not surprisingly, conventions sprung up to meet this demand. Bookings at the Miami Beach convention center doubled between 1949–50 and 1950–51 and doubled again in 1951–52.[93] The high demand for convention options continued throughout the 1950s. By the end of the 1950s, *The Economist* observed that "the annual convention is of course no novelty. For years these holiday jaunts, masked as educational meetings and therefore properly chargeable to the costs of doing business, have helped to support big resort hotels with convenient golf courses attached."[94] The entertainment aspect of the deductible convention business became so significant that some groups looked for venues where they could get attendees to focus on work a bit more. According to the Furness Bermuda Line, for example, the percentage of its cruise bookings attributed to conventions jumped from 18 percent in 1958 to 26 percent in 1959, an increase attributed to the fact that there "are no golf courses attached" to cruise ships at sea.[95]

As conventions, annual sales meetings, and industry trade associations multiplied, it was easy for the average taxpayer to find a business excuse to expense a family vacation. Indeed, you were considered a chump if you did otherwise. Hal Foust, a columnist for the *Chicago Daily Tribune* writing from Miami Beach, exclaimed that "if you haven't contrived a business trip to this playground, you're missing something. That's the way more and more smart operators are paying for visits here – classifying travel and hotel bills as business expenses deductible as such on income tax returns. Uncle Sam, in other words, is catching more and more of the checks around here."[96] The

[91] Id. at 176–78.
[92] Id. at 178.
[93] Hal Foust, *Tax Deductions Can Pay for Trip to Sunny South*, CHI. DAILY TRIB., Feb. 22, 1952, at B4.
[94] *Life at Uncle Sam's Expense*, THE ECONOMIST, April 18, 1959, at 234, 235.
[95] Id. at 235.
[96] Foust, *supra* note 93, at B4.

organizers of these meetings were all too willing to accommodate this desire for deductible pleasure trips. One vice-president of an insurance company that was holding an annual meeting in Fort Monroe, Virginia told the hotel manager that "while we hold two business sessions during our four-day convention, business is secondary. The main object is to give our people a good time. Specifically, I would be interested in knowing the fishing accommodations . . ."[97]

A few companies literally built vacation resorts to be used by their employees. In one example, the Slaymaker Lock Company of Lancaster, Pennsylvania, acquired a farm and stone house and spent almost three times the price to turn the house into a "recreation lodge."[98] It then conveyed the property to a trust controlled by an association of the foreman of the company. Under the trust, the property was to be maintained for the exclusive use and enjoyment of the employees, which the Tax Court held in 1952 to be sufficient to classify it as a deductible business expense. According to the court, "petitioner's volume of business more than quadrupled what it had been during the prewar years." Since it "had to compete with other industries in the area likewise engaged in war activities" and its wages were largely fixed by the wartime wage stabilization regulations, it used the recreation lodge "as a means of holding old employees, to attract new employees, and to cut down its labor turnover."[99] The court may have been fooled by the taxpayer in this and other similar cases. As one commentator noted, "ostensibly" these properties were used by employees, but they "actually [were] for the use of a key stockholder-officer as a country home. An annual barbeque picnic for the employees is staged in the hope that such a red herring will cause the Internal Revenue Service to lose the scent."[100]

Some employers even opened business locations to provide an excuse for travel. For example, Ray Kroc, the owner of the fast food franchisor McDonald's, bought a large ranch in Santa Ynez, California in the mid-1960s as a vacation spot for company executives, but, at the advice of tax counsel, installed a test kitchen on site and made the property the headquarters for his newly created foundation.[101] A more conventional variant of this strategy was opening a branch office. In 1957, the Internal Revenue

97 Stern, *supra* note 24, at 114–15.

98 Slaymaker Lock Company v. Commissioner, 18 T.C. 1001 (1952).

99 Id.

100 Henry Cassorte Smith, *Watch Your Expense Accounts*, 36 Harv. Bus. Rev. 120, 121 (1958).

101 Lisa Napoli, *The Ranch that Big Macs Built*, LA Curbed, Nov. 17, 2016.

Service advised field agents that "one area which requires close attention involves the use of alleged branch offices in resort cities for the sole purpose of sending business executives to such cities for vacation."[102] According to one account, it was "a growing practice . . . for a small firm to maintain an unused office as a 'front' in a resort area."[103] This "phony branch office . . . gives executives an excuse to deduct travel expenses for visits ostensibly made to the branch office."[104] In reality, however, "these visits can be a cloak for personal vacation trips."[105]

## The Push for Reform

It was an open secret that expense accounts were a catch-all for tax dodging. One columnist for the *New York Times* called the expense account "one of the uneasy national jokes of our time . . . it has become one of the greenest of playing fields for that all-American exercise in sportsmanship, getting around the income tax."[106] Under what some described as "expense account morality . . . a company has a lodge to entertain customer-executives in the South Sea Isles. Or there's a yacht for meetings of the board of directors. Or duck-hunting blind with bar attached. Or airplanes to whisk men away to pleasure dates as well as business dates."[107] One Internal Revenue Service agent described myriad potentially abusive "items that turn up regularly on expense accounts," including "upkeep of their homes, entertainment in their homes, clothes for their wives, and services provided for business associates – services such as furnishing chartered planes or railroad cars, limousines and chauffeurs, or supplying private secretaries complete with typewriters and dictating machines."[108]

What differentiated expense account abuse is that it was not limited to the super rich. As one contemporary commentator put it, "at the very top of the social pyramid" of billionaires and demi-billionaires, "tax-dodging is often looked upon as a sort of sport," but "in the next-to-highest brackets . . . tax evasion is cultivated as a fine art, if not an exact science,"

102 I.R.-Circular No. 57–85 (June 20, 1957).

103 *Expense-Account Scandal*, U.S. News & World Report, Jan. 25, 1960, at 50, 52.

104 Id.

105 Id.

106 Lynes, *supra* note 58, at 201.

107 J. A. Livingston, *Business Outlook: Wives Can Be Tax Deductible*, Wall St. J., May 2, 1956, at 27.

108 Gehman, *supra* note 48, at 45.

citing expense accounts as "a real 'old faithful' in this game."[109] William Graham Balter, a Los Angeles lawyer and the author of a 1953 treatise on tax fraud, cited "padding of business entertainment expenses" as one example of "tax evasion unfortunately practiced on a wide scale by rich and poor alike."[110]

Business interests claimed that these reports of abuse exaggerated the magnitude of the problem. As Clarence Randall, a former chairman of Inland Steel Company and an adviser to Presidents Dwight Eisenhower and John F. Kennedy observed, "this orgiastic abuse of the expense account is by no means universal, or even in a broad sense characteristic of our business community today."[111] Executive and employee compensation attorney Henry Rothschild told the House Ways and Means Committee's Panel on Income Tax Revision that "there is some disagreement among members of this panel as to the existence of a real expense account problem . . . the published statistics are based on pure estimates, and hearsay rather than true research."[112] Texaco attorney Edward Schlaudt testified before the Panel that "on the basis of my own experience . . . I refuse to believe that there is really any significant expense account abuse merely because there have been some loose charges and lurid magazine articles in the last few years."[113] In part, Schlaudt's logic rested on the fact that companies had good reasons to scrutinize expense account spending, given the pressure from stockholders to increase profits.[114] After all, if it did not make good business sense to permit lavish expense accounts, a deduction, even at the high post–World War II income tax rates applicable to corporations, would not make sense either. Even Randall, however, conceded that it was "a spectacular and alarming trend, participated in by enough companies and individuals to put all of us upon caution for the good reputation of business men as a class."[115]

109 Millikin, *supra* note 68, at 24.

110 Harry Graham Balter, Fraud Under Federal Tax Law 16 (2d ed. 1953).

111 Clarence B. Randall, *The Myth of the Magic Expense Account*, Dun's Rev., Aug. 1960, at 39, 40.

112 Income Tax Revision: Panel Discussion before the House Committee on Ways & Means, House of Representations, 86th Cong., 1st Sess., Ideas and Suggestions Submitted to the Committee on Ways and Means on the Broad Subject of the Revision of the Federal Income Tax Structure, Dec. 2, 1959, at 587 (testimony of Henry Rothschild) ("Income Tax Revision").

113 Id. at 590 (testimony of Edward J. Schlaudt).

114 Id. at 590–91.

115 Randall, *supra* note 111, at 40.

The Internal Revenue Service also had its doubts about expense account abuses. Dana Latham, who had been appointed Commissioner in 1958, conceded at a meeting of the Tax Executives Institute in 1959, that "while the Service obviously cannot determine with certainty the full extent of this problem, indications at hand would imply that these criticized practices are not nearly as widespread as this publicity suggests."[116] Experts tended to agree. Professor William Hoffman wrote in 1960 that "[t]he best authority would seem to concede that, although all is not well in this area, expense account abuses have been greatly exaggerated."[117]

Even if stories about the abuse of the expense account were overblown, they made for good copy, helping to normalize abuse. As one accountant argued, "the so-called expense account abuses became fashionable subjects for cartoonists, columnists and feature writers. Through such mediums the man on the street has probably been led to believe that the extreme cases he reads about are commonplace and typical."[118] They gave the average person a peek into the heretofore unknown world of expense accounts. Treasury noted in a 1961 report that "the millions of taxpayers who are not so fortunate as to have an expense account . . . are reading and hearing more and more of expense-account abuses."[119] The report explained that "the portrait presented by these articles is that of a privileged class which has become known as the 'expense-account society' – a society made up of individuals who, because of the liberality of our tax laws, practically live on expense accounts."[120]

The fear was that expenses account abuses were inspiring copycats among average taxpayers. One columnist noted that "[w]hen government officials, professional men, and corporation officials engage in self-serving practices, and use the expense account to raise their standards of living at taxpayer expense, they bring down on themselves not only censure," but the tax structure itself.[121] "If they shrink from paying

116 Dana Latham, *The Internal Revenue Service: Recent Developments and Some Current Problems*, 12 TAX EXECUTIVE 7, 11 (1959).

117 Hoffman, *supra* note 18, at 25.

118 B. Kenneth Sanden, *Guidelines for Handling the Reporting of Business Expenses and Reimbursements*, 38 TAXES 972, 972–73 (1960). See Income Tax Revision, *supra* note 112, at 587 (testimony of Henry Rotschild) (noting that the stories are "flamboyant" and "sensational").

119 Study on Entertainment Expenses, *supra* note 37, Exhibit V, at 236.

120 Id.

121 J. A. Livingston, *Business Outlook: Adams' Plight Symbol of our Amoral Times*, WASH. POST AND TIMES HERALD, June 20, 1958, at B9.

taxes, if they condone misapplication of the expenses account, why shouldn't everyone?"[122] Another noted that the "laboring man is as willing to falsify his tax return as his richer brother," suggesting that the "social pressure" to avoid taxes is like a repeat of Prohibition.[123]

For those unable or unwilling to join in, stories of expense account abuses served to fan the flames of discontent. As *San Francisco Chronicle* columnist Lucius Beebe observed, the lavish and unnecessary expenditures "is the aspect of expense account civilization that is most distasteful to people of ordinary means and prudent ways with money, even if they have it in ample abundance."[124] Big businesses, Beebe continued, "make more enemies among a class of people naturally sympathetic to corporate vastness than all the radical agitators and socialists put together."[125] As lawyer and novelist Louis Auchincloss remarked in a letter to the editor in the *New York Times*, "the vice of the system is . . . in the privilege of a few to dine and wine at the expense of the taxpayer."[126] Russell Lynes expressed a similar sentiment, lamenting that "the tax structure seems to create one ethic for certain business men whose services are greatly in demand by corporations and another for the rest of us . . . [Such a businessman] looks slightly ridiculous to a great many of us, for it is we who in the long run pay our taxes to keep him in the style to which he would like to become accustomed."[127] These observations may have led a writer in the *New York Times Magazine* to observe that "the group portrait of expense-account society presents a rather curious picture. To a great many people, it inevitably looks and will continue to look like the *society of kept men*."[128]

The real problem may not have been envy of the wealthy, but envy of people who got to act like they were wealthy. As Norman Lipoff observed, "expense account spending creates a group in our society which appears wealthy not primarily because they have money, but because they are able to spend it."[129] One "taxpayer in the moderate income bracket" relayed

122 Id. at B9.
123 Rene A. Wormser, *The Third American Revolution: A Reform Movement Gone Wrong*, 39 A.B.A. J. 389, 439 (1953).
124 Lucius Beebe, *Expense Account Caviar*, San Fran. Chron., March 20, 1961, at 36.
125 Id.
126 Louis Auchincloss, *Letter to the Editor, Deductions for Entertaining*, N.Y. Times, Dec. 6, 1960, at 40.
127 Lynes, *supra* note 58, at 201.
128 Hellerstein, *supra* note 50, at 126 (italics in original).
129 Lipoff, *supra* note 57, at 187.

an anecdote that illustrated how the unequal distribution of expense accounts created problems:

> My neighbor has a big expense allowance. Every now and then he invites my wife and me to dinner and the theater. Sometimes he takes our boy along with his own son to a baseball game. When we protest at the cost he says, "Don't give it a thought. Uncle Sam is paying for it." The catch comes when we try to reciprocate. I have no big expense account. When we entertain this man in return, it comes out of our own pockets. We simply can't afford to entertain as lavishly as he does.[130]

Clarence Randall saw this as the fundamental issue underlying the "rising public indignation" over lavish expense account living:

> An ordinary fellow – say, an executive from a public utility where every penny is scrubbed before it is spent – takes his wife out to dinner for the one big evening of the year. He finds at the next table a neighbor who has just ordered his third bottle of champagne, although he is known to be two payments behind on his car. And the ordinary decent citizen doesn't like what he sees. He cannot deduct his wife's dinner from his personal income tax as an expense, and he resents watching someone else live it up for free. So, when they hear about it second-hand from waiters and hat-check girls, do teachers and policemen and others who have just had a pay raise denied. So do I. And so does anyone else who understands and values the free enterprise system.[131]

Some disgruntled taxpayers reacted by tattling on their tax dodging neighbors. According to one agent in Detroit, "we get from 200 to 250 letters a month from people who say something like 'I pay my taxes but so-and-so down the street told me he didn't pay taxes on such-and-such.'"[132] The agent continued, "these people aren't being snoopy. They're downright indignant that they're carrying their load and others aren't."[133]

Critics even blamed expense accounts for the rising cost of travel and entertainment. The theory was that "the spendthrift attitude of those who are paying only a portion of the cost as a result of the business expense deduction," led to a degree of price insensitivity that permitted

130 *Expense-Account Scandal*, U.S. News & World Report, Jan. 25, 1960, at 50.
131 Randall, *supra* note 111, at 39, 40.
132 *Tax Dodgers: Stiffer Enforcement Deters Some Cheaters, But Many Persevere*, Wall St. J., April 11, 1957, at 1.
133 Id. *See Expense-Account Scandal*, U.S. News & World Report, Jan. 25, 1960, at 50 (noting "the rising number of complaints from taxpayers who do not have expense accounts and are irked by the ostentatious living of some of those who enjoy expense deductions.").

establishments to raise their prices.[134] Expense accounts were blamed for everything from "the climbing prices of beefsteaks and theatre tickets," to the high price of airline fares and hotel suites.[135] According to Representative Al Ullman, an Oregon Democrat, "the average citizen traveling on his own money is pretty well priced out of the market when it comes to big city nightclubs, some hotels, and other types of amusement, because those are living pretty much on expense account money and it has a very definite inflationary effect on our economy."[136]

The growing outrage may be why Treasury reportedly considered the abuse of the business expense deductions as one of the most worrying tax dodging maneuver.[137] As one commentator noted, the most significant consequence was "the effect on the morale of taxpayers who have no expense accounts and feel they are getting a raw deal."[138] The Commissioner of Internal Revenue agreed, reportedly expressing "particularly concern[] over improper practices existing in the handling of expense accounts, because this is the type of abuse that arouses deep resentment in the hearts of those who do not have similar privileges."[139] Others echoed these sentiments, suggesting that "[i]n a tax system that depends largely upon the voluntary self-assessment of the individual, the morale of the entire taxpaying public is always of crucial importance."[140]

## Enforcement Efforts

The Internal Revenue Service had threatened to crack down expense account abuse for years, but they were considered "window dressing" or a "bluff."[141] In 1957, the Service resolved to step up enforcement efforts. An Internal Revenue Service Circular distributed to field agents conducting audits noted that "for some time our field agents have been alerted to abuses by income taxpayers in claiming deductions for travel and entertainment which could not be justified as ordinary and necessary

134 Lipoff, *supra* note 57, at 187.

135 *Life at Uncle Sam's Expense*, *supra* note 93, at 234–35; Lucius Beebe, *Expense Account Caviar*, San Fran. Chron., March 20, 1961, at 36.

136 1961 House Hearings, *supra* note 52, at 1611.

137 Robert Lubar, *A Plan for Tax Reform*, Fortune, March 1959, at 92.

138 Id.

139 Hoffman, *supra* note 18, at 27.

140 Id.; John D. Pomfret, *"Expense Account Living" Coming Under Close Scrutiny*, N.Y. Times, Dec. 10, 1962, at 13.

141 *"What is a 'Business Expense?"* U.S. News & World Report, Sept. 25, 1953, at 108, 113.

business expenses."[142] Consequently, the Circular continued, "we have been taking a close look at expense deductions claimed involving such items as club dues, entertainment, travel, maintenance of automobiles, yachts, and airplanes, maintenance of company-supported residences, and so forth."[143]

Internal Revenue Commissioner Russell Harrington emphasized the focus on expense account deductions in a speech on September 5, 1957.[144] Harrington identified "the accounting for blanket expense account allowances by employers" as a particular "trouble spot," noting that they "may raise questions of actual, verifiable expenses of the recipient as against additional compensation to him."[145] According to Harrington, "dubious instances that have come to our attention include deductions, as expenses, of purported business trips by executives vacationing at resort hotels, expenses of hunting trips, expenses of attending sporting events in distant cities, and for other non-business expenses under the guise of business trips."[146] Particularly troubling was "the increasing tendency to misstate, 'pad,' and even cheat" on their expense accounts, effectively reducing tax revenues and effectively "placing a burden on the honest taxpayer."[147]

The problem with relying upon enforcement was it only covered businesses. Individuals did not have to disclose that they were beneficiaries of expense accounts on their own returns. In 1958, the Internal Revenue Service sought to remedy this by adding line 6(a) to individual income tax returns, which asked taxpayers to "list and explain all reimbursable business expenses."[148] There had been a question in the Form 1040 similar to Line 6(a) as early as 1921, but it had been dropped in 1944.[149]

142 I.R.-Circular No. 57–85 (June 20, 1957).
143 Id.
144 How Income Tax Returns are Audited, 1957 Standard Fed. Tax Rep. 52001, ¶8646, at 54,809 (1957).
145 Id.
146 How Income Tax Returns are Audited, *supra* note 144, at 54,809.
147 Henry Cassorte Smith, *Watch Your Expense Accounts*, 36 HARV. BUS. REV. 120 (1958).
148 Barcella, *supra* note 23, at 48; Alvin Shuster, *Expense Account Gets Top Billing*, N.Y. TIMES, Jan. 1, 1958, at 17.
149 Caplin, *supra* note 24, at 948; Shuster, *supra* note 148, at 17. The Service insisted individuals were still instructed to report that information even without the question, "but the requirement was in small print and frequently ignored." Caplin, *supra* note 24, at 948; *Expense Accounts: Firms Check Outlays Closer, Hunt Ways to Soften Tax Crackdown*, WALL ST. J., Feb. 14, 1958, at 1.

The Line 6(a) proposal, however, proved too controversial.[150] Apparently, the attempt to place the responsibility on the individual with an expense account "to justify all of his business spending ... touched a tender political nerve" that could not be resolved.[151] This led to a new policy designed to "shift[] to the employer the obligation of policing most expense account allowances."[152] In April 1960, Internal Revenue Commissioner Dana Latham announced a comprehensive travel and entertainment enforcement initiative that placed the burden on businesses.[153] The Service required businesses to disclose on their tax returns "an expense account schedule for certain officers, partners and highly-paid employees," and to disclose whether they are claiming any deductions associated with a "hunting lodge, ranch or farm, fishing camp, resort property, or any other similar facility."[154] According to Latham, "any corporation which does claim a deduction [concerning those specific items] probably will have its tax return audited."[155] The following year, the Treasury Secretary reported to Congress that nearly half of all returns claiming travel and entertainment expense deductions contained errors.[156]

There was evidence that these enforcement initiatives efforts had some effect. Businessmen, according to a *Wall Street Journal* survey conducted in 1962, reported that the "use of these tax-deductible accounts as 'swindle sheets' is declining," in part because of the "concerted campaign" IRS agents began in 1960 "to scrutinize expense-account deductions more

150 Initially, it was just delayed from 1957 to 1958, but it was ultimately dropped altogether in favor of a Regulation limiting disclosure to an employee "who does not account to his employer for his expense money." *Expense Accounts: Firms Check Outlays Closer, Hunt Ways to Soften Tax Crackdown*, WALL ST. J., Feb. 14, 1958, at 1; Malcolm Reed, *Uncle Sam v. The Expense Account*, 39 TAXES 329, 331 (1961); *Tax Ruling Is Changed*, BALTIMORE SUN, March 12, 1958, at 4; Caplin, *supra* note 24, at 948–49.

151 *Expense-Account Scandal*, U.S. NEWS & WORLD REPORT, Jan. 25, 1960, at 50.

152 Caplin, *supra* note 24, at 948.

153 Id. at 949.

154 Id.; Reinhold Groh, *Travel and Entertainment Expenses*, 39 TAXES 253, 254 (1961); *Expense Accounts to Get Tougher Tax Inspection*, WASH. POST TIMES HERALD, Dec. 30, 1959, at A2. *See* B. Kenneth Sanden, *Guidelines for Handling the Reporting of Business Expenses and Reimbursements*, 38 TAXES 972, 973 (1960) (noting that it required expense account allowances detailed for the twenty-five highest-paid officers of a corporation or partners of a partnership and the proprietor and five highest paid employees of a sole proprietorship).

155 *Expense Accounts to Get Tougher Tax Inspection*, WASH. POST TIMES HERALD, Dec. 30, 1959, at A2.

156 Caplin, *supra* note 24, at 951–52.

closely."[157] Nevertheless, even after "a decade of administrative effort" to "ferret out the unwanted expenses,"[158] IRS Commissioner Mortimer Caplin observed that "the T&E [Travel and Entertainment] problem ... remains serious."[159]

One obstacle to enforcement efforts was the courts, which applied what some considered "an all too generous conception of where the line should be drawn between personal and business expense."[160] In one infamous example, a couple who owned Sanitary Farms Dairy deducted the entire cost of an African safari as an advertising expense for their business.[161] Boarding a plan in Erie, Pennsylvania on May 28, 1950, they made stops in London, Paris, and Rome – taking motion pictures in each – before heading to Africa to a "big game hunt" where they reportedly "killed a number of animals" and captured several, including a tiger and two leopards for the Erie Zoo, all while filming portions of their trip before returning in November of 1950.[162] Upon returning, the couple invited wholesale customers and others to their farm to watch an edited film of their trip and inspect their game trophies.[163] Although the court conceded that "the cost of a big game hunt in Africa does not sound like an ordinary and necessary business expense of a dairy business in Erie, Pennsylvania," it found in favor of the taxpayers.[164] Perhaps anticipating the obvious objections, the judge wrote that while the couple "admittedly enjoyed hunting, ... enjoyment of one's work does not make that work a mere personal hobby or the cost of a hunting trip income to the hunter. There is evidence that this trip represented hard work on the part of the [taxpayers], undertaken for the benefit of the Dairy, rather than as a frolic of their own."[165] As NYU Law Professor Jerome Hellerstein sarcastically noted when commenting on this portion of the opinion, "it was purely coincidental that the president loved to hunt big game."[166]

157 *Expense Accounts: New Tax Rules Likely to Further Cut Abuses*, WALL ST. J., Oct. 11, 1962, at 1.
158 Caplin, *supra* note 24, at 953; HELLERSTEIN, *supra* note 50, at 129.
159 Caplin, *supra* note 24, at 964.
160 HELLERSTEIN, *supra* note 50, at 129.
161 Sanitary Farms Dairy, Inc. v. Commissioner, 25 T.C. 463 (1955).
162 Daniel Candee Knickerbocker, Jr., *Entertainment and Related Deductions Under the Revenue Act of 1962*, 31 FORDHAM L. REV. 639 (1963).
163 Sanitary Farms Dairy, Inc. v. Commissioner, 25 T.C. 465–66 (1955).
164 Id. at 467.
165 Id. at 468.
166 HELLERSTEIN, *supra* note 50, at 130.

The *Sanitary Farms* case was often cited as evidence of the futility of enforcement efforts in addressing the abuses of entertainment deductions. The Internal Revenue Service complained that "when existing law allows the cost of a safari to Africa, undertaken by a hunting enthusiast and his wife, to be deducted on the ground that it provides advertising for dairy milk, one cannot expect revenue agents to successfully question the business necessity of duck hunting or night-clubbing with business associates."[167]

## Legislation

With enforcement efforts stymied, reformers pushed legislative reforms. In theory, the government could have lowered the rates and therefore the benefits of deductions.[168] As Rudick explained, if a corporate executive's tax bracket was reduced from 90 percent to 60 percent, "he would be less likely to suggest to his employer corporation that instead of giving him a raise, they should supply and maintain for him a city apartment."[169]

Rather than address the incentives for pursuing questionable deductions, reformers tried to narrow what was deductible.[170] President John F. Kennedy's 1961 tax message to Congress specifically targeted the "widespread abuse" of expense accounts.[171] He argued that "too many individuals have devised means of deducting too many personal living expenses as business expenses."[172] Bemoaning the fact that "expense account living has become a byword in the American scene," Kennedy vowed that "the slogan – 'It's deductible' – should" be eliminated from the lexicon.[173]

Under Kennedy's proposal, expenses for "the amusement, recreation, or similar pleasurable diversion of any individual," would be completely

167 Knickerbocker, Jr., *supra* note 162, at 640 (quoting Hearings on the Tax Recommendations of the President Before the House Committee on Ways and Means, 87th Cong., 1st Sess. 166 (1961)).

168 *See* Income Tax Revision, *supra* note 112, at 589 (statement of Harry Rudick) ("the unnecessary and unwise – in my opinion – range of progression in the upper individual tax brackets contributes significantly to the problem of entertainment and travel expenses"); Lipoff, *supra* note 57, at 188 ("The high progressive tax rate is undoubtedly a major impetus to the use and abuse of expense accounts").

169 Id.

170 The Senate did pass a measure designed to restrict expense account deductions, but it died in the House and Congress instead directed the Internal Revenue Service to conduct further study of the issue. STERN, *supra* note 23, at 116.

171 President John F. Kennedy's Special Message to Congress on Taxation, April 20, 1961.

172 Id.

173 Id.

nondeductible, as would expenses on facilities used primarily for those purposes and club dues for "social, athletic, or sporting clubs or similar organizations."[174] Treasury Secretary Dillon indicated that this would include expenses for "entertaining guests at nightclubs, theaters, country clubs, prizefights, and on hunting and fishing trips."[175] It would also bar a deduction for spending on more mundane things, such as "automobiles, airplanes, apartments, and hotel suites" to the extent they were used "as a substitute for personal living and family expenses."[176]

Meals and beverages posed particularly thorny problems for reformers eager to police the personal/business borderline. As executive compensation experts asked, "[e]very executive and his family must eat; but should the entire cost of a dinner, often more elaborate than usual, become a tax deduction because a business guest is entertained at the table?"[177] "Or," the experts continued, "should the deduction be limited to the amount attributable to the guest's share of the meal or to the shares of both the guest and the executive? Or should a deduction for the host be limited to the difference between the cost of his ordinary dinner and the more elaborate dinner of which partakes because of the business guest?"[178] Under what was known as the Sutter Doctrine, courts created a rebuttable presumption against a deduction for food and beverages, only permitting it where the taxpayer could establish that it was different or more than what they would spend on themselves,[179] but this was so difficult to prove that strict enforcement would have effectively made these expenses non-deductible.[180]

Kennedy's proposal explicitly made meals non-deductible, with three exceptions. First, it permitted a deduction for meals provided to employees, but only on the business premises of the employer.[181] Second, it permitted a deduction for meals incurred while traveling away from home on business, but only with respect to the portion of the trip that was related to its business purpose.[182] Third, and most significantly, it

174 Hearings on President Kennedy's Special Message, *supra* note 39, at 73–74 (1962) (Statement of Treasury Secretary Dillon).

175 Id.

176 Id. at 73.

177 Rothschild & Sobernheim, *supra* note 15, at 1379.

178 Id.

179 *See* Sutter v. Commissioner, 21 T.C. 170, 173 (1953)

180 David W. Bellin, *Taxation: Federal Income: Limited Deductibility of Entertainment Expenses*, 52 MICH. L. REV. 1042, 1044–45 (1954).

181 Hearings on President Kennedy's Special Message, *supra* note 39, at 74.

182 Id. Transportation was also deductible with respect to such business trips.

permitted a deduction for food and beverages provided as part of a business meeting, but only if the meeting involved "discussions or similar activities which are directly related to the operation of the taxpayer's business and which are not furnished for the principal purpose of creating good will."[183] This would effectively disallow "cocktail parties and other functions which are primarily of a social or entertainment character for the purpose of creating good will."[184] Treasury Secretary Dillon also explained that this final exception would likely be accompanied by a proviso that the expenses not exceed a certain amount per day, which he pegged at the $4–$7 range.[185]

## The Persistence of the Expense Account Society

The response to Kennedy's proposal reflected just how deep-seated the expense account society had become. Opponents argued that the proposed limits on expense account deductibility would decimate entire industries. The restaurant industry was particularly vocal about the effect on its members. The National Restaurant Association estimated that "over $2 billion a year is reported as business expenses for food and beverages."[186] These expenses were often concentrated in certain areas, making the effect of their demise even more devastating. According to one estimate, in 1957 "some 80 per cent of luncheons served at top Manhattan restaurants like '21,' Le Pavilion and Chambord ... are expensed."[187]

In hearings, the National Restaurant Association's attorney, Thomas Powell, testified that "business entertaining would be entirely eliminated under the Administration's proposals except in very limited cases."[188] According to Power, that was because such expenses would only be deductible if the meal was consumed during the business meeting. "A meal furnished to a customer for the principal purpose of facilitating good will," which Power suggested was the primary basis for most business meals consumed in restaurants, "would not fit within these limitations even though they are reasonable, legitimate business expenses, and certainly are necessary for the proper conduct of

183 Id.
184 Id.
185 Id.
186 Hellerstein, *supra* note 50, at 132.
187 Brown, *supra* note 86, at 87.
188 1961 House Hearings, *supra* note 52, at 1611.

America's business today."[189] The consequence, Power explained, is that "much of the food and beverage entertainment business would be eliminated because it would be incurred at a time obviously not conducive for the discussion of business. For example, the majority of the banquet business in the restaurant industry would be eliminated."[190] The National Restaurant Association estimated that "$800 million in wages and tips of 200,000 employees in the business would be threatened."[191]

New York restaurateur, Vincent Sardi, Jr., echoed and expanded on Power's prediction, stating that "we cannot exist in midtown Manhattan with people who just live in that area. We must bring in people to New York to support the hotel, the theaters, the restaurants, and all this business. If we eliminate or curtail extensively this business travel, we are wiping out this whole form of business throughout the entire country."[192] Representative John Byrnes of Wisconsin asked Sardi "what you are suggesting is that if the Treasury recommendations, as presented to us, are put into effect, midtown Manhattan would become a distressed area, and that they would have to seek relief through the legislation we just passed to retrain personnel" for different jobs elsewhere?[193] Sardi responded "that may sound like an exaggeration, Congressman, but it really isn't, and it isn't just midtown Manhattan," suggesting that midtown Chicago would be similarly affected.[194] According to Sardi, "the restaurant industry is in a state of recession right now not only in New York, but throughout the country. Part of it, of course, has been due to the scare of this expense account. There has been a drastic curtailment and a drastic holding back to see what is going to happen."[195]

Members of the restaurant industry were not alone in predicting doom without expense account spending. John Lesure, a representative of the American Hotel Association, claimed that the proposal would devastate the hotel industry, especially given an anticipated decline in convention business. "In an industry in which the net income for 1960 was only 3.2 percent of its revenue, and that depends upon business travel for 60 percent of that revenue, a loss of as little as 5 percent of its business

[189] Id.
[190] Id. at 1612.
[191] HELLERSTEIN, *supra* note 50, at 132.
[192] 1961 House Hearings, *supra* note 51, at 1617.
[193] Id. at 1625.
[194] Id. at 1625.
[195] Id. at 1620.

could be fatal."[196] Representative Milton Glenn, a Republican from New Jersey whose district included Atlantic City, underscored this point, testifying that "any curtailment of the use of an expense account will be disastrous to the economy of the New Jersey resort areas."[197]

Proponents of the permissive rules for deducting entertainment expenses protested the notion that it financed personal consumption. The National Restaurant Association's Thomas Power conceded that "these expenses afford some advantage of a personal nature," but argued that this personal advantage was "grossly exaggerated."[198] Power asserted that "it is not the advantage that the person who has never experienced an expense account would imagine it to be ... The majority of men that must constantly travel or consistently entertain at the so-called plush cocktail parties, restaurants, social functions, etc., become very tired of this mode of living."[199]

Although business representatives were careful to align themselves with those concerned about "abuse," they painted such abuses as outliers, distinct from what their members, customers and clients were doing. John Lesure prefaced his testimony on behalf of the hotel industry to the Ways and Means Committee by noting that "we do not in any way approve of the abuses that may have occurred in recent years when taxpayers have attempted to deduct as business expenses the cost of an African safari, or the maintenance of yachts or hunting lodges."[200] Of course, a neutral observer might have recognized that Lesure's definition of abuse was limited to those types of experiences that did not require the use of a hotel. Nevertheless, Lesure "object[ed] strenuously to the establishment of arbitrary restrictions on legitimate business expenses," which presumably included hotel stays at his members' establishments.[201] Others defined abuse as being about bad actors and therefore not appropriate for across-the-board changes. Clarence Turner, an accountant speaking on behalf of the Council of State Chambers of Commerce, opined that "the abuse of expense accounts is confined to a relatively few persons."[202] "I have found" Turner recounted, "the vast majority of businessmen trying honestly and

196 Id. at 1645.
197 Id. at 1649 (Statement of Rep. Milton Glenn (R-N.J.).
198 Id. at 1614.
199 Id. at 1614.
200 Id. at 1643 (statement of John Lesure, American Hotel Association).
201 Id.
202 Id. at 1661 (statement of Clarence L. Turner, Council of State Chambers of Commerce).

conscientiously to separate personal from business expense and report the latter accurately."[203]

Kennedy's plan found some support in Congress,[204] but opponents succeeded in preserving most of the tax structure that supported the expense account society. As Jerome Hellerstein colorfully declared, the "proposals to restrict entertainment expenses were torn to shreds by Congress."[205] "What came out of Capitol Hill," Hellerstein explained, "was in essence a reaffirmation of the rule that business-entertainment expenses are to be allowed, plus some new standards for judging whether an expense is truly a business expense, and a tightening up of the records required to be kept to prove that the expenditures were actually made."[206] The travel and entertainment rules adopted in the 1962 Act may have been "the culmination of a long campaign by the Treasury Department to put an end to 'expense account living,'"[207] but they hardly fulfilled the campaign's mission.

Under the 1962 Act, entertainment had to be "directly related to the active conduct" of the taxpayer's trade or business or, if the entertainment directly preceded or followed "a substantial and bona fide business discussion," then the entertainment expense must be "associated with" the active conduct of the taxpayer's trade or business.[208] Although taxpayers had to show some business relationship to an entertainment expense even prior to 1962, the intention was that the 1962 amendment would require the taxpayer establish "a greater degree of proximate relation" than he had previously.[209] Congress intended that the deduction would be denied "where the possibility of the expenditure resulting in the production of income was remote," but this was hardly a high standard.[210]

That does not mean that observers thought the 1962 Act's reform provisions would have no effect. As Hellerstein explained, "the new law

[203] Id.

[204] For instance, Senator Paul Douglas, a Democrat from Illinois, called the deduction for expense accounts and entertainment "one of the grossest abuses in American business." Legislative History of H.R. 10650, 87th Cong., The Revenue Act of 1962, Pub. L. 87–834, 90th Cong., 1st Sess. 2942 (1967) (statement of Sen. Paul Douglas).

[205] HELLERSTEIN, *supra* note 50, at 135.

[206] Id.

[207] Dennis R. Powell, *Note, Effect of the 1962 Revenue Act on Travel, Entertainment, and Gift Deductions*, 38 NOTRE DAME LAW. 447, 447 (1963).

[208] I.R.C., § 274(a)(1)(A) (1954 Code).

[209] Knickerbocker, Jr., *supra* note 162, at 642.

[210] Id.

will undoubtedly curtail some of the worst abuses in extravagant living off the income-tax gravy train. The costs of African safaris and fishing cruises will now be difficult, if not impossible, to sustain for most taxpayers."[211] It also required more detailed record keeping, which Hellerstein predicted would "produce disallowances of unsubstantiated amounts of nondeductible expenditures that they have been getting away with for years."[212]

All of this led to "unprecedented" concern among businessmen and their advisers about the nature of the regulations being drafted to implement the 1962 Act.[213] Herbert Eagle, an insurance company executive, expressed concern that the documentation requirements would alter the "psyche of the go-get-'em salesman."[214] According to Eagle, "the substantiation requirement would tend to submerge the creative extrovert salesman in a deadening sea of detailed record keeping."[215] Hearings on these rules were moved to a larger hall and expanded from one to two days to accommodate the large number of witnesses hoping to soften the proposed regulations.[216] A total of fifty-one witnesses appeared on behalf of business interests during the Ways and Means Committee hearings and another 2,000 wrote letters criticizing the regulations.[217] Businessmen formally resented what they considered to be an attempt "to penetrate further into the affairs that businessmen ... feel is properly the business of business,"[218] but "there occasionally was an undercurrent of shocked realization that the good old days might really be gone after all."[219]

Notwithstanding this concern, few thought this was the end of the expense account society. Many believed the new restrictions "added nothing of any substance to the law" because the language used in the new provisions was similar to what had been used by courts in enforcing the preexisting law.[220] As long as taxpayers engaged in "shop talk" and

211 HELLERSTEIN, *supra* note 50, at 136.
212 Id. at 137–38.
213 Robert Metz, *Businessmen Protest Changes in Expense-Account Tax Rules*, N.Y. TIMES, Dec. 3, 1962, at 49.
214 Ronald J. Ostrow, *Area Executives Take Up Gauntlet Over Expense Account Deductions*, L.A. TIMES, Dec. 9, 1962, at K1, K3.
215 Id.
216 Metz, *Businessmen Protest Changes*, *supra* note 213, at 49.
217 John D. Pomfret, *"Expense Account Living" Coming Under Close Scrutiny*, N.Y. TIMES, Dec. 10, 1962, at 13.
218 Ostrow, *supra* note 214, at K1.
219 Pomfret, *supra* note 217, at 13.
220 Knickerbocker, *supra* note 162, at 660.

kept appropriate records, they could continue to entertain as normal. As Hellerstein explained, "the standards are too vague and uncertain and will, I suspect, result in the continued allowance as deductible of too much of what is in truth personal living expense."[221]

The documentation rules were more of an irritant than a real obstacle. Commissioner Mortimer Caplin explained that "many companies demand much greater detail from their employees" than what the documentation rules required.[222] Moreover, the truly dishonest taxpayers who exaggerated their expenses or made them up completely were just as likely to create fraudulent documentation as to forgo the activity altogether.[223] The prevailing sentiment seemed to be that if the law exceeded the commonly accepted view of what amount of tax avoidance was acceptable, it would simply be ignored. As one New York businessman warned, "if the government is determined to kill hunting lodges, pseudo business planes and phony business trips to Europe – that's great, but if they're going to start nickel snatching, denying a business lunch and modest entertaining of clients, they'll be deceived, denied and defeated."[224]

The 1962 Act appeared to demonstrate the difficulty of legislating away what was already culturally entrenched. As practitioners Michael Emmanuel and Norman Lipoff explained, "seldom has a new statute slashed so broadly across the practices and customs of the business community."[225] In effect, the statute was an attempt "for the first time to curb business practices which, over the span of a generation, had become a way of life."[226] Not surprisingly given its place in American society, the phrase "it's deductible" was not "vanishing from the American scene" as President Kennedy had hoped, but it was reportedly "no longer being uttered in such offhand fashion, nor quite so frequently,

221 Hellerstein, *supra* note 50, at 138.

222 Mortimer Caplin, *Letters to the Editor, Caplin and Congress*, Wall St. J., Jan. 17, 1963, at 14.

223 Ostrow, *supra* note 214, at K3. *See Expense Accounts: New Tax Rules Likely to Further Cut Abuses*, Wall St. J., Oct. 11, 1962, at 1, 14 (noting that "a few cheaters . . . may have hit on a way to beat" the documentation requirement, such as one "Long Island executive who, by arrangement with his deliveryman, never pays the bill for daily deliveries of bread and cakes to his house until it hits $100 or $150," which IRS agents had accepted in the past, "reasoning that if he paid $150 at one time for bakery goods he must have held a party.").

224 Metz, *Businessmen Protest Changes*, *supra* note 213, at 49, 52.

225 Emmanuel & Lipoff, *supra* note 41, at 487.

226 Id.

as it has been over the" previous two decades."[227] By 1964, Congress had already repealed an aspect of the new rules that had required allocation of transportation expenses between the time spent on a more than one-week trip for business and personal reasons.[228] It was not long before columnists were once again advising individuals with "travel fever" about the myriad ways they could cultivate a business connection in their desired destination and document it appropriately to ensure that much of it would be deductible.[229] The expense account society, it seemed, had emerged largely unscathed.

If the use of the expense account changed much after 1962, it was likely because of an evolution in business practices and societal norms rather than the new rules. As Commissioner Caplin observed in 1963, firms were already beginning to demand more documentation for business expenses than what the Treasury Regulations required.[230] With profits dropping in some industries, it was not surprising that business entertainment spending would eventually draw the attention of bean counters. For example, the *New York Times* reported in 1964 that "net profits as a percentage of gross income by advertising agencies tumbled from 5.4 per cent in 1953 to 3.3 per cent a decade later, and business entertainment was one obvious area for cost reductions."[231] A 1962 *Wall Street Journal* survey of expense account practices reported that "Government efforts have been reinforced by many companies, which have set up tight expense-control systems of their own. Caught in a growing squeeze on profit margins, these concerns have concluded they can no longer afford even tax-deductible extravagance."[232] The new tax rules therefore may have hastened the decline of the completely no-rules expense account in these instances, but not without business' cooperation. Indeed, they may have used the new rules as a convenient excuse for making changes they already wanted to make.

[227] Eileen Shanahan, *Expense Accounts: To Strict?* N.Y. TIMES, May 12, 1963, at E8. *See* Peter Bart, *Advertising: Entertainment is Less Lavish*, N.Y. TIMES, March 8, 1964, at F12 (noting that subtle changes were occurring in entertainment spending, although prompted by factors other than tax in many cases).

[228] William A. Klein, *The Deductibility of Transportation Expenses of a Combination Business and Pleasure Trip – a Conceptual Analysis*, 18 STAN. L. REV. 1099, 1177 (1966).

[229] Robert McKay, *Combine Travel, Business for Tax Break*, CHI. TRIB., Feb. 18, 1968, at N6.

[230] Caplin, *Letters to the Editor*, *supra* note 222, at 14.

[231] Peter Bart, *Advertising: Entertainment is Less Lavish*, N.Y. TIMES, March 8, 1964, at F12.

[232] *Expense Accounts: New Tax Rules Likely to Further Cut Abuses; Firms Crack Down Too*, WALL ST. J., Oct. 11, 1962, at 1.

Despite regular assaults, the deduction for business meals and entertainment persisted throughout the last half-century. Although there were several attempts to eliminate or substantially reform the deduction for business entertainment expenses,[233] they only whittled away at business entertainment's tax preference.[234] It was not eliminated entirely until 2017.[235] Even then the preference for business meals was restored at a higher level of deductibility in 2020.[236] As in prior efforts to eliminate it, the expense account society proved to be resilient.

[233] *See* Jimmy Carter, *Tax Reduction and Reform Message to Congress*, Jan. 20, 1978; Edward Cowan, *Tax Plan Expected to Halve the Deduction for Business Meals*, N.Y. TIMES, Sept. 28, 1977, at 1. Academics have long encouraged such efforts. *See* Schmalbeck & Soled, *supra* note 27, at 763; Wendy Gerzog Shaller, *Limited Deductions for Mixed Personal/Business Expenses: Curb Current Abuses and Restore Some Progressivity into the Tax Code*, 41 CATH. U. L. REV. 581, 605 (1992).

[234] Deductibility was capped in 1986 when there was a blanket disallowance of 20 percent of expenses and again in 1993 at a 50 percent disallowance. Revenue Reconciliation Act of 1993, which was part of the Omnibus Budget Reconciliation Act of 1993, P.L. 103–66, section 13209(a); P.L. 99–514, section 142 (1986).

[235] As part of President Donald Trump's Tax Cuts and Jobs Act, Congress removed the deduction for expenses for activities deemed to constitute "entertainment, amusement, or recreation" to help to pay for tax cuts elsewhere in the bill. I.R.C. §274(a)(1)(A).

[236] Under the Taxpayer Certainty and Disaster Relief Tax Act of 2020, as a pandemic relief measure, all business-related "food or beverages provided by a restaurant" prior to January 1, 2023, were eligible for a 100 percent deduction. Rules Committee Print 116–68, Text of the House Amendment to the Senate Amendment to H.R. 133 of the Consolidated Appropriations Act of 2021, Dec. 21, 2021, § 210 (Amending 274(n)(2)).

# 7

## Manufactured Tax Populism?

### The Campaign against Dividend and Interest Withholding

In 1962, President John F. Kennedy called for Congress "to apply to dividends and to interest the same withholding requirements we have long applied to wages."[1] Kennedy was concerned about the tax dodging that had been allowed to run rampant during the 1950s, which included a $3.3 billion shortfall between dividends and interest paid and reported on income tax returns.[2] By requiring withholding, Kennedy hoped to close what was considered one of the "major tax-escape routes for the upper-income brackets."[3]

Kennedy's withholding proposal was not expected to sail through Congress easily, but it was not expected to be controversial among regular taxpayers.[4] Wage earners were accustomed to withholding since Congress started requiring it during World War II to help quickly address the wartime revenue needs, control inflation from the massive rise in defense spending, and aid in the transition of the income tax from a class tax to a mass tax.[5] Many states had also adopted similar

[1] John F. Kennedy, Annual Message to Congress on the State of the Union, Jan. 11, 1962.

[2] *The Tax Bill Battle: Withhold - Or Not?*, NEWSWEEK, June 4, 1962, at 78. Cf. PHILIP M. STERN, THE GREAT TREASURY RAID 168 (1964) (citing a $4 billion shortfall).

[3] JULIAN E. ZELIZER, TAXING AMERICA: WILBUR D. MILLS, CONGRESS, AND THE STATE, 1945–1975 187 (1998). The other two "tax-escape routes" cited were foreign tax havens and capital gains rates. Id.

[4] Opposition to dividend and interest withholding during World War II and the early 1950s primarily came from corporations, banks, and trade groups rather than individuals. Joseph A. Pechman, *Withholding for Interest and Dividends*, in TAX REVISION COMPENDIUM, COMPENDIUM OF PAPERS ON BROADENING THE TAX BASE, submitted to the Committee on Ways and Means 1479, 1481–84 (Nov. 16, 1959).

[5] Current Tax Payment Act of 1943, Pub. L. No. 78–120, §2, 57 Stat. 126, 128 (1943); LAWRENCE ZELENAK, FIGURING OUT THE TAX: CONGRESS, TREASURY, AND THE DESIGN OF THE EARLY MODERN INCOME TAX 52–60 (2018); Charlotte Twight, *Evolution of Federal Income Tax Withholding: The Machinery of Institutional Change*, 14 CATO J. 359, 369–81 (1995); Carolyn C. Jones, *Class Tax to Mass Tax: The Role of Propaganda in the Expansion of the Income Tax During World War II*, 37 BUFF. L. REV. 685, 697 (1988); Richard L. Doernberg, *The Case Against Withholding*, 61 TEX. L. REV. 595, 602 (1982).

withholding tax systems, generally with much success.[6] Moreover, unlike wage withholding, dividend and interest withholding would hit wealthy taxpayers harder than regular taxpayers.[7]

Despite this history, Kennedy's dividend and interest withholding proposal was so wildly unpopular that it threatened to kill the 1962 tax bill altogether.[8] Congressional offices were "bombarded" by "an unprecedented avalanche" of letters from constituents in opposition to the proposal,[9] with some Senators receiving thousands of letters a day in what they called the most mail they had ever received on a single issue.[10] Congress relented and stripped the dividend and interest withholding provision from the bill in favor of new reporting requirements.

Why did dividend and interest withholding generate such a reaction? This chapter explains that the resistance, although initially organized by businesses and their lobbyists,[11] reflected something deeper than a typical "astroturf," or fake grassroots, movement.[12] Letter writers appeared to be genuinely concerned about what some characterized as the "gentle robbery" of dividend and interest withholding.[13] More broadly, the popular reaction to the withholding proposal illustrated a general tension in the government's antitax dodging efforts. Regular taxpayers resented that the rich had so many ways to dodge taxes, but they did not want one of *their* only ways – nonreporting of dividends and interest – foreclosed. Instead of driving a wedge between the rich and the middle class by focusing on capital rather than labor income, the battle over dividend and interest withholding symbolized how the two groups became aligned in their opposition to the government's efforts to combat tax dodging.

[6] Austin C. Wehrwein, *Withholding Tax Favored Widely*, N.Y. TIMES, Jan. 25, 1959, at 42.
[7] STERN, *supra* note 2, at 171.
[8] *Anti-Dividend Tax Letters Flood Senate*, CHI. DAILY TRIB., April 22, 1962, at B3; *The Tax Battle: Withhold – Or Not? supra* note 2.
[9] *The Tax Battle: Withhold – Or Not? supra* note 2.
[10] Douglas B. Cornell, *Tax Foes Lying, Says President*, ATL. CONST., May 10, 1962, at 1, 6.
[11] CATHIE J. MARTIN, SHIFTING THE BURDEN: THE STRUGGLE OVER GROWTH AND CORPORATE TAXATION 63 (1991); 108 CONG. REC. 22970 (1962) (statement of Sen. Proxmire).
[12] See KEN KOLLMAN, OUTSIDE LOBBYING: PUBLIC OPINION AND INTEREST GROUP STRATEGIES 13 (1998) (distinguishing an "astroturf" movement from a real grassroots movement).
[13] Editorial, *The Art of Gentle Robbery*, CHI. DAILY TRIB., April 24, 1961, at 16.

## A History of Withholding Efforts Through the Mid-Twentieth Century

### *Early Income Taxation*

Governments have resorted to third party withholding as a collection mechanism for dividends, interest, and wages since the earliest days of the income tax.[14] When the English Parliament adopted an income tax in 1799 during the Napoleonic Wars, it produced less than 60 percent of the expected revenue because of evasion.[15] To combat this, they employed "stoppage-at-the-source" methods in 1803 when the income tax was reintroduced.[16] The new tax imposed withholding on income from "public office or employment."[17] It also used the corporate income tax as a withholding device by requiring that it be paid out of on the "annual profits and gains" of the company "before any dividend shall have been paid," while permitting corporations to take from the dividends before paid to shareholders "a proportionate deduction in respect of the duty charged."[18]

Much like in England, the Union side during the Civil War applied withholding to the salaries of government employees.[19] In addition, an entity-level corporate income tax effectively operated as a withholding tax for the Union's individual income tax.[20] It included both a dividend tax on businesses in the banking and insurance industries and a dividend and interest tax on businesses in the transportation area.[21] In each case,

[14] For a general discussion of the pre-1943 withholding provisions, but not of their interest and dividend withholding aspects, *see* Ajay K. Mehrotra, *"From Contested Concept to Cornerstone of Administrative Practice:" Social Learning and the Early History of U.S. Tax Withholding*, 7 Colum. J. Tax L. 144 (2016).

[15] Meade Emory, *The Early English Income Tax: A Heritage for the Contemporary*, 9 Am. J. Leg. Hist. 291, 301 (1965).

[16] Steven A. Bank, Anglo-American Corporate Taxation: Tracing the Common Roots of Divergent Approaches 19–26 (2011).

[17] Id. at 24–25; Income Tax Act of 1803, 43 Geo. III c. 122, sec. 127. An informal system of withholding may have taken place for nongovernment employees too. According to Arthur Hope-Jones, "large corporations, such as the Bank of England, the East India Company, the Royal Exchange and London Insurance Companies may have assisted" in the collection of income tax by withholding on employee salaries "before the employees were paid." Arthur Hope-Jones, Income Tax in the Napoleonic Wars 22 (1939).

[18] Bank, Anglo-American Corporate Taxation, *supra* note 16, at 24–25.

[19] Lillian Doris, American Way in Taxation: Internal Revenue 1862–1963 115–16 (1963).

[20] Steven A. Bank, From Sword to Shield: The Transformation of the Corporate Income Tax, 1861 to Present 21–23 (2010).

[21] Act of July 1, 1862, ch. 119, §§ 81, 82, 12 Stat. 469–70. (1862); Act of June 30, 1864, ch. 173, §§ 120, 122, 13 Stat. 223, 283–84.

although the tax was levied on the corporation itself, the funds due could be withheld from the dividends or interest paid to shareholders or bondholders in order to pay the tax.[22] It was, therefore, commonly understood as a withholding mechanism.[23] As Senator John Sherman, a Republican from Ohio and a member of the Senate Finance Committee, explained in 1864, "[w]e are levying taxes on the citizens through the corporations. We make these corporations merely agents of ours to collect the tax from individuals."[24] Although the Civil War-era withholding system was "crude and nascent," it was relatively successful, accounting for 40 percent of the amounts raised from the income tax.[25] It also was tacitly approved by the Supreme Court in a case that challenged the constitutionality of the withholding mechanism.[26]

In 1894, Congress enacted an income tax that once again utilized the withholding principle. As with its mid-century predecessor, the 1894 Act required withholding for government employees with sufficient income to be subject to the tax.[27] Instead of imposing a dividend or interest tax, however, corporations were subject to an entity-level flat two percent tax on all of their income.[28] Even here, however, the corporate tax was a part of the withholding scheme because most corporations distributed all of their profits as dividends every year.[29] Since individuals were not required to pay tax on dividends received, the entity level tax was effectively a way to collect the tax on dividends at the corporate level.[30] Although the income tax was struck down as unconstitutional by the Supreme Court before it could be

22 BANK, FROM SWORD TO SHIELD, *supra* note 20, at 19–20; Act of June 30, 1864, §§ 120, 122, 13 Stat. at 283–84.

23 DORIS, *supra* note 19, at 116; FREDERIC C. HOWE, TAXATION AND TAXES IN THE UNITED STATES UNDER THE INTERNAL REVENUE SYSTEM, 1791–1895, 96–97 (1896).

24 CONG. GLOBE, 38th Cong. 1st Sess. 2499 (1864).

25 Mehrotra, *From Contested Concept*, *supra* note 14, at 152.

26 United States v. Balt. & Ohio R. R., 84 U.S. 322, 324–25 (1872). *See* Mehrotra, *From Contested Concept*, *supra* note 14, at 156–57 (explaining that although the case upheld the challenge because the City of Baltimore was the creditor and would not be subject to tax on the interest received, it acknowledged that the result would have been different if the City had been a trustee for a private individual in whose hands the income would be taxable).

27 Revenue Act of 1894, ch. 349, § 33, 28 Stat. 509, 559 (1894).

28 Id. at § 32, 28 Stat. at 556.

29 BANK, FROM SWORD TO SHIELD, *supra* note 20, at 48–49.

30 Id. at 54–55.

implemented,[31] many of its details, including the withholding scheme, provide a template for future legislation.[32]

### *Post-Sixteenth Amendment*

When Congress enacted the first post-Sixteenth Amendment income tax in 1913, it adopted "the most extensive application . . . of the collection-at-source method" possible to increase revenues and reduce evasion.[33] Called "the new law's most salient, if not its most popular feature,"[34] the withholding scheme covered all wage earners who earned more than the $3,000 minimum, rather than just government employees.[35] It covered interest, but only foreign, rather than domestic, dividends.[36] Withholding was more complicated under the 1913 Act than its nineteenth-century predecessors because of the graduated rates. To deal with that, Congress imposed a flat rate "normal," or base, tax of 1 percent and a surtax applied at progressive rates up to 6 percent,[37] applying withholding only to the normal rate.[38]

To implement withholding, Treasury needed a system that accounted for the fact only 2 percent of individuals made more than the $3,000 exemption.[39] For salaries, this was simple. Employers paying more than $3,000 to an individual taxpayer withheld an amount equal to the normal rate.[40] Interest was more challenging because payers might not know whether a recipient had earned at least $3,000. Treasury issued regulations addressing that, stating that "any person subject to the normal tax . . . wishing to avail himself or herself of the exemption . . . must file with

[31] Pollock v. Farmers' Loan and Trust Co., 157 U.S. 429, 572 (1895).

[32] BANK, FROM SWORD TO SHIELD, *supra* note 20, at 85; Mehrotra, *From Contested Concept*, *supra* note 14, at 159.

[33] DORIS, *supra* note 19, at 118. *See* Mehrotra, *From Contested Concept*, *supra* note 14, at 159 (calling it "an ambitious attempt to capture nearly all of the 'normal' tax through the process of withholding.").

[34] Garrard Glenn, *The Income Tax Law and Deduction at the Source*, 13 COLUM. L. REV. 714, 715 (1913).

[35] Mehrotra, *From Contested Concept*, *supra* note 14, at 159.

[36] ROY G. BLAKEY & GLADYS C. BLAKEY, THE FEDERAL INCOME TAX 98 (1940). The theory was the earnings and profits used to pay domestic dividends were already taxed under the corporate income tax. BANK, FROM SWORD TO SHIELD, *supra* note 20, at 83; Anuj C. Desai, *What a History of Tax Withholding Tells Us about the Relationship Between Statutes and Constitutional Law*, 108 NW. U. L. REV. 859, 884 (2014).

[37] Act of Oct 3, 1913, ch. 16, § II(B), 38 Stat. 166, 167–68.

[38] Glenn, *supra* note 34, at 715; ZELENAK, *supra* note 5, at 31.

[39] Mehrotra, *From Contested Concept*, *supra* note 14, at 158.

[40] Id. at 159; Act of Oct. 3, 1913, ch. 16, § II(B), 38 Stat. at 169.

the withholding agent, not later than 30 days prior to the day on which the return of his income is due, a notice" certifying his exemption.[41] This method, however, was cumbersome,[42] not to mention creating potential liability for the bond issuer.[43] This may have fueled some of the later opposition to withholding.

Although the Supreme Court upheld the constitutionality of withholding under the 1913 Act,[44] the system was highly unpopular.[45] Economist Roy G. Blakey observed that "perhaps no feature of the income tax law has caused more unfavorable criticism than the stoppage-at-the-source provision, which throws much of the burden of collecting the government's revenue upon banks, trust companies, corporations, and other agents."[46] Both the Treasury Secretary and the Commissioner of Internal Revenue recommended ending withholding,[47] influenced perhaps in part by the criticism and in part by the revelations that the percentage of revenues brought in through withholding fell far short of what was expected.[48] In the Revenue Act of 1917, withholding was replaced with third party information reporting for payments that exceeded the individual personal exemption.[49]

### *New Deal and World War II*

Withholding was revived during the New Deal to fund retirement plans under both the Social Security Act of 1935 and the Railroad Retirement Act of 1937.[50] Neither involved the income tax, but they offered proof of concept.[51] As Professor Anuj Desai noted, "it demonstrated that

41 Glenn, *supra* note 34, at 721 (quoting the Regulations of October 31, 1913).
42 Desai, *supra* note 36, at 885–86.
43 Id. at 886, fn. 130.
44 *Brushaber v. United States* 240 U.S. 1, 24, 26 (1916); Doernberg, *supra* note 5, at 599–600.
45 Id. at 600; Mehrotra, *From Contested Concept*, *supra* note 14, at 160, 162–64; Ajay K. Mehrotra, Making the Modern American Fiscal State: Law, Politics, and the Rise of Progressive Taxation, 1877–1929 287–89 (2013).
46 Roy G. Blakey, *The New Revenue Act*, 6 Am. Econ. Rev. 837, 842 (1916). A major criticism was it withheld only on the normal tax and not the surtax too. Zelenak, *supra* note 5, at 34.
47 Doernberg, *supra* note 5, at 600.
48 Desai, *supra* note 36, at 887; Doris, *supra* note 19, at 119.
49 Revenue Act of 1917, Pub. L. No. 65-63, §3, 40 Stat. 300, 301–02 (1917). Withholding continued for "tax-free covenant bonds" and for nonresident aliens. Robert H. Montgomery, Income Tax Procedure 314–15 (1919); Doris, *supra* note 19, at 119.
50 Doris, *supra* note 19, at 119–20.
51 Id.

withholding was administratively possible – for both the government and employers. This laid the groundwork for the full-scale adoption of withholding enacted during World War II."[52]

Withholding was not initially part of Congress' wartime income tax expansion, despite the need to collect taxes from a significantly larger base of taxpayers because of the lowered exemptions.[53] Treasury presented a withholding plan that included dividends and interest in 1941 and reintroduced it in 1942, where it was adopted by the House.[54] In his statement to the House Ways and Means Committee, Treasury Secretary Henry Morgenthau noted that the "best available expedient" for enforcing the expanded income taxes proposed would be a "provision for collecting at the source for those incomes that are paid periodically, including wages, salaries, bond interest, and dividends."[55] The Commissioner of Internal Revenue, Guy Helvering, threw a "dash of very cold water" on the proposal, however, by predicting "much difficulty" in implementing withholding.[56]

Treasury persisted in part because of the argument that withholding could help combat inflation by siphoning off some of the nation's purchasing power.[57] Thus, although the Senate rejected the House Bill and its withholding provision, it did include withholding in its proposed so-called "Victory Tax," which Congress adopted as part of the Revenue Act of 1942.[58] This imposed a 5 percent flat rate tax on the gross income of individuals above a small exemption amount of $624 with fewer deductions, resulting in 13 million new taxpayers.[59] This provided a "foot in the door" for the broader adoption of withholding.[60] Within a year, under the Current Tax Payment Act of 1943,[61] Congress enacted a withholding provision that covered all wages. Treasury advocated withholding for

52 Desai, *supra* note 36, at 889.

53 Steven A. Bank, Kirk J. Stark, & Joseph J. Thorndike, War and Taxes 86 (2008).

54 Doernberg, *supra* note 5, at 600.

55 Randolph E. Paul, Taxation in the United States 330 (1954).

56 Id. at 330–31.

57 Bank, Stark & Thorndike, *supra* note 53, at 99–100; Zelenak, *supra* note 5, at 53.

58 Zelenak, *supra* note 5, at 56–57; Revenue Act of 1942, Pub. L. No. 77-753, 56 Stat. 798 (1942).

59 Bank, Stark & Thorndike, *supra* note 53, at 99.

60 Dennis J. Ventry, Jr., & Joseph J. Thorndike, *The Plan that Slogans Built: The Revenue Act of 1943*, Tax History Project, Sept. 1, 1997.

61 Current Tax Payment Act of 1943, Pub. L. No. 78-68, §§ 2(a), 6, 57 Stat. 126 (1943).

dividends, but not interest, in addition to wages.[62] The final act, however, covered wages only and omitted both dividends and interest.[63]

Dividend and interest withholding was strenuously opposed by business interests – particularly banks, savings and loans, and corporate financial officers – who complained about the burden of furnishing bondholders or stockholders with receipts for amounts withheld and processing certificates of exemption from withholding on coupon bonds for bond issuers.[64] In its proposals, Treasury tried to simplify things by exempting interest on coupon bonds and dividends from credit unions, savings and loans, and bank and farm cooperatives,[65] but the Senate Finance Committee instead excluded dividends and interest altogether.[66] With wage withholding less controversial,[67] Congress appeared to take the path of least resistance.

### *1950s*

There were calls for revisiting dividend and interest withholding after World War II,[68] but Congress did not heed these calls until the early 1950s. In 1950, the House passed a bill that would extend withholding to dividends only,[69] effectively returning to the 1943 Treasury proposal. This was the first time withholding had been proposed because of concerns about unreported income, in this case from dividends. According to the Ways and Means Committee, "a substantial percentage of the dividends paid out by the corporations of this country is not declared as taxable income."[70] The Committee found that there was a dividend tax gap of approximately $800 million in 1947, after deducting dividends paid to tax-exempt organizations and individuals whose incomes fell below the exemption.[71] It did not attribute this tax gap to tax evasion, per se,

62 Doernberg, *supra* note 5, at 601.
63 Id.
64 Id. at 600.
65 Id. at 601.
66 Id.
67 *See* id. at 602 (only 6 percent of surveyed employers viewed it unfavorably and labor groups like the CIO supported it). Randolph Paul said Treasury received letters expressing opposition, but he attributed most objections to misunderstanding withholding. PAUL, TAXATION IN THE UNITED STATES, *supra* note 55, at 348.
68 *See, e.g.*, Joseph A. Schafer, *The Withholding System Needs Revision*, 26 TAXES 432, 439 (1948).
69 Revenue Act of 1950, S. Rep. No. 2375, 81st Cong., 2d Sess. (1950).
70 H.R. Rep. No. 2319, 81st Cong., 2d Sess., 1950-2 C.B. 380, 406 (June 23, 1950).
71 Id.

but rather to "errors of omission."[72] Notably, it concluded that information returns or audits were insufficient for closing this tax gap.[73]

Rather than adopting the House's dividend withholding proposal, the Senate sought to address some of the issues it raised about current methods of detecting underpayments. For instance, the Senate Finance Committee recognized that the $100 limitation on information reporting for dividends "tends to encourage carelessness on his part, if not deliberate evasion" and that the lack of dividend itemization on individual returns "tends to reduce the accuracy of the reporting of income."[74] It claimed, however, that it had received reassurance from the Commissioner that it would "revise the existing regulations so as to require complete reporting" of dividends, rather than merely those that exceeded the limit, and that it "will amend the income tax return form so that the itemization of dividends will be required in the 1950 tax returns filed in 1951."[75] According to the Committee, "these administrative changes will help to correct the problem at which the proposal for withholding on dividends was aimed," making withholding unnecessary.[76]

Notwithstanding the Senate Finance Committee's rejection of dividend withholding, the House provision was originally approved in Conference.[77] A day later, however, the conferees reversed course and removed dividend withholding.[78] The explanation for the change was that the Senate traded the withholding provision for two provisions in its bill – one involving the taxation of family partnerships and the other favorable tax treatment for profits on the sale or lease of oil or other mineral rights – that were "widely criticized as 'grabs' for privileged taxpayers."[79] In theory, the dividend tax gap was deemed to be less objectionable, but reportedly business interests' complaints about the burden of complying with the withholding requirement were what swayed the conferees.[80] Senator Hubert Humphrey, in a speech that assailed the Senate bill and tax loopholes generally, specifically "deplored" the omission of the dividend

72 Id.
73 Id.
74 Senate Rep. No. 2375, 81st Cong., 2d Sess., 1950-2 C.B. 483, 521 (Aug. 22, 1950).
75 Id.
76 Id.
77 John D. Morris, *Withholding Levy of 10% on Dividends Wins in Conference*, N.Y. Times, Sept. 20, 1950, at 1.
78 John D. Morris, *Decision Reversed on Tax-Rise Bill; No Dividends Levy*, N.Y. Times, Sept. 21, 1950, at 1.
79 Id.
80 *See* Godfrey N. Nelson, *Dividend Tax Bill Takes a New Slant*, N.Y. Times, May 6, 1951.

withholding provision.[81] Nevertheless, the Senate passed the bill without dividend withholding.[82]

In 1951, the House tried again, passing a bill that required withholding for both dividends and interest.[83] At this point, the tax gap on both dividends and interest was reportedly $3 billion and the Internal Revenue Bureau urged Congress to enact withholding as an enforcement measure.[84] Business interests again opposed withholding. Trade groups like the American Bankers Association, the New Jersey State Bankers Association, the Pennsylvania Bankers Association, and the New York State Bankers Association expressed concern about the House proposal.[85] Critics raised several objections, such as that it would tax depositors with incomes below the exemption level or that it would discourage purchases of certain bonds or participation in cooperative organizations.[86] In response, Ways and Means redrafted the bill to include myriad exemptions,[87] but this only fueled complaints about the administrative burden without fully addressing the objections.[88] Opponents also

81 Paul, Taxation in the United States, *supra* note 55, at 564. *Cf.* Hubert H. Humphrey, Tax Loopholes 17–19 (1952) (discussing the tax loopholes in the 1950 Revenue Act, including the absence of a dividend and interest withholding provision).

82 Lily Kahng, *Investment Income Withholding in the United States and Germany*, 10 Fla. Tax Rev. 315, 325 (2010).

83 H.R. Rep. No. 586, 82nd Cong. (1951). Joseph A. Pechman, *Withholding for Interest and Dividends*, in Tax Revision Compendium, Compendium of Papers on Broadening the Tax Base, submitted to the Committee on Ways and Means 1479 (Nov. 16, 1969).

84 Sen. Rep. No. 781, 82d Cong., 1st Sess., 1951–2 C.B. 458, 504 (Sept. 18, 1951); *Congress Group Urged to Support Withholding Tax on Interest and Dividends to Raise $250 Million*, Wall St. J., Feb. 7, 1951, at 3.

85 *Bankers Association Hits Proposal for Withholding Levy on Dividends*, Wall St. J., July 19, 1951, at 4; *Tax Protest Made by Jersey Bankers*, N.Y. Times, May 26, 1951, at 32; George A. Mooney, *Threat of New Heavy Burden of Paper Work in New Tax Proposals a Big Worry to Banks*, N.Y. Times, July 8, 1951, at 1.

86 *Tax Protest*, *supra* note 85, at 32; *Withholding Taxes*, Wash. Post, May 18, 1951, at 20, *Good and Bad in Tax Proposals*, L.A. Times, June 13, 1951, at A4; Harold Walsh, *Dividend Withholding Tax Would Hit Small Investor*, L.A. Times, June 21, 1951, at A10; *No More Withholding Taxes*, Wall St. J., April 6, 1951, at 6; "Woman Accountant," *Letter to the Editor, Withholding Taxes*, Chi. Daily Trib., June 2, 1951, at 10.

87 Exemptions were offered for US Savings Bonds, postal savings certificates of deposit, and interest or dividends paid by savings and loan associations, building and loan associations, cooperative banks, homestead associations, credit unions, and other similar organizations. *Tax Bill Changes Stay House Action*, N.Y. Times, June 15, 1951, at 12; Godfrey N. Nelson, *Inequities Cited in House Tax Bill*, N.Y. Times, June 24, 1951, at 113.

88 Mooney, *Threat of New Heavy Burden*, *supra* note 85, at 1, 4; John D. Morris, *Rise in Income Tax Near 12% is Likely in Conferees' Plan*, N.Y. Times, Oct. 11, 1951, at 1, 44; *Inconveniencing Everybody*, Wall St. J., May 1, 1951, at 8.

claimed that the whole exercise was unnecessary since the Bureau of Internal Revenue already had the information necessary to go after the unreported income.[89]

The opposition rhetoric was often overheated. One former US Representative and current Illinois State Representative claimed that the exemption of government bonds from withholding as "another step down the socialist road that England has traveled."[90] The president of a group called the Investor's League, which purported to represent small investors, "said the proposal smacks of 'police state' methods."[91] A banking executive called it "one of the most far-reaching tax legislation proposals that has ever been proposed in the history of our nation. It would be the only law of which we have every heard that imposed a penalty on the innocent in order to catch the guilty."[92]

Ultimately, the Sente Finance Committee rejected the withholding provisions. Chairman Walter George, a Democrat from Georgia, claimed that withholding was both an unnecessary and harsh remedy in light of other alternatives for closing the tax gap.[93] House conferees eventually dropped the proposal as part of an "old-fashion horse-trading" in favor of making retroactive a provision clarifying the treatment of family partnerships,[94] an issue of interest primarily for wealthy tax dodgers.[95] Consequently, withholding was not included in the final legislation.[96]

## The Kennedy Administration's Move for Dividend and Interest Withholding

### *Push toward Legislation*

In 1959, House Ways and Means Committee Chair Wilbur Mills announced that Congress needed to consider closing avenues for tax dodging, including

89 *Why More Tax Red Tape*, WALL ST. J., May 21, 1951, at 6.

90 John Fisher, *Hits Tax Bill as a Step to Socialization*, CHI. DAILY TRIB., June 15, 1951, at B 5 (quoting Rep. Noah Mason, R-Ill.).

91 *Dividend Tax Held Insult to Investors*, WASH. POST, July 11, 1951, at 2 (quoting William Jackman).

92 *Bankers Association Hits Proposal*, *supra* note 85, at 4.

93 Sen. Rep. No. 781, 82d Cong., 1st Sess., 1951-2 C.B. 458, 504 (Sept. 18, 1951); PAUL, TAXATION IN THE UNITED STATES, *supra* note 55, at 606–07.

94 *Conferees Drop Withholding Levy on Interest, Dividends, Royalties*, WALL ST. J., Oct. 11, 1951, at 4.

95 Robert K. Lifton, *The Family Partnership: Here We Go Again*, 7 TAX L. REV. 461 (1951).

96 Morris, *Rise in Income Tax*, *supra* note 88, at 1; Revenue Act of 1951, S. Rep. No. 781, 82nd Cong. (1951); Kahng, *supra* note 82, at 325.

the nonpayment of taxes on dividends and interest.[97] A Treasury study of income tax returns revealed that almost $4.5 billion worth of dividends and interest had gone unreported in 1956, resulting in a loss of approximately $500 million in tax revenue.[98] The tax gap on dividends was estimated to be fourteen percent, while the gap for interest was almost 50 percent.[99]

Treasury first launched a dual education and enforcement campaign to try to voluntarily increase reporting.[100] The Internal Revenue Service printed 42 million notices explaining the taxability of dividends and interest, which it then asked corporations and banks to distribute to their stockholders and depositors.[101] The Service also changed the Form 1040 to specifically include the words "dividends" and "interest" in bold type,[102] while declaring that "underreported and unreported dividend and interest payments" would be "a major target of income tax audit checks" during 1960.[103] In the dawn of the computer age, it also began working on an "electronic data processing system" to match interest and dividends with their recipients to help catch nonreporters.[104]

Treasury believed that its education and enforcement strategies were starting to work,[105] but the election of Democratic President John F. Kennedy in November 1960 ushered in renewed support for dividend and interest withholding.[106] Given reports during the presidential

97 Alan L. Otten, *Specialists Mull Ways to Close 'Loopholes' in Present Taxes*, WALL ST. J., Jan. 7, 1959, at 1, 9.

98 Richard E. Mooney, *Loophole Noted in Dividend Tax*, N.Y. TIMES, Sept. 19, 1959, at 7.

99 Id.

100 *IRS Moves to Cut Dividend Tax Loss*, WASH. POST TIMES HERALD, Dec. 11, 1959, at C7.

101 John D. Morris, *Tax on Dividends May Be Withheld*, N.Y. TIMES, Feb. 29, 1960, at 19; *IRS Moves*, *supra* note 100, at C7; Richard E. Mooney, *U.S. Seeking Unreported Taxes*, N.Y. TIMES, Nov. 23, 1959, at 48; *Map Tax Drive on Dividends and Interest*, CHI TRIB., Nov. 23, 1959, at C10. Fred Scribner, the Undersecretary of the Treasury, "cautioned corporations and banks that Congress might force them to withhold taxes from dividends and interest if they didn't help promote voluntary compliance with the tax laws." *IRS Moves*, *supra* note 100, at C7.

102 *Map Tax Drive*, *supra* note 101, at C10.

103 Robert Metz, *Interest Income to Be Target of U.S. Tax Return Scrutiny*, N.Y. TIMES, Feb. 15, 1960, at 35; *Income Tax Drive Aims at Dividends Loophole*, L.A. TIMES, Feb. 17, 1960, at 27.

104 *Income Tax Drive Aims at Dividends Loophole*, *supra* note 103, at 27. For background on the use of the electronic data processing system by the IRS, see William H. Smith, *Electronic Data Processing and Federal Tax Administration*, 54 PROC. ANN. CONF. ON TAX'N, NAT'L TAX ASS'N 205 (1961).

105 *See Treasury Encouraged by Rise in Taxpayers Voluntarily Reporting Dividends, Interest*, WALL ST. J., Dec. 23, 1960, at 16 (returns reporting dividends increased 16 percent and returns reporting interest increased 26 percent).

106 Robert Metz, *Study May Lead to Tax Changes*, N.Y. TIMES, Jan. 9, 1961, at 85.

campaign that the government was losing a billion dollars in tax revenue each year from the failure to collect on dividends and interest,[107] new IRS Commissioner Mortimer Caplin "scoffed" at claims by the Eisenhower Administration that reporting had increased significantly because of Treasury's efforts.[108] Moreover, Treasury changed its tune regarding the efficacy of its educational program. Douglas Dillon, the new Treasury Secretary, concluded in his 1961 Annual Report that "[T]his gap in tax payments cannot be closed by taxpayer educational programs nor by attempts to apply other collection techniques to the millions of separate dividend and interest transactions. An automatic system similar to tax withholding for employee compensation is essential."[109]

Thus, it was not surprising that Kennedy's planned to submit a bill that contained a provision for dividend and interest withholding.[110] As Kennedy told Congress in a special message on taxation,

> [T]he application of the withholding principle has remained incomplete. Withholding does not apply to dividends and interest, with the result that substantial amounts of such income, particularly interest, improperly escape taxation. . . . This is patently unfair to those who must as a result bear a larger share of the tax burden. Recipients of dividends and interest should pay their tax no less than those who receive wage and salary income, and the tax should be paid just as promptly. Large continued avoidance of tax on the part of some has a steadily demoralizing effect on the compliance of others.[111]

Under his proposal, which he expected would raise $600 million, dividends and interest would be subject to withholding at a 20 percent rate.[112] To ease compliance burdens, payers would not be required to issue withholding statements and accommodation would be made for recipients not otherwise subject to tax.[113]

107 Dexter M. Keezer, *Our Scandalous Income-Tax Snarl*, L.A. TIMES, April 10, 1960, at G19.
108 John A. Grimes, *Tax Agency Calls Drive to Spur Voluntary Reporting of Dividends, Interest a Failure*, WALL ST. J., March 29, 1961, at 4 (quoting Caplin).
109 ANNUAL REPORT OF THE SECRETARY OF THE TREASURY ON THE STATE OF THE FINANCES FOR THE FISCAL YEAR ENDED JUNE 30, 1961, at 25.
110 Richard E. Mooney, *Kennedy to Urge Business Tax Aid to Spur Investing*, N.Y. TIMES, April 9, 1961, at 1.
111 *President John F. Kennedy's Special Message to the Congress on Taxation*, April 20, 1961.
112 Id.
113 Id.

### *Business Opposition*

Business leaders vigorously opposed dividend and interest withholding, viewing it as an assault on savings and investment.[114] Norman Strunk, executive vice president of the United States Savings and Loan League called it a "tax on thrift," while Gaylord Freeman, president of the First National Bank of Chicago complained that it would be "discriminatory."[115] The Vice President of New York's First National City Bank argued that "taking off 20% of a man's interest, without any identification, no W-2 withholding form, no detail at all, no statement to the customer – that's just outright confiscation."[116] Edward McCormick, the president of the American Stock Exchange, argued that dividend withholding would be particularly unfair for "retired persons with low incomes, who because of available exemptions and generally applicable deductions are not required to pay a tax."[117]

They were also concerned about the administrative burden that banks and other financial institutions would bear. Although the proposal relieved them of the obligation of issuing receipts,[118] they would still need to collect and remit the taxes from depositors' interest payments. One representative of the American Bankers Association called the plan "unduly burdensome and costly" for banks and savings institutions, while being "inequitable and confusing for taxpayers."[119] Another explained that "no practical, workable withholding system has yet been proposed which would not contribute to confusion and irritation on the part of ordinary taxpayers and would not impose unreasonable hardships or inequities" on individuals and financial institutions.[120] Businesses complained about being "pressed into service as a tax collector . . . at its own expense."[121]

[114] *Kennedy's Tax Plan on Dividends Assailed*, ATL. CONST., April 21, 1961, at 50; *Wall Street Rips Kennedy Taxing Plan*, CHI. DAILY TRIB., April 21, 1961, at C9; *Business Criticism of Plans to Withhold Dividends Expected at Hearings this Week*, WALL ST. J., May 22, 1961, at 3.

[115] Louis Dombrowski, *Withholding of Dividend Tax Ripped*, CHI. DAILY TRIB., March 31, 1961, at C5.

[116] Editorial, *Saving Under Suspicion*, WALL ST. J., May 25, 1961, at 18.

[117] *Reaction to Tax Plan is Mixed; Dividend Proposal Draws Fire*, N.Y. TIMES, April 21, 1961, at 20 (quoting McCormick).

[118] Robert Metz, *Dissent on Tax Plans*, N.Y. TIMES, July 24, 1961, at 27.

[119] *A.B.A. Oppose Tax Withholding*, CHI. DAILY TRIB., May 27, 1961, at C5.

[120] *Banks' Views Mixed on Withholding Taxes on Interest, Dividends*, WALL ST. J., May 29, 1961, at 2.

[121] Id. at 2 (quoting Robert J. Landoll, the Controller's Institute of America); *Tax Plan's Effect*, CHI. DAILY TRIB., June 25, 1961, at N_B6; *Questions Withholding Tax on Dividend Plan*, CHI. TRIB., June 25, 1961, at S_B6.

Financial institutions offered dire predictions about the consequences of withholding. There were reports that depositors, fearing or even "resenting" the withholding proposal, were withdrawing their funds and purchasing savings bonds.[122] While interest on bonds would also be subject to withholding, they could delay that until maturity or even indefinitely under policies permitting holders to renew their bonds.[123] This would reduce the funds available to lend to customers, which they claimed would raise interest rates and the "the cost of home mortgage loans and other types of credit."[124] One bank executive warned that "for every dollar withheld from interest and dividends paid by savings banks and savings and loan associations, the supply of money invested in home mortgages by these institutions would be reduced by 75 cents or more."[125] A New York banker estimated the amount of money that savings and loans in the state of New York would have to remit each year would be approximately $160 million – "enough to finance the purchase of 10,000 homes."[126]

After stalling during the fall of 1961,[127] President Kennedy reissued his call for dividend and interest withholding in his 1962 State of the Union Address.[128] With Kennedy's push, the withholding proposal moved swiftly through the House. Ways and Means adopted the withholding proposal with a 20 percent rate that exempted savers under age eighteen or over age sixty-five if they filed statements with their banks or savings institutions.[129] Observers believed that "it would take a massive effort on the part of corporations, savings institutions and investors to dissuade the legislators from their course."[130] The House passed the bill with the dividend and interest withholding provision intact, despite Republican attempts to remove it.[131]

122 Robert Metz, *Tax Escape Seen in Savings Bonds*, N.Y. TIMES, Oct. 29, 1961, at 1, 18.
123 Id. at 1, 18.
124 *Questions Withholding Tax on Dividend Plan*, CHI. TRIB., June 25, 1961, at S_B6.
125 *Sidelights: Job Peril Seen in Withholding*, N.Y. TIMES, Feb. 13, 1962, at 48 (quoting Gerald J. Peffert, vice president and controller of Dime Savings Bank of Brooklyn).
126 *The Tax Bill Battle: Withhold – Or Not?* NEWSWEEK, June 4, 1962, at 79.
127 After the Ways and Means Committee appeared to be against withholding, a compromise measure emerged to reduce the withholding rate and exempt minors, but no action was taken on it. *Dividend Tax Plan Wins Tentative Nod*, WASH. POST TIMES HERALD, July 15, 1961, at B18.
128 *Text of Address on State of Union*, L.A. TIMES, Jan. 12, 1962, at 16.
129 Vincent J. Burke, *Interest, Dividend Tax Withholding Backed*, WASH. POST TIMES HERALD, Feb. 24, 1962, at A2.
130 Robert Metz, *Withholding Bill for Taxes Gaining*, N.Y. TIMES, Jan. 28, 1962, at 1.
131 John D. Morris, *House Approves Kennedy's Plan of Tax Revision*, N.Y. TIMES, March 30, 1962, at 1.

As in 1961, the proposal met fierce opposition, but this time it came directly from taxpayers rather than businesses. Politicians faced a literal "deluge" of letters to politicians from individuals opposed to withholding.[132] Described as "a grass-roots revolt of surprising intensity cutting across party lines,"[133] some senators reported that they received "3,000 letters of protest a day," with several saying "it is the biggest volume of mail they ever have gotten on one subject."[134] Democratic Senator Paul Douglas said he "received over 40,000 letters from constituents in Illinois protesting against the withholding tax,"[135] with 10,000 letters reportedly coming in the first week of the Senate Finance Committee hearings.[136] Senator Clifford Case, a Republican from New Jersey who had received 5,000 letters in a single day, had to hire part-time help to answer the letters, while Senate Postmaster David D. Jenkins announced that Senate mail delivery volume had doubled during the Finance Committee hearings.[137] All told, Senate Finance Committee chair Harry Byrd, a Democrat from Virginia, reported that "he had received 100,000 letters opposing the proposal."[138]

Few thought the letter-writers were acting on their own initiative. Democrats "said they believed the mail flood resulted from an organized campaign."[139] Senators reported receiving notes from depositors "scribbled on the back of the letter making the request from the financial institution" or "on the back of forms supplied by savings and loan and banking institutions."[140] The *Washington Post* canvassed Senators of both parties and concluded that "there is abundant evidence that many of their constituents wrote in only after reading statements on the subject from their savings institution."[141] With more than 50 percent of the population having interest-bearing accounts or bond or stock

[132] *Anti-Dividend, supra* note 8, at B3.

[133] Robert D. Novak, *Grassroots Report: Voter Revolt is Raging Over Plan to Withhold Interest, Dividend Tax*, WALL ST. J., May 2, 1962, at 1.

[134] Cornell, *supra* note 10, at 6.

[135] Hearings before the Committee on Finance, United States Senate, 87th Cong., 2d Sess., on H.R. 10650, Revenue Act of 1962 4357 (May 11, 1962) (Sen. Paul Douglas, D-Ill.)

[136] *Anti-Dividend, supra* note 8, at B3.

[137] Robert C. Albright, *Confusion on Tax Bill Keeps Senators Busy*, WASH. POST, May 4, 1962, at A15.

[138] *Dividend Withholding Defeat Seen in Senate*, L.A. TIMES, July 29, 1962, at D2.

[139] *Anti-Dividend, supra* note 8, at B3 (citing Senators Paul Douglas, D-Ill., and Harrison A. Williams, Jr., D-N.J.).

[140] Id.; Robert C. Albright, *Confusion on Tax Bill Keeps Senators Busy*, WASH. POST, May 4, 1962, at A15.

[141] Id.

investments as of 1961,[142] it was not surprising that businesses turned to the average saver and investor as a potential ally in their fight against withholding.

The start of the campaign against interest withholding could be traced to a precise date – March 26, 1962 – when a subcommittee of the United States Savings & Loan League decided to seek the aid of their customers in opposing the bill.[143] It paired a letter-writing campaign with a campaign against one of the bill's other proposals that would raise taxes on savings and loans.[144] On March 30, the League's executive vice president, Norman Strunk, sent letters to the League's 4,800 members announcing the campaign and providing them with sample letters that they were encouraged to use to write letters to their 30 million depositors.[145] "Member institutions from coast to coast took up the battle" after receiving the League's request.[146] They send "Dear-Saver" letters to their depositors, arguing that using withholding to stop tax dodging was like "trying to weed the garden with a bulldozer."[147]

Stock exchanges and mutual funds started a similar, but less organized, campaign against dividend withholding even earlier. After a survey revealed in 1961 that most shareholders opposed withholding,[148] New York Stock Exchange president Keith Funston called listed corporations "to urge their shareowners to get in touch with their respective congressmen" and reported that the Pacific Stock Exchange was doing the same thing on the west coast.[149] At the same time, the Association of Stock Exchange Firms conducted "a full-fledged drive across the country on a regional level."[150] Mutual funds also tried "to arouse shareholders against" dividend withholding, including inserts in their quarterly

[142] Richard E. Mooney, *Congress is Given Tax Plan Seeking Aid for Business*, N.Y. TIMES, April 12, 1961, at 1, 18.

[143] James McCartney, *Big Lobby Push Born in Chicago: Decided Fate of Withholding Taxes on Dividends, Interest*, CHI. DAILY NEWS, Oct. 8, 1962). The article was described in and entered into the Congressional Record by Democratic Senator William Proxmire of Wisconsin as evidence of the lobbying problem in Washington. 108 CONG. REC. 22969, 22971 (1962).

[144] Id.

[145] Id.

[146] Id.

[147] STERN, *supra* note 2, at 171.

[148] *Funston Says Survey Backs Big Board Stand on Dividend Tax Rise*, WALL ST. J., April 17, 1961, at 6.

[149] Harold Walsh, Ranks Form to Stop *Higher Dividend Tax*, L.A. TIMES, April 21, 1961, at B7.

[150] Id.

statements "advising shareholders to write their Senators."[151] One insert included the following excerpts:

> You may want to write your Senator in Congress right now about something of vital importance to you which is being decided now. At issue is a bill to withhold 20 per cent of your dividend and interest income. The bill passed the House by a small margin, but it is still being deliberated in the Senate.
>
> Withholding as applied to wages and salaries has proven quite successful. Withholding applied to dividends and interest would, we feel, be unjust, ineffective and enormously complicated and confusing. While the bill would have the benefit of reducing tax evasion, we feel that there are many other alternatives to dividend-interest withholding which would not carry the same hardships to individual taxpayers.[152]

Another insert in the quarterly report of a mutual fund told investors "A short letter – or even a postcard – just a sentence or two to your Congressman and Senator can mean a lot."[153] A securities dealer services publication "recommended that all salesmen warn their clients about the dangers and get them to write their Senators protesting such proposed legislation."[154]

The letter writing campaign appeared to make an impression even on liberal members of the Senate. According to one report, "Democratic members of Congress, . . . surprised at the widespread opposition to the Administration's plan for withholding taxes on dividend and interest income," were taking notice.[155] Senator Paul Douglas later recalled, "we heard rumblings of opposition, but I must admit we were not prepared for the storm that followed."[156] Consequently, *The Wall Street Journal* reported, "the real cause of the withholding plan's present problems is an uprising against it by liberals and moderates. This rebellion reflects an influx of anti-withholding letters matched in recent years only by protests against President Truman's dismissal of Gen. MacArthur and the Senate's censure of Sen. McCarthy."[157]

151 Gene Smith, *Mutual Funds: Drive Against Tax Bill of U.S.*, N.Y. TIMES, May 7, 1962, at 50.

152 Id., at 50 (quoting letter from David L. Babson Management Corporation, sponsor of the Aberdeen Fund).

153 Id.

154 Id.

155 Editorial, *Political Withholding*, WALL ST. J., May 4, 1962, at 12.

156 Paul H. Douglas, *The Problem of Tax Loopholes (Or: My Eighteen Years in a Quandary)*, 37 AM. SCHOLAR 21, 25 (1967–68).

157 Robert D. Novak, *Tax Bill's Troubles*, WALL ST. J., May 2, 1962, at 13.

Democrats' wavering reflected the letter writing campaign's potential to be "a campaign issue of some potency."[158] One Senator, described as a "liberal-leaning Southern[er]," candidly explained his stance this way: "In all honesty, the Treasury has some pretty good arguments for withholding. But this is something the people just plain don't want, and I'm not going to vote for it, particularly in a year when I'm running for re-election. That's what I tell the Treasury."[159]

Another said "it could be the kind of issue that hurts you, especially with people who aren't vitally concerned with other issues."[160] These fears later proved to be well-grounded, as dividend and interest withholding became a key issue in a Democratic House primary run-off election in the fall of 1962 in a district covering Atlanta and several surrounding counties,[161] with the two candidates each running newspaper advertisements claiming that the other had supported withholding.[162]

This led some senators to publicly announce their opposition, including Edward Long, a stalwart Democrat from Missouri facing an election challenge, and Administration supporter Stephen Young of Ohio,[163] while Senator Warren Magnuson of Washington, reportedly "dispatched 10,000 letters branding the withholding plan as unconstitutional."[164] Other senators privately suggested that Kennedy drop, or at least shelve, the proposal.[165] Senate Democrats became "so concerned about the flood of mail" that about twenty-five senators[166] decided to ask Senate leaders to privately urge Kennedy to intervene.[167]

158 Novak, *Voter Revolt*, *supra* note 133, at 18.

159 Novak, *Tax Bill's Troubles*, *supra* note 157, at 13 (quoting from the Senator)

160 Novak, *Voter Revolt*, *supra* note 133, at 18.

161 M. Kent Jennings & L. Harmon Zeigler, *A Moderate's Victory in a Southern Congressional District*, 28 Pub. Opinion Q. 595, 596 (1964).

162 *See Display Ad 6*, Atl. Const., Sept. 25, 1962, at 7 (advertisement from incumbent James C. Davis, charging his opponent Charles Weltner with endorsing the withholding proposal at a speech before a local civic club); *Display Ad 91*, Atl. Const., Sept. 26, 1962, at 24 (advertisement from challenger Charles Weltner calling Davis' accusations "double talk." In his ad, Weltner clarified that he said he "opposed such withholding unless no adequate tax collection method could be found" and claiming that Davis had voted in favor of the withholding proposal in March).

163 Novak, *Tax Bill's Troubles*, *supra* note 157, at 13.

164 Id.

165 *Senators Urge Kennedy to Scrap New Tax Plan*, L.A. Times, May 7, 1962, at 22.

166 Robert C. Albright, *Confusion on Tax Bill Keeps Senators Busy*, Wash. Post, May 4, 1962, at A15

167 Id.; *Senators Urge*, *supra* note 165, at 22.

Kennedy lashed out at withholding's opponents.[168] He "charged [savings institutions] with inspiring a mailing campaign by implying that the measure constituted a new tax, suggesting it would create a 'mountain of red tape,' and saying it would create hardship for widows, orphans and the elderly."[169] According to Kennedy, this organized campaign had "misinformed millions of people" about the proposal, erroneously claiming that it would "take money unjustly from honest taxpayers" or "harm the elderly ... or others on low income."[170] Other members of the Administration echoed this theme. Treasury Secretary Douglas Dillon declared in a speech in late May at the University of Pennsylvania that the campaign against withholding set new records for distortion of the facts and has created widespread public misunderstanding."[171]

Kennedy's sharp rebuke appeared to have an effect among business opponents. "Fear[ing] that a continued fight against the withholding plan would endanger a compromise formula for the taxation of savings and loan associations," the United States Savings and Loan League abruptly changed course after initiating the letter-writing campaign a few months earlier.[172] In early June, it started "quietly informing Senators that the bulk of the savings and loan community, though still opposed to the withholding plan, is now resigned to swallowing the provisions in the overriding interest of promoting favorable Senate action on the bill as a whole."[173] Delaware Senator John J. Williams, the top ranking Republican on the Finance Committee, went so far to imply that the Administration was involved in wrongdoing, remarking that "this has the appearance of either an attempt to blackmail a group for its support" or

[168] Cornell, *Tax Foes, supra* note 10, at 6; *Kennedy, in Bid to Stem Grass Roots Revolt, Defends Withholding of Taxes on Dividends*, WALL ST. J., May 10, 1962, at 3.

[169] Robert Metz, *Taxes and Dividends*, N.Y. TIMES, May 14, 1962, at 57.

[170] *President Hits Back*, N.Y. TIMES, May 13, 1962, at E2; Cornell, *Tax Foes, supra* note 10, at 6.

[171] Novak, *Tax Bill's Troubles, supra* note 157, at 13.

[172] John D. Morris, *Savings Men Drop Fight to Prevent Tax Withholding*, N.Y. TIMES, June 10, 1962, at 1, 32; *Lobby Drops Battle on Dividend Tax, Fearing JFK Slap*, WASH. POST TIME HERALD, June 11, 1962, at A7. Kennedy proposed to change a provision that allowed savings and loan associations and mutual savings banks to establish tax deductible bad debt reserves of as much as 12 percent, as compared with only 2–3 percent for commercial banks, which allowed them to insulate more of their earnings from taxation. Edward O'Toole, *Battle Over Tax Laws Looms Between Big Banks and Rivals*, N.Y. TIMES, Nov. 26, 1961, at F1; *Taxation of Mutual Savings Banks and Savings and Loan Associations*, Hearings before the Committee on Ways and Means, House of Representatives, 87th Cong., 1st Sess. 28 (Aug. 9, 1961) (statement of Federal Home Loan Bank Board).

[173] Morris, *Savings Men, supra* note 172, at 1.

"a 300 million dollar deal with the association in return for their support."[174]

Regular taxpayers remained unconvinced. The *Washington Post Times Herald* reported that "the surge of opposition mail continues in a concentrated flood."[175] Letter writers were inspired by Democratic Senator Harry Byrd's decision to break ranks with the president on withholding.[176] By the summer of 1962, the anti-withholding forces gained the upper hand. In August, the Senate "overwhelmingly rejected" the withholding proposal.[177] House conferees made a "perfunctory demand" to reinstate some form of dividend and interest withholding, but it was quickly dropped in favor of requiring information reporting on interest and dividends in excess of $10.[178]

Kennedy lamented the absence of withholding in the Revenue Act of 1962, which established a new investment tax credit and erected limits on deductions for entertainment expenses but not without mentioning the omission.[179] He suggested he would reintroduce withholding in the new Congress,[180] but this was quickly dropped to give more time for a trial of the stricter information reporting requirements.[181] Treasury was directed to provide annual reports to Congress "on how successful the system is in combating tax avoidance."[182]

## Understanding the Popular Opposition

Although the industry letter-writing campaign focused taxpayer attention on the issue, it seemed improbable that it would be enough to sustain opposition. In part because of the obvious self-interest of

174 *Raises Query of 'Blackmail' in Tax Fight*, CHI. DAILY TRIB., June 12, 1962, at B7.

175 *Mail Opposition to Dividend Tax Plan Increases*, WASH. POST TIMES HERALD, May 23, 1962, at A7.

176 *Withheld Interest Tax is Opposed by Byrd*, WASH. POST TIMES HERALD, May 20, 1962, at A2; *Mail Opposition*, *supra* note 175, at A7.

177 *Senate Crushes Plan to Withhold Tax on Dividends*, WALL ST. J., Aug. 30, 1962, at 1; Joe Hall, *Dividend Withholding Taken Out of Tax Bill*, ATL. CONST., Aug. 30, 1962, at 16.

178 Robert D. Novak, *Conferees Vote Tax Bill Diluting Outlay Credit Plan, Eliminating Proposal for Withholding on Dividends*, WALL ST. J., Sept. 26, 1962, at 3. Rumors suggested they might push for only dividend withholding in conference, but it never happened. *Conferees Plan New Effort on Dividends Tax*, L.A. TIMES, Sept 9, 1962, at G2.

179 John F. Kennedy, Statement by the President Upon Signing the Revenue Act, October 16, 1962.

180 Id.

181 *Treasury May Not Request Dividend Withholding Tax*, WALL ST. J., Nov. 12, 1962, at 1.

182 Novak, *Conferees Vote*, WALL ST. J., Sept. 26, 1962, at 3.

promoters, top-down attempts to generate grassroots opposition are rarely successful.[183] Organized grass-roots letter-writing campaigns are often viewed as an attempt to camouflage special interest group lobbying by creating the impression of popular support.[184] If people see through letter-writing campaigns to the self-interest of the organizers, the effort is destined to fail.

There is little doubt that the corporations and financial institutions opposing withholding were self-interested. First, withholding would saddle them with administrative costs.[185] They had to withhold the proper amount from each payment of interest and dividends, remit it to the government on behalf of the intended recipient, keep track of those payments, and provide some form of notice to the depositor or stockholder of the amount withheld, all of which imposed costs on the payors.[186] Second, withholding deprived them of the use of the funds.[187] As Senator Douglas observed, when depositors leave the interest in their accounts or stockholders reinvest their dividends, the payors "get an automatic snowballing of capital" from which they can generate profits.[188] Third, they risked losing customers and stockholders because of withholding. Investment bankers used the used the withholding proposal to lure people to move their money into tax-exempt municipal bonds.[189] As one individual warned in a letter to the editor in the *Chicago Daily Tribune*, "[r]egardless of how the bill is sugar-coated … I feel certain that the average citizen will merely interpret the result of the bill to be a reduction of the rates of dividends and interest paid him by banks, corporations, and savings and loan associations. This

183 Kollman, *supra* note 12, at 33.

184 Id. at 79–81; Ronald J. Hrebenar , Interest Group Politics in America 158–59 (3rd ed. 1997).

185 Hearings before the Committee on Ways and Means, House of Representatives, 87th Cong., 1st Sess., on the President's 1961 Tax Recommendations, 2325–2331 (May 26, 1961) (testimony of Robert K. Wilmouth, member of the Savings Operations Committee of the Savings Division of the American Bankers Association).

186 *But see* Bernard D. Nossiter, *Maverick Bank Likes Withholding*, Wash. Post Times Herald, April 20, 1962, at B9 (John Sadlik of the Franklin National Bank of Mineola, Long Island claimed that the "extra cost would be 'insignificant.'").

187 Douglas, *The Problem of Tax Loopholes*, *supra* note 156, at 27.

188 108 Cong. Rec. 17779 (1962) (Statement of Sen. Douglas).

189 *See Display Ad 55*, Atl. Const., July 19, 1962, at 41 (encouraging municipal bond investments, which "would not be affected even if we should have income tax withholding on interest and dividends").

will place the government savings bond in an enviable competitive position for the savings dollar."[190]

Moreover, defeating withholding provided few benefits to the average letter writer.[191] Only 10 percent of 1959 tax returns included dividends, but 80 percent of those dividends went to individuals with incomes of $100,000 per year or more.[192] Indeed, taxpayers making $100,000 or more received 30 percent or more of their adjusted gross income as dividends, while those in the $1 million bracket received over 48 percent of their adjusted gross income from dividends.[193] Interest income was a bit more evenly distributed, but only 1 percent of the total returns filed – those with incomes of over $20,000 per year – accounted for 55 percent of all interest.[194]

Despite the obvious self-interest of its sponsors and the disproportionate benefit for high bracket taxpayers, the campaign struck a nerve with average taxpayers.[195] One Senator described the opposition in his home state to withholding as "hotter than a firecracker."[196] A retired Air Force officer wrote to the *Chicago Daily Tribune* that "the pot is beginning to boil among the little people," noting that "if the 18 million people affected can be aroused, the issue could be political dynamite."[197] Some of the outrage was based on misconceptions about the proposal,[198] which businesses pushing the letter-writing campaign helped to create,[199] but

190 William E. Trude, *Letter to the Editor, Withholding Taxes*, CHI. DAILY TRIB., April 18, 1961, at 20.

191 Novak, *Tax Bill's Troubles*, *supra* note 157, at 13. See 108 CONG. REC. 17776 (1962) (statement of Sen. Douglas) ("it is not the widows and orphans . . . [but] the recipients of large incomes who are in the main" affected by dividend and interest withholding).

192 108 CONG. REC. at 17776–17777.

193 Id.

194 Id. at 17777.

195 Novak, *Voter Revolt*, *supra* note 133, at 1.

196 Id. (quoting Senator Markle of Maine).

197 George E. Stratemeyer, *Voice of the People, Kennedy's Mistake?* CHI. DAILY TRIB., May 25, 1962, at 20.

198 *See Revenue Act of 1962, Hearings before the Senate Committee on Finance*, United States Senate, 87th Cong. 2d Sess. on H.R. 10650 4357-4360 (May 11, 1962) (statement of Sen. Paul Douglas) (describing "five key points of misunderstanding about the withholding provisions," including that it was a new tax rather than a collection mechanism of the current income tax, that it applied to the principal and not just the interest, that there would be over-withholding for nonfilers even though there were exemptions, that it would shift administrative costs to businesses even though they had decided to not require them to send notices to depositors/stockholders, and that it was unnecessary because of the impending implementation of electronic data processing).

199 *See* STERN, *supra* note 2, at 296 (describing a "Dear Saver" letter from the U.S. Savings and Loan League about "the proposed withholding tax"); *Display Ad 214*, L.A. TIMES,

there were a number of factors beyond that which contributed to making it such a populist issue.

First, millions of people were potentially affected by the withholding proposal. According to one estimate, "more than half the population [had] savings accounts, savings bonds, corporate bonds or stocks."[200] That includes nonfilers, but "more than 75 million special notices were mailed to recipients of dividends and interest" as part of the education program that Treasury initiated before Kennedy introduced his withholding proposal, suggesting both the number of affected taxpayers and the public awareness of the issue, was high.[201] As the *Wall Street Journal* noted, the fact that "many millions of ordinary Americans now own stocks and many millions more of moderate means have either savings accounts or stocks or both" meant that Congress should not have been surprised at the "widespread opposition" to the Administration's plan.[202]

Second, lower bracket taxpayers felt targeted by the withholding proposal. In part, this was because they *were* being targeted. Kennedy's proposal was supposed to hit lower bracket taxpayers harder than other taxpayers. Under the income tax, the lowest rate was 20 percent on income up to $2,000, rising to 91 percent on income over $300,000.[203] This meant that the 20 percent withholding rate captured all, or more than all for someone who was not required to file, of the tax due from low bracket taxpayers, but only a fraction of what was due from high bracket taxpayers.[204] Stanley Surrey, the Assistant Secretary of the Treasury in charge of Tax Policy in the Kennedy Administration and a former Harvard Law School tax professor, suggested in a 1961 interview that this was intentional: "we feel that if we have this automatic machinery for getting at those in the lower brackets, we can concentrate on other methods of enforcement to ensure compliance from those in the upper brackets."[205]

May 28, 1961, at SF5 (an advertisement from the North Hollywood Federal Savings and Loan Association warning about "this withholding tax against your savings").

200 Richard E. Mooney, *Tax Bill is Ready for House Floor*, N.Y. TIMES, Feb. 28, 1962, at 1, 17.

201 Dana Latham, *Internal Revenue Administration: 1960*, 14 BULL. AM. BAR ASS'N, SECTION OF TAX'N 7, 16 (1960).

202 Editorial, *Political Withholding*, WALL ST. J., May 4, 1962, at 12.

203 Tax Foundation, Historical U.S. Federal Individual Income Tax Rates & Brackets, 1862–2021 (1963 income year), https://taxfoundation.org/data/all/federal/historical-income-tax-rates-brackets/.

204 Robert Metz, *The Politics of Tax Reform*, 9 CHALLENGE 6 (1961).

205 Interview, *Stanley S. Surrey: The Role of the Tax System*, 9 CHALLENGE 20, 21 (1961).

Third, lower bracket taxpayers viewed withholding as a form of "self-help" to counter the fact that the "chosen few" could avoid taxes by investing in domestic tax shelters and foreign tax havens.[206] A 1950s-era insurance consultant captured the essence of this view:

> The income-tax law is stacked against the professional and the little man in favor of businessmen and owners of stocks, bonds, and other property. ... While overstating deductions and omitting dividends or interest income will not set things right, no one ... can properly criticize the disfavored taxpayers from using these devices to offset in a small measure the injustices of the tax laws.[207]

As George Sokolsky of the *Washington Post* noted, one of the reasons the withholding proposal was "something to be angry about" is "because it strikes directly at those who do not have much money."[208] Sokolsky asked "if they want to soak the rich, why don't they go after the numbered accounts in Swiss banks?"[209]

By contrast, dividends and interest were among the few areas where middle and lower-bracket taxpayers had a chance to dodge taxes. As one contemporary commentator observed: "The Little Guy, whose wage or salary is his only source of income, really is in a tough spot. He'll have a hard time dreaming up any kind of tax-saving device. If only he owned a few stocks and bonds – that's the one field where he can practice a bit of 'withholding' of one's own."[210]

There is some evidence that they took advantage of this. Economist Daniel Holland examined the gap in dividend reporting over time and observed that "the zeal with which people reported their dividend income declined markedly between 1939 and 1952,"[211] which he attributed to the change in tax rates over the same period.[212] Holland surmised that "more taxpayers were pushed below the margin of honesty as it became more profitable not to report dividend receipts."[213] Most significantly, there was "a general tendency for the importance of underreporting to vary inversely with income class," with underreporting higher among the

206 Humphrey, *Tax Loopholes*, *supra* note 81, at 10.
207 Jerome R. Hellerstein, Taxes, Loopholes, and Morals 241–42 (1963).
208 George Sokolsky, *These Days ... How to Protect Yourself*, Wash. Post Times Herald, April 7, 1962, at A13.
209 Id.
210 H. F. Millikin, The Prudent Man: Tax Dodging as an Art 153 (1963).
211 Daniel M. Holland, *Dividend Underreporting on Tax Returns*, 13 J. Fin. 238, 246 (1958).
212 Id. at 247.
213 Id. at 250.

lower-income classes.[214] Although some underreporting in the lower-income groups could "be laid to carelessness and poor record-keeping rather than purposeful evasion," Holland concluded that since "over-reporting errors averaged only half as much or less than underreporting errors" many lower-bracket taxpayers may have deliberately underreported their dividends to dodge taxes.[215]

Fourth, taxpayers resented that withholding seemed to be more about revenue-raising than tax dodging. Many felt it was designed to obscure an effort to increase taxes on the already "overburdened" average citizen.[216] One columnist reported the "growing feeling" that withholding mechanisms were "mischievous and trouble-making devices which only help hide from the average individuals the extent to which he is being taxed."[217] Another complained that "the proposal to put a withholding tax on interest and dividends may look like a scheme to soak the rich to get after the tax-dodger. In fact, it will be a hardship on the widow and orphans, on those who have inherited small amounts and have to live on interest and dividends."[218] It is little wonder that in a survey of editors of small-town newspapers and weeklies approximately two-thirds were opposed to dividend and interest withholding.[219]

To make things worse, it appeared that withholding's revenue was intended to pay for more tax breaks for the wealthy.[220] In 1962, Kennedy told Ways and Means Committee Chairman Wilbur Mills that "the single-most important provision in the bill would provide a tax credit for new investment in machinery and equipment,"[221] which most viewed primarily as a benefit for high bracket taxpayers.[222]

214 Id. at 253–54.

215 Id. at 256.

216 H. F. Schilling, Letter to the Editor, *Withholding Tax on Dividends: Its Benefits are Pure Guesswork*, L.A. TIMES, May 21, 1962, at A5; Abigail Cole, *Letter to the Editor, Bread and Water*, WASH. POST TIMES HERALD, May 11, 1962, at A20.

217 Bill Henry, *The Opposition is Bi-Partisan*, L.A. TIMES, May 22, 1962, at A1.

218 Sokolsky, *supra* note 208, at A13.

219 Editorial, *America the Gullible?*, WALL ST. J., May 11, 1962, at 14 (citing a survey by the *American Press*, a trade magazine for newspapers).

220 Harold Walsh, *Ranks Form to Stop Higher Dividend Tax*, L.A. TIMES, April 21, 1961, at B7.

221 *Kennedy's Letter to Mills on the Tax Bill*, N.Y. TIMES, March 23, 1962, at 15 (quoting Kennedy's letter to Mills).

222 J. Reid Hambrick, *The Illusion of Tax Reform*, 1963 DUKE L.J. 56, 67 (1963); Robert E. Rosacker & Richard W. Metcalf, *United States Federal Tax Policy Surrounding the Investment Tax Credit: A Review of Legislative Intent and Empirical Research Findings over Thirty Years (1962–1991)*, 9 AKRON TAX J. 59, 65 (1992).

Withholding, by contrast, was described as a way of funding the new investment tax credit,[223] fulfilling Kennedy's pledge to submit a balanced budget for 1963 "even if it required a tax increase."[224] Republicans highlighted the inequity, claiming that the tax bill would provide a "'tax bonanza' to owners of gambling casinos, bars and race horses while imposing hardships on millions of people with savings accounts."[225]

This suspicion about the true motives behind withholding reflected a broader antigovernment sentiment. As one individual wrote to the *Los Angeles Times*, "there is already too much government interference in the nation's enterprises."[226] According to this writer, "there is a growing resentment as to the way in which our finances are being managed, or rather mismanaged by the administration, and its encroachments on all phases of business and incomes in the form of taxation."[227] Another compared it to "conscription" in a letter written to the *Wall Street Journal*, asking whether the government has the right to "conscript the services of private citizens at the expense of private enterprises."[228]

Even if withholding helped to curb tax dodgers, not everyone viewed them as enemies. As one observer noted, "taxes are so heavy and so complicated that the average citizen has more sympathy than he should have, perhaps, for the tax dodger."[229] Another commented that "[e]verybody wants a smaller tax bill, and the collective response of taxpayers generally to this aspiration is sympathetic."[230] It was true, of course, that some law-abiding citizens resented this attitude. As one individual remarked in a letter to the editor of the *Wall Street Journal*, "I find it infuriating to hear people say that they 'never bother to report dividend or interest income.' I suspect that these are the same people who are

223 Walsh, *Ranks Form*, *supra* note 220, at B7; *Program for Economy: Tax on Dividends*, N. Y. TIMES, Feb. 25, 1962, at E2; SHELDON D. POLLACK , THE FAILURE OF U.S. TAX POLICY 73–74 (1996).

224 Richard E. Mooney, *Budget Debate Grows Sharper*, N.Y. TIMES, Nov. 5, 1961, at E6.

225 *G.O.P Says Tax Bill Aids Bars but Hurts Millions with Savings*, N.Y. TIMES, March 28, 1962, at 19.

226 E.D., *Letter to the Editor, Withholding*, L.A. TIMES, July 20, 1962, at A5.

227 Id.

228 Margaret M. Mitchell, *Is it Ethical?* WALL ST. J., May 22, 1962, at 14.

229 *Tidal Wave of Protests Rolls in on Dividend Holding Plan*, CHI. DAILY TRIB., May 27, 1962, at 39.

230 Metz, *The Politics of Tax Reform*, *supra* note 204, at 8.

opposing" the withholding proposal.[231] This apparent erosion of confidence in the tax system was part of Kennedy's concern when he focused his 1963 tax message on removing some of the "complexities and inequities which undermine the morale of the taxpayer."[232] Nevertheless, withholding for dividends and interest was unlikely to be an approach that would garner much popular support or boost taxpayer morale. Indeed, it only served to align high and low bracket in their opposition to serious efforts to curtail tax dodging.

***

The anti-withholding campaign struck a chord with middle class taxpayers who felt that they had been left behind in the hollowing out of the tax base. Not only did millions of people own dividend-paying stocks or interest-bearing investments, but withholding proposal's low flat rate effectively targeted lower bracket taxpayers. By linking it with an investment tax credit, Kennedy and his fellow Democrats in Congress deprived withholding of much of its moral force and encouraged the self-help rationale that contributed to the middle-class tax dodging of the era.[233] Consequently, the rejection of dividend and interest withholding was as much about populist ambivalence toward tax dodging as it was about the letter-writing campaign that sparked the movement.

This populist ambivalence continued when renewed concerns about the tax gap led to a revival of the dividend and interest withholding proposal in the 1970s and 1980s, first by Democratic President Jimmy Carter and then by Republican President Ronald Reagan.[234] Congress even went so far as to briefly adopt a withholding requirement in 1982,[235] but after an opposition campaign that resembled the one that took place two decades earlier in 1962, Congress "acquiesced to the opposition" and

[231] Edward J. Seligman, *Letter to the Editor, Dividend Tax*, WALL ST. J., July 21, 1961, at 6.

[232] *Text of President Kennedy's Message to Congress on Tax Reduction and Revision*, N.Y. TIMES, Jan. 25, 1963, at 6.

[233] This grievance over an individual's relative tax burden is not limited to the 1960s–1980s. *See* VANESSA WILLIAMSON, WHY AMERICANS ARE PROUD TO PAY TAXES 3 (2017) (noting that in a 2015 survey 67 percent of Americans reported that what bothered them most about taxes was the feeling that someone else was not paying their fair share).

[234] Twight, *supra* note 5, at 385–90; *Miller Urges Withholding of Tax on Interest*, L.A. TIMES, April 30, 1982, at A2; Bill Neikirk, *Withholding Tax Plan for Interest*, CHI. TRIB., Jan. 28, 1982, at 1.

[235] Deborah Rankin, *A Closer Look at the New Tax Law*, N.Y. TIMES, Oct. 10, 1982.

passed a measure to repeal withholding over Reagan's threat of a veto.[236] To this day, withholding generally applies only to wages, and not to dividends and interest.[237] Instead, dividends and interest are subject to the less effective, but less intrusive, enforcement method of third party information reporting.[238]

[236] *Congress Passes Repeal of Interest Withholding*, N.Y. TIMES, July 29, 1983, at D7.

[237] Kahng, *supra* note 82, at 322–26. Exceptions include backup withholding for taxpayers who have failed to report dividend or interest income in the past, *see* I.R.C. § 3406(a)(1)(C), or withholding on income paid to nonresident aliens and foreign entities, *see* I.R.C. §§ 1441, 1442, 1446.

[238] Although nonreporting is better with information reporting (7 percent) than self-reporting (63 percent), both are worse than withholding (1 percent). INTERNAL REVENUE SERVICE, TAX GAP ESTIMATES FOR TAX YEARS 2008–2010 Figure 1, Attachment 3 (April 2016).

# Conclusion

## A Tax Cut of the Worst Kind

Contrary to what modern observers might have you believe, tax dodging during the 1950s and 1960s was more about tax cuts than tax increases. Faced with a high tax rate it did not support, but, for political reasons, it could not lower, Congress did the next best thing. It riddled the tax laws with "leaks, loopholes, exemptions, and preferences," while looking the other way at much of the widespread "income-tax chiseling" in American society and only occasionally passing watered down legislation targeting the more high-profile tax dodging schemes.[1] In effect, it cut the tax rates implicitly, rather than explicitly, which amounted to a tax cut of the worst kind. It was not transparent, it was not evenly distributed among the taxpayers or even targeted to achieve any policy objective in some cases, and, because it was too unpredictable for taxpayers to rely upon for planning purposes, it was inefficient. It did lower taxes for some, but in the process it reduced tax morale, erected a system of tax preferences that exacerbated complexity, and it led to the rise of tax dodging as a cultural phenomenon. Moreover, even when tax rates were cut explicitly in later years, the cuts were paired with more implicit tax cuts that prompted taxpayers to leverage some of the mid-century developments in tax dodging to spark the next tax dodging wave of the 1970s and 1980s.

### Implicit Rather Than Explicit Tax Cuts

During World War, the popular consensus in favor of high marginal rates was widespread. According to a Gallup Poll in February 1944, an astounding 90 percent of respondents told pollsters that their tax burden was fair.[2] After the war, however, that consensus in favor of high rates

[1] Jerome R. Hellerstein, Taxes, Loopholes and Morals 16, 232 (1963).

[2] Gallup Poll, Feb. 1944, cited in *Public Opinion on Taxes, 1937 to Today* 22 (2012), AEI Public Opinion Series at 4 (Updated April 2012).

began to dissipate.[3] Between February 1944 and November 1946, when Gallup again asked individuals whether their tax burden was fair, only 60 percent of respondents answered in the affirmative.[4] Among the wealthiest respondents, the percentage had dipped from 77 percent to 54 percent over the same period.[5] Corporations had a similar response, shedding their muted wartime reaction to the dramatic increase in the corporate tax burden in favor of a concerted push for reform after it ended.[6]

Many Republicans pushed for postwar tax cuts. They argued that the high progressive tax rates "fostered class discrimination and threatened tyrannies of the majority."[7] As Minnesota Representative Harold Knutson, the incoming chairman of the House Ways and Means Committee, explained in proposing across-the-board tax cuts in 1946, the bill "puts the ax to punitive taxes designed by alien minds and whizzed through subservient congresses. . . . For years we Republicans have been warning that the short-haired women and long-haired men of alien minds in the administrative branch of government were trying to wreck the American way of life and install a hybrid oligarchy at Washington through confiscatory taxation."[8] These efforts, however, proved unsuccessful as policy experts argued the high tax rates were necessary in the immediate aftermath of the war as a check against inflation spurred by postwar consumer spending and others argued that the spending funded by taxes was necessary to forestall recession as military spending ramped down.[9]

The campaign for tax cuts returned in 1952 after the election of Dwight D. Eisenhower, who was the first Republican President in two decades and only the second Congress since 1933 to have a Republican

[3] Kenneth Scheve & David Stasavage, Taxing the Rich: A History of Fiscal Fairness in the United States and Europe 191 (2016).

[4] Gallup Poll, Nov. 1946, cited in *Public Opinion on Taxes, 1937 to Today*, *supra* note 2, at.5.

[5] Scheve & Stasavage, *supra* note 3, at 191.

[6] Steven A. Bank, From Sword to Shield: The Transformation of the Corporate Income Tax, 1861 to Present 191 (2010); *Tax Report*, Wall St. J., Jan. 30, 1946, at 1; Steven A. Bank, *The Rise and Fall of Post-World War II Corporate Tax Reform*, 73 L. & Contemp. Probs. 207, 209–14 (2010).

[7] Dennis J. Ventry, Jr., *Equity Versus Efficiency and the U.S. Tax System in Historical Perspective*, in Tax Justice: The Ongoing Debate 25, 37 (Joseph J. Thorndike & Dennis J. Ventry, eds., 2002).

[8] John F. Witte, The Politics and Development of the Federal Income Tax 132 (1985).

[9] Joseph J. Thorndike, *Soak-the-Rich Republicans: The Persistence of High Tax Rates in the 1950s*, 66 Tax L. Rev. 761, 775 (2013).

majority.[10] Not surprisingly, Congressional Republicans "pressed the new president to cut taxes as soon as possible."[11] The problem was that Eisenhower insisted on "budget discipline" amidst bipartisan support for significantly expanding Social Security.[12] In Eisenhower's first State of the Union Address in 1953, he emphasized that "the first order of business is the elimination of the annual deficit," noting that "[r]eduction of taxes will be justified only as we can show we can succeed in bringing the budget under control."[13] Eisenhower even persuaded Congress to retain the corporate tax rate at 52 percent, instead of the 47 percent rate that had already been approved under the previous Democrat-controlled Congress.[14] Although Eisenhower did advise that Congress to "[w]ork toward the earliest possible reduction of the tax burden" and acknowledged that "the tax structure as a whole demands review," this clearly was not his focus. Joseph Thorndike explained that "Eisenhower consistently prioritized fiscal responsibility over tax cuts, despite paying lip service to the latter" and Congress, despite being controlled by Republicans throughout most of the period when the top rate was at 91 percent, "were unwilling to challenge the fundamentals of the war-forged tax regime."[15]

Another obstacle to tax cuts may been the bad optics if the first thing Republicans did upon regaining control of Congress after twenty years was to reduce the top marginal rates.[16] As Surrey wrote, "conservative governments fear the political consequences of rate reduction for the wealthy although their effective tax burden would be lessened."[17] Perhaps

[10] Robert D. Hormats, The Price of Liberty: Paying for America's Wars 193 (2007).

[11] Id.

[12] Julian E. Zelizer, Taxing America: Wilbur E. Mills, Congress, and the State, 1945–1975 79, 87 (1998); Hormats, *supra* note 10, at 174.

[13] *Annual Message to the Congress on the State of the Union, Feb. 2, 1953*, in Eisenhower Presidential Library, Presidential Speeches, 1953 State of the Union Address.

[14] Marc Linder, *Eisenhower-Era Marxist Confiscatory Taxation: Requiem for the Rhetoric of Rate Reduction for the Rich*, 70 Tul. L. Rev. 905, 917 (1996). Eisenhower also pushed for a delay of the expiration of the excess profits tax enacted during the Korean War. Karl O'Lessker, *The New President Makes a Budget: From Eisenhower to Bush*, 12 Pub. Budget & Financing 3, 4 (1992); Raymond J. Saulnier, Constructive Years: The U.S. Economy under Eisenhower 9 (1991).

[15] Joseph J. Thorndike, *Timelines in Tax History: Tax Codes, Tax Reform, and Tax Preferences*, 177 Tax Notes 499 (2022).

[16] William E. Foster, *Partisan Politics and Income Tax Rates*, 2013 Mich. St. L. Rev. 703, 713 (2013); Ventry, Jr., *supra*, note 7, at 30.

[17] Stanley S. Surrey, *The Congress and the Tax Lobbyist: How Special Tax Provisions Get Enacted*, 70 Harv. L. Rev. 1145, 1150 (1957).

as proof of this effect, Democrats called Republicans "the party of the bigshots [with] no sympathy for the laboring man" and accused them of going back to Mellon-era "trickle-down" economics in the 1954 revision to the Internal Revenue Code when the top marginal rate only dropped from 92 percent to 91 percent.[18] Even tax cut supporters felt it was "politically impossible to decrease the rate of progression."[19] This political reality did not change when Democrats narrowly regained control of Congress in the mid-term elections in 1954. They did not have the votes to overcome Eisenhower's objection to tax rate cuts.[20] Northwestern Law professor William Cary called "high taxes and some progression" simply "a part of the facts of life" in 1955.[21]

That does not mean that members of Congress were unsympathetic to the plight of taxpayers subject to those high rates. Surrey explained that "the average congressmen does not basically believe in the present rates of income tax in the upper brackets. When he sees them applied to individual cases, he thinks them too high and therefore unfair."[22] Cameron Hawley, a corporate executive, opined that "the majority of Congressmen feel in their hearts that present income tax rates are grossly unfair to business enterprises and high-rating individuals. Political expediency, of course, counsels against openly reducing rates in those brackets, but conscience nudges our legislators in this endless granting of special preferential exceptions."[23]

Since broad rate cuts were not politically feasible,[24] "the natural outcome," Surrey explained, was "indirect reduction through special provisions."[25] Surrey called this problem "income-tax schizophrenia," where Congress' generous exemptions from its high rates implied that it did not believe those high rates should actually be imposed.[26] John W. Byrnes, a Wisconsin Republican member of the House Ways and

18 100 Cong. Rec. 15, 310 (1954) (statement of Rep. Russell Long); id. at 12,536 (statement of Rep. Johnson (CO). Linder, *supra* note 14, at 833.

19 Eugene Neil Feingold, The Internal Revenue Act of 1954: Policy and Politics 272 (1960) (unpublished Ph.D. Dissertation, Princeton University).

20 James M. Verdier, *The President, Congress, and Tax Reform: Patterns Over Three Decades*, 499 ANNALS OF THE AM. ACAD. POLI. SCI. 114, 116 (1988).

21 William L. Cary, *Pressure Groups and the Revenue Code: A Requiem in Honor of the Departing Uniformity of the Tax Laws*, 68 HARV. L. REV. 745, 776 (1955).

22 Surrey, *The Congress and the Tax Lobbyist*, *supra* note 17, at 1150.

23 Cameron Hawley, *Morality vs. Legality*, 27 PA. BAR ASS'N Q. 230, 238–39 (1956).

24 *See* Surrey, *The Congress and the Tax Lobbyist*, *supra* note 17, at 1150–51.

25 Id. at 1150.

26 Stanley S. Surrey, *Do Income-Tax Exemptions Make Sense?* COLLIERS, March 30, 1956, at 26, 29.

Means Committee conceded in a radio broadcast that many so-called loopholes "were specifically put in there by the Congress because of the fact of the extreme high rates."[27] Even Roswell Magill, the former Assistant Secretary to the Treasury under Roosevelt and Morgenthau had "abandoned some of the antiloophole zeal that had animated his service in the New Deal."[28] Magill argued that loopholes were necessary as a form of rough justice against the high postwar rates: "The trouble is that, so long as high surtax rates persist, special provisions are essential to give the tax law reasonably fair application."[29]

Special interest groups took advantage of this attitude. Economist Roy Blough reported that at a tax hearing in 1947 no fewer than 150 lobbying groups representing business, labor, agricultural, and professional interests sought to protect their tax benefits and obtain new ones.[30] During the 1950s, this was a running theme as "the perfection and enactment of tax loopholes, credits, and exemptions became one of Washington's principal cottage industries."[31] Congress enacted so-called "rifle shot" provisions to protect the tax benefits of specific prominent taxpayers, like Louis B. Mayer and Charles Merrill.[32] Politicians became so brazen with these custom-designed loopholes that they sometimes left clues to the identity of the recipient in the statute itself. That seemed to be the case in a provision in the Tax Reform Act of 1969 that was designed to exclusively benefit a single radio station located in the home state of Louisiana of the provision's sponsor, Senate Finance Committee chairman Russell Long, with the call letters of the station spelled out in the first letter of the first word of

27 Feingold, *supra* note 19, at 272–73 (quoting Rep. Byrnes).

28 Joseph J. Thorndike, *Profiles in Tax History: Roswell Magill*, TAX NOTES, Jan. 25, 2008.

29 Roswell Magill, *High Taxes and Growth*, WALL ST. J, July 5, 1960.

30 ROY BLOUGH, THE FEDERAL TAXING PROCESS 27 (1952).

31 KEVIN PHILLIPS, WEALTH AND DEMOCRACY: A POLITICAL HISTORY OF THE AMERICAN RICH 220 (2002).

32 Surrey, *The Congress and the Tax Lobbyist*, *supra* note 22, at 1147 (referring to the "Louis B. Mayer Amendment"); Lawrence Zelenak, *Are Rifle Shot Transition Rules and Other Ad Hoc Tax Legislation Constitutional?* 44 TAX L. REV. 563, 564–65 (1989); Feingold, *supra* note 19, at 229; PHILIP N. STERN, THE GREAT TREASURY RAID 44–45 (1964). For Merrill, the provision exempted income from a charitable trust created by a will, but only if the testator died between August 15, 1954 and January 1, 1957, and only if the income was received by the charitable trust by virtue of its status as a limited partner in a partnership and certain other requirements were met, all of which made it exceedingly unlikely it could apply to anyone other than Merrill. Note, *Tax Equity and Ad Hoc Legislation*, 84 HARV. L. REV. 640, n. 3 (1971).

each subsection in the provision.[33] The Senate bill for the 1969 Act reportedly contained at least fifteen of these "hand-tailored amendments," each what Phillip Sterm called a "Private Agreement, Privately Arrived At," because neither the information upon which the provision was based, nor the fact that it was designed to benefit a specific taxpayer, were disclosed.[34]

Special preferences were so prevalent that one satirist wrote an essay in the *Wall Street Journal* entitled "The Last Taxpayer," which "envisioned a future where Congress had exempted first this and then that group of taxpayers until there was left just one man who was subject to taxation."[35] Of course, Congress acted if it was unaware of the joke, often proposing new deductions that would take special preferences to the extreme. Representative Herbert Zelenko, a Democrat from New York, went so far as to introduce a bill that proposed a deduction for "human depletion" starting at age forty-five.[36] Under Zelenko's "Over-the-Hill Tax Shelter"

[33] The provision exempted income of charitable organizations earned by businesses operated by the organization that were not part of its charitable purpose, but only in the case of a business –

> (A) which consists of providing services under license issued by a Federal regulatory agency,
> (B) which is carried on by a religious order or by an educational organization ... maintained by such religious order, and which was so carried on before May 27, 1959, and
> (C) less than 10 percent of the net income of which for each taxable year is used for activities which are not related to the purpose constituting the basis for the religious order's exemption.

I.R.C. §512(b)(15). Reportedly, Long had a staffer draft the provision so that the first letter of the text in each subsection spelled out – WWL – which were the call letters of the CBS TV station in New Orleans owned by Loyola University that was the object of the provision. PHILIP STERN, THE RAPE OF THE TAXPAYER 40 (1974).

[34] Id. at 37, 40. As Stern points out, private laws are not necessarily unique or problematic as a way to "grant[] legislative relief to designated individuals." Id. at 42. Louis Eisenstein justified these by noting that "[j]ust as those who are similarly situated should not be differently taxed, those who are differently situated should not be similarly taxed. Hence the ideology is always available to sanctify a special dispensation if an excuse is required ... even when the dispensation is carefully contrived for only one taxpayer." LOUIS EISENSTEIN, THE IDEOLOGIES OF TAXATION 156 (1961). The complaint in cases such as Mayer, Merrill and the ones proposed in the 1969 tax bill was about the lack of disclosure and the inequitable way that the provisions are granted to those with influence. Id. at 161; STERN, THE RAPE OF THE TAXPAYER, *supra* note 33, at 42.

[35] William H. Grimes, *The Last Taxpayer*, WALL ST. J., Aug. 25, 1958, at 6.

[36] Mortimer M. Caplin, *Threats to the Integrity of Our Tax System*, 44 VA. L. REV. 839, 850, n.26 (1958).

proposal, taxpayers would be entitled to a deduction equal to one percent of earned income multiplied by a number equal to the number of years of their age minus forty-four.[37] *Billboard* reported that "singers, comedians, and other show people will say 'amen' to a proposed deduction for 'depletion of human resources' by Representative Zelenko."[38]

Many observers called the maintenance of high progressive rates in the face of these generous tax deductions, which primarily benefitted the wealthy, a form of bait-and-switch that "misleads the taxpaying public as to the progressivity of the rate structure."[39] As early as 1938, economist Henry Simons had written that the exemptions in the pre–World War II income tax system were set so high that "one senses here a grand scheme of deception, whereby enormous surtaxes are voted in exchange for promises that they will not be made effective. Thus, politicians may point with pride to the rates, while quietly reminding their wealthy constituents of the loopholes."[40] By the 1950s and 1960s, Jerome Hellerstein called it "a colossal delusion,"[41] while David Bazelon described the high rates as "a kind of spiritual consolation prize to the 20-percent fellows."[42] It is little wonder that economist Harold Groves wrote in a report to Congress that there is a "widely-shared" impression that "Congress deliberately throws a high-rate scale to the public as a demagogic bone and then as deliberately allows escapes from taxes that make these rates specious."[43]

## The Corrosive Effect of Implicit Tax Cuts

One way to understand the corrosive effect on the tax system of cutting taxes implicitly through special preferences, loopholes, and lax enforcement is to examine why people engage in tax dodging in the first place. In a recent article, Professor Leandra Lederman used what accountants call the "fraud triangle" to help understand why people engage in tax

[37] Id.

[38] *Capitol Hill Snowed Under in Entertainment Bill Blizzard*, BILLBOARD, Jan. 19. 1959, at 4, 13.

[39] Arthur L. Berger, *Congress Inquires into Federal Tax Policy – the Joint Committee Symposium*, 17 U. PITT. L. REV. 594, 600 (1956).

[40] HENRY C. SIMONS, PERSONAL INCOME TAXATION: THE DEFINITION OF INCOME AS A PROBLEM OF FISCAL POLICY 219 (1938).

[41] HELLERSTEIN, *supra* note 1, at 16.

[42] DAVID BAZELON , THE PAPER ECONOMY 146 (1965).

[43] Harold Groves, *Special Provisions and the Economy*, *in* JOINT COMM. ON THE ECONOMIC REPORT, 84TH CONG., 1ST SESS. FEDERAL TAX POLICY FOR ECONOMIC GROWTH AND STABILITY 286, 289 (Joint Committee Print, 1955).

evasion,[44] which draws largely upon the mid-century work of criminologist and sociologist Donald Cressey.[45] In a study involving interviews with people who were convicted of embezzlement or a similar crime involving a violation of a position of trust that they had accepted in good faith, Cressey endeavored to explain why people who conceive of themselves as good nevertheless do bad things. He concluded that

> [t]rusted persons become trust violators when they conceive of themselves as having a financial problem which is non-shareable, are aware that this problem can be secretly resolved by violation of the position of financial trust, and are able to apply to their own conduct in that situation verbalizations which enable them to adjust their conceptions of themselves as trusted persons with their conceptions of themselves as users of the entrusted funds or property.[46]

This framework was later applied to fraud crimes with the simpler rubric of (1) Perceived Pressure or Incentives (often financial), (2) Opportunity, and (3) Rationalization.[47]

As Lederman contended, it "is not a big stretch" to apply the elements of the fraud triangle to tax evasion, which is both a type of fraud and a type of conversion of funds that rightly belong to another like in the embezzlement context.[48] Tax dodging is, of course, broader than tax evasion since it refers to both legal and illegal means of reducing your taxes. Nevertheless, the fraud triangle offers helpful insights even if you confine tax dodging to schemes designed to take advantage of favorable tax provisions that Congress did not anticipate and to the kinds of

44 Leandra Lederman, *The Fraud Triangle and Tax Evasion*, 106 IOWA L. REV. 1153 (2021).

45 Id. at 1156–57.

46 DONALD R. CRESSEY, OTHER PEOPLE'S MONEY: A STUDY IN THE SOCIAL PSYCHOLOGY OF EMBEZZLEMENT 30 (1953).

47 Alexander Schuchter & Michael Levi, *The Fraud Triangle Revisited*, 29 SEC. J. 107, 108 (2016); Clinton Free, *Looking Through the Fraud Triangle: A Review and Call for New Directions*, 23 MEDITARI ACCT. RES. 175, 177 (2015). Sometimes, a fourth element is added (forming a diamond) – Capability – which asks whether an individual has the "personal traits and abilities" to commit the fraud even if the other elements are present. David T. Wolfe & Dana R. Hermanson, *The Fraud Diamond: Considering the Four Elements of Fraud*, 74 THE CPA J. 38 (2004). The American Institute of Certified Public Accountants adopted the fraud triangle's framework to explain and predict the conditions for fraud in Statements on Auditing Standards No. 99 and the International Audited and Assurance Standards Board adopted it in International Standards on Auditing 240. CODIFICATION OF ACCT. STANDARDS & PROCS., Statement on Auditing Standards No. 99, 17 (Am. Inst. Of Certified Pub. Accts, 2002); *Auditor's Responsibility to Consider Fraud in an Audit of Financial Statements*, INT'L AUDITING & ASSURANCE STANDARDS BD. (Feb. 2004).

48 Lederman, *supra* note 44, at 1182–83.

income tax "chiseling" that taxpayers undertook to overclaim deductions and under-declare income,[49] and think of the perfectly legal special preferences, loopholes, and lax enforcement as providing context for the decisions to evade.

The application of the first two elements of the fraud triangle – pressure/incentive and opportunity – to tax dodging is self-evident. Taxpayers often perceive financial pressure from tax liability.[50] Even in the absence of financial pressure, the "lure of saving money" or even of avoiding the financial and psychological costs of compliance offers an incentive to engage in tax dodging.[51] Similarly, opportunity is generally present in tax dodging, much like in embezzlement, because so much of the tax system is based upon voluntary compliance.[52] This includes taxpayer decisions about the classification of receipts and expenditures. Although these decisions are subject to review, it is quite uncommon. Less than 1 percent of tax returns filed by individuals are audited each year, and the rate is even lower for those with income below $1 million who do not claim the Earned Income Tax Credit.[53] Moreover, most of those audits are correspondence audits involving a few targeted items, rather than field audits that are more comprehensive.[54]

The rationalization element of the fraud triangle not only applies to tax dodging, but it helps to explain how tax dodging became so prominent in the 1950s and 1960s. Cressey explained that rationalization was the process by which violators are enabled to look upon the violations "(a) as essentially non-criminal, (b) as justified, or (c) as part of a general irresponsibility for which he is not completely accountable."[55] The theory is that rationalizations are necessary for so-called "white-collar crime" because those contemplating doing it will be unable to "square their self-perception as 'good people' with" what committing the crime.[56] In the tax

[49] Martti Vihanto, *Tax Evasion and the Psychology of the Social Contract*, 32 J. Socio-Econ. 111, 113 (2003) (noting that evasion of in the individual income tax "typically manifests itself as undeclared earnings . . . and as exaggerated deductions in the tax return.").

[50] James A. Tackett, Joe Antenucci, & Fran Wolf, *A Criminological Perspective of Tax Evasion*, 110 Tax Notes 654, 655 (2006).

[51] Id. at 655–56; Lederman, *supra* note 44, at 1185.

[52] Tackett, Antenucci, & Wolf, *supra* note 50, at 656.

[53] Congressional Research Service, *Distribution of IRS Audits by Income and Race* (updated Nov. 6, 2023).

[54] Id.

[55] Cressey, *supra* note 46, at 93.

[56] Todd Haugh, *Overcriminalization's New Harm Paradigm*, 68 Vand. L. Rev. 1191, 1196 (2015).

dodging context, most people who exaggerate a deduction here or there or omit some item of income received in cash do not see themselves as criminals.[57] They do so because they rationalize their behavior as justifiable or defensible in one or more ways. As Randolph Paul observed, "[r]ationalization is constantly at work in the law of tax avoidance."[58] According to Tackett et al., "the overwhelming rationalization used in tax evasion is the lack of equity in the tax system," which often appears in one of three forms: "uneven tax burden, fiscal irresponsibility by the government, and lack of enforcement."[59] All three of these forms of rationalizations popped up in mid-century America tax dodging.

The "uneven tax burden" or inequity rationalization was commonly heard during the 1950s and 1960s. Indeed, perceived inequity is a constant theme in the tax context. Provisions that are passed by Congress to benefit an individual group often appear to be unfair to people who are not members of the favored group.[60] Louis Eisenstein wrote, "[s]ince equity includes the equal distribution of dispensations, the question for equity is necessarily a search without end. As a prior dispensation is extended, a new discrimination is created; and the demand for equity is inevitably soon heard once more."[61]

The inequity concern was often about horizontal rather than vertical inequity. Kiplinger's *Changing Times* reminded readers that "[i]t's not just the people in the high brackets who get the tax breaks," urging them to consider "the fellow down the block who earns the same salary as you. While you put in eight hours a day at the office, he's eating at the poshest restaurants, seeing the best shows, taking his wife to conventions, vacationing at the company's lodge, joining the country club – all at his boss's expense."[62] As the magazine complained, "he's enjoying a higher standard of living than you. Yet he may not pay a cent more in taxes."[63] Mortimer Caplin, the Commissioner of Internal Revenue from 1961 through 1964, observed that "[i]ndividuals frequently hear of

57 Tackett, Antenucci, & Wolf, *supra* note 50, at 656.

58 Randolph E. Paul, *Restatement of the Law of Tax Avoidance*, in STUDIES IN FEDERAL TAXATION: TAXATION WITHOUT MISREPRESENTATION 93 (1937).

59 Id.

60 Walter W. Heller, *Limitations of the Federal Individual Income Tax*, 7 J. FIN. 185, 192 (1952).

61 EISENSTEIN, *supra* note 34, at 167.

62 *Let's Fix Up Those Crazy Income Tax Laws!*, CHANGING TIMES: THE KIPLINGER MAGAZINE, March 1960, at 25, 26.

63 Id. Perhaps in reaction to this perceived inequity, readers wrote in to say "I've heard that the Internal Revenue Service hires people to turn in income tax evaders How do I apply

expense accounts, fringe benefits, and persons earning huge sums but paying little taxes. The remark made the other day by a salaried employee is typical: 'Why does everyone have a loophole but me? Why shouldn't I have a window to crawl out of?'"[64]

The seemingly endless parade of special tax provisions added to the tax laws fed the inequity rationalization. As William Cary wrote, "[t]he more preferential the legislation written into the Code, the greater the opportunity for others to claim they are being discriminated against."[65] The problem was that most Congressmen "want to be helpful to their constituents and others and are therefore sympathetic to taxpayers who assert that they are being unfairly treated."[66] Since taking away benefits from the people who already have them would "satisfy neither group. The result is that asserted inequities are eliminated by extending privilege to additional groups, rather than by withdrawing them from others."[67]

Not only did special treatment begat more special treatment, but it created the justification for individuals unable to qualify for any special treatment to resort to tax dodging.[68] Hellerstein related a conversation he had with a building contractor who told him that "if you want to get anything like a fair shake as a taxpayer, you've got to try to get by with everything you can on your tax return, and then be ready to take care of the revenue agent. Otherwise you'll end up holding the bag."[69] Similarly, a 1950s-era insurance consultant complained that

> the income-tax law is stacked against the professional and the little man in favor of businessmen and owners of stocks, bonds and other property. . . . While overstating deductions or omitting dividends or interest income will not set things right, no one . . . can properly criticize the disfavored taxpayers from using these devices to offset in a small measure the injustices of the tax law.[70]

Meanwhile, while the little guys complained about the favored few, corporations complained that they "have long been discriminated against in federal taxation" because of the double taxation of corporate income.[71]

for this job?" *Your Questions Answered*, CHANGING TIMES: THE KIPLINGER MAGAZINE, August 1959, at 30.

64 Caplin, *supra* note 36, at 840.
65 Cary, *supra* note 21, at 774–75.
66 Feingold, *supra* note 19, at 275–76.
67 Id. at 276.
68 Surrey, *Do Income-Tax Exemptions Make Sense?*, *supra* note 26, at 28.
69 HELLERSTEIN, *supra* note 1, at 241.
70 Id. at 241–42.
71 *Unequal Taxation*, CHI. DAILY TRIB., March 13, 1943, at 12.

They argued that their treatment was particularly unfair compared to an individual proprietorship where "a man of large means is able, as he is under present law, to offset profits on one of his personally owned ventures with losses on another."[72]

While fiscal irresponsibility generally was a common complaint, revelations about government corruption in the postwar era were a very public and specific brand of that in the tax dodging context. One of the most significant scandals in the history of the federal income tax, which led to the reorganization of the Bureau of Internal Revenue into the Internal Revenue Service, occurred in the late 1940s and early 1950s.[73] A Congressional investigation "exposed corruption reaching from the auditing field agents to the top officials," leading to the imprisonment of two of the sixty-four Internal Revenue Collectors scattered around the country, the resignation of seven others, and the conviction of Joseph D. Nunan, Jr., the former Commissioner of Internal Revenue, for nonpayment of taxes during a period that overlapped with his term of office.[74] Such impropriety was not limited to the Bureau of Internal Revenue either. The Assistant Attorney General in charge of the Tax Division of the Justice Department admitted that he accepted fur coats from a law firm that represented a tax matter before him and received commissions from person under investigation by his office.[75] Government officials believed these revelations could lead to more tax dodging. As Helen Fuller of the *New Republic* reported, "[t]here is grave fear in government of the effect which further disclosures of crookedness may have on the willingness of millions of citizens to pay taxes they owe their country."[76]

Another common rationalization used during this period was the perceived "lack of enforcement" of the tax laws. In his 1937 message to Congress in support of legislation to attack tax evasion, Franklin D. Roosevelt said "[t]he example of successful tax dodging by

72 Id. This complaint may have been rooted in the repeal of the consolidated return provisions for all but railroad corporations in the 1930s. Steven A. Bank, *When We Taxed the Pyramids*, 41 Fla. St. U. L. Rev. 39, 49–53 (2013).

73 Joseph J. Thorndike, *Truman's IRS Commissioner was Evading Taxes While in Office*, 152 Tax Notes 1767 (2016).

74 Id.; Hellerstein, *supra* note 1, at 240–41.

75 Hellerstein, *supra* note 1, at 241.

76 Helen Fuller, *The Tax Thieves of 1951*, New Republic, Nov. 11, 1951, at 9, 10. *Cf.* Joel Slemrod, *Trust in Public Finance*, in Public Finance and Public Policy in the New Century 49 (Sijbren Cnossen and Hans-Werner Sinn, eds., 2003) (showing the correlation between attitudes toward tax evasion and trust in government).

a minority of very rich individuals breeds efforts by others to dodge ... tax laws."[77] In a sense, this was just another form of the inequity rationalization. Offenders often explained that what they were doing was nothing in comparison to what others did without punishment. As one contemporary commentator noted, "[p]ossibly the worst breach of all in the equity of the income tax is the differential escape from taxation of legally taxable income."[78] Hellerstein, for example, recounted from a dinner party conversation, "one of our guests ... declared that he had no pangs of conscience whatever in overstating his business-expense deductions, because that's the only way he can come anywhere near paying his fair share of the income tax. Most people, he knows, 'get away with murder,' and chisel on a far larger scale than he does."[79] The dinner guest continued, "I'm not cheating Uncle Sam one bit when I overstate my deductions in my modest way. I'm merely correcting a small part of the injustice done me by lax enforcement of the tax laws. I'd be delighted to pay every penny the law calls for, if they'd really go after the big fish, because everybody's rates would go down."[80]

Robert Metz of the *New York Times* reported that government officials were worried about this phenomenon: "Treasury is concerned that when a man notices that his neighbor does better on a comparable income through an expense account, he will become dissatisfied. The income-tax system is built upon the 'voluntary compliance' of individual taxpayers and, if taxpayer morale is affected by seeming inequities, the system may crumble."[81] Treasury periodically made a public show of announcing it was going to go after tax dodgers,[82] but it usually complained that it was hamstrung by "soft" judges and lawyers who argued that "cheating the government on a tax return is much less

77 Franklin D. Roosevelt, Message to Congress on Tax Evasion Prevention, June 1, 1937.

78 Heller, *supra* note 60, at 195.

79 HELLERSTEIN, *supra* note 1, at 240.

80 Id.

81 Robert Metz, *Cut in Tax Rate Termed Possible,* N.Y. TIMES, Dec. 11, 1960, at F1, F12. A similar phenomenon occurred in Britain soon after World War I, where Inland Revenue reported to a Royal Commission created to survey the income tax that it was concerned about "the taxpayers lack of a sense of social disgrace – not least because they assumed that other taxpayers were doing the same." MARTIN DAUNTON, JUST TAXES: THE POLITICS OF TAXATION IN BRITAIN, 1914–1979 110 (2002).

82 Rodney Crowther, *Tax-Evading Gamblers to be Hunted,* The Sun (Baltimore), April 1, 1951, at 1; *U.S. to Push Hunt for Tax Evaders,* N.Y. TIMES, March 14, 1953, at 21; Richard E. Mooney, *Crackdown is Aimed at Tax Evaders,* ATL. CONST., March 14, 1953, at 1.

reprehensible than larceny."[83] One modern observer suggested that lax enforcement helped spread the use of tax shelters in the entertainment industry, noting that "the blind eye cast on their tax shelters by the U.S. Treasury may have encouraged their behavior. Throughout the war years, the Treasury Department has been aware of Hollywood's trend in using collapsible corporations, but Secretary of the Treasury Morgenthau has chosen to ignore the matter."[84]

This cycle of high-profile tax dodging and special preferences, self-help efforts, and a lack of trust in tax enforcement all contributed to a general decline in taxpaying morale. Taxpayers did not want to become one of the "patsies" House Ways and Means Chairman Wilbur Mills contrasted against the tax system's "coddled pets."[85] "Cutting corners" or "income-tax chiseling" became "socially acceptable" and "respectable."[86] Indeed, Hellerstein reported that "it's not uncommon to hear people boast of how they got away with this or that unwarranted deduction."[87] Holdouts were considered chumps, while tax dodging became culturally and structurally embedded in mid-century American society.[88]

By the end of the 1960s, public frustration with the tax system had reached a boiling point. Although much of this frustration was with local property taxation,[89] federal income tax loopholes drew public ire as well. Taxpayers were particularly upset with the decision under the Revenue and Expenditure Control Act of 1968 to impose a surtax to pay for the Vietnam war and preserve President Lyndon B. Johnson's Great Society social welfare program instead of closing loopholes.[90] In 1969, 83 percent of respondents to a Harris Poll agreed with the statement that "there are

[83] Clark Mollenhoff, *Drive Seeks Prison for Tax Evaders*, MINNEAPOLIS SUNDAY TRIB., Sept. 18, 1955, at 4; Clark Mollenhoff, *Prison is Least Worry for Tax Cheaters*, WASH. POST, July 19, 1953, at B7.

[84] Eric Hoyt, *Hollywood and the Income Tax, 1929–1955*, 22 FILM HIST.: AN INT'L J. 5, 14 (2010).

[85] FERDINAND LUNDBERG, THE RICH AND THE SUPER-RICH 391 (1968).

[86] HELLERSTEIN, *supra* note 1, at 219, 232.

[87] Id. at 219.

[88] LUNDBERG, *supra* note 85, at 391.

[89] Josh Mound, *Stirrings of Revolt: Regressive Levies, the Pocketbook Squeeze, and the 1960s Roots of the 1970s Tax Revolt*, 32 J. POL'Y HIST. 105, 107 (2020).

[90] Seichiro Mozume, *Tax Expenditures and the Tax Reform Act of 1969 in the United States*, 46 SOC. SCI. HIST. 93, 101 (2022); STEVEN A. BANK, KIRK J. STARK & JOSEPH J. THORNDIKE, WAR AND TAXES 132–37 (2008); Rowland Evans & Robert. Novak, *Johnson in Dilemma Over Tax Boost as Liberals Seek to Close Loopholes*, WASH. POST TIMES HERALD, Aug. 24, 1967, at A21; James N. Fazio, Letter to the Editor, *Plug Loopholes Before Hiking Income Tax*, NEWSDAY, July 28, 1967, at 28.

a lot of tax loopholes for the rich to avoid taxes" and 62 percent responded that they would "feel better about the taxes" they paid "if many of the tax loopholes for the rich were closed."[91] A few years later, author Philip Stern suggested that the "public unrest about the tax system" reflected in the Harris Poll results had been "sparked in large measure . . . by the 1969 revelation by outgoing Treasury Secretary Joseph Barr that 155 Americans making more than $200,000 were paying no tax whatever."[92]

In 1973, one poor Treasury attorney, perhaps disgusted by the carve-outs, loopholes, special provisions, and general gutting of the tax base, appeared to register protest in a rather passive-aggressive manner by inserting a hidden message in one provision of the Treasury Regulations. In this instance, an Example was inserted into the Regulation implementing a provision under Section 167 on the sale of property subject to accelerated depreciation allowances. Accelerated depreciation was considered fundamental to tax shelters and was under attack during this period.[93] As is customary, the Example identified the depreciable assets with a single capital letter for ease of discussion, but rather than using letters like A, B, C, and D, the Example identified each of the assets as K, R, A, and P, in that order.[94] Presumably, the drafter of the Regulation sought to call a spade a spade, or, in this case, crap as K.R.A.P.

## The Cycle Repeats

Notwithstanding the frustration with the tax system that emerged from the 1950s and 1960s, the tax dodging cycle repeated with the explosion of the tax shelter industry in the 1970s and early-to-mid

[91] Louis Harris, *Majority is Critical of Tax Loopholes*, WASH. POST, Sept. 22, 1969, at A7.
[92] STERN, THE RAPE OF THE TAXPAYER, *supra* note 33, at xi.
[93] Anthony Yudis, *To Retain or Plug Loopholes*, BOSTON GLOBE, April 20, 1969, at B47.
[94] T.D. 7272, 1973-1 C.B. 82 (1.167(a)-11(d)(3)(iv)(b), example 1). The full text of the regulation is as follows:

> Example (1). Corporation X has a multiple asset vintage account of 1971 consisting of assets K, R, A, and P all of which are section 1245 property. The unadjusted basis of the account is $40,000. The unadjusted basis of asset A is $10,000. When the reserve for depreciation for the account is $20,000, asset A is sold in an extraordinary retirement for $8,000 in cash. The $10,000 unadjusted basis of asset A is removed from the account and the $5,000 depreciation allowable for asset A is removed from the reserve for depreciation. Gain in the amount of $3,000 (to which section 1245 applies) is recognized upon the sale of asset A.

1980s.[95] At the time, an executive at investment firm E. F. Hutton called the interest in investing in tax shelters "phenomenal. Everybody is tired of paying taxes. Doctors, lawyers, you name them. The sort of people interested in tax shelters goes across the board."[96] Even after the top marginal rate dropped, the *New York Times* still reported that tax shelters were "booming."[97] As one measure of tax shelter activity, the Joint Committee on Taxation found that taxpayers invested roughly $8.4 billion in what were called "'public program' tax-advantaged investments," or limited partnerships registered with the Securities and Exchange Commission, as against $5.5 billion in 1982."[98]

Somewhat paradoxically, this rise in tax shelter activity occurred at a time of explicit statutory tax cuts. The drop in the top marginal tax rates – from 91 percent during the 1950s and early 1960s to 70 percent by the 1970s,[99] and, again to 50 percent by the early 1980s[100] – was expected to lower demand for tax dodging, but that did not happen.[101] There were two explanations. First, the top rate dropped for the wealthy, but the middle class ended up worse off, which increased their interest in tax dodging. Second, although these tax cuts were explicit, they were accompanied by implicit tax cuts from the creation of new loopholes or

[95] Some have asserted that tax shelters are not the same as "tax dodges." *See* James C. Corman, *Use and Misuse of Tax Shelters: The Congress and Tax Reforms*, 49 NOTRE DAME LAW. 509, 510 (1974). As used in this book, tax dodging is broad enough to encompass both legislative provisions designed to permit taxpayers to reduce their taxes, which Corman might have suggested constituted "legitimate" tax shelters, and abuses of those provisions or schemes designed to take advantage of unintentional gaps in the Tax Code, which Corman might have characterized as "tax dodges."

[96] Robert Kearns, *Not Every Tax Shelter Plan Can Ward off Taxman's Bite*, CHI. TRIB., March 4, 1980, at C3, C12.

[97] Robert D. Hershey, Jr., *The Boom in Tax Shelters*, N.Y. TIMES, July 19, 1983, at D1.

[98] Joint Committee on Taxation, *Proposals Relating to Tax Shelters and Other Tax-Motivated Transactions*, scheduled for Hearings before the Committee on Ways and means on February 22 and 28, 1984) at 6 (citing Robert A. Stranger & Co., The Stranger Report, February 1984) ("Joint Committee Report").

[99] Rev. Act of 1964, Pub. L. No. 88–272, § 111, 78 Stat. 19, 20–21 (setting the top marginal rate at 70 percent).

[100] Economic Recover Tax Act of 1981, Pub. L. No. 97–34, § 101, 95 Stat. 172, 176 (investment income); Tax Reform Act of 1969, Pub. L. No. 91–172, § 804, 83 Stat. 487, 685–86 (earned income).

[101] *See* Jerry Knight, *Tax Shelters Still Work But So Does the IRS*, WASH. POST, Nov. 8, 1981, at G11 ("Tax shelters were supposed to slip off their foundations when the maximum federal income tax rate was cut from 70 percent to 50 percent this year, but that hasn't happened.").

expansion of existing ones that gave many taxpayers both the opportunity and justification to pursue tax dodging.

### *Middle Class Demand for Tax Dodging*

In the 1970s, the middle class fell victim in part to what was called, "tax bracket creep."[102] They may not have felt wealthier, but they paid more taxes in part because some portion of their income was taxed at a higher bracket. Between 1971 and 1981, the average tax rate of individuals rose from 24 to 32.1 percent,[103] while the percentage of taxpayers paying a marginal rate above 35 percent increased from 1 percent in 1964 to 13.7 percent in 1981.[104] Going back even farther, whereas 90 percent of taxpayers in 1954 were subject to the lowest tax rate of 20 percent, almost 50 percent of the taxpayers in 1981 were subject to a tax rate higher than 20 percent.[105] By 1981, a single individual with income of $41,500 or a married couple with joint income of $60,000 for the first time had been pushed into the 50 percent tax bracket.[106]

Although middle class taxpayers may not have immediately invested in tax shelters because of a change in their tax burden,[107] it did not take long. In 1977, George E. Warner, the head of the corporate financing department for the National Association of Securities Dealers, explained that the effects of the tax bracket creep had made many middle class taxpayers "increasingly interested in lightening their tax burden."[108] *U.S. News & World Report* observed that "increasing numbers of people with moderate incomes are looking into a subject once considered the

[102] Bill Sing, *Middle Class Retreating to Tax Shelters*, L.A. TIMES, Mar. 5, 1981, at A17; W. ELLIOT BROWNLEE, FEDERAL TAXATION IN AMERICA: A HISTORY 156, 172 (3rd ed. 2016); Kearns, *supra*, note 96, at C12. Some of this bracket creep was the result of inflation, which was remedied to some extent, but not completely, by increasing the threshold at which income was taxed at the next highest marginal rate. CONGRESSIONAL BUDGET OFFICE, INDEXING THE INDIVIDUAL INCOME TAX FOR INFLATION 14–15 (1980).

[103] Joint Committee Report, *supra* note 98, at 11.

[104] Daniel L. Simmons, *The Tax Reform Act of 1986: An Overview*, 1987 B.Y.U. L. REV. 151, 157.

[105] Id. at 156–57.

[106] Sing, *supra* note 102, at A20.

[107] The Joint Committee on Taxation suggested that there may have been a "lagged response" to this increase in average rates over the decade. Joint Committee Report, *supra* note 98, at 11.

[108] Deborah Rankin, *Taxes & Accounting: Some Persistent Tax Shelters*, N.Y. TIMES, Dec. 27, 1977, at 57.

exclusive province of the rich – tax shelters."[109] By 1980, the effects of tax bracket creep were supercharging this interest. The number of taxpayers subject to the 50 percent tax bracket had quadrupled since 1973,[110] which one partner at the accounting firm of Peat, Marwick explained was the rate at which most people "start worrying about how to avoid a hefty tax bill."[111]

Tax advisers, many of whom traced their origins to the rise in interest in tax dodging during the 1950s and 1960s, stepped in to serve these new prospective middle-class clients. As Robert D. Hershey, Jr, reported in 1983 for the *New York Times*: "[a] large network of financial entrepreneurs, promoters, advisers and salesmen has gradually developed. That network is constantly creating new products and trying to sell them to a tax-conscious and sometimes gullible public."[112] Even conservative financial firms that previously had been hesitant about promoting tax shelters, especially to less sophisticated investors, got into the act.[113] Middle class taxpayers eagerly took advantage of all these options. According to the *Los Angeles Times*, "[m]ore middle-class taxpayers are going to accountants, financial advisors, or tax lawyers – and paying sometimes huge fees – to make sure they claim every allowable tax deduction."[114]

The middle class also resorted to the kind of self-help guides that became popular in the 1950s and 1960s. Indeed, J. K. Lasser's *Your Income Tax* remained a perennial bestseller and sold its entire run – over one million copies – in the first three months alone in 1977 as the average person tried to figure out the changes wrought by the Tax Reform Act of 1976, which had been focused on curbing tax shelters.[115] A new crop of authors also helped to demystify and normalize tax shelters and other tax dodging techniques with advice books. In the 1978 book, *Tax Shelters: A Complete Guide*, for example, which "was written to make the

109 *Tax Shelters Gaining Favor with the Not-So-Rich, Too*, U.S. News & World Report, Aug. 30, 1976, at 70.

110 Sing, *supra* note 102, at A20.

111 Kearns, *supra* note 96, at C12. *See* Rankin, *Some Persistent Tax Shelters*, *supra* note 108, at 58 ("most experts recommend that an individual be in the 50 percent tax bracket . . . before considering such a move.").

112 Hershey, Jr., *supra*, note 97, at D1.

113 Id. Their reluctance was partly overcome by aggressive tax opinions secured by shelter promoters. Dennis J. Ventry, Jr., *Tax Shelter Opinions Threatened the Tax System in the 1970s*, Tax Notes, May 22, 2006, at 947; Donald L. Korb, *Schemes, Shelters and Abusive Transactions*, 2005 Tax Notes Today 29–61 (Feb. 11, 2005) (Part II.B).

114 Sing, *supra* note 102, at A20.

115 *How to Beat Taxes*, Forbes, March 15, 1977, at 120; Lawrence J. Lee, *Tax Shelters under the Tax Reform Act of 1976*, 22 Vill. L. Rev. 223, 223–26 (1976–1977).

subject of tax shelters comprehensible to the average investment-oriented layperson," the authors answered the question "Are tax shelters legal and proper?" with the reassuring response "Legal, without question."[116] Middle class investors could even get tax shelter tips from tax and investment specialists, such as Robert Stanger, who left Merrill Lynch's tax incentive department to publish several pamphlets and books on tax shelter investing, including one targeted at novices entitled *Tax Shelters: The Bottom Line*, or William G. Brennan, formerly of the accounting firm of Arthur Anderson, who published a monthly newsletter focused on tax shelters.[117]

Tax advisers marketed tax shelters specifically to middle-class taxpayers. According to the *Wall Street Journal*, "[t]ax shelters, once considered the exclusive province of the rich, now are being marketed to the masses. With inflation and so-called bracket creep propelling many Americans into more burdensome tax situations, tax sheltering is becoming a mass industry, if not a national pastime."[118] Similarly, *The Economist* reported that part of the reason that tax shelter investors were no longer "limited to the very rich and the haute bourgeoisie" and "increasingly include the middle class" was because of "the active promotion of shelters" to those prospective investors.[119]

Not only were tax shelters no longer the exclusive province of the rich, but they spread to new markets. If the Black community was the growth market for tax dodging opportunities in the 1950s and 1960s, women were in the 1970s and 1980s. Financial planning columns started to appear in so-called "women's" magazines that discussed tax saving tips, including tax shelters. Jane Bryant Quinn, a noted financial writer, authored a column in the magazine *Woman's Day*, including several on tax shelters, such as one that recommended "Three Tax Shelters Everyone Should Check Out" and another that was titled "Tax Shelters: Not Just for the Rich."[120] Julian

[116] Robert and Carol Tannenhauser, Tax Shelters: A Complete Guide (1978) (author's note, 16).

[117] Arthur M. Louis, *The Risks and Rewards or Tax Shelters*, Fortune, Oct. 1, 1985, at 73, 76; Daniel F. Cuff, *The Oracle of Shelters*, N.Y. Times, Nov. 20, 1983; Robert A. Stanger, Tax Shelters: The Bottom Line (1982); Bruce W. Fraser, *Where to Get More Tax-Shelter Data*, Christian Science Monitor, Sept. 21, 1984.

[118] Jonathan Kwitny, *Risky Havens: Tax Shelters Attract Attention of Masses – and of the Revenuers*, Wall St. J., June 29, 1984, at 1.

[119] *Psst – Wanna Shelter?*, The Economist, March 10, 1984, at 38, 41.

[120] Jane Bryant Quinn, *Three Tax Shelters Everyone Should Check Out*, Woman's Day, Feb. 5, 1985, at 16; Jane Bryant Quinn, *Tax Shelters: Not Just for the Rich*, Woman's Day, April 24, 1984, at 21.

Block, a tax attorney, wrote articles on tax shelters for both *Good Housekeeping* and *Woman's Day*, where he explained that "[m]any people think tax shelters are only for the very wealthy – those whose tax brackets are so high they can afford to invest in risky ventures. But taxpayers with moderate incomes can also benefit from a wide variety of tax shelters today."[121] Even the fashion magazine *Vogue* discussed tax shelters in a "Managing Your Money" column geared toward women.[122]

To make it accessible to these new investors, promoters created new investment structures that allowed easier price points for entry. During this period, public syndications of tax shelter investments emerged, with "minimum subscriptions as low as $2,500 or $5,000, and in a few cases, only $1,000–$1,500."[123] Although not accessible for everyone, even the top end of this range, $5,000, was the kind of investment that was within reach for a segment of people traditionally considered part of the middle class.[124] Of course, these public syndications were "so weighted by promotional fees and other front-end loads" that it was hard to make a profit even after tax.[125] Nevertheless, tax professionals, who often advised on deals that they themselves were promoting,[126] convinced many unsophisticated investors eager to get the same tax deals as the rich that they were good deals. It should not be surprising, therefore, that "the boom in sheltering" was "coming not from the wealthy, but from ... young, middle-income wage earners who are getting regular pay raises, but that inflation and tax 'bracket creep' nonetheless made then worse off than before."[127] Indeed, by 1985, the *Washington Post* noted that tax shelters "have proliferated so much in the last 15 years" that they have become "a basic feature of American life."[128]

121 Julian Block, *Tax Shelters for Middle Incomes*, WOMAN'S DAY, March 11, 1980, at 28; Julian Block, *Tax Shelters for Anyone*, GOOD HOUSEKEEPING, Oct. 1978, at 265.

122 *See, e.g.*, Lisa Gubernick, *Managing Your Money: Tax Shelters: What You Should Know*, VOGUE, April 1984, at 130.

123 Mitchell Gordon, *More Tax Shelters: Weighing the Rewards and Risks in Schemes to Balk the IRS*, BARRON'S NAT'L BUS. AND FIN. WEEKLY, Oct. 1, 1973, at 5.

124 According to the Federal Reserve Board's Survey of Consumer Finances for 1983, the average amount of liquid assets, which included checking, money market, and savings accounts, as well as individual retirement accounts, Keoghs, certificates of deposit and savings bonds, held by individuals was above $5,000 for the majority of those surveyed. *Survey of Consumer Finances, 1983*, FEDERAL RESERVE BULLETIN, Sept. 1984, at 679, 680 (tbl. 1) and 686 (tbl. 10).

125 Gordon, *supra* note 123, at 5.

126 Id.

127 Sing, *supra* note 102, at A20. See *Tax Shelters Gain Despite Cut in Rates*, CHI. TRIB., Aug. 9, 1983, at C3.

128 Dale Russakoff, *Influential Tax-Shelter Industry Concludes its Busiest Time of Year*, WASH. POST, Jan. 1, 1985, at A7.

### *The Corrosive Effect of Pairing Explicit Tax Cuts with Implicit Ones*

The tax cuts enacted in the 1960s and again in the early 1980s were explicit, but they were accompanied or soon followed by implicit tax cuts. This was true even though the government also closed some loopholes while it cut the top statutory rates. The problem was that it deliberately or unintentionally left others open or created or liberalized new avenues for tax dodging, which "made some shelters more attractive," thereby diverting tax shelter money into those areas and away from others.[129] As tax lawyer and future law professor Martin Ginsburg accurately predicted in his testimony before the House Committee on Ways and Means in 1973, "advisers to the wealthy will devote enormous ingenuity to developing and tailoring new devices to meet the dictates of revised law. 1969's orange groves became 1970's almond orchard became 1972's rosebush nursery."[130] The effect of this ad hoc approach to tax preferences was to undercut the transparency of the magnitude of the cuts to the top rates and continue the corrosive cycle of tax dodging.

In one example of this effect, during the late 1960s there was concern the high costs and investment risks associated with oil production would lead to a shortfall.[131] Perhaps not coincidentally, the Tax Reform Act of 1969 targeted loopholes and enacted a minimum tax that House Ways and Means Committee Chair Wilbur Mills called "a second line of defense against special preferences and deals,"[132] but, from the perspective of tax advisors, "the law barely touched the oil and gas development

[129] Hershey, *supra* note 97, at D6; Andrew Tobias, *The Fables and Follies of Tax Shelters*, ESQUIRE, March 27, 1979, at 75.

[130] Martin D. Ginsburg, Panel Discussions on Tax Reform Before the Committee on Ways and Means, U.S. House of Representatives, 93rd Cong., 1st Sess., at 879, 887–88 (1973) ("1973 Ways and Means Tax Reform Panel").

[131] Frank W. Corrigan, *Finding Shelter for the Wealthy*, NEWSDAY, Jan. 11, 1971, at 68.

[132] Wilbur D. Mills, *The Tax Reform Act of 1969*, 4 IND. LEGAL F. 26, 30 (1970–71). By 1973, however, the minimum tax was considered ineffective. Tax attorney Kenneth A. Goldman, who had worked as an Attorney-Advisor in the Treasury Department's Office of Tax Legislative Counsel, called the minimum tax "a good concept," but told the House Ways and Means Committee in 1973 that "the present features of it have virtually emasculated the effect that the public thought it was getting in 1969." Goldman, 1973 Ways and Means Tax Reform Panel, *supra* note 130, at 855, 856. Martin Ginsburg concluded that the "minimum tax has done little if anything to depress the tax shelter market." Ginsburg, 1973 Ways and Means Tax Reform Panel, *supra* note 130, at 883 (prepared statement of Martin D. Ginsburg). *See* Alan S. Murray & Jeffrey H. Birnbaum, *Lawmakers, Lobbyists and the Unlikely Triumph of Tax Reform*, 2 CONGRESS & THE PRESIDENCY 185, 185 (1988) ("The 1969 reform act was largely reversed by 1971.").

funds, except to cut the depreciation allowance slightly."[133] Indeed, their view was that "oil and gas investments received rather favorable treatment," in part because the Act allowed depletion allowances for oil shale and for production from continental shelf areas,[134] and it did not include intangible drilling and development costs as a preference item under the minimum tax.[135] The result, *Newsday* reported in 1971, was that "most tax shelter money is being funneled into these [oil and gas development] funds."[136] Congress attempted to stem the tide with the Tax Reform Act of 1976,[137] which ostensibly "limit[ed] the attractiveness of drilling shelters," but rising prices as a result of the energy crisis "put a bloom on investments in oil, gas and coal."[138]

By the early 1980s, the *New York Times* reported that "[r]eal estate shelters have prospered as a result" of "a grab-bag of benefits bestowed upon property owners by the 1981 tax law."[139] Under the Economic Recovery Tax Act of 1981 (ERTA), Congress shortened the accelerated depreciation system's recovery period from as long as thirty to fifty years to only fifteen years using the new Accelerated Cost Recovery System (ACRS) and allowed a 175 percent declining balance method for calculating the depreciation deduction each year, both of which were considered "significant benefits to the real estate industry" by permitting the faster recovery of costs.[140] While ACRS was touted as a simplification

[133] Thomas F. Cunnane, *Tax Shelter Investments After the 1969 Tax Reform Act*, 49 TAXES: THE TAX MAG. 450, 450 (1971). Under the Act, the percentage depletion allowance, which is the deduction allowed for the decline in the value of the oil and gas in the ground from the drilling, was reduced from 27.5 percent to 22 percent. Tax Reform Act of 1969, H.R. 13270, P.L. 91-172, §501(b)(1).

[134] Cunnane, *supra* note 133, at 457. Tax Reform Act of 1969, *supra* note 133, at § 502 (amending §613(c)(4) of the Int. Rev. Code of 1954) and § 505 (adding Code § 638).

[135] J. Waddy Bullion, 1973 Ways and Means Tax Reform Panel, *supra* note 130, at 868, 869 (noting that although the Senate included intangible drilling and development costs as a preference item, the House omitted it and the provision was removed in conference).

[136] Corrigan, *supra* note 131, at 68.

[137] *See* Tax Reform Act of 1976, H.R. 10612, P.L. 94-455, §205. This rules previously only required the recapture upon sale of oil and gas property of deductions attributable to the depreciation of tangible personal property. This section required the recapture of intangible drilling and development costs as well. STAFF OF THE JT. CMTE ON TAX'N, SUMMARY OF THE TAX REFORM ACT OF 1976 at 4-5 (Oct. 4, 1976).

[138] James A. Rousmaniere, Jr., *Tax Shelter Opportunities Boom in Spite of New Law*, THE SUN (Baltimore), Feb. 9, 1977, at A9.

[139] Deborah Rankin, *The Advantage in Real Estate Shelters*, N.Y. TIMES, Aug. 15, 1982, at F13.

[140] Howard L. Braitman, James J. Klink, & Bernard M. Shapiro, *Real Estate Industry Benefits from ERTA 1981*, 52 CPA J. 32 (1982).

measure, Harvard Law Professor William Andrews complained that its main purpose, in combination with a newly liberalized investment tax credit, was "to create new mountains of wealth for distribution in the form of tax deductions through the tax shelter industry."[141] The net effect of these legislative developments was that investment in oil and gas drilling "plummeted" and investments in real estate shelters rose.[142]

This type of tax dodge shifting occurred within the same industry as well. In the movie industry, for example, the government's efforts to combat runaway production in the 1950s and 1960s led to the search for alternative methods of bringing down the tax liabilities associated with film production. Producers turned to film financing tax shelters, which paired partnerships of high-income investors eager for depreciation deductions to offset their outside income with film studios looking for alternative sources of capital.[143] These shelters have been described as "an apotheosis of these incipient practices, serving both as a means to reduce the tax liability of high-earning individuals [often outside the entertainment industry] and as an alternative strategy for motion picture financing."[144] In this sense, loophole closing for film and other tax dodges in the 1970s and early 1980s were sometimes like the mid-century high tax rates: "full of sound and fury," but often "signifying nothing."[145]

The continued parade of tax legislation offering new or better tax preferences for certain industries and individuals only fueled the same types of rationalizations that encouraged tax dodging in the 1950s and 1960s under the fraud triangle analysis. First, Congress' attempt to spur investment further via the Tax Code legitimized tax dodging in the minds of the average taxpayer. By 1983, the *New York Times* observed, "[t]ax shelters have achieved wide social acceptability."[146] Moreover, when combined with the foundation for tax dodging that had been built in

141 William D. Andrews, *The Economic Recovery Tax Act of 1981*, 68 CORNELL L. REV. 421, 424–25 (1983). *See* John F. Witte, *The Tax Reform Act of 1986: A New Era in Tax Politics*, 19 AM. POL. Q. 438, 443 (1991) (calling ERTA a "strident antireform bill," which resulted in revenue loss estimated at $239 billion over 5 years because of tax cuts paired with new and expanded tax preference items).

142 Rankin, *The Advantage on Real Estate Tax Shelters*, *supra* note 139, at F13.

143 *See* Jt. Committee on Internal Rev. Tax'n, *Tax Shelters: Movie Films*, prepared for the use of the Committee on Ways and Means 1 (1975) (generally describing the operation of this type of shelter).

144 London Palmer, *Between the Movie and the Money: Packaging the 1970s Motion Picture Tax Shelter*, 9 MEDIA INDUS. 1, 4 (2022).

145 William Shakespeare, THE TRAGEDY OF MACBETH, Act V, scene 5, line 30 in Folgers Shakespeare Library edition 179 (Barbara A. Mowat & Paul Wersteine, eds., 2003).

146 Hershey, *supra* note 97, at D6.

the 1950s and 1960s, tax shelters had become socially desirable. "They are proudly mentioned in cocktail-party conversation by status-seeking investors, leading others to become interested."[147] An accountant at the national firm of Coopers & Lybrand confirmed this account, relating that some of his clients had become tax shelter investors in part because they "like the idea of being able to talk to their friends about their cattle in Wyoming."[148]

This "social acceptability" rationalization was aided by the fact that the term "tax shelter" was attached to so many things that people were doing already.[149] As two income tax consultants mentioned in response to a question about ways for people to shelter their income, "individuals covered by a corporate or government pension plan already are getting tax shelter for a part of their earnings."[150] Congress had even increased the options available – including creating Individual Retirement Accounts (IRA) for workers in firms that did not offer tax-deferred pensions or Keogh tax-deferred plans for self-employed individuals – which were openly "described as "tax shelters," "tax shelter pensions," or "tax-sheltered retirement plans" in news stories about their growing popularity and advisability.[151] Economist Robert Samuelson called the adoption of the IRA "a shelter … concocted that would, in theory, be available to most working Americans."[152] Promoters also pointed out that municipal bond interest was tax-exempt and investing in real estate could provide preferential capital gains income at sale and a hedge against inflation.[153]

Second, new tax shelter investors justified their tax dodging with the same inequity rationalization that tax dodgers used in the 1950s and 1960s. They did not necessarily object to tax dodging; rather, if the wealthy were going to be allowed to do it, they wanted to have the same privilege. Representative James Corman complained that "[t]he national sense of tax inequity is grounded in the taxpayer's belief that he is 'entitled to the privilege of paying as little as

[147] Id.
[148] Gordon, *supra* note 123, at 5.
[149] *You Needn't be Rich to Shelter Your Income*, U.S. NEWS & WORLD REPORT, Aug. 7, 1978, at 75 (interview with Stephen Wales and William Keller, income-tax consultants and faculty members at Ferris State College).
[150] Id.
[151] Id.; Quinn, *Three Tax Shelters*, *supra* note 120, at 16; *Tax Shelter Pensions on Rise*, BALTIMORE SUN, June 17, 1975, at A11.
[152] Robert J. Samuelson, *The Twilight of Tax Shelters?* NEWSWEEK, June 2, 1986, at 52.
[153] *You Needn't be Rich to Shelter Your Income*, *supra* note 149, at 76.

somebody else.'"[154] Part of this was because "[a]s they read of 'loopholes' by which the well-to-do reduce their income tax payments," many asked the same question that was asked by mid-century tax dodgers, "where's my tax shelter?"[155] As one columnist explained, "ordinary people" know that "wealthy people can use or avoid the tax laws to stay wealthy" and they want know how to do it themselves.[156] One middle class taxpayer – a union pipefitter – explained that he invested in a tax shelter because "[t]he rich guy and the elite, they can afford the tax lawyers and advisers . . . I pay 20% of my income where a man earning $500,000 a year doesn't pay anything."[157] Similarly, a retired schoolteacher said that he invested in a tax shelter after watching people at an expensive country club "fly up in their airplanes and eat meals and play golf and write everything off."[158] He decided that "the people who work every day and get checks, they pay taxes for the country," so why not do what the rich people do who "have accountants and they never pay for anything."[159]

Promoters used middle class frustration over the inequity of tax dodges as part of their appeal to prospective customers. The union pipefitter, for example, reported that he was told that his tax shelter investment was "for the working guy that's trying to get ahead, to get into the same thing" that the wealthy used to dodge taxes.[160] Even if promoters did not mention it, ordinary people saw it everywhere they looked, including popular culture. In one episode of the popular 1970s sitcom, *All in the Family*, the protagonist Archie Bunker defended his failure to pay taxes on income he earned driving a taxi on weekends by saying "the big millionaires have their tax shelters – this is mine."[161] According to Justice Department tax attorney Carolyn Parr, "[a]verage people read that rich people are avoiding taxes and the promoters tell them, 'You can do that, too.'"[162]

[154] Corman, *supra* note 95, at 511 (quoting Louis Eisenstein, *Some Second Thoughts on Tax Ideologies*, 23 N.Y.U. Inst. on Fed. Tax 1 (1965)).

[155] *You Don't Have to Be Rich to use Tax Loophole on Gifts*, Chi. Trib., Nov. 30, 1975, at A20.

[156] Robert G. Kaiser, *So You Want to Play the Tax Shelter Game?* Hartford Courant, Dec. 27, 1983, at B9.

[157] Kwitny, *supra* note 118, at 1.

[158] Id. at 26.

[159] Id.

[160] Id.

[161] *All in the Family: Archie's Fraud* (CBS television broadcast, Sept. 23, 1972); Ernest Conine, *Tax Shelters Help a Few, Hurt a Lot*, Atl. Const., Dec. 25, 1973, at 18D.

[162] Kwitny, *supra* note 118, at 1.

Finally, a growing loss of confidence in the tax system may have allowed shelter investors to rationalize their tax dodging. One writer noted, only partly tongue-in-cheek, "[e]very patriotic American feels it his bounden duty to search and seize all possible tax shelters" in order "to foil the insidious forces of the IRS."[163] More generally, others rationalized their decision to invest in tax shelters because of their growing distrust of the government. One tax shelter attorney reported that "[s]ome grow so angry over the idea of Uncle Sam taking their money, they'd rather lose it in a crap shoot – if it's deductible."[164] As Martin Ginsburg noted in 1973 during a House Ways and Means Committee meeting discussing tax reform, "when a taxpayer revolts, he does not storm the office of the District Director; in our system of self-assessment, he adjusts his tax assessment by assessing himself less."[165]

The government itself worried that public perception of its failure was contributing to the tax shelter boom. In 1984, the Joint Committee on Taxation wrote that "the highly visible marketing of tax shelters, and the accompanying belief that the Internal Revenue Service cannot deal with them, may erode taxpayer's confidence in the fairness and effectiveness of the tax system."[166] As the Joint Committee explained, "[t]he widespread use of tax shelters deprives the system of its claim to fairness and retards the administrative and judicial processes to the point that penalties seem neither certain nor costly," which reduces taxpayer incentives to comply with the tax laws."[167] The growth of tax shelters served to further undercut taxpayer confidence in the system, inducing more people to participate in the tax dodging. The Joint Committee concluded that "[t]he rise of the tax-shelter industry may have contributed significantly to the general deterioration in compliance by undermining taxpayer confidence in the fairness and effectiveness of the tax laws."[168] In this case, the government's inability or unwillingness to control tax shelters only contributed to this narrative. Stanford Ross, a former Treasury official, lamented that "the government has for longer and longer times tolerated shelters and, in the name of reform, passed acts that scarcely touched them. The response is predictable."[169]

163 S.L. Varnado, *Foiling the IRS*, NAT'L REV., April 16, 1976, at 396.
164 Gordon, *supra* note 123, at 5.
165 Ginsburg, 1973 Ways and Means Tax Reform Panel, *supra* note 130, at 881.
166 Gordon, *supra* note 123, at 7.
167 Id.
168 Joint Committee Report, *supra* note 98, at 6.
169 Russakoff, *supra* note 128, at A7.

To address concerns about out-of-control tax dodging, Congress passed the Tax Reform Act of 1986, which was called a "legislative miracle" because it accomplished the seemingly impossible task of pairing implicit tax cuts with explicit tax cuts by reducing tax preferences in the Internal Revenue Code, cutting both the top marginal tax rate and the number of tax brackets, and increasing exemptions and the standard deduction.[170] Under the 1986 Act, the top marginal rate for individuals was reduced from 50 percent to 28 percent,[171] while the capital gains preference and investment tax credit were eliminated, the deductibility of things like so-called "passive activity losses," interest expenses, miscellaneous and non-reimbursed employee business expenses, business meals and entertainment, and Individual Retirement Account contributions were all scaled back, and the Accelerated Cost Recovery System was modified to lengthen the times for taxpayers to recovery their original investments through depreciation deductions.[172] Some of these changes were intended to reduce tax preferences, while others were designed to protect against the abuse of remaining provisions. The theory was that while some people might lose their favorite tax preference, the drop in the overall tax rate would largely compensate them for it. The hope was that it would also restore transparency and some measure of equity and confidence to the system. As Joseph Pechman confidently proclaimed after its passage, the 1986 Act "will greatly improve the fairness of the tax system and remove major distortions from the economy."[173]

There is some evidence that the 1986 Act succeeded in reducing tax dodging.[174] It limited opportunities by repealing some of the deductions that taxpayers might have overclaimed and incentivizing taxpayers to

[170] Jeffrey H. Birnbaum & Alan S. Murray, Showdown at Gucci Gulch: Lawmakers, Lobbyists, and the Unlikely Triumph of Tax Reform 285 (1987); Karyl A. Kinsey & Harold G. Grasmick, *Did the Tax Reform Act of 1986 Improve Compliance? Three Studies of Pre- and Post-TRA Compliance Attitudes*, 15 L. & Pol'y 293, 293–94, 295 (1993); Simmons, *supra* note 104, at 164.

[171] Tax Reform Act of 1986, Pub. L. 99–514, § 101, 100 Stat. 2085, 2096. The 28 percent rate was modified by a "bubble" in that there was a phaseout of the lower 15 percent bracket above certain income levels, resulting in a 33 percent top rate until an individual paid a 28 percent effective rate on all income. Brownlee, *supra* note 102, at 204; Simmons, *supra* note 104, at 164.

[172] Sheldon D. Pollack, The Failure of U.S. Tax Policy: Revenue and Politics 104–05 (1996); Ajay K. Mehortra & Dominic Bayer, *The Promise and Limits of Fundamental Tax Reform: Contrasting the 1986 Tax Reform Act with the 2017 Tax Cuts and Jobs Act*, 53 U.C. Davis L. Rev. Online 93, 101, 103 (2019).

[173] Joseph A. Pechman, *Tax Reform: Theory and Practice*, 1 J. Econ. Persp. 11, 17 (1987).

[174] Kinsey & Grasmick, *supra* note 170, at 293.

take the standard deduction rather than itemizing.[175] It also lengthened depreciation schedules and lowered rates generally, which reduced the value of investing in many tax shelter transactions. All told, there were seventy-two provisions of the Act that either substantially restricted or eliminated tax preference items, which political scientist John Witte observed was "approximately equal the total number of tax expenditures that had been repealed from 1913 through 1985."[176] For tax shelters specifically, the limit on deductibility of passive activity losses was significant. Passive losses were the main attraction for investors in tax shelter partnerships seeking depreciation deductions and other flow-through tax benefits to offset their income from their regular occupations. Requiring investors to "materially participate" to use those losses was inconsistent with both the premise of passive investment and the legal structure of the tax shelter's limited partnership, which prohibited active participation under state law.[177] As IRS Deputy Chief Counsel Peter K. Scott said in an interview in 1988, "[t]he passive loss rules pretty much put the final nail in the coffin, in terms of the tax shelter business."[178] One study concluded, based upon the declines in public sales and net income of limited partnerships, that "[t]here is little doubt that investments in tax shelters have all but disappeared since the enactment of" the 1986 Act.[179]

Perhaps more importantly, the 1986 Act appeared to increase the perceived fairness of the income tax system. According to a 1984 national survey of taxpayers prepared for the Internal Revenue Service, 80 percent of respondents agreed with the statement that "the tax system benefits the rich and is unfair to the ordinary working man or woman."[180] After the 1986 Act, however, this attitude appeared to change. Although the 1986 Act was not particularly popular among a "skeptical public," researchers reported that by the early 1990s "attitudes more directly related to tax

175 Id. at 294–96.

176 Witte, *The Tax Reform Act of 1986*, *supra* note 141, at 443.

177 Section 469 made this clear by establishing that "no interest in a limited partnership as a limited partner shall be treated as an interest with respect to which a taxpayer materially participates." I.R.C. §469(h)(2); Lester D. Bailey, *Passive Activity Losses and Credits*, 17 U. Balt. L Rev. 390, 395 (1988).

178 Michael Moriarty & R. Eliot Rosen, *An Interview with IRS Deputy Chief Counsel Peter K. Scott*, 39 Tax Notes 920 (1988).

179 Andrew A. Samwick, *Tax Shelters and Passive Losses After the Tax Reform Act of 1986*, in Empirical Foundations of Household Taxation 193, 194 (Martin Feldstein & James Poterba, eds., 1996).

180 Yankelovich, Skelly, and White, Inc., Taxpayer Survey 198 (1984).

compliance and to general evaluations of the tax system have become more positive."[181] This, in turn, increased taxpayers' willingness to comply with the tax laws. Karyl Kinsey and Harold Grasmick concluded from an analysis of survey data and IRS data on aggregate returns that there was "a phenomenon of changing attitudes and perceptions toward the federal income system" after the 1986 Act was passed, creating an "improved normative climate for tax compliance."[182] Not only were more people willing to comply with the tax laws, they "were less likely to excuse tax cheating in others."[183] This is not surprising since perceptions about the fairness of a tax system have been shown to affect compliance across different cultures and societies.[184]

Notwithstanding these immediate effects, the Tax Reform Act of 1986 ultimately failed to deliver on some of its most ambitious goals. As Professor Michael Graetz wrote two decades later, the "changes wrought by the 1986 act have proven neither revolutionary nor stable."[185] The compromise between lower rates and ending tax preferences was broken before "the ink had hardly dried" on the legislation, with rate increases and new tax preferences enacted soon after.[186] Moreover, while the individual tax shelter market dried up, the corporate tax shelter market flourished, motivated in part by corporations' desire to avoid the consequences of the 1986 Act's repeal of the *General Utilities* doctrine, which had allowed corporations to distribute appreciated assets without entity-level gain recognition.[187]

181 John T. Scholz, Kathleen M. McGraw & Marco R. Steenbergen, *Will Taxpayers Ever Like Taxes? Responses to the U.S. Tax Reform Act of 1986*, 4 J. ECON. PSYCHOL. 625, 626 (1992).

182 Kinsey & Grasmick, *supra* note 170, at 319.

183 Id. at 318–19.

184 Ronald G. Cummings, Jorge Martinez-Vazquez, Michael McKee & Benno Torgler, *Tax Morale Affects Tax Compliance: Evidence from Surveys and an Artefactual Field Experiment*, 70 J. ECON. BEHAVIOR & ORG. 447, 448 (2009).

185 Michael J. Graetz, *Tax Reform Unraveling*, 21 J. ECON. PERSP. 69, 69 (2007).

186 Id. at 71.

187 James S. Eustice, *Abusive Corporate tax Shelters: Old Brine in New Bottles*, 55 TAX L. REV. 135, 142 (2002). The doctrine was named after a Supreme Court decision in which the Court permitted a corporation to avoid recognition of gain on the distribution of a highly appreciated stock interest when it declared an in-kind dividend of the stock. General Utilities & Operating Co. v. Helvering, 296 U.S. 200 (1935). By 1986, the doctrine had already been eroded by prior legislation and its application was limited to liquidating distributions, certain dividend distributions and deemed asset sales in an election made under Section 338. Eric M. Zolt, *The* General Utilities *Doctrine: Examining the Scope of the Repeal* in 40th Annual Federal Tax Conference of the University of Chicago Law School, 65 TAXES: THE TAX MAG. 819, 821 (1987).

## The Legacy of Mid-Century Tax Dodging

Although the brazenly public mid-century tax dodging may have faded, many of the practices adopted during this period remain. Conventions and business meetings continue to be held at resorts and exotic locales with plenty of entertainment options onsite or nearby.[188] Sports arenas, stadiums, and even golf courses have been literally redesigned to accommodate the kind of luxury boxes and suites that businesses can use to entertain clients before and during games.[189] Many of the compensation techniques developed or expanded between the 1950s and 1980s in part to allow corporate executives to dodge taxes on their income, such as stock options and restricted stock, fringe benefits, deferred compensation in the form of pensions and Individual Retirement Accounts, and other retirement plan options, are completely mainstream today.[190] Loan-out corporations, which were brought to the forefront by Charles Laughton of *Mutiny on the Bounty* fame in the 1930s, remain a popular business structure for entertainers and athletes to license their intellectual property rights.[191] Indeed, the persistence of these and other techniques and business customs popularized between the 1950s and 1980s during radically different tax rate environments is perhaps the greatest evidence of the lasting cultural influence of mid-century tax dodging.

[188] *See* Dawn Gilbertson, *Balancing Work and Play at Conferences*, WALL ST. J., Oct. 24, 2024, at A12 ("Conferences and corporate retreats are back, and with them the heaping side of scheduled fun."); Kate King, *Corporate Retreats Lift Hotel Business*, WALL ST. J., Oct. 15, 2024, at B1 ("Companies also are spending big at the hotels and resorts where their employees are staying ... group spending on dining and entertainment reached a record in the second quarter.").

[189] *See* Alan Blinder, Kevin Draper & Doug Mills, *Opulent Sanctums for the Affluent Fan*, N. Y. TIMES, April 13, 2024, at B7 ("Premium hospitality at sporting events is still dominated by corporations, which buy the seats to entertain current clients and woo potential ones.").

[190] Irv Becker & Tony Wu, *Recent and Emerging Trends in CEO Pay*, DIRECTORS & BOARDS, June 24, 2024; Jennifer Williams, *Stock Incentives Lift Pay of CFO's*, WALL ST. J., June 25, 2024, at B1; Congressional Research Service, *U.S. Retirement Assets: Data in Brief*, Sept. 20, 2023, at 1, Fig. 1.

[191] Katie Kilkenny, *Gavin Newsom Signs Union-Supported Bill Safeguarding Entertainment Loan-Out Companies*, HOLLYWOOD REPORTER, Sept. 30, 2024.

# INDEX

For EU product safety concerns, contact us at Calle de José Abascal, 56–1°,
28003 Madrid, Spain or eugpsr@cambridge.org.

www.ingramcontent.com/pod-product-compliance
Ingram Content Group UK Ltd.
Pitfield, Milton Keynes, MK11 3LW, UK
UKHW022004220926
475880UK00004B/241
* 9 7 8 1 0 0 9 7 0 1 9 5 2 *